WOMEN AS SITES OF CULTURE

Women as Sites of Culture

Women's roles in cultural formation from the
Renaissance to the Twentieth Century

Edited by
SUSAN SHIFRIN

Ashgate

Published by
Ashgate Publishing Limited
Gower House
Croft Road
Aldershot
Hampshire GU11 3HR
England

Ashgate Publishing Company
131 Main Street
Burlington, VT 05401-5600 USA

Ashgate website: http://www.ashgate.com

British Library Cataloguing in Publication Data
Women as sites of culture : women's roles in cultural
    formation from the Renaissance to the twentieth-century
    1. Women - History - Renaissance, 1450-1600 2. Women -
    History - Modern period, 1600- 3. Women in literature
    4.Women - Social conditions 5. Women - Public opinion -
    History
    I. Shifrin, Susan
    305.4'2'09

Library of Congress Control Number: 2001099664

ISBN 0 7546 0311 3

Printed and bound in Great Britain by MPG Books Ltd, Bodmin, Cornwall

Contents

List of Figures

List of Contributors

SUDIPTO CHATTERJEE is Assistant Professor of Drama at Tufts University, Boston. He received his PhD in Performance Studies from New York University. His essay included here has been extracted from a chapter in his forthcoming book *The Colonial Stage(d): Hybridity, Woman and the Nation in 19th Century Bengali Theatre*. His scholarly work has been published in several anthologies and journals internationally. Originally from Calcutta, Chatterjee is also a playwright-performer-director-filmmaker whose work has been seen in India, Bangladesh, the United States, Australia, and the United Kingdom.

ELIZABETH V. CHEW is Associate Curator of Collections at Monticello in Charlottesville, Virginia. Chew received her PhD in art history from the University of North Carolina. Her dissertation examines female architectural patronage and art collecting in seventeenth-century Britain. Her research interests include the relationships among architecture, material culture, and gender and family identities in early modern Britain and America. She has an essay on the Countess of Arundel's collection at Tart Hall forthcoming in *The Evolution of English Collecting*, from Yale University Press.

LISA PLUMMER CRAFTON is Professor of English at the State University of West Georgia. Her scholarly expertise is in British Romantic literature and women's literature. Her most recent publications include the edited volume *The French Revolution Debate in English Literature and Culture* (Greenwood Press, 1997) and '"Insipid Decency": Modesty and Female Sexuality in Wollstonecraft' in *European Romantic Review* (Summer 2000).

ROBIN DEROSA is currently completing her doctorate in English at Tufts University. Her dissertation, titled 'Scholars, Specters, and Sightseers: The Salem Witch Trials and American Memory,' concerns the relationships between the history of colonial New England and current-day tourist productions. Her work deals with theories of performativity and the connections between identity and theatricality. She has recently published work in *The Rocky Mountain Review of Language and Literature, In-Between: Essays & Studies in Literary Criticism,* and *Postscript.* She also has an essay on Olaudah Equiano forthcoming in *The Connecticut Review.*

REINA GREEN is currently completing her dissertation on constructions of listening in early modern drama in the Department of English, Dalhousie University. She has published on Mary Sidney's *Tragedy of Antonie* and on early modern women translators with Brown University's 'Renaissance Women Online' and has an article forthcoming in *Studies in English Literature* on listening in *The Tragedy of Mariam* and *The Duchess of Malfi*.

LISA JOHNSON received her PhD in English from Binghamton University, where she recently completed a dissertation on positive re-readings of the female body in American literature. Her research interests include feminist theory and female sexuality, the subject of the forthcoming collection to be published by Four Walls, Eight Windows, *Jane Sexes It Up: True Confessions of Feminist Desire*, for which she is the editor. She now teaches composition at the State University of West Georgia.

ETSUKO KATO is an assistant professor in the Department of International Studies at International Christian University in Tokyo. She received her PhD in anthropology from the University of Toronto, after which she held a post-doctoral research post at the University of British Columbia. Her dissertation on the present-day practice of the tea ceremony was based on field research carried out from 1998 to 1999. She has published several articles and presented a number of papers focusing on the Japanese tea ceremony and Japanese culture. Her research interests include traditional Japanese culture in modern times, the rise of Japanese cultural nationalism following World War II, and how these interrelate with notions of gender.

RUTH ELLEN KOCHER is Assistant Professor of American Literature, specializing in African American Literature, at Southern Illinois University at Edwardsville. Her first book, *Desdemona's Fire*, was published by Lotus Press in 1999 and won the Naomi Long Madgett Poetry Award. Her most recent article, co-authored with Keith Miller and titled 'Narrativizing Oratory in Frederick Douglass' Narrative of the *Life of Frederick Douglass*,' appeared in *Approaches to Teaching Frederick Douglass*, from the Modern Language Association Series on Teaching World Literature (Fall 1999).

SUSAN LAMB is Assistant Professor of English at University of Toronto at Scarborough. She is finishing a book, titled *Bringing Travel Home*, on the intersections among gender, tourism, and literature, and has published articles on the subject in journals such *as Studies in Eighteenth-Century Culture* and *Comparative Drama*. She also works on the connections between drama and the novel in the eighteenth century.

LYNN LUBAMERSKY received her PhD in history at Indiana University and is now Assistant Professor of History at Boise State University. Lubamersky is currently revising her dissertation, *Women in Family Politics*, for publication as a book. She has published an article titled 'Women and Political Patronage in the Politics of the Polish-Lithuanian Commonwealth' in *The Polish Review* (1999), as well as several book reviews in *The Polish Review* and *The Slavic Review*.

ELIZABETH MCCARTNEY is a visiting assistant professor at The Robert D. Clark Honors College, University of Oregon. She is completing a two-volume study on the use of emotion in political theory and royal ceremonial in late-medieval and early modern France.

MARJORIE OCH received her doctorate in art history from Bryn Mawr College and is now Associate Professor of Art History at Mary Washington College. Her essay here on Vittoria Colonna is a continuation of the work she did in her dissertation. A related article appears in *Beyond Isabella* (eds. Reiss and Wilkins, 2001). Och is currently working on Colonna's patronage of a women's religious community in Rome, as well as on Giorgio Vasari's descriptions in his *Lives of the Artist...* of the influence of travel on artists.

CHRISTOPHER ORCHARD is Associate Professor of English at Indiana University of Pennsylvania, where he teaches Shakespeare, Renaissance studies and contemporary British literature. His research interests focus on literature and politics of the English Civil War, Civil War drama and masques, women's writing and writing about women in the 1640s and 1650s, the politics of translation, and the reception of Ben Jonson during the same period. His most recent publication was a contributing article to Brown University's Women's Writing Project concerning *A Petition to Parliament* (1642).

KRISTINE PELEG is a doctoral candidate in the department of English Literature at the University of Arizona, where she is writing a dissertation on women pioneers in the Upper Midwest. She received her masters degree in Political Science from Hebrew University in Jerusalem.

ALISON PIEPMEIER is a lecturer in the English Department and Women's Studies Program at Vanderbilt University. She received her PhD in English from Vanderbilt University. Her dissertation is entitled *Out in Public: Configurations of Women's Bodies in Nineteenth-Century America*. While most of her research involves nineteenth-century American woman writers, she is currently co-editing a book with Rory Dicker called *Catching a Wave: Reclaiming Feminism for theTwenty-first Century*.

ROSS J. PUDALOFF is a member of the faculty of English at Wayne State University. He is coeditor of *The Ends of Theory* and the author of essays on, among others, Jonathan Edwards, Richard Wright, William Byrd, and Henry

David Thoreau. He published an earlier essay on Anne Hutchinson and the Antinomian Controversy, titled 'Sign and Subject: Antinomianism in Massachusetts Bay,' in *Semiotica* 54 (1985).

LOUISE RYAN is a senior lecturer in sociology at the University of Central Lancashire in England. She is currently working on a research project based at the Irish Studies Centre at the University of North London. She has published widely in such journals as *Gender and History, Feminist Review, Women's Studies International Forum*, and the *Journal of Gender Studies*. Her book *Irish Feminism and the Vote* was published by Folens, Dublin in 1996. She is currently working on a book titled *Embodying the Nation: Gender and National Identities in the Irish Printed Media, 1920s-1930s*, Edwin Mellen Press, New York, to be published in 2001.

SUSAN SHIFRIN is an art historian specializing in the field of early modern portraiture. She received her PhD in art history from Bryn Mawr College, and has worked as a curator and freelance collections manager at a number of museums and academic institutions, as well as teaching and writing in the fields of art history and women's studies. Shifrin is currently a Visiting Fellow at the Center for Visual Culture at Bryn Mawr College, where she is preparing an exhibition titled 'Picturing Women: Historical Works and Contemporary Responses' that will open at several Philadelphia-area institutions in 2004. She is also completing the manuscript for a book titled *'That fair Copy drawn...': Configuring Biography, Iconography and Likeness in Seventeenth-Century Portraits of Women.*

Introduction

Susan Shifrin

When the essays that form the core of each of the four sections that follow were presented at the annual meeting of the Group for Early Modern Cultural Studies several years ago, they created a cohesive and tightly-focused group of explorations of early modern, largely European and Anglo-American women's roles as sites and 'sights' of culture. What emerged during the presentation of these studies and the conversations that ensued among presenters and discussants was that the themes of 'siting' and 'sighting' — particularly from the specific, gendered viewpoint we had chosen to adopt — went broader and deeper than any of us had envisioned in preparing for our panel. We were all invigorated and empowered to return to our own work and expand our investigations of these themes. In addition, we were all intrigued to further explore their ramifications on a broader geographical and chronological scale. This collection of eighteen essays marks a milestone in the progress of those further explorations.

Refracted through the disciplinary lenses and methodologies of the literary historian, the anthropologist, the historian, the literary critic, and the art historian, the pertinence of our themes emerges in relation to the roles women have played in interrogating, forming, informing, and reforming political discourse, cultural tradition and ceremony, social mores, and the patronage and definition of art since the Renaissance. The female body as the basis for and site of political and nationalistic metaphor constitutes the focus of the first set of essays. Christopher Orchard examines various visualizations and configurations of the female body as one basis of discourse during the period of the English Civil War. Alison Piepmeier analyzes Sojourner Truth's siting of her own body — both in figurative and pragmatic terms — within the context of the uniquely American, nineteenth-century tall-tale tradition, thereby accentuating the potency of the female body both as a physical and discursive force. In a related project, Lisa Plummer Crafton investigates Maxine Hong Kingston's inscription of the Asian American female body as a site of nationalistic and cultural conflict, situated at the crossroads of traditional and post-modern storytelling. Intervening between these two chapters, Louise Ryan's essay investigates the interrelations among the female body, Irish nationalism of the 1920s, and the rhetorical configuration and manipulation in Irish newspapers of the sometimes celebratory, always troublesome notion of femaleness peculiar to the period of the 1920s, known as the 'flapper.' Closing this first section of the book, Lisa Johnson writes a self-reflexive critique of post-modern, American notions of white womanhood. Siting her own perspective as informed by the influences of personal experience on the one hand and the burgeoning body of critical literature in the area of 'whiteness studies' and third-wave feminism on the other, Johnson, like the other contributors to this section, also locates her topic within the contexts of nationalist discourse, metaphor embodied, and storytelling. She contextualizes her early twenty-first century analysis through reference to nineteenth-century American literary traditions exemplified by Henry James' *Daisy Miller*.

The second section of the book is devoted to the 'spectacle' of women staged and 'sighted' within the context of ritual ceremony or theatrical representation. Once again, the influence exercised on the formation and reformation of culture by women's physical and figurative bodies and their societally pre- and proscribed natures forms the thematic crux of these essays. Elizabeth McCartney's essay reconsiders the role of the royal widow and regent in Renaissance France as political agent, a role that in conventional historiography has been constituted as minimal. Through her close study of the records of court ceremonial associated with the mourning of deceased sixteenth-century French monarchs and the enthronement of their under-age successors, McCartney re-reads this ceremonial staging of the widow's/regent's body as of substantial religious, nationalistic and political significance. Reina Green analyzes representations of the mythic/historical figure of Cleopatra in a range of sixteenth- and seventeenth-century plays, exploring what she terms the 'eroticization of virtue' in their multivalent and sometimes ambivalent characterizations of the Queen of Egypt as simultaneously exemplary of spousal virtues and of the vices of the transgressor of conventionally feminine and domestic harmony. Susan Lamb engages in the related project of tracing the fortunes of the Shakespearean figure of Ophelia in the eighteenth century. Lamb analyzes for their embodiment of notions of womanhood and virtue in eighteenth-century English society Ophelia's varied representations as sexually explicit transgressor and virtuous madwoman (and the various and often overlapping shades of each in- between) in eighteenth-century stage performances of Hamlet, visual characterizations of Ophelia in print and in paint, and novelistic appropriations of her character and name. Sudipto Chatterjee, in turn, recounts and analyzes the crisis of nationalist, political, and gendered hierarchies that occurred at the dramatic moment in the late-nineteenth-century history of Indian theater when Bengali theater sought for the first time to admit women to the stage. Chatterjee explores the ramifications of the fact that this transgression of theatrical and gendered convention was embodied in and heightened by the female prostitutes who served as the first woman players on the Bengali stage. Finally, again considering the ways in which the conventions of feminine rank and nature inform and reform cultural ceremony, Etsuko Kato investigates in the concluding essay of this section how the changing role of women in the traditional tea ceremony has changed the ceremony itself and the ways in which it has functioned and been perceived during the modern era in Japan.

The third set of essays investigates and delineates the paradigmatic roles of notable women in Renaissance Italy, sixteenth- and seventeenth-century England, and the sixteenth- through eighteenth-century Polish-Lithuanian Commonwealth as cultural resources: that is to say, as the motivators, makers, and matter of cultural creation. Marjorie Och considers the case of Vittoria Colonna, Renaissance patron of the arts and poet in her own right, whose medallic portraits Och reads as markers of Colonna's appropriation of and encompassment in the culture of humanism burgeoning in Italy during her lifetime. Elizabeth Chew lays out the case of Lady Anne Clifford, Countess of Dorset, Pembroke, and Montgomery. Representing Clifford as paradigmatic for those notable sixteenth- and seventeenth-century Englishwomen who made their enduring, self-reflexive marks on their societies by siting themselves within architectural and artistic programs that reflected and memorialized their own aesthetics and cultural values, Chew demonstrates the ways in which her subject overcame the cultural erasure to which early modern Englishwomen were often subject, inflecting lastingly the English culture that eyed her resourcefulness with a certain degree of distrust and dismay. Susan Shifrin analyzes the visual and literary record revealing Hortense Mancini, Duchess Mazarin and Louise de Kéroualle, Duchess of Portsmouth as sites of political agency at the Restoration court of Charles II of England. In addition, Shifrin explores the notion that these women's prerogative as illicit intimates of the king, as well as their renown throughout England and Europe as inveterate transgressors of the boundaries of propriety prescribed for their gender, allowed contemporary chroniclers to authenticate their accounts of the English court by siting these women as prominent players within them. Lynn Lubamersky, also exploring the roles of renegade but still somehow exemplary women as cultural icons and as the material of cultural mythmaking, writes in the final essay of this section about the remarkable figure of the mythic/historical 'wild woman' of the Polish-Lithuanian Commonwealth. Lubamersky traces the evolution of this figure embodying both cultural myth and historical fact in the Commonwealth's reservoirs of lore, song, biography, and poetry, from ancient Amazons to eighteenth-century noblewomen on the frontiers of the Commonwealth, casting off the shackles of restrained womanhood to defend and preserve the nationalistic and cultural integrity of their community while providing others with the resource of their stories to inspire them to do the same.

The final section of the book is devoted to articulations of the female voice as the site of cultural authority. It is comprised of a set of essays concerned with sound and silence, both: with the celebration of woman's voice, and its muting or silencing altogether. Ross Pudaloff writes of Anne Hutchinson, accused in seventeenth-century New England of the crimes of speaking for herself, for her own religious beliefs, and doing so in public, and then called upon to simultaneously defend and condemn herself in open court by raising her own voice to articulate that defense, thus demonstrating the paradox of the articulate, authoritative woman whose capacity for self-expression was her greatest weapon and her silencing its greatest antidote. Robin DeRosa addresses a nineteenth-century extrapolation of some of these same issues of sound, silence, and self-expression as embodied in the persona and writings of the English poet Anna Leticia Barbauld and the critical fortunes of her work both in her own day and in the twentieth century. DeRosa examines the notion that Barbauld was burdened during her own lifetime and continues to be burdened by late- and post-modern critics with the charge of not being 'woman enough': in her own day, not woman enough to keep silent rather than write, and in ours, not woman enough to have issued through her poetry what we, at the end of the twentieth century, would dignify as a full-blown feminist battle cry. Kristine Peleg continues the thematic focus on the paradoxes of women's eloquent speech and silence with her analysis of the ramifications of women's exclusion from vocal participation in Israel's ongoing Remembrance Day ceremonies. Ruth Ellen Kocher's essay, bringing to a close both this set of essays and the collection as a whole, draws together the thematic strands of women's bodily presence as the subtext of polemics, the ceremonial staging of women as spectacle, women as sources, inspiration, and facilitators of cultural creation, and women's voices as the site of cultural authority. Kocher's analysis of the narrative testimonies of JoAnn Gibson Robinson in her *Boycott Memoir* contextualizes this twentieth-century African American woman's memoirs of the Civil Rights movement in the United States by siting it within the rhetorical tradition of the nineteenth-century slave narrative. Through her own bodily presence at and participation in the events of the 1960s, asserted throughout her text, Robinson is said to certify the verity of her account and to site herself as an authorized chronicler. Through her cataloguing of the dates, locations, and events of the movement, she is said to locate herself as both a participant in and viewer of what may be called the powerful spectacle of the movement's progress. And by the authority vested in Robinson as she bears witness in her own voice from within the very matter of her text, informing and reforming prior texts on her subject, Robinson's memoirs exemplify what all the writers in this last section have articulated as women's voicing of cultural authority.

In the progress from the first section of the book, which treats the subject of women's bodies as the metaphorical and vernacular vehicles for (largely male) polemical discourse; and the second section, which reviews perceptions and receptions of women 'sighted' in the spectacles of stage, ceremony, and ritual; to the third section, which attends to women's agency in the production and dissemination of cultural creation; the final set of essays marks an arrival of sorts at women's voiced recognition of their own authority and the conflicts of policy, religion, race, and authorship to which that recognition gives rise. It is a progress that is neither straightforward nor uninterrupted. The path from early-modern to late- and post-modern is meandering and multivalent rather than unveering, and while Kocher's essay marks a late-modern consummation of the themes of 'siting' and 'sighting' in Gibson's memoirs — a consummation that fully asserts and authorizes the authenticity and potency of women as sites of culture — there is little of this theme exemplified in Gibson's work that cannot be found in at least partial form throughout the early, late, and post-modern Anglo-American, African-American, Asian-American, English, French, Indian, Irish, Israeli, Italian, Japanese, and Lithuanian subjects addressed in our full range of essays. We wish to leave our readers, finally, with the cultural diversity and commonality of these themes, and their pertinence to the study of women's places in the world.

PART I

The Female Body as the Site of Polemics

1   The Rhetoric of Corporeality and the Political Subject: Containing the Dissenting Female Body in Civil War England

Christopher Orchard

The contributors to this volume study women who embody a wide range of socio-economic examples, ranging from prostitutes in nineteenth-century India to aristocrats in seventeenth-century Europe. While this essay focuses on the seventeenth century and on women in Europe, it mainly concentrates on lesser known, less socially-prominent English women in a particular time period — that of the English Civil War of the 1640s — who did not enjoy the same highly visible presence of their social superiors, whether they were aristocrats or queens. The idea of visibility is central to understanding this essay collection with its key concepts of 'sighting' and 'siting.' As an articulation of these concepts, this essay explores how the sight of women protesting to the English Parliament in the 1640s provoked male authors to locate and then disable the radical potential of the female body. This was achieved first by taking rhetorical control of specific, dissenting female bodies and second, by labeling those bodies merely as metaphorical sites at which the political differences between Royalists and Parliamentarians could be fought out.

It has been an assumption of many literary historians that the English Civil War (1642-49), fought between the Royalist supporters of Charles I and supporters of Parliament, was characterized as a period of turmoil and innovation. This has been validated by studies with titles such as Christopher Hill's 1991 *The World Turned Upside Down*, with its implication of an upheaval of societal norms. Yet recently, historians such as G.E. Aylmer and Conrad Russell have questioned this assertion.[1] Indeed, although it is easy to trace the radical *effects* of the war, such as the regicide, the abolition of the monarchy, and the establishment of a commonwealth government in 1649, the years prior to these momentous occurrences address the tangible failure of more substantive political reform.

It is the contention of this essay that this predilection for modified political reform typified male reaction to the involvement of women in politics in the 1640s. In the first half of the essay, I build on current scholarly discourse concerning women petitioners and their documented public appeals to king and Parliament for redress of various ills. Following the pioneering essay by Ellen McArthur early in the twentieth century, much recent scholarship has examined the rhetorical and political content of petitions and their public reception, particularly as expressed in contemporary newsbooks, pamphlets that contained news with a satirical edge.[2]   Articles by Patricia Higgins, Ann Marie McEntee and Susan Hughes have revealed a lack of consensus about whether such petitions demonstrate their authors' acceptance of their inferior social positions or their manipulation of cultural convention in order to undermine it.[3] McEntee has also explored how newsbooks sought to equate women's political presence with a public display of their sexuality. In general, both McEntee and Hughes limit the scope of their studies to tracing the politics of and reaction to women who supported the Leveller movement, radical in its intent to establish a universal franchise in England. While I do discuss below the case of Mary Overton, the wife of a Leveller, I am more concerned here with broadening the social spectrum encompassed in these studies to include middle-class citizens, expressly for the purpose of exploring how these texts, whether written by men or women, reflect male anxieties about a highly visible female interaction with political crisis across the board. Motivated by the desire to see acts of female radicalism contained, male writers consciously (in pamphlets that satirized female public behavior) and unconsciously (in official Parliamentary responses to the requests of women petitioners) undermined acts of female advocacy. I will argue that by validating the sight of women articulating issues of political content *only* from within the domestic sphere, these authors could preserve the patriarchal locus of political power.[4]

Ironically, as the second half of the essay shows, there *was* a consistent female presence in Parliament but only one embodied in the figurative language of political discourse. While a body of female petitioners was protesting outside the Houses of Parliament, the female body was used as an analogy to describe the Royalist and Parliamentarian reaction to legislative decisions being made *inside* the House. What is interesting here is the consensual preference for this analogy. This observation marks my departure from recent scholarly work. It is my contention that the discourses of political factionalism generated by the events of these years were disguising a more subtle consensual agreement that inscribed the female body as a passive subject that followed prescriptive gender codes of behavior. In other words, the ideological bifurcation that had divided citizens along religious, political and class lines did not preclude both Royalist and Parliamentarian writers from employing the same analogy, that of the female body, to describe political crisis. Recent scholarly work does not fully acknowledge the way in which metaphorical perspectives of the female body complemented more overt observations of women's protest in demonstrating a male consensus across the political spectrum that sought to denigrate the female political body. My reading of these rhetorical patterns suggests the coexistence of contradictory political impulses: a period of strife that manifested itself as ideological disagreement also signified a continuum in gender relations. The sharing of a gender metaphor suggested a joint political desire to sustain rather than challenge certain established orthodoxies.

This comprehensive use by both Royalists and Parliamentarians of the female body is ignored by recent theoretical analyses of the docile female body. Many accounts of Foucault's approaches to femininity argue that the contemporary female body is shaped by an intrusive state, through advertising and other means. They investigate how women respond either negatively by engaging in self-surveillance — by focusing on body shape through exercise and dieting, for instance — or positively by investing in strategies of resistance.[5] However, such criticism does not consider instances, both contemporary and historical, where women do not respond at all. Neither do these theoretical perspectives address the metaphorical rather than physical representation of the docile body, although this has begun to be addressed by twentieth-century cartographic analyses of the seventeenth-century body. Such work asserts that descriptions of the male political body use a rhetorical language that denies the presence and voice of women in its conceptual framework.[6] However, by and large, this criticism focuses on canonical texts of political theory — almost exclusively on Hobbes's *Leviathan* and Filmer's *Patriarcha*. It ignores less canonical and more popular discourses such as Civil War newsbooks and pamphlets in which male authors use corporeal images of women to describe the contestation of political meaning. This essay will take issue with the critical assumption that women's 'corporeal specificity marks them as inappropriate analogues to the political body.'[7] On the contrary, I will argue that the discourses of mid-seventeenth-century debates indicated that the pervasive presence of the female body was regarded as a consistently apposite means to determine political legitimacy.

The Protesting Female Body

The first half of this essay explores the strategies employed by male authors to ridicule merchants' wives, housewives and the wives of radicals for their attempts at political articulation. The vociferous presence and sighting of literate middle-class women on English streets led male writers to satirize the very idea that *ordinary* women *could* get access to a political locus — the house of Commons or Parliament — that in a real sense was inaccessible to them.

During the early years of the Civil War, the pervasive presence of women's involvement in politics was perceptibly felt. Prognosticators such as the Parliamentarian astrologer William Lilly used specific planetary movements to convince his readership of a feminine influence in international

politics. In a pamphlet, Lilly suggested that the position of the moon in both
houses 'doth assure us that the greatest state-actions of Europe will be
mannaged [*sic*] by a woman or women.'[8] This was already occurring in
England according to some Parliamentary writers. *Mercurius Britanicus*,
edited by the Parliamentarian journalist Marchamont Nedham, mocked the
one-sided relationship between Charles I and his wife Henrietta Maria, arguing
that her involvement in Parliamentary politics had transgressed conventional
gender boundaries. When the editor of a Royalist newsbook, *Mercurius
Aulicus*, taunted women who had formed committees to help the Parliamentary
cause, Nedham replied : 'Master *Aulicus* if our Ladies have legislative power, I
am sure some of your Ladies have a *Soveraigne power*, if ours compell their
own sex, yours *compell* another sex, which is not so naturall, we know who
can rule her husband at *Oxford*...I tell you we doubt here whether this be the
year of the kings raigne or the Queens.'[9] This taunt was reiterated nearly two
years later with the seizure of Charles I's cabinet of private correspondence
after the battle of Naseby. Nedham suggested that Charles I had surrendered
the breeches (wearing the pants in the family) by being ruled wholly by his
wife.[10]

It was precisely women who desired to have a role in the *public*
management of political affairs who produced the most vehement reaction.
And these women were not typically of such a high rank as Henrietta Maria's.
In England, and in London in particular, women's intrusion into traditionally
masculine spheres of public influence was most clearly seen in women who
petitioned to Parliament, often on behalf of their families. These women
argued that their motivation for petitioning was based on an anxiety that the
war would deprive them of their husbands and their manpower.[11] Yet their
agenda also threatened to destabilize society. In early 1647, a ballad writer
viewed dissenting women's mere presence on the streets as a confirmation of
the social upheavals of the 1640s. The ballad, entitled 'Anarchy,' anticipated
the consequences of allowing women the chance to protest: 'Come Females of
each degree, / Stretch your throats, bring in your votes / And make for the
Anarchy.'[12] In other words, the sight of them vociferously protesting was
enough to precipitate a subversion of all order.

Many pamphlets that record women's petitions do not indicate how
these petitions were received. Those that do suggest a reaction to women's
public presence that varied from the threat of real physical violence to the
women facing hostile crowds on the streets of London to the interested but
ultimately dismissive language of official government discourse. Perhaps this
disdainful attitude typified male reaction to female protest, which explains
what happened to Mary Overton in the same year that 'Anarchy' was
published. Overton petitioned to Parliament in 1647 to protest the
imprisonment of her husband, the Leveller Richard Overton in Newgate prison
and then Overton herself in Bridewell prison, both for protesting the tyrannical
procedures of Parliament. Overton presented her thoughts in a pamphlet that

detailed less the reasons why she or her husband should be released than a description of how she was vilified for *publicly* voicing her grievances. She recalled in graphic detail how she was 'most inhumanely and barbarously dragged headlong up the stones through all the dirt and the mire in the streets, and by the way was most unjustly reproached and vilified by officers, with the scandalous, infamous names of wicked whore, strumpet, &c.'[13] Overton was labeled as a lascivious woman simply because of her having been seen in public speaking on behalf of her husband. Her treatment exemplified not only the physical maltreatment of the protesting female body but also the harsh language to which the dissenting female voice was subject.

Official government reaction to petitioning women was more subtle but no less derogatory. In 1642, just months before the Civil War began, tensions were running high in London for several reasons. A petition circulated by one Anne Stagg, described in the petition as a gentlewoman and a brewer's wife, articulated the concerns of women citizens about the spread of Catholicism from Ireland, where reports of widespread massacres of Protestants the previous October had created hysteria on the mainland. What is significant about this petition is the way in which the women petitioners appropriated the role of councillors to Charles I in advising means of resolving this tension rather than simply expressing their concerns. The printed version of this petition concluded with a response from John Pym, the speaker of the House, who was a Parliamentary hero when Anne Stagg delivered the petition to Parliament on 4 February 1642. Three weeks prior to the delivery of this petition, Charles I had entered the House demanding the arrest of Pym and four other members. The members had fled only to be escorted back in triumph a week later. As a vociferous and highly visible advocate of Parliament and a critic of royal prerogative, Pym might have been expected to express sympathy with the content of the petition and hence the political cause of the petitioners. However, although Pym's response indicates that the House of Commons read and considered the petition, its text reveals more Parliament's concerns with the gathering of women in public places than with the issues broached by the women authors of the petition. Amidst the *pro forma* rhetoric embodied in the acceptance of the petition is a request that seeks to subsume the political activism of these women in conventional patterns of domestic behaviour that are regarded as more fitting to their gender. After validating their requests as 'lawfull desires,' Pym added this request: 'We intreat you to repaire to your Houses, and turne your Petition which you have delivered here, into Prayers at home for us.'[14] Couched as a reasonable directive, Pym's orders encapsulate the rhetoric of containment. The intent is to transform matters of political urgency expressed in public into acts of domestic piety. By espousing solitary inner petitioning, Pym sought to divert the women petitioners from maintaining a collective and visible presence at the heart of patriarchal political power.

This attempt at containing protest was in keeping with other attempts to confine the threat that such women were perceived to pose. Newsbooks ridiculed the notion of women petitioning by invariably attaching sexual innuendo to their requests. Tropes that represented women as sexual objects subverted serious political protest. The Royalist newsbook *Mercurius Pragmaticus* reported that one group of women petitioners, frustrated in their desire to present their petition to Parliament, ran up and down 'like a company of gossips, and shewed their petitions to everyone. One of them shewing it to a Gentleman, she bad him stand to it, for this is an open time, upon which the blade swore that if she were handsome, he would stand to her.'[15] The anecdote was worth telling, the newsbook implied, because of its comedic value. Yet the implication of the anecdote was more telling still: the militancy of the female challenge was offset by the repartee of the male respondent. This was conveyed by exploiting the ambiguity of the direction to 'stand.' Whereas the female petitioner intended it to represent her defiance of prescribed gender behaviour — justified by the 'open time' — the male respondent intended it to mean an assertive male gesture, an erection. Through this display of masculine wit, militant female protest was rendered harmless and the conventions of gendered relationships restored.[16]

It is evident that both the legislative male body of Parliament and the male body as represented in the newsbook were engaged in strategies designed to block female political access. While the former sought to avoid any female penetration of the patriarchal legal body, the latter was represented as offering penetration as a means of dissipating the female desire for voicing dissent. Both instances clearly indicated an anxiety about women's proximity to the male-dominated locus of power. The consequences of such gender usurpation were viewed as no less far-reaching than the end of the world. For what else could be signified since 'Adam was now seen struting out of Eve?'[17] The author of this pronouncement was Henry Neville, who, in 1647, produced two pamphlets of a satirical tone that had as their subject matter government by women. In them, Neville imagined that women had indeed gained access to the male body politic in order to assert their own political ascendancy. This enabled him to articulate male anxiety about female penetration and to assuage it by ridiculing the sight of women as legislators, seeking thereby to rhetorically contain the influence of female protest.

Initially, these pamphlets seemed to take seriously the political activism that had been apparent in all of the women's petitioning to Parliament. In *The Parliament of Women*, for example, the female protagonists were described as determined to make laws that ensured that women's view of events would not be silenced: 'our tales shall be heard.'[18] Self-representation compensated for their inability to fight: 'though we want weapons and are abridged of their armes, yet they shall know that / we have the Law in our owne hands, and in our own cases we shall be our owne lawyers and plead our own right.'[19] As a Parliamentarian in the 1640s who would be appointed a member of the influential Council of State in 1651, Neville's voicing here of women's political autonomy appeared to associate him with democratic principles of meritocracy and egalitarianism.[20]   However, the title page of this pamphlet signified the jocular treatment of this apparent threat to male legislative power. It declared that the intentions of this parliament of women were to pass laws that would enable them to live in more ease, pride, and wantonness, to ensure that they achieved sovereignty over their husbands. In a predictable gesture toward gender stereotypes, the Parliamentary session imagined in the pamphlet deteriorated into garrulous anarchy. Neville sardonically declared his surprise that this session of Parliament had lasted as long as it had: 'it was a wonder among women, they suffered one to speak at once.'[21] Furthermore, the author concluded his text by asserting that politics was a matter exclusively the prerogative of men. While the text condemned members of this Parliament of women for their levity and inconstancy, it commended the son of the fictive Matron (the female equivalent of the speaker of the House) for his silence and taciturnity in refusing to divulge to his mother the speeches made by the real, non-fictive and exclusively male Parliament at Westminster. This textual strategy served three purposes: first, it assured the male reader that this female-dominated parliament was merely a simulacrum of the 'real' thing; second, by locating their activities within the parlour of a house, Neville domesticated and contained the legislative session. He located it within the confines of the traditional female space, a strategy familiar from other male responses to petitions; third, it asserted that politics was an arcane patriarchal mystery to which women had no access.

Neville's rhetoric consistently expressed political action as sexual innuendo. Orders passed by the Parliament of Women encouraged libertinism. The absence of men, occasioned, as the text explained, by their active service on the battlefield, produced a legislative order (dated 13 August 1647 by Neville to convey the impression of authenticity) that instructed 'any women venereously inclined, and capable of more than is put upon her, to use the ayd and assistance, not onely of the men of her own Nation, but also of any other Forraigner.'[22] Neville's text mocked the potential for power-sharing, relating that, when the Parliament at Westminster requested that the ladies concur with their order forbidding malignant ministers from preaching in the pulpit, the women were keenly debating instead the word 'enter' and considered only those divines who had 'entered their pulpits to their exceeding comfort.'[23] Clearly, the text suggested, women could not be trusted to participate in the serious business of politics, and could only be seen and see themselves as sexual objects or lascivious bodies serving their husbands and, by implication, the state. In this respect republican rhetoric about women's connection with power was as disparaging as the rhetoric of Royalist newsbooks. [24]

The Passive Political Body

Henry Neville's fictional account of women accessing a male prerogative was offered in contrast to an absence of actual power enjoyed by women during a period of social upheaval. As the reception of Anne Stagg's petition suggests, there was no true intent of allowing a broad body of women access to the chamber where political decision-making took place.[25]

In the second half of this essay, I will examine how these strategies of controlling the radical articulation of political protest *by* a female body of petitioners was mirrored by male writers who spoke *through* the female body as they debated whether Parliament had any legitimate right to pass legislative ordinances. In moving from the politics of the street to the politics of the legislative chamber, all female articulation was rendered silent. Therefore it will be my contention that while women's presence in Parliament, a presence that was denied to the women petitioners discussed in the first half of the essay, was discernible, women were there only by proxy, through analogy. The denigrating images with which Royalists and Parliamentarians alike described this passive body, as they articulated different concepts of political legitimacy, metonymically embodied the status of such women in general in mid-seventeenth-century England.

The use of gender relations to describe politics was a commonplace of Civil War discourse. Domestic tropes were consistently regarded as apposite analogies. As negotiations between Charles I and Parliament continued into 1648, one commentator remarked: 'I know no comparison doth run better, or more fit than that of a man and his wife, with the King, and his Parliament.'[26] It was striking, however, that this comparison did not extend to descriptions of the royal and the Parliamentarian bodies. The lack of reference to the maleness of the king was compensated by the attention given to the feminine nature of Parliament. And the analogy was not favourable. Pamphlets and newsbooks of the 1640s consistently made negative comparisons between the female body and the political status of the nation. Writers commonly characterized political dissent as materialized by the body, and figured female corporeality as an image of internal strife within the body politic. This particularly implicated the maternal body whose signs of heterodoxy were said to be discernible at the birth of her child. The maternal transgression of correct religious and political beliefs was understood to leave its physical mark in the production of offspring inevitably malformed and disfigured, exemplifying what Mitchell and Synder have described as 'deformities of the surface (signalling) an ideologically inflected body.'[27] The title page to the 1645 pamphlet *A Declaration of A Strange And Wonderful Monster* depicted a headless child with a face upon its breast. This monstrosity was viewed as a consequence of the mother's having made the wrong political decision.[28] The punning author informed the reader that the mother had cursed the Parliament and vowed to have a child without a head rather than it should be a roundhead.[29]   The text validated this occurrence by revealing the mother's papist inclinations, her marriage to a papist and the use of her house by heretics.   She was criticized for supporting the king and for declaring that Puritans and Independents — that is, those believing in non-hierarchical churches — should be hanged.   This account was printed by Parliament to show the effect of the hand of God on those who derided them.   Such an admonitory narrative reveals that Parliamentary writers were just as prone as Royalist writers to castigate those women who deviated from their paradigm of orthodox gender behavior.

Dissent was lineal, as the political sins of the mother were often passed on to the daughter.   Freakish female offspring became allegories for political dissent.   Richard Brathwaite's political romance *Panthalia* contains a story from the west of England that occurred shortly before Charles I's execution. Brathwaite used the story as a moral for the turmoil of the body politic of the 1640s:

> a Female child was born, that from the belly upward was a Twin, having two heads, two breasts and four arms; and the one part did that which the other did not: so while the one did eat, the other would not; and whilest the one slept, the other waked. And having lived in this manner (as a prodigy to nature) for some certain time, the one died, the other surviving; which afterwards through the stench of the other, died also. That which by this prodigious event, had been formerly predicted, was by as fearful an issue not long after seconded, in production of those state combustions, whereto no age was ever exemplary.[30]

The female body, distorted and monstrous, was regarded, then, as precipitating and signifying political disturbance.

And it was at tense moments of political impasse that such monstrous offspring occurred. 1647 was a year notable for a series of failed negotiations between king and Parliament.   The Parliamentary army, which was in a volatile mood because of Parliament's plans to disband it, acted as a crucial third political player. Its leadership had produced radical political proposals and soon took over the power of Parliament when the army marched into London in September 1647. The Parliamentary army's increasing frustration at Parliament's inability to become more hawkish in its negotiations with Charles I influenced Parliament's decision in January 1648 to suspend its addresses to the king. The Royalist newsbook *Mercurius Aulicus* referred to the printed declaration of this intention as 'a dreadful monster with a headlesse Trunk: the blessed issue of an adulterous and bloody Parliament after the tedious labour of seven years.'[31] All political enactments carried out under the aegis of Parliamentary assent were figured as monstrous offspring, while its body, the House of Commons, was depicted as an unfaithful female exposed for a protracted viewing. Ironically, the following year, this Parliament would substitute the real for the symbolic: Charles' headless trunk, lying on the scaffold, would signify 'the blessed issue' that Parliament finally delivered to the nation.

Aulicus's equation of unacceptable political negotiations with pregnancy and deformity was a typical strategy, subscribing to what Jonathan Sawday has described as a common practice of cutting up female bodies in texts 'in order to be circulated as a specifically male knowledge of women.'[32] Nowhere was the sight of the female body figured through the language of reproduction used more comprehensively than in articulating the question of whether Parliament had the legal right to pass legislation in the absence of the king. This legal question had arisen because Charles I had absented himself from all political decision-making when he fled to Oxford at the end of 1642, not to return to London again until his execution seven years later. Royalists claimed that political illegitimacies and the defeat of Parliamentary laws were to be expected in the absence of the royal progenitor. The Royalist divine and dramatist Jaspar Mayne argued that Parliament could not make or repeal laws without the king:

> Since for *either*, or both *Houses* to produce a *statute Law* by *themselves*, hath alwaies, in this state, been thought a *Birth* as *Monstrous* as if a *child* should be *begotten* by a *Mother* upon *herselfe*. *They* are usually the *Matrice* and *Womb*, where *Lawes* receive their first *Impregnation*, and are *shap't* and *formed* for the *publique*; But...it hath alwaies been acknowledged by the *Law*...that the *King* is thus farre *Pater Patriae*; that these *lawes* are but *abortive* unless his *consent* passe upon them.[33]

Monarchical paternity was thus deemed essential to ensure healthy legal offspring whereas the feminized Parliament was depicted as merely the passive receptacle that awaited such 'passing' and disinterested moments of royal approval. Early the following year, *Mercurius Aulicus* referred to any ordinance of Parliament as

> truly begotten in the adulterous wombe of their inconstant braine; and no sooner brought forth: but it is presented like a puppet on the publique stage of the kingdome for fooles and knaves to look at; yet at the best 'tis a bastard without the assent of majesty, and that's the reason that it perisheth through neglect; being either smothered in the birth, or after production dyes for want of strength, before it gains maturity.[34]

Figured in Royalist texts as the female partner of the king, Parliament was depicted here as a maternal figure of unfaithfulness and fickleness, regularly exposing itself to shame in public, uncaring towards its political offspring and unable to ensure their survival. The author castigated the House of Commons for suspending its protracted negotiations with Charles I. Parliament was politically unfaithful and capable of producing only verbally deficient proposals in the absence of the inscriber of a proficient rhetorical style. The implication here was that only Charles' presence as patriarchal progenitor with his signature on the feminine body of the nation could ensure legislative legitimacy.[35]

In retaliation, Parliamentarian pamphlets sought to correct this impression by emphasizing not only the legitimacy of their legislative offspring but their healthy survival rate. When John Cleveland defined an ordinance as 'a Law still-borne; dropt, before quickned by the Royal assent,' Parliament retorted *in A Full Answer to a scandalous pamphlet*. The author defended the legitimacy of the perfectly formed and virile ordinances produced in the absence of the monarch: 'Thus are our Ordinances no subventantious, or abortive births, but reall, mature, and *Herculean* Infants, destin'd and brought forth, to strangle those serpents, sent out by malignant *Juno*, to destroy our Religion, and Liberties.'[36] This statement challenged the Royalist depiction of Parliament as an unproductive and inefficient female body that could not bring its births to full term or ensure their survival. Here Parliamentarian legal acts were mythologized as feminized political bodies that not only produced substantive offspring but virile and aggressive male offspring intent on thwarting insidious monarchical schemes, which were characterized as malevolently female in origin. As important as the pamphlet's masculine posturing was the author's implication that the royal progenitor was superfluous. These ordinances were mature and therefore did not require patriarchal fiat.[37] John Milton would substantiate this claim after the regicide in his *Eikonoklastes*, a reply to the influential *Eikon Basilike*, thought to have been authored by Charles I. Milton contended that as Parliament made kings, therefore Charles 'ought then to have so thought of a Parlament, if he count it not Male, as of his Mother.' As a consequence, 'what can it be less then actual tyranny to affirme waking, that the Parlament, which is his Mother, can neither conceive or bring forth *any autoritative Act* without his Masculine coition.'[38] Milton used a different approach, with his implications of incest logically and wittily negating the necessity of royal assent, than did *A Full Answer*. Yet both texts testified to Parliament's use of generative metaphors and of the female body to challenge Royalists' use of the same metaphors as a means of legitimating patriarchal power.

It is evident that despite Parliamentary writers' favorable representations of the maternal body, its value as a political trope was unquestioned. Satirized or defended, the construction of the female body as a passive site of contested meaning was an accepted aspect of political discourse. Its pervasive presence was indicated by the way in which it extended beyond the legal precincts of London. In James Howell's 1645 pamphlet *England's Tears For The Present Wars*, the maternal body was used to represent the whole of England, personified as a distressed mother addressing her daughter, London. As a feminized body, England was subject to masculine imprecatory actions.   Howell depicted a female subject physically debilitated by the intrusions of her children, who she had felt 'lacerate and rip up (viper like) the womb that brought them forth, to tear the paps that gave them suck.'[39]   In recalling previous civil wars, England recounted that, during the War of the Roses, 'there was a Monster with two heads…I mean during that time that I had two kings at once, *Edward the 4*, and *Henry the 6* within me…in five years I had twelve Battails fought within my entrails… .'[40]   The maternal body was construed by Howell as a site of the grotesque, a passive container for internal dissent, and the battleground for male contestation.

Howell did not exclude himself from this patriarchal fantasy of marking the female body.   His personification of England concluded her lament, 'If I and my Monarchy miscarry, I desire that my Epitath may be written…by my dearly beloved childe'[41]; Howell then appended his name. Stepping in as the royal apologist for the absent monarchical father, Howell paternally inscribed and voiced as text the sentiments of a personified female whose body had been marked and identified with the inscriptions of her belligerent male offspring.   The end result of Howell's mapping of the female body as an analogy for the whole nation was a systematically sadistic violation of this body.   Anatomized by uncivil practices, the figure of the female body spoke powerfully of the cultural violence the nation had visited upon itself.

Such narratives indicate that the seventeenth-century use of the metaphor of the female body to describe political crisis drew attention to the very practices by which Englishwomen were generally accorded a subordinate status.[42]   This is most evident in the pronounced docileness of the female form subjected to wilful acts of punitive desecration, as described by Howell, and exposed to public viewing as the Royalist pamphlets proposed.   Such a patriarchal discourse also embodied the rhetorical power of analogy.   In this context, the female body functioned as a useful analogy by means of which newsbook writers and pamphleteers could articulate the contestation of power between Royalists and Parliamentarians.   Such strategies relegated women to non-speaking parts within the locus of power — that very Parliament rendered metaphorically female by these same authors.   Further, by steering dissenting women away from Parliament and back towards their homes, as Neville's pamphlets and Stagg's petition have shown, Royalist and Parliamentarian writers alike indicated that questioning a political paradigm — the relationship between king and Parliament — did not necessarily entail reconsidering a cultural counterpart to that paradigm: that of the place of women in Civil War Britain.

Notes

[1]   G.E. Aylmer, *Rebellion or Revolution?: England 1640-1660* (Oxford: Oxford University Press, 1987); Conrad Russell, *The Causes of the English Civil War: The Ford Lectures*

Delivered in the University of Oxford, 1987-1988 (Oxford: Oxford University Press, 1990).

[2] See Ellen McArthur's essay 'Women Petitioners and the Long Parliament,' *English Historical Review* 24 (1919): 698-709.

[3] See Patricia Higgins, 'The Reactions of Women, with special references to women petitioners' in *Politics, Religion and the English Civil War*, ed. Brian Manning (London: Edward Arnold, 1973), 179-97; Ann Marie McEntee, ' "The [Un]Civill-Sisterhood of Oranges and Lemons": Female Petitioners and Demonstrators, 1642-3' in *Pamphlet Wars.Prose in the English Revolution*, ed. James Holstun (London: Frank Cass, 1992), 92-3; Ann Hughes, 'Gender and Politics in Leveller Literature' in *Political Culture and Cultural Politics in Early Modern England : essays presented to David Underdown*, eds. Susan D. Amussen and Mark A. Kishlansky (Manchester: Manchester University, 1995), 162-89. For a detailed bibliography of articles about women petitioners *see British Women's History. A Bibliographical Guide*, compiled by June Hannam, Ann Hughes and Pauline Stafford (Manchester: Manchester University Press, 1996) and *Women and the Literature of the Seventeenth Century. An Annotated Bibliography based on Wing's Short-title Catalogue*, compiled by Hilda L. Smith and Susan Cardinale (New York: Greenwood Press, 1990).

[4] McEntee is right to suggest that '[n]ewspaper accounts of the petitioners' activities...attempted to discredit women's political power by relocating them in a traditionally gendered realm...' (op.cit., 93).

[5] For an overview of Foucault and feminism, see Monique Deveaux , 'Feminism and Enpowerment. A Critical Reading of Foucault,' *Feminist Studies* 20, no. 2 (1994): 223-39.

[6] Hilda Smith, for example, talks about gendered language in terms of how pronoun references hint at women's possible but not definitive presence in the corporate nature of the political body. Her concern is whether men, when they talk about politics, understand it to include women and how they would imply it if so. See Smith, ed., *Women Writers and The Early Modern British Political Condition* (Cambridge: Cambridge University Press, 1998).

[7] Moira Gatens, 'Corporeal representation in/and the body politic' in *Cartographies. Poststructuralism and the Mapping Of Bodies and Spaces*, eds. Rosalyn Diprose and Robyn Ferrell (North Sydney, Australia: Allen and Unwin, 1991), 82.

[8] *Mercurius Anglicus, junior* (London, 1644), Sig. B7^r.

[9] *Mercurius Britanicus* (September 1643), 42. Royalists had set up their headquarters in Oxford towards the end of 1642 and it would remain the center of their political operations until the surrender of the city in 1645.

[10] *Mercurius Britanicus* (July 1645), 817-8.

[11] See, for instance, *The Humble Petition of many thousands of wives and matrons of the City of London...For the cessation and finall conclusion of these civill wars, and for the restitution and revocation of their husbands* (London, 1643). It is often difficult to determine the true authorship and tone of such petitions. In this pamphlet, the wives and matrons of London criticize 'malicious and ungracious reports' (A2v) that misrepresent their sex as talking too much, wearing the breeches in the house and consuming their husbands' estates. Nevertheless, despite this consciousness of the gendered stereotype, their desire is less for more equitable treatment than for libidinous satisfaction. As their husbands return from the war lame and impotent, a relaxation on monogamy would enable them to do their bit for the monarchy: 'to bring forth children every yeare to increase the number of the kings liege people and faithful subjects' (Sig. A4v). Smith and Cardinale have noted that *The Humble Petition* pamphlet is 'one of many semi-pornographic tracts supposedly written by lustful women who miss their absent husbands' (op. cit., 209).

[12] 'Anarchy' (London, 1647).

[13] *The petition of Mary Overton, Prisoner in Bridewell, to the House of Commons* (London, 1647), Sig. A4^r.

[14] *A True Copie of the Petition of the Gentlewomen, and Tradesmens-wives, in and about the City of London* (London, 1642), 7.

[15] *Mercurius Pragmaticus* (April 1648), 16.

[16] See McEntee's commentary on how newsbooks developed 'the notion of women's power as exclusively sexual' (op.cit., 93).

[17] Henry Neville, *Parliament of Ladies* (London, 1647), Sig. B3^r.

[18] Neville, *Parliament of Women* (London, 1647), Sig. A3^v.

[19] Ibid.

[20] For a review of Neville's republicanism, see Susan Wiseman, ' "Adam, the Father of all Flesh,' Porno-Political Rhetoric and Political Theory in and After the English Civil War' in *Pamphlet Wars: Prose in the English Revolution*, ed. James Holstun (London: Frank Cass, 1992), 135. Wiseman's essay focuses on the connections between sexual satire and political theory. Wiseman's focus on satires of male republicans that fused their politics with sexual licentiousness turns on its head the way in which republicans like Neville were fusing women's politics with sexual licence.

[21] Neville, *Parliament of Women*, Sig. A2^v.

[22] Neville, *Parliament of Women*, Sig. B2^v.

[23] Neville, *Parliament of Women*, Sig. A3^r.

[24] Wiseman makes the astute observation that what worried Neville was the commingling of women's political interests with their presumed sexual interests, a merger that would necessarily result in their inability to determine which political side in the conflict had more merit. See Wiseman, op. cit., 147.

[25] This strategy of excluding a corpus of female citizens from power was markedly distinguishable from the political access once exercised by a single woman, Elizabeth I. It is likely that the pejorative references of later male writers to the vocal and visible activism of the female body were informed by the rhetoric of Elizabeth's detractors, who had reviled during and following her reign the unnatural and transgressive potency of a female ruler. The later commentaries studied here drew on similar vocabularies to disqualify women from achieving in even a limited way the kind of political power to which the female monarch had once obtained privileged access. For a discussion of this rhetoric of dissent, see Julia Walker, ed., *Dissing Elizabeth: Negative Representations of Gloriana* (Durham and London: Duke University Press, 1998). Particularly pertinent to my essay are Susan Doran's essay entitled 'Why did Elizabeth not marry?' (30-59) and Carole Levin's essay entitled ' "We shall never have a merry world while the Queene lyveth": Gender, Monarchy and The Power of Words' (77-95).

[26] Arthur Nethercote, *Parables Reflecting Upon The Times* (London, 1648), 7.

[27] David Mitchell and Sharon I. Synder., eds., *The Body and Physical Difference: Discourses of Disability* (Ann Arbor: University of Michigan Press, 1997), 6.

[28] Diane Purkiss argues that 'the literature on monstrous births abounds with tales of women who produced abnormal infants because their imaginations were fixed on something inappropriate at the moment of conception.' See Purkiss, 'Producing the Voice, Consuming the Body' in *Women, Writing, History 1640-1740*, ed. Isobel Grundy and Susan Wiseman (Athens: University of Georgia Press, 1992), 154.

[29] This designation was associated with the pudding bowl haircut favored by Parliamentary soldiers.

[30] Richard Brathwaite, *Panthalia* (London, 1659), Sig. R5v.

[31] *Mercurius Aulicus*, vol. 1 (London, 1648), Sig. C2^v.

[32] Jonathan Sawday, *The Body Emblazoned: Dissection and the Human Body In Renaissance Culture* (London: Routledge, 1995), 212.

[33] Jaspar Mayne, *The Peoples War* (1647), Sig. B4^r.

[34] *Mercurius Aulicus*, vol. 1, Sig. A4^r.

[35] According to Foucault, 'In a society like that of the seventeenth century, the King's body wasn't a metaphor, but a political reality. Its physical presence was necessary for the functioning of the monarchy.' See Foucault, *Power/Knowledge: Selected Interviews & Other Writings 1972-1977*, ed. Colin Gordon (New York: Pantheon Books, 1980), 55. From a Parliamentary perspective, however, the king, by his very absence, could only be referred to in a metaphorical sense. The royal material body was as distant from the

political process as were the women through whose metaphorical bodies contentious debate was articulated.

[36] John Cleveland, *Character of A London Diurnall* (London, 1644), Sig. A2^r; *A Full Answer to a scandalous pamphlet Intituled A Character...* (London, 1645), Sig. A3^v.

[37] This had been suggested within a few years of the onset of the Civil War. William Ball was a political theorist who sought to eradicate the zealous opinions of both Parliamentarians and Royalists in order to encourage dialogue between the warring sides. He did believe though that Parliament had the right to pass legislation for altruistic reasons: 'yet his [the king's] dissent doth not nor cannot frustrate, or make void an ordinance concluded of and avouched by both Houses of Parliament, and generally accepted of by the whole, or major part of the kingdome, and the reason is, because the Parliament is the representative Body of the kingdome, intrusted by the kingdome, and may therefore conclude of, and constitute what shall seem expedient for the good of the kingdome.' Ball, *Tracatus De Jure Regnandi & Regni. Or, the sphere of Government, According to the law of God, Nature, and Nations* (London, 1645), 9.

[38] John Milton, *The Complete Prose Works of John Milton*, ed. Merritt Y. Hughes, vol. 3 (New Haven: Yale University Press, 1962), 467. Taking up Milton's association of a masculine Parliament with a feminine king, the Royalist Joseph Jane commented that 'Parliaments can be noe Mothers to kings, that are created by kings. The king is by the law of England Father of the Countrey, & the life, and soule of the law... .' Jane, *The Image Unbroaken* (London, 1651), 186. Jane believed in a patriarchal lineage of monarchy that was self-generative and in no need of female assistance.

[39] James Howell, *England's Tears For The Present Wars* (London 1645), 180.

[40] Ibid.

[41] Howell, 191.

[42] Many feminist theorists argue that these patriarchal practices have been overlooked. See in particular Sandra Lee Bartky's article entitled 'Foucault, Femininity, and Patriarchal Power' in *Feminism and Foucault. Reflections on Resistance*, eds. Irene Diamond and Lee Quinby (Boston: Northeastern Press, 1988), 63-4.

2 'As Strong as Any Man': Sojourner Truth's Tall Tale Embodiment

Alison Piepmeier

Sojourner Truth was an abolitionist and feminist activist who used her many public speeches to construct her body as a site of culture in the public eye. As an African American and freed slave, she did not have untroubled access to the defining rhetorical models of white female identity in nineteenth-century America. The author of this essay argues that Truth enacted a critique of certain nineteenth-century ideals of womanhood by identifying herself with a different discourse, that of the tall tale. The essay examines one particular moment of Truth's corporeal self-construction, her 1851 speech at the Akron Woman Rights Convention, the speech commonly known as 'Ar'n't I a Woman?' By defining herself in this speech as a kind of tall-tale figure, Truth is shown to have enacted a deliberate and politically revisionary construction of her body, representing herself as a powerful, physically capable, economically self-sufficient person who was emphatically and defiantly a woman. Examining Truth within the rubric of the tall tale genre, the author argues, reveals her strategic negotiation of public discourses as a means of constructing female selfhood as heroic.

> I want to say a few words about this matter. I am a woman's rights. I have as much muscle as any man, and can do as much work as any man. I have plowed and reaped and husked and chopped and mowed, and can any man do more than that? I have heard much about the sexes being equal; I can carry as much as any man, and can eat as much too, if I can get it. I am as strong as any man that is now.

So begins Sojourner Truth's most famous speech, alternately called 'Ar'n't I a Woman?' and 'Ain't I a Woman?,' which she presented to the Akron Woman Rights Convention in 1851. This best-known of all Truth's public utterances has been widely anthologized in the twentieth century; it is the production for which Truth is best known. These first lines demonstrate Truth's insistence on engaging with women's rights at the most material level, the level of the body. Truth configures herself as a powerfully physical form, capable of feats of strength equal to that of any man. If Truth's words are interpreted within that most familiar of nineteenth-century constructs of womanly existence — true womanhood — her speech seems shocking, ahead of its time, and indeed it was. But true womanhood is not the most productive context within which to understand Truth's Akron speech or her other public acts. In this speech and elsewhere in her speeches and the reports of her life written by others, Truth uses and revises the tall tale form to construct her bodily identity.

Truth (1797-1883) was a public speaker for most of her life, traveling around the country first as a preacher and later as a political speaker advocating abolition and women's rights. Thus her public body was configured on stage, before mostly white audiences. As an illiterate woman, she had limited control over the written texts that were produced in response to her speeches, so her voice became an important extension of her body, allowing her body to bespeak itself onstage. Through her acts of speech, Truth constructed a public body unlike her material body but which became a substitute for it.[1] By utilizing the tall tale discourse, Truth avoided both negative models of black female embodiment and oppressive discourses of white female embodiment while still defining for herself a highly corporeal and dramatically public life.

The models of black female embodiment available in the nineteenth century were problematic, to say the least. Black women were represented in much scientific literature as overly sexual and animalistic. Pro-slavery rhetoric characterized blacks as having bodies especially suited for oppressive labor.[2] Even abolitionist discourse frequently characterized black women in terms of their deviation from the true womanly ideal and emphasized their victimization and their suffering. Thus, Truth faced a host of troubling representations of African American female bodies as she began her career as a public speaker, and she had to navigate her way through these models as she attempted to represent her own bodily identity.

The most positive model available, the one which least threatened Truth's safety — what one critic calls 'the already canonized figure of the suffering slave, particularly the sexually degraded slave woman' presented by abolitionist writers — still carried with it a host of troubling implications, not least of which was the way the discourses of sentiment and suffering shaped black women's stories.[3] Late twentieth-century critics tend to replicate this approach, interpreting the work of women writers, especially African American women, in terms of victimization. However, this type of approach is inadequate to represent Truth, who deliberately positioned herself outside these discourses. Truth does not seem to have seen herself as a victim at all; instead, she presented herself as a tall tale hero. The genre of the tall tale allowed Truth to capitalize on the ways in which she deviated from the assumed norms of true womanhood and sentimentalism while still making herself a figure appealing to a white, middle-class audience.

By examining Truth's constructed embodiment in light of the tall tale elements evident within that construction, we can more fully explore Truth's anti-sentimental configurations of her body and her life. The genre of the tall tale allowed her to address, in Hazel Carby's terms, 'the depth of the polarity between ideologies of black and white womanhood';[4] as many critics have noted, white and black women experienced and were subject to very different expectations and ideals of womanhood. Truth could articulate this particular polarity by aligning herself with the tall tale, which values the very qualities true womanhood forbids: power, outspokenness, strength, even violence and vulgarity.

However, it is important to note that this particular polarity does not define Truth entirely. Truth's relationship to white ideologies was not exclusively confrontational. By positioning herself within the tall tale genre, Truth was identifying herself with a genre that was primarily peopled by white characters and was familiar to most nineteenth-century white and black Americans. Her use of the tall tale thus allowed her to confront certain ideologies while remaining a familiar and friendly figure to her audience, and this dual standpoint helped her to establish the authority necessary to allow her to enact her critique of American culture. Although Truth did make strategic revisions of the tall tale model in her self-construction, this essay will examine how she aligned herself with the model to heroicize herself and thus better equip herself to propound her message of women's rights and racial equality.[5]

One of Truth's best known speeches, commonly called 'Ar'n't I a Woman?,' is a contested site, because competing versions of her speech, primarily that printed in the *Anti-Slavery Bugle* and that recorded by Frances Gage, offer significantly different representations of Truth.[6] These differences, however, need not deter us from the study of Truth's self-identifying statements; rather, to examine the interactions of the multiple voices evident in both versions of the speech is to achieve insights into the multiplicity of discourses in nineteenth-century culture. In addition, such study reveals the ways in which a black woman's words are used and transformed within this culture as well as the ways these words interact with the culture. The two versions of Truth's speech may seem contradictory; however, the goal of this essay is not to emphasize their opposition, much less to choose a 'winner's version,' but to examine the two texts in concert, looking at their differences as productive of Truth's changing cultural presence.

Truth made her most famous speech at the 1851 Woman Rights Convention in Akron, Ohio. Shortly after the convention, several periodicals reported the speech. The *Anti-Slavery Bugle* printed the fullest transcription of it on 21 June 1851.[7] The full text from the *Anti-Slavery Bugle* follows.

> One of the most unique and interesting speeches of the Convention was made by Sojourner Truth, an emancipated slave. It is impossible to transfer it to paper, or convey any adequate idea of the effect it produced upon the audience. Those only can appreciate it who saw her powerful form, her whole-souled, earnest gestures, and listened to her strong and

truthful tones.   She came forward to the platform and addressing the President said with great simplicity: 'May I say a few words?' Receiving an affirmative answer, she proceeded; 'I want to say a few words about this matter. I am a woman's rights. I have as much muscle as any man, and can do as much work as any man. I have plowed and reaped and husked and chopped and mowed, and can any man do more than that? I have heard much about the sexes being equal; I can carry as much as any man, and can eat as much too, if I can get it. I am as strong as any man that is now. As for intellect, all I can say is, if woman have a pint and man a quart — why can't she have her little pint full? You need not be afraid to give us our rights for fear we will take too much, — for we can't take more than our pint'll hold. The poor men seem to be all in confusion, and don't know what to do. Why children, if you have woman's rights give it to her and you will feel better. You will have your own rights, and they won't be so much trouble. I can't read, but I can hear. I have heard the bible and have learned that Eve caused man to sin. Well if woman upset the world, do give her a chance to set it right side up again. The Lady has spoken about Jesus, how he never spurned woman from him, and she was right. When Lazarus died, Mary and Martha came to him with faith and love and besought him to raise their brother. And Jesus wept — and Lazarus came forth. And how came Jesus into the world? Through God who created him and woman who bore him. Man, where is your part? But the women are coming up, blessed be God, and a few of the men are coming with them. But man is in a tight place, the poor slave is on him, woman is coming on him, and he is surely between a hawk and a buzzard.'[8]

Anyone familiar with the popularized Truth will notice that this version is very different from the 'Ar'n't I a Woman?' speech as it has made its way onto twentieth-century posters and into books. The *Bugle* version, in fact, appears nowhere in Truth's narrative or her *Book of Life*; the version that appears there is that recorded by Frances Gage. Gage presided over the Woman Rights Convention and therefore stands in a position of some authority in terms of Truth's words. However, Gage's version of Truth's speech was not printed until 1863 — twelve years after the convention itself — and it is significantly different than the version printed, as one critic notes, 'less than thirty days after she delivered it.'[9]

The textual issues surrounding these two versions of Truth's speech are complex.[10]   Although problematic, Gage's version of the speech brought Truth's voice into circulation.[11]   Gage offered physical description of Truth's vocal tone and physical gestures and thus deployed Truth's dramatic physical presence and her ideas. As Painter points out, twentieth-century 'Americans of goodwill deeply need the colossal Sojourner Truth' deployed in Gage's version.[12]   Thus, this discussion will have recourse to both versions of the speech. Rather than acting in opposition, the two versions work together to show the way one woman entered the nineteenth-century public consciousness and identified herself with the tall tale in order to define herself as heroic and powerful rather than as sentimental or freakish.

Truth and the Tall Tale Tradition

Truth's Akron speech shows her as an orator engaging with many different nineteenth-century discourses. Several critics, for instance, have discussed Truth's negotiations of such discourses as religion and racial categorization in her speeches. Others have discussed African American women's negotiations of the sentimental and of true womanhood, discussions that have important bearings on Truth's work.[13]   The tall tale comprises a particularly vivid discourse that Truth utilized to represent herself in her Akron speech, an aspect of the speech not previously noted by critics.[14]

Tall tales flourished in nineteenth-century American folklore. Tall humor emerged as a distinctly American form around the time of the American Revolution and thrived during the nineteenth century. Although not a form of folklore indigenous to America, tall humor and the tall tale became identified with America during the nineteenth century. As one critic asserts, 'Americans adopted tall talk as a national idiom and the tall tale as a national form of humorous storytelling.'[15]   The exaggeration and boasting characteristic of tall humor were particularly suited to expressing the incongruity between America's expectations for itself and the realities of life in the new country. Certainly noting this incongruity was one of Truth's major goals in her speeches, a goal that fitted well with the techniques of tall tales and tall talk.

The tall tale is a particularly oral form, which made it an accessible and welcoming form for the illiterate Truth. Carleton Mabee posits that Truth deployed her engagement with the spoken word as a significant component of her public self-construction: 'In a sense she molded her public image around her illiteracy, using it to dramatize herself and shape her life, turning her illiteracy from a handicap into a significant element of her charm.'[16]   Although the idea of illiteracy as 'charm' is debatable, Mabee offers the valid suggestion that this aspect of Truth's public embodiment may have been a conscious cultural negotiation. Truth's inability to read could become an asset within the world of the tall tale, which valorized acts of speaking and which circulated primarily through the spoken word.[17]

Tall tale bodies constitute the only access listeners have to the characters themselves; tall tale characters are pure embodiment, with no inner life at all. They are the bodies of the frontier, confronting natural forces and negotiating often chaotic landscapes. Most nineteenth-century tall tales feature white men boasting about their feats of hunting, fishing, or brute strength; the protagonists may brag about prowess in such areas as holding their breath or eating an enormous amount of food. They are thus figures in direct opposition to the goals and ideals of the developing nineteenth-century middle-class culture. Their physical brutality and the comedic tone of their tales make tall tale characters a dramatic inversion of the ideals of sentimental womanhood, such as purity, domesticity, middle-class propriety, and the self-contained body. These rewritings of dominant cultural ideologies made the tall tale a potential site of authority; as Carroll Smith-Rosenberg notes, 'power emanated from the violation of categories and the fusion with chaos' evident in tall tales.[18] By aligning herself with the discourse of the tall tale, a speaker like Truth could gain access to this power to enact a critique of particular cultural standards.

The protagonists or heroes of tall tales come in many forms, from the purely fictional to those figures whose exploits may be fictional but whose existence as real people is verifiable.[19] Perhaps the epitome of the folk hero and the tall tale protagonist who was both a real person and an exaggerated fictionalized character is David Crockett. Crockett was, of course, a real person; however, he is remembered less for his real-life exploits than for the legends that grew up around him both during his life and after his death, legends which he created, allowed, and promoted. In these ways, Crockett is an analogous figure to Sojourner Truth.[20]

Truth's use of tall tales in constructing her public body is made clearer through comparison to the Crockett legend, which provides useful parallels to Truth's constructed public image of her corporeality. Crockett's legend was constructed around elements central to the tall tale in general: conflict and comedy, both of which played out and through the protagonist's excessive body. These are elements that Truth utilized in her public presentation of her own body. Crockett's legend was forming during the time that Truth began and then solidified her public speaking career, from the 1830s through the 1850s. While I do not draw a direct causal relationship — I am not suggesting, for instance, that Truth based her public embodiment on the Davy Crockett stories — I do think that Truth was participating in or inserting herself into the same public discourse that inflected Crockett's legend.[21] As Mabee explains, 'Truth often seemed willing to let friendly myths develop around her, myths that might make her a more fascinating advocate of the causes she supported.'[22] Painter, too, emphasizes Truth's role in fashioning her image, explaining that she 'created and marketed the persona of a charismatic woman who had been a slave, and it is precisely through her marketing of herself or, as she put it, her selling the shadow to support her substance, that her name is known today.'[23] By using and revising the tall tale formula to construct her own embodiment, Truth made use of a pre-existing cultural trope which validated the very physical differences that could otherwise have hindered her communication of her message.

Truth's body is constructed within the discourse of the unconventional, excessive tall tale body. The *Bugle* version of her speech opens, 'I am a woman's rights.' This powerful statement, not only of personal identity, but of alliance with a struggle for justice, shows Truth not only striving for women's rights, but presenting herself as their incarnation.   This is the sort of exaggerated, dramatic speech characteristic of tall tales; Truth's proclamation that she is 'a woman's rights' is analogous to Crockett's claims to be 'half-horse, half-alligator and a bit of snapping turtle.'[24]   She then proceeds to describe herself in terms sharply different from those espoused by the rhetoric of true womanhood and the sentimental.   According to the familiar precepts of true womanhood outlined by Barbara Welter, a true woman is delicate, unable to do physical labor, and governs the domestic realm.[25]   Truth defines herself in this part of her speech according to her labor, asserting that she can perform all of the physical acts a man can, stressing, 'I am as strong as any man that is now.'   Rather than skirting the issue of sexual equality, one that raises questions even today, she meets it head on and brings it to the material level, the level of the body, saying, 'I have heard much about the sexes being equal; I can carry as much as any man, and can eat as much, too, if I can get it.'   In Gage's version of the speech her claims become more brutally physical as she claims she 'can bear de lash as well' as any man, boasting of her body's ability to withstand abuse.

This kind of bravado would have been familiar to Truth's audience from the tall tale; bravado is one of the means by which the excessive body is routinely defined within the genre.   Characters like Davy Crockett asserted their identities by boasting of their abilities; for instance, in the first Crockett comic almanac, Crockett is reported as saying he 'can run faster, — jump higher, — squat lower, — dive deeper, — stay under longer, — and come out drier, than any man in the whole country.'[26]   Similarly, in an 1836 almanac, Crockett faces an opponent with the following claim: 'Says I, stranger! I'm the boy that can double up a dozen of you. I'm a whole team just from the roaring river.   — I've rode through a crab apple orchard on a streak of lightning. I've squatted lower than a toad; and jumped higher than a maple tree; I'm all brimstone but my head, and that's aquafortis.'[27]   An important part of the tall tale character's identity is his ability to intimidate his opponents through a show of confidence and braggadocio known as the 'frontier boast.' While the claims are generally so extreme as to be impossible and therefore humorous, within the world of the tale they are considered literally true, and outside the world of the tale they establish the speaker as a clever adversary.

By defining herself in terms that would have been so unwomanly as to be almost laughable in the mid-century — claiming to 'have as much muscle as any man' and to be able to 'carry as much as any man, and…eat as much too' — Truth utilized tall-tale bravado and aligned herself with tall tale characters.   She defined her body according to the conventional tall tale configuration of excessive strength.   At the same time, Truth superseded the tall tale genre, because while her boasts may have seemed absurd to her audience, they had a grounding in physical truth.   During her time as a slave,

Truth had been required to do physical labor that the average middle-class white woman would have found impossible. Although at the time of her Akron speech, Truth was probably no longer physically capable of this kind of labor, her assertions were more than empty or humorous boasts. The purpose of tall tale exaggeration, or tall talk, is to drive home the distance between the real and the ideal worlds. Truth's 'exaggeration' was true, so she represented a real body that undermined the ideal and showed this idea — true womanhood — to be lacking.

In addition to her claims to physical strength, Truth's boast that she 'can eat as much as any man' identifies her with the discourse of the tall tale. Eating is a very important activity within tall tales; the excessive tall tale body is excessive in its ability to eat — both grotesque kinds of food and massive quantities. Crockett, for instance, regularly described his diet. As a child, he explained, 'I would take up a roasted duck by the neck and gnaw the meat off the bones before the rest had time to set down to the table.'[28] Bear's meat is a favorite food within these almanac tales, often cooked by such unusual means as with 'a piece of sunrise' or 'a flash o'lightning.'[29] Crockett's wife drank 'eagle's egg nog,' and the whole family ate 'bush eels' — rattlesnakes.[30] The amount of food a character eats is also a means of emphasizing physical strength; Crockett described a mid-day snack as 'a sandwich, which was composed of half a bear's ham, two spare ribs, a loaf of bread, and a quart of whiskey.'[31] Truth made only one reference to food in her Akron speech, but this brief reference to her ability to eat would instantly have suggested the discourse of the tall tale to her listeners and would have further identified her body with the excessive tall tale bodies. At a time when middle-class table manners were being propounded in such documents as Catharine Beecher's *A Treatise on Domestic Economy* (1842) and in women's magazines like *Godey's Lady's Book*, Truth was participating in a discourse that flouted etiquette and validated eating as a show of carnal strength. By proclaiming her ability to eat, Truth was equating her physical prowess with men's, suggesting therein that she deserved the nourishment men received, confounding the sexist foundations of the cultural directive that women eat little.

Rather than conforming to sentimental standards for women's embodiment, Truth defined herself within a genre that values physical excess and power. Gage's version makes this redefining of the female body particularly clear, for in this version Truth says, ' "Look at me. Look at my arm," and she bared her right arm to the shoulder, showing its tremendous muscular power.' In this version, Truth actually displays her body, manifesting her physical strength. Because Gage's version of the speech is a document meant to be read, her description of Truth's 'tremendous muscular power' has an even more emphatic effect, allowing her readers to imagine Truth as an almost superhuman body.

By showing her audience her muscular arm, Truth aligns herself with the bodily skill and power of Crockett and other tall tale protagonists. In addition, as several critics have noted, she evokes the image of the slave woman on the auction block whose body is displayed for purchase and appropriating it for her own uses. She exposes her arm, not to demonstrate her value in the slave market but to illustrate her power and to define her body in terms different than those that might be applied to her. The force represented in her arm is not evidence of her ability to do physical labor for someone else but is, as for Crockett and other tall tale characters' bodies, evidence of her heroic status.

Without proper contextualization, Truth's claims to physical strength could be read as a reification of her subaltern status as an African American woman whose body was only considered socially valuable if she was able to labor for others. As Carby explains, 'Strength and ability to bear fatigue, argued to be so distasteful a presence in a white woman, were positive features to be emphasized in the promotion and selling of a black female field hand at slave auction.'[32] Indeed, one of Truth's masters had bragged about Truth's strength, telling a friend, ' "*that* wench" (pointing to Isabel [Truth]) "is better to me than a *man* — for she will do a good family's washing in the night, and be ready in the morning to go into the field, where she will do as much at raking and binding as my best hands." '[33] His claim clearly demonstrates the dual role black women were expected to fulfill, that characterized by male physical strength (working in the fields) and that by feminine domesticity (doing the laundry), as well as the value of their labor and strength within the context of both masculine and feminine arenas of work. However, rather than contradict her master's claim by emphasizing the ways in which she might fit within traditional models of womanhood, Truth embraces his characterization of her strength. Importantly, she appropriates this strength for her own purposes, to define herself as a hero and undercut the sexual stereotypes governing black and white women's lives.

By identifying herself with the strength of the tall tale body, arguing, 'I have as much muscle as any man, and can do as much work as any man,' Truth undercut dominant nineteenth-century assumptions about women's embodiment. Her self-definition in terms of strength and labor implied a new envisioning of women's roles. Rather than simply reacting against the nineteenth-century agenda for women, Truth suggested an agenda of her own, one that presented women as a legitimate presence in the world of economic production. Her insistence that she had 'plowed and planted and gathered into barns, and no man could head me' and that she 'could work as much and eat as much as a man' positioned her explicitly as a laborer. She herself could be responsible for the whole process of growing food, from the initial plowing and planting to the final harvesting and storing. She presented herself not as a worker on an assembly line but as an autonomous producer. Truth's speech worked in direct contradiction to the ideals of true womanhood, not only through the actions she described but through her repeated comparison of her body to the body of a man. Her forceful opposition of feminine ideals demystified the ideals, showing that they were not natural attributes of women in that she, as a woman, was not bound by them. She deployed a new ideal of womanhood by explicitly comparing her body to a male body, emphasizing that she had *the same* strength and ability as 'any man' but was still a woman. Truth used this kind of tall talk to construct her own body in a way that dislodged 'true woman' rhetoric.

Truth's actual body was probably five feet, eleven inches in height, dark black, and somewhat muscular (although her right hand had been injured while she was a slave and so was somewhat debilitated). Her tall tale body, however, was formidable — extremely powerful, able to stun a crowd into silence and outdo any man's body. Truth presented her audience with an interpretive script, and this script was profoundly influential; through her self-presentation and representation as a tall tale protagonist, Truth helped her audience and those who reported about her to see her not as a tired, injured older woman but as a tall-tale hero. By aligning her body with the discourse of tall tales, Truth shaped not only her own words but the descriptions others gave of her, and thus destabilized racist and sexist rhetorics. As a tall tale figure, she was able to command a wider audience than she might have as a sentimental figure. She was able to assume authority as a speaker and configure a public bodily presence far more powerful and far-reaching than her material body.

Acknowledgements

Thanks to Cecelia Tichi, Teresa Goddu, and Thadious Davis for helping me to develop this essay.

Notes

[1]   Truth's use of the tall tale to define her body is exemplified in her speeches, but her public life as constituted in print was more complex. For instance, she utilized images of domesticity to define her body in her many *cartes de visite*, photographs of herself that she sold and distributed at her speeches and later in lieu of speeches when she was too ill to travel.

[2]   See Deborah Gray White, *Ar'n't I a Woman? Female Slaves in the Plantation South* (1985) and Hazel Carby, *Reconstructing Womanhood: The Emergence of the Afro-American Woman Novelist* (New York: Oxford University Press, 1987).

[3]   Fanny Nudelman, 'Harriet Jacobs and the Sentimental Politics of Female Suffering,' *ELH* 59 (1992): 941.

[4]   Carby, 32.

[5]   For an evaluation of Truth's revisions of the tall tale model, see the longer version of this essay in Alison Piepmeier, 'Out in Public: Configurations of Women's Bodies in Nineteenth-Century America' (Ph.D. diss., Vanderbilt University, 2000).

[6]   The two versions of Truth's speech I will discuss are 'Women's Rights Convention: Sojourner Truth,' *Anti-Slavery Bugle* [Salem, OH], 21 June 1851, hereafter referred to as the *Bugle* version, and Mrs. F. D. Gage, 'Sojourner Truth,' *Independent*, 23 April 1863, 1, hereafter referred to as the Gage version. These textual differences involve not only

dialect (Gage's version shows Truth speaking in a Southern dialect reminiscent of *Uncle Tom's Cabin*, while the *Bugle* version does not) but reflections of exactly what Truth said and in what order. In addition, the version transcribed by the *Anti-Slavery Bugle* focuses primarily on Truth's words, while Gage's version includes Gage's commentary on Truth's gestures and on the reaction of her audience.

[7] Before this speech was reprinted in the Schomburg Library's 1991 edition of Truth's narrative, it was only available in the original *Anti-Slavery Bugle*.

[8] 'Women's Rights Convention: Sojourner Truth.' This version of Truth's speech is now also available in C. Peter Ripley, ed., *Black Abolitionist Papers* (© 1985) and in Suzanne Pullon Fitch and Roseann M. Mandziuk, *Sojourner Truth as Orator: Wit, Story, and Song* (Westport, CT: Greenwood Press, 1997).

[9] Jeffrey Stewart, introduction to *Narrative of Sojourner Truth:A Bondswoman of Olden Time, with a History of her Labors and Correspondence Drawn from her 'Book of Life,'* by Sojourner Truth (1878; New York: Oxford University Press, 1991), xxxiv.

[10] Gage's version is different in style, form, and even in some content, from the version the *Bugle* printed. In fact, it is stylistically different from many of the quotes from Truth printed elsewhere in her narrative. In Gage's version appears the refrain, 'Ar'n't I a woman?' Gage represents Truth as continually referring to blacks as 'niggers' throughout the speech (something Truth does nowhere else in her narrative or *Book of Life* and something that surely would have been repellent to her), and she portrays Truth as a feisty but somewhat stupid woman. Because of what we assume to be her distortion of Truth's language and the stereotypical images of black womanhood her version evokes, Gage's text is problematic. Although Gage seems to have distorted Truth's words to fit the current stereotypes of black dialect, Gage's is the well-known version of the speech, a version that many of Truth's nineteenth-century admirers would have read; it is through Gage, in fact, that the speech received the name by which it is still known.

[11] Gage's version of the speech appeared in Elizabeth Cady Stanton's *History of Women Suffrage* in 1881, and a recent children's book about Truth is called *Sojourner Truth: Ain't I a Woman* (McKissack, 1992). In addition, both Deborah Gray White and bell hooks have used the phrase 'ain't I a woman' or 'ar'n't I a woman' in the titles of critical books. In the chapter entitled 'Ar'n't I a Woman?' of her biography of Truth, Painter discusses Gage's motivation in crafting her version of Truth's speech as she did. See Nell Painter, *Sojourner Truth: A Life, A Symbol* (New York: Oxford University Press, 1996).

[12] Painter, 284.

[13] For discussions of religion and racial categorization, see Painter, and Fitch and Mandziuk. For sentimentality and true womanhood, see Nudelman and Carby.

[14] In fact, very little critical discussion exists on either fictional women represented in tall tales or actual women who utilized the techniques of tall talk and tall humor in representing themselves. See Michael A. Lofaro, 'Riproarious Shemales: Legendary Women in the Tall Tale World of the Davy Crockett Almanacs,' in *Crockett at 200: New Perspectives on the Man and the Myth*, eds. Michael A. Lofaro and Joe Cummings (Knoxville: University of Tennessee Press, 1989), 148-149, fns. 6-7, for a listing of the work that has been done.

[15] Henry B. Wonham, *Mark Twain and the Art of the Tall Tale*, (New York: Oxford University Press, 1993), 21.

[16] Carlton Mabee, *Sojourner Truth: Slave, Prophet, Legend* (New York: New York University Press, 1993), 65.

[17] In addition to its dissemination through oral channels, tall humor was also communicated through many newspapers, magazines, and comic almanacs.

[18] Carroll Smith-Rosenberg, *Disorderly Conduct: Visions of Gender in Victorian America*, (New York: Oxford University Press, 1985), 97.

[19] See Wonham, *op. cit.* and Michael A. Lofaro, ed., *Davy Crockett:The Man, the Legend, the Legacy, 1786-1986* (Knoxville, TN: University of Tennessee Press, 1985). See Richard Dorson, *America in Legend: Folklore from the Colonial Period to the Present*

(New York: Pantheon Books, 1973) on authentic early nineteenth-century American folk heroes.

[20] Crockett served in the military under Andrew Jackson in 1813 and 1814, and was a representative to the United States Congress from 1827 until 1831 and then from 1833 until 1835. He d·ed at the Alamo in 1836. Several important factors contributed to Crockett's fame, including James Kirke Paulding's very popular play *The Lion of the West* (1831), biographies and autobiographies that appeared between 1833 and 1836 and featured tall embellishment, and the 1835-1856 *Davy Crockett's Almanacks*, comic magazines that represented Crockett as a tall tale hero.

[21] Because Crockett's tall tales have been the subject of a substantial base of research, something which Truth's tall tale persona has not, the Crockett legend offers useful critical apparatus that may be applied to Truth.

[22] Mabee, 68.

[23] Painter, 'Representing Truth: Sojourner Truth's Knowing and Being Known,' *The Journal of American History* 81 (1994): 470.

[24] Quoted in Dorson, *America in Legend*, 77.

[25] For further information, see Welter, *Dimity Convictions: The American Woman in the Nineteenth Century* (Athens: University of Ohio Press, 1976).

[26] Richard Dorson, *Davy Crockett: American Comic Legend* (New York: Arno Press, 1977), 29. Dorson's book remains the most widely-used anthology of Crockett's almanac stories.

[27] Quoted in Michael A. Lofaro, 'The Hidden "Hero" of the Nashville Crockett Almanacs' in *Davy Crockett: The Man, the Legend, the Legacy, 1786-1986*, 55.

[28] Dorson, *Crockett*, 6.

[29] Dorson, *Crockett*, 17, xvii.

[30] Lofaro, 'Riproarious Shemales,' 132. Dorson, *Crockett*, 29.

[31] Dorson, *Crockett*, 6.

[32] Carby, 25.

[33] Sojourner Truth, *Narrative of Sojourner Truth: A Bondswoman of Olden Time, with a History of her Labors and Correspondence Drawn from her 'Book of Life'* (1878; New York: Oxford University Press, 1991), 33.

3 Flappers and Shawls: The Female Embodiment of Irish National Identity in the 1920s

Louise Ryan

In engaging with the theme of women as sites of culture, this essay focuses on the 1920s 'flapper' in the specific environment of the post-colonial southern Irish state. The author argues that this symbol of modern womanhood was a contested site onto which were mapped competing notions of Irish femininity. While traditional nationalist and religious groups used the flapper to embody all that was wrong with the modern, decadent world, other interest groups celebrated the flapper as the site of consumerism, individualism and modernity. In addition, the author demonstrates that while usually associated with the modern city, the siting and sighting of the flapper in rural Irish society brought this controversial female archetype to the very heart of Irish national identity.

The Modern Girl
(extract)

Her feet are so very little
Her hands are so very white
Her jewels so very heavy
And her head so very light

Her colour is made of cosmetics–
Though this she'll never own
Her body is mostly cotton,
And her heart is wholly stone.

She falls in love with a fellow,
who smells with a foreign air;
He marries her for her money,
They are a well-matched pair.
— *John Marcus O'Sullivan*[1]

In the newly established Irish Free State of the 1920s, the flapper or 'modern girl' was a highly contested and deeply controversial symbol of womanhood.[2] Within 'Irish Ireland' nationalist and Catholic discourses the modern girl represented disobedience, vice, immorality and was ultimately constructed as un-Irish, foreign and pagan.   Her embodiment of foreign fashions and lifestyles threatened to destabilize Irish identity and thus undermine the new nation.   National daily newspapers published in Dublin, the capital city, regularly reported concerns about flappers. But such accounts tended to locate modern, fashionable, independent young women in urban centers.[3]   These configurations suggest interwoven gendered dichotomies of urban versus rural, modern versus traditional, sinful versus virtuous.

This chapter engages with these dichotomies by examining representations of the archetypal flapper/modern girl in the provincial press in the southern Irish Free State in the mid to late 1920s.   This study of a previously neglected area of inquiry will raise questions about not only the prevalence of the flapper archetype in rural Ireland but also the construction of this symbol of womanhood in the context of Irish cultural and national identity. Press representations are complex and multifaceted; advertisements, women's pages and feature articles indicate the range and diversity of perspectives that simultaneously celebrated and condemned women's independence and modernity.

Embodying the Nation

Nationalism is a gendered project within which women have been ascribed particular roles and responsibilities.[4]   While it is important not to ignore the active and often violent roles that women have played and continue to play in nationalist movements, women's more usual roles have tended to emphasize passivity and dependency.[5]   As Anthias and Yuval-Davis have theorized, women are represented as symbols of the nation, as mothers of the nation, as transmitters of cultural traditions and as boundary markers between nations.[6] I will argue that it is in this nationalist context that the Irish flapper needs to be located and understood.

The particular religious, social, cultural and political context of the Irish Free State informed the specific constructions and interpretations of the flapper. Following a protracted campaign for Irish independence from Britain that culminated in the Anglo-Irish war of 1919-1921, the southern Irish Free State came into being on 6 December 1922.   This newly established, newly partitioned, semi-independent nation had a lot of work to do to justify its existence and legitimate its demand for complete sovereignty. I have noted elsewhere that, as a new nation, the Free State sought to assert its legitimacy by defining a unique culture and identity that marked Irish people apart and distinct from British people.[7]

Nonetheless, Irish culture in the 1920s was greatly influenced by British forms of entertainment and media, as well as by the growing enthusiasm for Hollywood films.[8]   The government and the powerful Catholic hierarchy attempted to define their authority by restoring traditional order.   This carefully constructed notion of 'traditional' Gaelic, Catholic Ireland was one in which women were to play a very specific role.   Part of this nationalist project was an attempt to distance Ireland from the unflattering and degrading stereotypes that had formed such a core aspect of the colonial experience.[9] Therefore, there was a strong emphasis on the cultural purity, virtue, integrity and honor of the nation.   Idealized womanhood was to embody these virtues and so become 'the badge of respectability' of the new nation-state.   Thus Irish women in general, married mothers and virginal young women in particular, were ascribed the thankless task of representing the purity and uniqueness of Irish national culture and identity.[10]

However, as I have argued at length elsewhere, the gendering of national characteristics was a complex and contradictory process.[11]   For example, Irish women who did not conform to the norms of traditional femininity were used to symbolize national weakness and susceptibility to foreign corruption.   To borrow Meaney's phrase, women became simultaneously the 'bearers of national honor' but also the 'scapegoats of national identity.'[12]   Irish male religious and political leaders asserted their own masculine authority through their attempts to police and contain women's sinful and wayward bodies.   Fashionable, adventurous young women embodied the decadence that threatened not only to undermine masculine authority but also to destabilize the fragile culture of the Irish nation-state.

In Search of the Flapper

In attempting to locate and analyse the specific representations of the flapper — also called the 'modern girl' in the Irish Free State — I have previously explored the mainstream national daily press.[13]   The images in such publications usually focused on urban contexts rather than offering a broader account of the flapper throughout the rest of the nation.   Thus, in an effort to understand the true extent of the flapper image in the country as a whole, I have chosen to concentrate here on the provincial press.   I have selected two primary examples: the largest provincial paper, the *Cork Examiner*, a daily paper, and one of the more fervent cultural nationalist papers, the *Limerick Leader*, published thrice weekly.   In addition, I have selected five weekly papers; the *Kerryman*, based in Tralee but circulated throughout the counties of Kerry, Clare and North Cork, the *Connacht Tribune* and its sister paper the *Connacht Sentinel*, based in Galway but with a wide circulation throughout the West of Ireland, the *Sligo Champion*, and the *Wicklow People*.   Though not claiming this to represent a completely exhaustive survey, I would suggest that together, these papers do cover most of the country outside of the metropolitan centre of Dublin and, of course, the North of Ireland.

In an attempt to make my study manageable, while at the same time aiming to include a good range of issues and topics, I have concentrated on the period between 1926 and 1928. Because the media were dominated by coverage of the armed struggle between 1919 and 1923, there seemed little point in analyzing images of frivolous flappers in the early twenties.[14] The mid-to-late twenties are important because this time encompassed not only an attempt to return to 'normality' but also a visible project of nation building and defining national cultural identity.

On 6 March 1926, the *Connacht Tribune* carried an eye-catching headline, 'Flappers and Shawls.'[15] This headed a column of local court reports, only one of which had any connection with the bold headline. In the trial of a woman for non-payment of bills, the prosecuting barrister asked if she had bought a coat for her daughter. She said no, to which he replied 'what does she put over her blouse, is it a shawl? Very few of the flappers now would be content with a shawl (laughter).' On 24 April 1926, the same paper carried an equally dramatic headline, 'Armed Amazons.'[16] This referred to a dispute over land rights in county Galway. The Civic Guards (police), having arrested several men from the area, were attacked by 'a party of women and girls mostly of the flapper age, armed with sticks and carrying baskets of stale eggs.' In both of these articles, the term flapper is used very generally to refer to young women. In the first article, it refers to clothing and fashion, but in the second, it is vague and may simply refer to age and physical appearance. However, what the articles do suggest is the extent to which the term was in common use in the Irish provincial press.

While these particular references to the flapper were all fairly innocuous, the more usual connotations were extremely negative. Concerns with flapper immorality and immodesty usually focused on her clothes. Her short skirts and sleeveless dresses symbolized not only her modernity but also her vanity. In exposing so much of her flesh, the flapper was a danger to all decent society. On 20 October 1928, the *Wicklow People* published a sermon given by Father Degen in which he addressed the topic of modern fashions. 'Worship of the body takes the place of religion in women who are inordinately vain. The mortal soul is treated as non-existent, and nothing is recognized as sinful except dowdiness. In the case of some women their ambition appears to be to drag men's hearts about on a string.'[17]

The elevation of the body above the soul is an exact reverse of Catholic doctrine and so this image of women who worship their bodies but neglect their souls not only constructs them as vain but as anti-Catholic and doomed to eternal damnation. As Mica Nava has argued, there was a growing suspicion that women derived a libidinous pleasure from 'the physical adornment and nurturing of the self.'[18] Furthermore, women who took such pains over their physical appearance not only endangered their own souls but were also a danger to men. They teased men and broke their hearts. This image of modern women was very common and will be explored in more detail later. For now, let us continue with Father Degen. In attempting to explain this phenomenon, he turned to mothers, asking 'What is your ideal of womanly perfection? Would you really prefer your daughters to imitate the daring sartorial suggestiveness of the modern flapper rather than the modesty, sweetness and gentleness of our Blessed Lady?'[19]

It was common for the flapper to be set up in direct opposition to the modesty of Mary the mother of God. As Maryann Valiulis writes, '[t]he flapper was juxtaposed to the young girl who was innocent and vulnerable. Ecclesiastical discourse thus defined women in the traditional Madonna/Eve split — a dualism which is an integral part of catholic teaching.'[20] Flappers were constructed as wild and uncontrolled daughters but also as poor prospects for marriage and motherhood. On 11 August 1928, the *Wicklow People* published an article on the 'modern young woman,' which focused on her many faults and failings.[21] Men wanted to marry 'a modest, intelligent girl,' 'a sensible, virtuous girl' with 'feminine charm.' Who would wish to marry 'a control defying,' 'good time', 'can anybody come?' flapper?' Here the flapper is seen as frivolous, wilful, superficial, and lacking in the feminine virtues of modesty and good sense.

This image of the immodest and wayward flapper underpinned many sermons and religious pamphlets reprinted in newspapers throughout the Irish Free State in the 1920s. On 7 May 1928, the *Cork Examiner*, the largest provincial newspaper, reported on a sermon by Dr. Roche, the Bishop of Ross.

> In modern times a bit of the spirit of paganism and love of pleasure are prominent features even in the life of good Catholics. It manifests itself particularly at present in regard to female dress. This failing is world-wide. It is not confined to one country or to one parish, or to one class of people, but the disease is prevalent in every land... our people have been caught in this snare of fashion, and in our towns and in the country too, at present, many of our young girls are dressed in a manner that is to men an occasion for sin.[22]

Bishop Roche highlighted the Church's fears about the 'love of pleasure,' which was linked to paganism and was, thus, in opposition to Catholicism. He laid all the blame for modern paganism firmly on the shoulders of young women; women were the carriers and the transmitters of this 'disease,' men seemed to be helpless victims. Interestingly, this quote also established the prevalence of modern fashionable girls in every area of Irish society; in every parish — town and countryside — and in every social class.

Pagan Fashions

On 2 May 1928, the *Limerick Leader* (page 3) reported that notices had been posted outside Catholic churches in the town of Ennis prohibiting the wearing of 'dresses less than 4 inches below the knee, dresses cut lower than the collar bone, dresses without sleeves sufficiently long to cover the arm as far as the wrist, and dresses of transparent material.'[23]

This was not unique but was part of an orchestrated attempt on the part of Church leaders and nationalist organizations to rid Irish society of 'immodest fashion.' In 1927, the Modest Dress and Deportment Crusade was founded in Limerick. This had the backing not only of the Catholic hierarchy in Ireland but also received messages of support from Rome. Churches in Italy were also attempting to bar women wearing 'inappropriate dress.'[24] Newspapers like the *Limerick Leader* also supported the Crusade. On 11 June 1928, the *Leader* editorial addressed the topic of female fashion.

> [Short] feminine garments...are not so numerously or brazenly evident in Limerick now as they were a year or two ago. This gratifying evidence of a return to decency and sanity is largely attributable to the modest dress crusade....The craze for nudity was catching on to a disgusting extent all over Ireland. In this new movement for decency Limerick has so far played a prominent and laudable part...Those who still flaunt in the streets the unbecoming habiliments that are more suited to the bathroom than to a public thoroughfare are now very few and are steadily growing less in number.[25]

The crusade also received the backing of other provincial papers. For example, on 7 April 1928, the *Sligo Champion* carried an article entitled 'A National Campaign for Modesty.'[26] In supporting the crusade, the report began 'Readers of the Sligo Champion who have not already heard of this new national movement will no doubt be glad to have news of it.' It was described in dramatic terms as 'a big push' to save the country from 'demoralising and denationalising influences.' The use of the term 'denationalising' located the modest dress crusade in the particular context of national identity and national sovereignty and so went beyond the narrow focus on modesty and decency in dress. At this moment in history, Ireland 'should prove that she is truly "a nation once again" and show her independence of foreign ascendancy.' The 'tyranny of fashion' was presented as a threat not just to decency but to the 'traditions of our land': 'It is a movement to ensure that 'Dark Rosaleen' shall, as the poet predicted, 'reign a queen' while the other nations of the world are grovelling in the paganism called the new civilisation which is merely a glorification of the animal nature of man and wholly opposed to the spiritual heritage of our race.'[27]

This quote is very revealing and suggests the relationship among nationhood, tradition, heritage, race, and sovereignty. Irish independence can only be maintained if the uniqueness of Irish culture is preserved from modern, foreign, pagan influences. This sets up a dichotomy of native purity and tradition versus outside impurity and modernity. These images are gendered in several ways. Firstly, this dichotomy is mapped onto the bodies of women — the pure, native girl versus the frivolous flapper. Secondly, Ireland, as a nation, is also represented by a female symbol 'Rosaleen,' who is a beautiful, pure, and innocent Irish girl. Thus women become inscribed within images of Ireland and images of Irishness. Women embody the essence of Irish cultural tradition, therefore it is essential that Irish womanhood is safeguarded from all moral corruption so that ultimately Ireland 'herself' can be preserved from foreign assimilation.

But where did these foreign fashions come from and who was responsible for them? In all the newspapers, modern fashions were presented as deeply alien, coming into Ireland from abroad. All the negative aspects of modern living, the jazz age, were associated with foreign influences, but the main sources of influence varied. Usually disreputable cinema influences came from Hollywood, salacious magazines and papers came from England, jazz was described as African, immodest fashions came from Paris. In 'Catholic Notes,' a regular weekly feature, the *Wicklow People* frequently explored the problems and sources of modern fashions. For example, on 15 May 1926, 'Catholic Notes' pointed out that 'vulgar fashions' were dictated by the 'underworld of Paris.'[28] The exact make-up of that underworld was more fully explained in 'Catholic Notes' on 21 January 1928: 'The women of Ireland will be pleased to hear that the designers of their dresses and the fashions are Jews and Freemasons from Paris and other great continental cities.' These were aiming to 'deChristianize society.' 'What is to be said of Catholic women in Ireland who co-operate in this infamous design by slavishly following every mode decreed by these tyrannical fashion-makers?'[29]

The insidious nature of these Parisian styles can be seen in a report published in the *Connacht Sentinel* on 28 February 1928, under the intriguing headline 'Parisian Style Frocks: Ceilidhe Fashions Criticized.' The Irish language movement, the Gaelic League, expressed its concern about the clothes that women wore to traditional Irish dances or 'ceilidhe.' Although the League was keen to promote Irish dances and Irish music in opposition to foreign cultural influences, it was frustrated to discover that even when young women did turn up to such events, they brought modern fashions with them: 'Ladies' Irish costumes are scarcely ever seen; all the cailini [girls] are attired in the very latest Parisian fashions.'[30]

Both the independence of women and that of the nation were undermined by the dictates of modern fashions. Women's freedom, like Ireland's freedom, was only possible through a return to religious values and traditional lifestyle. This argument represents a complete reversal of the usual way in which 1920's fashions were viewed, that is, as liberating for women, representing women's newly found political, educational and economic opportunities.[31] Coupled with the demise of constricting corsets, loose-fitting clothing and shorter skirts facilitated women's greater mobility and freedom of movement. According to the Catholic hierarchy and Irish cultural nationalists, however, modern fashions threatened to enslave women. In a report carried in both the *Connacht Tribune* and the *Sligo Champion*, Archbishop Gilmartin of Tuam was quoted as saying,

> We do not want to make you all monks and nuns. We do not want to ban your innocent recreations. All we want is that you would restrain yourselves from sinful excess, and not allow yourselves to become slaves to pagan fashions and sinful pleasures. We want you boys and girls to remake the beautiful Ireland of the past — an Ireland of brave, clean boys and pure girls; an Ireland of happy marriages and happy homes.[32]

Thus true happiness and freedom lay in the past, in heritage and tradition, not in the fashions and lifestyles of modernity.

Conflicting Images

Thus on first reading, it would appear simply that Irish provincial newspapers were united in their condemnation of modern fashions and modern flappers, seeking instead to elevate traditional womanhood to her rightful place as pure embodiment of a pure nation. However, this reading ignores some of the wider complexities around the image of the fashionable modern girl.

Two of the provincial papers in this study had regular women's pages — the *Kerryman*'s 'Women's Chat' and the *Cork Examiner*'s 'Woman's World.' These concentrated mostly on fashion advice, reviewing the latest from Paris, London and Hollywood. There were also regular references to 'the modern girl,' usually described in positive tones. On 13 August 1927, the *Kerryman* carried a fashion report under the sensational heading 'Trousers for women.'[33] Designers were refusing to shorten women's skirts any further despite the continuing pressures from women themselves. So in an attempt to solve the 'skirt length controversy,' designers were proposing a compromise in the form of trousers which would look like 'plus fours' drawn into the leg well below the knee. Later that month, 'Women's Chat' again returned to the topic of women's reluctance to return to more constricting dress. Designers were reported to be making 'considerable efforts to bring back the waist-line to its normal place but apparently nothing will induce women to look at boned corsets. These instruments of torture are being shown but as yet no one will buy anything more substantial than a band of woven silk elastic.'[34]

According to Mica Nava, there were many conflicting views about the consumer in the 1920s.[35]   As consumerism became increasingly feminized, opinions were divided about the powers of the consumer versus the powers of commercial and fashion industries. It is clearly apparent in the two articles cited above that the female consumer was being constructed as powerful and determined to get her own way. In both of these reports, the designers were not presented as 'heathens' setting out to 'de-Christianize' women. Instead, women were presented as assertive customers demanding the right to shorter and looser clothing than the designers would prefer.

Such images stood in stark contrast to those propounded by the Catholic hierarchy and the traditionalists.

However, the women's pages were sensitive to the many criticisms made against the 'modern girl' and did not always attempt to justify them. On some occasions, feature articles were critical of some of the excesses of modern life styles. On 15 June 1928, the *Cork Examiner*'s 'Woman's World' carried an article entitled 'When Girls Smoke': 'The girl who smokes habitually is the exception who proves the rule.   We hear a lot about the modern girl's cigarettes and cocktails; but it is merely a perverse desire to be ultramodern — really to shock the older people.' For every girl who smoked, the article claimed, six did not. Most modern girls realized that 'the cigarette habit can grow, and how, once formed, it can dull the complexion and teeth, besides staining the fingers.' The article concluded by saying that 'the majority of us prefer chocolates to "fags" and so long as our men friends buy "sweets for the sweet" we shall not ask for cigarettes.'[36] Apart from the obvious attempt here to distinguish between the 'ultramodern,' who border on the perverse, and the sweet modern girls, this article also situated the writer as a modern girl herself. This was common in the women's pages where features were frequently penned by 'A Modern Girl.' Thus both the reader and the writer were assumed to be modern girls and to share in a sense of what was acceptable, modern and fun. In that way, the women's pages adopted a chatty, friendly tone rather than an authoritative, judgmental tone. The dominant image to emerge from these pages was one of a healthy, unrestricted, independent, happy modern girl. Her clothing, dancing, bobbed hair, confident, assertive personality all symbolized her vitality and independence. However, it was precisely these features that represented her defiance and moral corruption in the eyes of religious leaders and traditionalists.

While the other provincial newspapers in this study did not have women's pages, that is not to imply that these papers represented a one-dimensional, monolithic, wholly negative view of the 'modern girl.' All the newspapers carried advertisements for fashion, films, dances and cigarettes that can be read as selling the modern life style. It was not uncommon for modern girls to be condemned on one page and then celebrated in advertisements on another page in the same newspaper. These tensions were apparent in relation to cigarettes. On 28 July 1928, the *Sligo Champion* published a poem by regular contributor Randall McDonnell:

'The Girls of Sligo' (extract)

...So Free from Fashion Sway
Dress Always in a Modest Way

...Unlike their sex in Dublin town
They have no Tobacco tricks

O the acme of perfection
and the pink of etiquette

Who ever met a Sligo Girl
who smoked a cigarette.[37]

This poem constructed Sligo girls as pure, modest and natural, untouched by modern fashions. They were very different from Dublin City women. It is questionable whether young Sligo women would have found it quite so flattering to be described as unfashionable and most unlike city women. However, this urban/rural dichotomy drew upon the stereotypical image of the West of Ireland as representing the true source of native tradition.[38] But it is apparent that not every one shared such a viewpoint.

Just one week later, on 4 August 1928, the *Sligo Champion* carried an advertisement for Gold Flake cigarettes, noting that they were Irish made (not foreign imports).[39] The advertisement featured a bobbed-haired modern girl playing tennis in a sleeveless, very short dress cut several inches above the knee. The image celebrated youth, health and vitality. Her clothing and cigarette symbolized her thorough modernity, her freedom, and her enjoyment of pleasure. This image was very common not only in cigarette advertising but also in a wide array of products. The use of such an image to sell Irish-made goods suggests the tensions among various interest groups within Irish society; the drive for commercial success versus the perceived threat to traditional order and authority. Regardless of the concerns expressed by the Catholic hierarchy, the female body was used to sell a range of diverse products. Advertisements were aimed at the large cross-section of the local community who read provincial papers, and this is reflected not only in the range of products but also in the range of prices. In accordance with the increasing feminization of consumerism, women were frequently targeted as consumers, not just for domestic essentials like washing powder but also for luxury goods.[40]

Conclusion

Drawing on notions of gendered nationalist discourses, this essay has attempted to locate and analyze the flapper within the specific setting of the rural Irish Free State. I have argued that the Irish flapper served very particular functions within nationalist and Catholic ideology in terms of defining Irishness, Irish womanhood and relations with foreign nations. Hence, in my view, the flapper helps to illustrate the tensions between former colonizer and colony: representing both the reality of British cultural influences in entertainment and lifestyles and the perceived threats that such influences posed to the uniqueness of Irish cultural identity.

Judging by the Irish provincial press, the flapper archetype was very powerful and pervasive even in remote rural areas. The Catholic hierarchy in particular seemed to have been very attached to this female image and may have helped to enhance its notoriety. A wide range of signifiers distinguished the 'modern girl': her smoking, drinking, clothes, bobbed hair, motor cars, her love of dancing and cinema. In different contexts, any one or all of these features could be emphasized. Such a useful symbol could not be left to dwell in far-off metropolitan centers like Dublin or London. Thus, I argue, it is simplistic to locate the flapper within a narrowly defined urban/rural dichotomy that constructs 'urban' as essentially degenerate and 'rural' as essentially pure. The flapper's transition of this dichotomy suggests the complexities and contradictions faced by rural Ireland in the early decades of independence. The flapper's existence in local, rural communities demonstrated that the apparent threats of modern excesses and the 'craze for pleasure' were everywhere; evil, sin, and temptation were 'all around us.' Constructed in opposition to the goodness and purity of the 'Irish cailín,' the mother of future generations, the transmitter of Irish cultural and religious values, the modern girl symbolized threats to national culture, national identity and ultimately to national stability. In her Parisian short skirts and Hollywood hairstyles, she visibly embodied all the dangers of foreign influences on the delicate and fragile essence of Irish womanhood and hence on the newly established Irish nation.

However, it is also apparent in the provincial press that while images of the modern girl were widely shared, interpretations of her varied. In particular sections of the newspapers such as fashion features, advertisements, women's pages, etc, the modern girl appeared as a very desirable image. Her youth, her flare for amusement, her loosely-fitted clothing, her health and vitality all symbolized freedom and independence. In addition, as a young woman without dependants, frequently employed in paid work, she represented the ultimate consumer of luxury goods — clothes, cosmetics, accessories. Therefore, the flapper was a site of cultural tensions embodying the conflicts between, on the one hand, cultural nationalists and the Catholic church working to minimize foreign tastes and fashions and, on the other hand, commercial interests and popular consumer demand that continued to promote and enjoy them.

Notes

[1] John Marcus O'Sullivan, 'The Modern Girl,' *Kerryman Newspaper*, 18 August 1928, p. 5.

[2] Louise Ryan, 'Negotiating Modernity and Traditions: Newspaper Debates On the 'Modern Girl' In the Irish Free State', *Journal of Gender Studies* 17, no.2 (1998): 181-97.

[3] Louise Ryan, 'Constructing "Irishwoman": Modern Girls and Comely Maidens,' *Irish Studies Review* 6, no. 3 (1998): 263-72.

[4] Anne McClintock, 'Family Feuds: Gender, Nationalism and the Family,' *Feminist Review* 44 (1993): 61-80.

[5] See Nira Yuval-Davis, *Gender and Nation* (London, Sage: 1998). See also Louise Ryan, 'Furies and Diehards: Women and Irish Republicanism In the Early Twentieth Century,' *Gender and History* 11, no.2 (1999): 256-75.

[6] Floya Anthias and Nira Yuval-Davis, *Racialised Boundaries* (London: Routledge, 1993).

[7] Breda Gray and Louise Ryan, '(Dis)locating "Woman" and Women In Representations Of Irish National Identity' in *Women and Irish Society: a Sociological Reader*, eds. Anne Byrne and Madeleine Leonard (Belfast: Beyond the Pale Publications, 1997).

[8] Terence Brown, *Ireland: A Social and Cultural History* (London: Fontana, 1987).

[9] Maryann Valiulis, 'Power, Gender and Identity in the Irish Free State' in *Irish Women's Voices: Past and Present*, eds. Joan Hoff and Moureen Coulte (Bloomington: Indiana University Press, 1995).

[10] See, for example, C.L. Innes, *Woman and Nation in Irish Literature and Society* (Hemel Hempstead: Harvester Wheatsheaf, 1993) and Gerardine Meaney, 'Sex and Nation: Women in Irish Culture and Politics' in *Irish Women's Studies Reader*, ed. Ailbhe Smyth (Dublin:Attic Press, 1993).

[11] See Gray and Ryan.

[12] Meaney, 233.

[13] Ryan, 'Negotiating Modernity and Traditions.'

[14] Ryan, 'Furies and Diehards.'

[15] The *Connacht Tribune*, 6 March 1926, p. 6.

[16] The *Connacht Tribune*, 24 April 1926, p. 5.

[17] The *Wicklow People*, 20 October 1928, p. 4.

[18] Mica Nava, 'Modernity Tamed? Women Shoppers and the Rationalisation Of Consumption In the Interwar Period,' *Australian Journal of Communication* 22, no. 2 (1995): 11.

[19] The *Wicklow People*, 20 October 1928, p. 4.

[20] Maryann Valiulis, 'Neither Feminist nor Flapper: the Ecclesiastical Construction of the Ideal Irish Woman' in *Chattel, Servant or Citizen: Women's Status in Church, State and Society*, eds. Mary O'Dowd and Sabine Wichert (Belfast: Institute of Irish Studies, 1995), 172.

[21] The *Wicklow People*, 11 August 1928, p. 4.

[22] The *Cork Examiner*, 7 May 1928, p. 7.

[23] The *Limerick Leader*, 2 May 1928, p. 3.

[24] Valiulis, 'Neither Feminists nor Flapper.'

[25] The *Limerick Leader*, 11 June 1928, p. 2.

[26] The *Sligo Champion*, 7 April 1928, p. 3.

[27] *Ibid.*

28   The *Wicklow People*, 15 May 1926, p. 4.
29   The *Wicklow People*, 21 January 1928, p. 4.
30   The *Connacht Sentinel* , 28 February 1928, p. 2.
31   Elizabeth Wilson, *Adorned in Dreams: Fashion and Modernity* (London: Virago, 1985).
32   The *Sligo Champion*, 18 February 1928, p. 2 and The *Connacht Tribune*, 18 February 1928, p. 3.
33   The *Kerryman*, 13 August 1927, p. 4.
34   The *Kerryman*, 27 August 1927, p. 11.
35   Nava, 'Modernity Tamed.'
36   The *Cork Examiner*, 15 June 1928, p. 4.
37   The *Sligo Champion*, 28 July 1928, p. 7.
38   Catherine Nash, 'Remapping and Renaming: New Cartographies Of Identity, Gender and Landscape In Ireland', *Feminist Review* 44 (1993): 39-57.
39   The *Sligo Champion*, 4 August 1928, p. 6.
40   Nava, 1995, 'Modernity Tamed.'

4 'We are going to carve revenge on your back': Language, Culture, and the Female Body in Kingston's *The Woman Warrior*

Lisa Plummer Crafton

Maxine Hong Kingston's The Woman Warrior... *grapples with cross-generational representations of the female body as a site of culture. The five narratives of the book interweave diverse female characters exiled from their cultural communities whose stories present the female body as a locus for conflicts between the forces of individual and cultural identity, forces caught up in cultural processes of instability, change, and renewal. This literary and cultural critical study argues that Kingston's text centers upon metaphorical representations of the female body as a repository for cultural values and that the narratives offer both destructive and constructive models of the relationship between Asian women and their cultures. Crafton uses the theoretical frameworks of feminist and cultural literary criticism to place* The Woman Warrior... *and her own study of it within the context of the critical debates that Kingston's work provokes, and by which readings of Kingston are continually informed. The author explores how Kingston's postmodern narrative techniques enact thematic concerns, emphasizing links between the female body and the power of language and, ultimately, the potential of writing from the body. Thus, Kingston's text emerges here as richly contributing to an exploration of how women serve as sites for both cultural inscription and cultural authority.*

As a focus of recent critical controversies, Maxine Hong Kingston's 1989 *The Woman Warrior: Memoirs of a Girlhood Among Ghosts* — perhaps the most well-known work of Asian-American literature — has few equals, provoking debate about genre, gender, and ethnicity. Just as the book's generic status as autobiography or fiction stimulates strong argument about its purposes, and, indeed, the very purposes of art, its embrace by white feminist critics provokes adamant responses by Chinese-American critics who censure the book's representation of Chinese culture. At times, both of these opposing camps reduce the book's representation of conflict either to women's experience or the Chinese and Chinese-American cultural experience. These critical debates, which inform much of the scholarship on *The Woman Warrior*..., can be reconciled, however, in a reading of the text that argues the female body as both a subject and an icon for cultural change, a topic few critics have discussed.[1] In fact, *The Woman Warrior* grapples with cross-generational representations of the female body as a site of culture. The five narratives of the book interweave diverse female characters exiled from their cultural communities whose stories present the body as a locus for conflicts between the forces of individual and cultural identity, forces caught up in cultural processes of instability, change, and renewal.[2] Enabling a negotiation between individual female and cultural identity, Kingston's text thematizes metaphorical representations of the body as a repository for cultural values; through this focus, the narratives offer both destructive and constructive models of the relationship between women and their cultures.[3] Consequently, Kingston's narrative techniques enact these thematic concerns as the text presents the problematic ways in which the female body is encoded by cultural conflicts.

Cultural conflicts, in fact, lie at the base of critical debates about the very genre of the text. Kingston's blend of fiction and autobiography concerns some Chinese-American critics, like Frank Chin and Katheryn Fong:

> I read your references to mythical and feudal China as fiction....Your fantasy stories are embellished versions of your mother's embellished versions of stories. As fiction, these stories are creatively written with graphic imagery and emotion. The problem is that non-Chinese are reading your fiction as true accounts of Chinese and Chinese-American history.[4]

These kinds of critiques stem, of course, from a set of assumptions about ethnic literature, grounded in a keen awareness of the sociopolitical climate of minority art in general, that somehow the perceived 'truthfulness' of the text carries with it a responsibility for the minority artist. Kingston, however, in her candid response to the reviews, 'Cultural Mis-readings by American Reviewers,' flatly denies that her art should at all times represent the Chinese-American cultural condition and rejects the constraints of ethnic representation:

> Why must I 'represent' anyone besides myself? Why should I be denied an individual artistic vision? And I do not think I wrote a 'negative' book as the Chinese-American reviewer said; but suppose I had. . . . I'm certain that some day when a great body of Chinese American writing becomes published and well-known, then readers will no longer have to put such a burden on each book that comes out.[5]

Even more interesting, however, than the conflict regarding the politicization of genre is the theoretical speculation that genre invokes. As literary theorist

Fredric Jameson argues, 'Genres are essentially literary institutions, or social contracts between a writer and a specific public, whose function is to specify the proper use of a particular cultural artifact.'[6] Rejecting the label of history or autobiography, Kingston specifies the genre in her subtitle: *Memoirs of a Girlhood Among Ghosts*. Kingston cites approvingly Johnson's definition of memoir as a form which can 'neither [be] dismiss[ed] as fiction nor quarrel[led] with as fact.'[7] More at stake than merely a label, Kingston's choice of memoir in effect 'constructs a new form of subjectivity...an ideographic selfhood.'[8] Acknowledging a number of fine theoretical discussions of Kingston's manipulations of autobiography -, Lee Quinby, in a literary study of the generic form of the memoir, differentiates between autobiography and memoirs in that autobiography promotes an 'I' that shares with confessional discourse an assumed interiority which is presumed to be unitary and continuous over time whereas memoirs construct a subjectivity where the 'I' is explicitly constituted in the collective presence of others and in their utterances and thus is overtly dialogical as well as multiple and discontinuous.[9] The genre of memoirs, then, names a type of writing that is a composite of many genres, many voices, an appropriate paradigm for the structure of *The Woman Warrior*, especially for its representation of the female body.

Summarizing the etymological history of the word 'memoirs,' Quinby highlights such definitions as 'note,' 'memorandum,' 'memento,' and, most significantly, 'memorial.' Kingston's text itself serves as a memorial, a record that continues to speak from the past, in that its narrator is haunted by stories of crimes against women and the Chinese people. These are not mutually-exclusive subjects as some literary critics have concluded, however; Kingston's unifying trope of the female body integrates these subjects in *its* role as a form of memorial. The female reproductive body itself, of course, assures a continuing lineage for a family, but a female is also expected to maintain and preserve custom, thus functioning as a cultural or social body as well. For the first, a woman is characterized as a sexualized body, but for the second, she becomes a part of the network of kinship and social bonds. In opposition to a Chinese culture that attempts to deny the embodied female, Kingston's text speaks the language from the body, in the vengeance enacted *upon* the body of No Name Woman, the revenge embodied *in* Fa Mu Lan, and the art manifested *by* Ts'Ai Yen's songs from the body. The book's teleology moves, then, from the female body as a site of cultural vengeance to its potential as a site for cultural renewal, as the narrator finds in her own stories the same age-old clashes between an autonomous female body and a patriarchal culture.

Occupying a unique position as both sexual and social body, the figure of woman is an apt site for the inscription of cultural values, but it also issues potentially disruptive language as well.[10] Language, oral and written, is the consistent subject of Kingston's memoirs, as many have noted, but often the female body speaks when the tongue cannot. Accentuating this dominant metaphor, Kingston tells of her mother's cutting her frenum[11]: 'She pushed my tongue up and sliced my frenum. Or maybe she cut it with a pair of nail scissors. I don't remember her doing it, only her telling me about it.'[12] This literal event functions as a thematizing statement in that Kingston's conflict with language 'originates in the memory of her mother's literally cutting the voice out of her.'[13] Kingston's exploration of her own use of language as a writer is interwoven with the sense that truths about her 'self' can only be realized through the telling. Interestingly, it is through her mother's re-telling that Kingston feels the sense of having a 'broken voice,' and it is against this mother's voice that she must relearn how to talk.[14] The first two chapters of *The Woman Warrior* prove that the narrator has not only relearned the language that her mother, in a sense, cut out of her but has learned to speak it through her body.

The story of No Name Woman is one told *about* the narrator's aunt — whose illicit sexual act and pregnancy by one other than her husband brands her with shame and leads to her suicide — and told *to* the young narrator on the occasion of her first menses. Explicitly, this one of her mother's stories issues a warning to her daughter against women's transgressive sexuality: 'Now that you have started to menstruate, what happened to her could happen to you. Don't humiliate us.'[15] More significantly, No Name Woman's bodily acts of adultery and suicide literally erase her name from the family; she is not to be spoken of. As a form of punishment and repression of the body, the narrator obeys this injunction against speaking for a time, but from the first sentence, her text transgresses this rule; as another critic argues, Kingston's story subverts 'the paternal law concerning language, sexuality, generation, and gender.'[16] Not only does the narrator record her aunt's existence, but she also sympathetically and imaginatively embellishes the story, which then, according to Smith, 'functions as a sign, like her aunt's enlarging belly, publicizing the potentially disruptive force of female textuality and the matrilineal descent of the texts.'[17] While the story is an act of empowerment for Kingston as a writer, more importantly her account gives both a body and voice to her aunt, essentially linking body and voice by doing so. Both the facts of the story and the narrator's fictional scenarios (in which she imagines her aunt as active lover rather than a passive victim) represent the destructive, hostile powers of cultural and tribal codes against the body and the potential power of the female body once allowed to speak.

In the narrator's account, the village raiders enact their vengeance upon the aunt's transgressive body by raiding the house, ruining the crops, slaughtering the animals, and marking the house with blood. Visceral and corporeal, their actions are clearly linked with destruction of the flesh (even the description of the people in the fields holding lanterns contains the metaphorical images of saw teeth, cutting through material, as Kingston refers to the files of people who 'like a great saw, teeth strung with lights...walked zigzag across our land, tearing the rice'), although they themselves seem disembodied in that they 'wore white masks.'[18] Subtly exposing the hypocrisy of the cultural codes, Kingston then goes on to allow her aunt a voice about and from her own body. She imagines her both as victim of rape (thus not culpable or deserving of the raid, even from the standpoint of village morality) and as an active lover who protects the father of her unborn child by refusing to give his name. To entice her lover, as Kingston imagines, the 'aunt combed individuality into her bob...guessing at the colors and shapes that would interest him.'[19]   And yet this physicality is represented not as lust but as creative energy that resists a woman's being cast only in the role of social body; thus the aunt becomes a prototype of female possibility. In contrast to her four brothers who are sent west 'out on the road,' she alone is expected to keep tradition: 'The heavy deep-rooted women were to maintain the past against the flood, safe for returning. But the rare urge west had fixed upon our family, and so my aunt crossed boundaries not delineated in space.'[20] Conflating the physical image of a body in space and that of a spirit crossing intangible boundaries, Kingston attributes to her aunt much more than bodily transgression. She uses this metaphor — 'crossing boundaries not delineated in space'— throughout the narration to suggest the link between the female body and spirit, especially in the childbirth scene. The aunt chooses the overt materiality of the pigsty as a place for her labor, but in between contractions, she is liberated from the spatial boundaries that have confined her:

> With forehead and knees against the earth, her body convulsed and then relaxed. She turned on her back, lay on the ground. The black well of sky and stars went out and out and out forever; her body and her complexity seemed to disappear. She was one of the stars, a bright dot in blackness, without a home...she felt pain return, focusing her body....For hours she lay on the ground, alternately body and space.[21]

Her spiritual journey to the 'black well of sky and stars' is echoed by her walk to the physical well where she takes the baby with her in suicide; Kingston describes it as an act of love, for 'mothers who love their children take them along.'[22] The narrator's memorializing account represents both the destructive ways in which culture inscribes the female body (whether one accepts the passive, 'heavy-rooted' role or chooses to cross boundaries) and the potential for writing one's self. The metaphor of her aunt as 'one being flaring up into violence' who could 'open up a black hole, a maelstrom that pulled in the sky' suggests a potential for all who dare to resist the containing horizons of their own village structure. [23]   The opening chapter of the book thus not only empowers the narrator's art — Kingston avows that she 'alone devotes[s] pages of paper to her'— but metaphorizes the female body as a site upon which culture imposes its vengeance, but which may subversively provide imaginative energy to 'cross boundaries not delineated in space.'

The crossing of boundaries climaxes, of course, in 'White Tigers,' where the cross-dressing Fa Mu Lan offers her body both as a tablet for cultural inscription and as a maternal source of knowledge and power. That her body is warrior and mother, simultaneously, exemplifies the dual, composite role of the female body. While her mother tells her the story of Fa Mu Lan to ensure her filial piety, the narrator connects the heroic acts of Fa Mu Lan, her own writing, and her mother's talk-story:

> Night after night my mother would talk-story until we fell asleep. I couldn't tell where the stories left off and the dreams began, her voice the voice of heroines in my sleep....At last I saw that I too had been in the presence of great power; my mother talking-story....I remembered that as a child I had followed my mother about the house, the two of us singing about how Fa Mu Lan fought gloriously and returned alive from war to settle in the village. I had forgotten this chant was once mine, given me by my mother who may not have known its power to remind.[24]

Fondly remembering a daughter singing around the house about the legendary heroine, Kingston makes the distinction that her mother may not have known the tale's 'power to remind.' There is also ample reason to believe that the narrator's version of the story is *not* the one told her by her mother; instead, Kingston revises the legend as a metaphorical statement about the power of the female body.

Critics who charge Kingston with fictionalizing the genre of autobiography (thus risking prompting naïve readers to mistake fiction for fact) point especially to this episode.[25] Kingston's adaptation of this traditional tale serves as a multivalent, multivocal narrative of a heroic warrior, but more importantly bespeaks the heroic art of self-expression through the body. Kingston's first revision to the traditional 'Ballad of Mulan' or 'Mulan Shi' is that instead of the heroine who joins the army only out of filial piety, a substitute for her aging father, Kingston's Fa Mu Lan is a 'chosen' one. Also, the tattooing of her body is taken from a well-known tale of Yue Fei, whose mother was said to have carved four characters (not entire passages) on his back to ensure his patriotic loyalty. Finally, the traditional Fa Mu Lan is never described as having been pregnant and given birth to a child while in male disguise. In fact, in the original version of the tale, the military campaigns comprise a lonely detour in her life, and the end of the poem finds her putting on makeup, ready to resume her interrupted female life.[26] In short, Kingston translates Fa Mu Lan from a defender of the establishment, both patriarchal and patriotic, to a subversive female 'warrior' whose body serves as both a material example of cultural inscription and a physical manifestation of the word/body as weapon.

In her first deviation from the traditional story, the narrator of 'White Tigers' memorializes her mother's stories of the legendary swordswoman and fantasizes about being chosen to be a warrior: 'The call would come from a bird that flew over our roof. In the brush drawings it looks like the ideograph for 'human,' two black wings...I would be a little girl of seven the day I followed the bird into the mountains.'[27] Underscoring the theme of inscription that structures the narrative, the narrator links the natural form of the body with language, as the bird resembles the Chinese ideograph for 'human.' In a sense, the link testifies that the narrator (who then mutates into Fa Mu Lan) is summoned to become fully 'human,' not simply a warrior. Kingston's complex narrative style is nowhere more compelling than here as the narrator moves from literal memory of her mother's stories, to imaginative fantasy that she too may be called one day, and to a first-person account of her imagined experience.

The traditional martial arts training for Kingston's fictional first-person narrator begins with her learning how silence and language coincide. While the old woman admonishes her to learn 'how to be quiet,' the training exercises teach her literally to use her body as a tool of inscription: 'I learned to move my fingers, hands, feet, head, and entire body in circles. I walked putting heel down first, toes pointing outward thirty to forty degrees, making the ideograph "eight," making the ideograph "human."'[28] Emulating the bird whose wings resemble the ideograph 'human,' the narrator begins a journey to learn the many voices of the body. In one of her visions, brought on by hunger, she makes the connection that a body in space designates much more than just itself:

> I saw...two people made of gold dancing the earth's dances. They turned so perfectly that together they were the axis of the earth's turning....I am watching the centuries pass in moments because suddenly I understand time...And I understand that working and hoeing are dancing; how peasant clothes are golden, as king's clothes are golden, how one of the dancers is always a man and the other a woman.[29]

Like No Name Woman, the narrator herself crosses boundaries 'not delineated in space'; spatiotemporal bonds are suspended here in a moment when she is both in her body (intense hunger) and outside of it. This phase of her training invokes her identification with ordinary people (peasants hoeing) and her commitment to the belief that she 'could stare at ordinary people and see their light and gold...see their dance.' That she is compelled to this perception of the link between individual and culture by being rooted in her own body is made clear as she explicitly acknowledges the cycles of her body as materializing that link: 'I bled and thought about the people to be killed; I bled and thought about the people to be born.' [30]

Kingston's second alteration of the traditional tale incorporates the story of the tattooed back of Yue Fei into the story of Fa Mu Lan. In this version, Fa Mu Lan presents herself as a female avenger, and the scene of inscription where her parents literally mark her body as a weapon is crucial to Kingston's argument about how the body functions as a site of both individual and cultural renewal. Waking Fa Mu Lan in the early morning, her parents take her to the family hall:

> Forebodingly, I caught a smell — metallic, the iron smell of blood, as when a woman gives birth, as at the sacrifice of a large animal, as when I menstruated and dreamed red dreams.
> ...'We are going to carve revenge on your back,' my father said. 'We'll write out oaths and names.'
> 'Wherever you go, whatever happens to you, people will know our sacrifice,' my mother said. 'And you'll never forget either.'[31]

The inscribed body functions as a sign of cultural identification and individual resistance at the same time. The words carved in blood are ones that will be of help to her people even if she is killed in battle, and thus even her dead body would be a 'weapon.' Furthering this analogy, Fa Mu Lan explains that her back is 'covered entirely with words in red and black files, like an army, like an army.'[32] Like the zig-zaw files of people swarming across the rice fields of No Name Woman, these words will enact vengeance, and while her martial exploits are literal, the most significant acts of the woman warrior occur where she speaks from the body.

Kingston casts no doubts upon the physical prowess of Fa Mu Lan, but like the men's clothes she must adopt even to engage in battle, her martial exploits in a sense mask the fact that most of her power comes from deep inside the body, not from military expertise. Kingston has said in an interview that her mission was to invent a new form of autobiography, which tells the inner life of women: 'One of the ways to keep ourselves alive is to recognize these invisible forces that are very powerful in ourselves.'[33] These invisible forces form the base of Fa Mu Lan's strength. During a charge, for example, she 'guide[s] the horse with her knees, freeing both hands for sword-work, spinning green and silver circles all around [her].'[34] Here, Kingston insinuates a supernatural cause of her strength; like No Name Woman in labor, the woman warrior works her body (guiding the horse with her knees) while metaphorically transforming space (spinning circles all around). Recounting one of the most perilous battles, she acknowledges that she sought out her repository of power, enabling her body to be not only a metaphorical weapon (the words on her back) but a literal one: 'I made a throwing gesture and the opposing army would fall, hurled across the battlefield. Hailstones as big as heads would shoot out of the sky and the lightning would stab like swords, but never at those on my side.'[35] Like the initial body writing that she learns in the mountains, these essential body gestures serve as performatives, coinciding with nature's own weapons, linking her female body to the cycles of the natural world. This connection between body and spirit culminates in the figure of the warrior poet who offers not only physical victories but spiritual ease for her comrades, singing songs at night that 'came out of the sky and into my head.'[36] Kingston's warrior, then, is a spiritual one, not simply a woman who takes on the armor of men. Therefore, Wong's claim that the 'very necessity of male disguise means that the narrator's fantasized challenge to patriarchy can never be complete' misses the point in that Fa Mu Lan embodies the strength of self-knowledge and the power that many women in different cultural disguises can invoke.[37]

Finally, Kingston's most significant revision of the traditional story emphasizes that Fa Mu Lan does not separate her role as public bearer of the cultural record from her role as private, sexualized body; instead of delaying the life of wife and mother, she chooses both pregnancy and birth in the course of battle. When Fa Mu Lan's husband — joined to her as a 'spirit bridegroom' in a wedding ceremony that she witnessed from afar as she trained in the mountains — appears in the camp one night, her role as defender of the cultural body is most overtly displaced by his recognition of her as a sexual body, as Kingston's poignant description emphasizes: 'He wept when he took off my shirt and saw the scar-words on my back. He loosened my hair and covered the words with it.'[38] Loosening her hair (which had been tied back 'in a man's fashion'), he reconnects her to her body and, for a moment, subordinates its function as cultural sign as he consciously covers the words of vengeance with her hair. Subsequently, she literally embodies both sexual/social roles as her pregnant naked body becomes a dual sign of female and cultural identity: 'Now when I was naked, I was a strange human being indeed — words carved on my back and the baby large in front.'[39] She retreats from battle only once, to give birth in a scene clearly reminiscent of the labor of No Name Woman, which stresses the limitless connection between the female body in labor and infinite space. As she narrates, 'In dark and silver dreams, I had seen him falling from the sky, each night closer to the earth, his soul a star. Just before labor began, the last star rays sank into my belly.'[40] In perhaps the oddest episode of her description, she and her husband tie the cut umbilical cord to the flagpole, thus literally uniting the flesh of the female, maternal body to the world of the woman warrior.

The construction of the warrior as maternal body, Kingston's clearest alteration to the original legend, also comes to inform the narrator's final reflections on her imagined experience as Fa Mu Lan. At the end of the chapter, after recounting her own trials as a woman warrior (marching at Berkeley in the sixties, struggling to be 'American feminine'), Kingston returns to the legend to claim the swordswoman figure for herself and to affirm that 'Marriage and childbirth strengthen the swordswoman, who is not a maid like Joan of Arc.'[41] This chapter's powerful representation is, in many ways, foundational for the whole text; not simply a legend that parallels the narrator's struggles, it is an emblem for potential 'swordswomen' readers. Cultural critic Amy Ling too dismissively comments that the story 'may be a glorious model for a girl to dream about' but is a 'gross exaggeration, a wish-fulfillment which the author indulges in with a smile on her face.'[42] To call this narrative an exaggeration is to miss the overt analogy that the narrator makes between herself and the woman warrior:

> The swordswoman and I are not so dissimilar. May my people understand the resemblance soon so that I can return to them. What we have in common are the words at our backs. The idioms for *revenge* are 'report a crime' and 'report to five families.' The reporting is the vengeance — not the beheading, not the gutting, but the words. And I have so many words — 'chink' words and 'gook' words —that they do not fit on my skin.[43]

Closing the final chapter, Kingston transforms the tale of Ts'ai Yen, a poet born in A.C.E. 175, into a parable about the potential of writing from the body. Captured at the age of twenty by a barbarian tribe, the scholar's daughter was captive for twelve years before her ransom and return to her native lands.[44] Yet, this writer-warrior — who bears two children with her barbarian captor and is thus, like the others, a mother-warrior as well — learns her song from listening to the dried reed flutes of her captors. More than just martial tunes, the music played in the camp in the silent desert night is a potent expression of art and yearning that affects Ts'ai Yen so profoundly that she amazingly finds within herself the power to replicate it. With no instruments of her own, she uses her voice, her body to imitate exactly the sound of the home-made instruments: 'Then, out of Ts'ai Yen's tent, which was apart from the others, the barbarians heard a woman's voice singing, as if to her babies, a song so high and clear, it matched the flutes.'[45] When Kingston concludes the book by explaining that Ts'ai Yen's song eventually became her poem 'Eighteen Stanzas for a Barbarian Reed Pipe,' she stresses that this is a song the Chinese sing to their own instruments, and she comments that it 'translated well.' This description of a song's harmonious translation from one context to another is often interpreted as referring to Kingston's reconciliation with the figure of the mother. Many critics have made this connection. The final chapter's personal narrative recounts Kingston's confrontation of her mother with a long list of grievances and conveys the sense that Kingston's newly strong self has enormous difficulty in 'translating' the dictates of her mother's Chinese culture into her own evolving Chinese-American one. Thus, her recognition that Ts'ai Yen's song 'translated well' can be read as a conciliatory moment that stands for her own translation of her mother's stories throughout the narrative. While this engagement with the relationship of the mother may be particularly resonant in the story of Ts'ai Yen, the line's simplicity — 'It translated well' — and its function as the final line in the book should not be overlooked. That is, a translation from one form of language to another, from the language of captors to that of the captive, underscores the text's emphatic and consistent concern with forms of language and our ability to 'read' them.

Just as Ts'ai Yen translates the music of her captor's desert flutes into songs for her own voice, Kingston's composite text translates many different forms of language from the body, representing subversive bodies as both cultural weapon and individual female force. That this is her subject, and not the militaristic celebration of a woman warrior, is clear in Kingston's uneasiness with the title of the book: 'I really don't like warriors...I guess I always have in my style a doubt about wars as a way of solving things.'[46] By the end, it is very clear that the narrator's mentor has evolved from Fa Mu Lan to Ts'ai Yen — from warrior to poet — but, in fact, the poet has always been her guiding spirit, as No Name Woman, Fa Mu Lan, and Ts-ai Yen are *all* figures of a poet who speaks her body. That Kingston follows their examples in her textual practice, by displacing boundaries and insisting on the presence of the body, enables us to say that their songs 'translated well.'

Notes

[1] It is possible to see gender and national identity as versions of one another. See Suzanne Juhasz, 'Maxine Hong Kingston: Narrative Technique and Female Identity,' in *Contemporary American Women Writers: Narrative Strategies*, ed. Catherine Rainwater (Lexington: University Press of Kentucky, 1985), 173-89. My focus on the body as a site for cultural conflict suggests a tangible space where individual/cultural roles and gender/ethnicity meet. For a different, theoretical exploration of how Kingston's text reconciles fixed opposition, see Leslie Rabine's 'No Lost Paradise: Social Gender and Symbolic Gender in the Writings of Maxine Hong Kingston,' *Signs* 12, no. 3 (1987): 471-92. Also, on physical mutilation in Kingston, see Deborah L. Madsen, '(Dis)Figuration: The Body as Icon in the Writings of Maxine Hong Kingston,' *The Yearbook of English Studies* 24 (1994): 237-50.

[2] My focus is limited to the figures of No Name Woman, Fa Mu Lan, and Ts'ai Yen, all women whose bodies become encoded with the signs of this conflict; for a useful analysis of Brave Orchid and Moon Orchid, see Margaret Miller, 'Threads of Identity in Maxine Hong Kingston's *The Woman Warrior*,' *Biography* 6, no. 1 (1983): 13-33.

[3] See Lee Quinby, 'The Subject of Memoirs: *The Woman Warrior*'s Technology of Ideographic Selfhood,' in *Critical Essays on Maxine Hong Kingston*, ed. Laura E. Skandera-Trombley. (New York: G. K. Hall, 1998), 125-45; King-Kok Cheung, '*The Woman Warrior* versus *The Chinaman Pacific*: Must a Chinese-American Critic Choose Between Feminism and Heroism?' in *Critical Essays on Maxine Hong Kingston*, ed. Laura E. Skandera-Trombley. (New York: G. K. Hall, 1998), 107-124.

[4] Katheryn M. Fong, 'To Maxine Hong Kingston: A Letter,' *Bulletin for Concerned Asian Scholars* 9, no. 4 (1977): 67. See also Mylan's charge of latent Orientalism in Sheryl Mylan, 'The Mother as Other: Orientalism in Maxine Hong Kingston's *The Woman Warrior*,' in *Women of Color: Mother-Daughter Relationships in 20th Century Literature*, ed. Elizabeth Brown-Guillory (Austin: University of Texas Press, 1996), 132-52.

[5] Kingston, 'Cultural Mis-readings by American Reviewers,' in *Critical Essays on Maxine Hong Kingston*, ed. Laura E. Skandera-Trombley. (New York: G. K. Hall, 1998), 101.

[6] Fredric Jameson, *The Political Unconscious: Narrative as a Socially Symbolic Act* (Ithaca: Cornell University Press, 1981), 106.

[7] Quoted in Kingston, 'Cultural Mis-readings,' 102.

[8] Quinby, 126.

9   See Quinby's summary on 126-7. Also see John Paul Eakin, *Fiction in Autobigraphy: Studies in the Art of Self-Invention* (Princeton: Princeton University Press, 1985) and Sidonie Smith, *A Poetics of Women's Autobiography: Marginality and the Fictions of Self-Representation* (Bloomington: Indiana University Press, 1987).

10   On language as liberation, see King-Kok Cheung, 'Don't Tell: Imposed Silences in *The Color Purple* and *The Woman Warrior*,' *PMLA* 103 (1988): 162-74.

11   The frenum is the membrane underneath the tongue that restricts its movement.

12   Kingston, *The Woman Warrior* (New York: Vintage, 1976), 164. All subsequent quotations from Kingston cite this source.

13   Smith, 168.

14   Many critics have analyzed the representation of the dominating mother; see especially Celeste Schenk, 'All of a Piece: Women's Poetry and Autobiography,' in *Life/Lines: Theorizing Women's Autobiography*, eds. Bella Brodzki and Celeste Schenke. (Ithaca: Cornell University Press, 1988), 107-30, for an analysis of the Ts'ai Yen episode as a return to the exiled mother as the source of poetry.

15   Kingston, *The Woman Warrior*, 5.

16   Rabine, 484.

17   Smith, 156.

18   Kingston, *The Woman Warrior*, 3-4. Kingston purposefully points out the paradox of village morality, of those who indulge the body and yet mask it, both figuratively and literally.

19   Kingston, *The Woman Warrior*, 9.

20   Kingston, *The Woman Warrior*, 8.

21   Kingston, *The Woman Warrior*, 14.

22   Kingston, *The Woman Warrior*, 15.

23   Kingston, *The Woman Warrior*, 12.

24   Kingston, *The Woman Warrior*, 19-20.

25   While Chin attacks Kingston's 'distortions,' Cheung counters that the 'distortions' are actually subversions. See Frank Chin, 'This Is Not an Autobiography,' *Genre* 18, no. 2 (1985): 109-30, and Cheung, '*The Woman Warrior*, esp. 112.

26   For these revisions to the legend of Fa Mu Lan, see Wong, esp. 149-50 and 160-61.

27   Kingston, *The Woman Warrior*, 20.

28   Kingston, *The Woman Warrior*, 23.

29   Kingston, *The Woman Warrior*, 27.

30   Kingston, *The Woman Warrior*, 33.

31   Kingston, *The Woman Warrior*, 34.

32   Kingston, *The Woman Warrior*, 35.

33   Quoted in Pin-Chia Feng, *The Female Bildungsroman by Toni Morrison and Maxine Hong Kingston* (NY: Peter Lang, 1998).

34   Kingston, *The Woman Warrior*, 37.

35   Kingston, *The Woman Warrior*, 38-9.

36   Kingston, *The Woman Warrior*, 37.

37   Sau-Ling Cynthia Wong, 'Autobiography as Guided Chinatown Tour? Maxine Hong Kingston's *The Woman Warrior* and the Chinese-American Autobiographical Controversy,' in *Critical Essays on Maxine Hong Kingston*, ed. Laura E. Skandera-Trombley. (NY: G. K. Hall, 1998), 146-67. The quotation is from 161.

38   Kingston, *The Woman Warrior*, 39.

39   Kingston, *The Woman Warrior*, 39-40.

40   Kingston, *The Woman Warrior*, 40.

41   Kingston, *The Woman Warrior*, 48.

42   Ling, 175. Amy Ling, 'Maxine Hong Kingston and the Dialogic Dilemna of Asian American Writers,' in *Critical Essays on Maxine Hong Kingston*, ed. Laura E. Skandera-Trombley (NY: G. K. Hall, 1998), 168-81. My reading also opposes Cheung's argument that she is 'problematic as a model since she can only exercise her power when in male armor.' See '*The Woman Warrior*,' esp. 116.

[43] Kingston, *The Woman Warrior*, 53. Quinby claims that the excess of words disrupts 'categories of containment through which the dominant and dominating regimes of power are constructed.' See 136.

[44] Ts'ai Yen has been interpreted as a stand-in for Kingston (as in David Li, 'The Naming of A Chinese-American I: Cross-Cultural Significations in *The Woman Warrior,*' *Criticism* 30, no. 4 (1988): 497-515), for Brave Orchid (as in Margit Wogowitsch, *Narrative Strategies and Multicultural Identity: Maxine Hong Kingston in Context* (Vienna, Austria: Braumuller, 1995), and for both alternately (as in Rabine).

[45] These quotations from Kingston are found on 208-9.

[46] Quoted in Cheung 117.

5 'If this is improper, ... then I am all improper, and you must give me up': Daisy Miller and Other Uppity White Women as Resistant Emblems of America

Lisa Johnson

In this essay, the author explores the site of the white, middle-class, female body at the center of American national symbolism as a potentially resistant (or 'uppity') force in literary history and contemporary pop culture. She points to several sightings of this body in postures of social revolt. Beginning with her own white, middle- class, female body as reader, Johnson looks for ways to see (or re-vision) this site not as a passive emblem of unquestioning nationalist pride or uncritical ethnocentrism but as a symbol come to life, speaking against the interpellation of the white female into sexist, racist, classist, and heterosexist cultural rubrics. Johnson seeks out textual and touristic sites in which a certain white female body has been used to represent the 'new world' as a parallel land to be penetrated and tamed by the European patriarchal systems of marriage and colonization, respectively. Referring to two focal examples — the Statue of Liberty and Henry James' treatment of the American Girl in his novella Daisy Miller — Johnson contends that a certain white, American woman has always agitated for more control over women's representation in relation to nationalist and imperialist agendas.

> I am learning to connect the dots. One dot for woman-hate, one for racism, one for classism, one for telling me who I can fuck. When I connect all the dots, it's a picture of me, a picture of privilege and the way it's disguised behind pretty white smiles.
>
> – Christine Doza, *Bloodlove*

Middle-class white American women have been used consistently to represent the whole of America and, more recently, the whole of feminism.[1] As both reader and citizen, it strikes me that I must determine how to engage with this inherited social position. Will I carry it forward with pride? (I'll never forget the electricity at my fingertips before every high school football game when I stood on the field, arms raised, suspended in the moment before signalling the band to begin 'The Star Spangled Banner.') Or will I bear it obliviously, thinking graduate school somehow excused me from the social power structure by giving me a peek behind its curtains? Or, finally, will I put it down altogether, finding some way, in Adrienne Rich's words, to turn it over?[2]   I bought a pair of Tommy Hilfiger shoes the other day. Tommy Hilfiger advertises its red-white-and-blue clothing line with an image of the quintessential American girl: young, white, blonde, blue-eyed. The girl every boy wants, and every girl wants to be. She is a girl I have flirted with becoming. Because I am close to the ideal (I am white, thin, heterosexual-ish), it becomes my choice (through artificial high-lights) to inhabit this monolithic American womanhood. Or not ('your hair's still dark,' Grandmother rumbled accusingly yesterday). I felt a slight and secret thrill as I slipped on those shoes, suddenly a Tommy Girl — it's so easy, so constructed, so slippery — staring back from the mirror; then came quick guilt and an urge to find some way in this article to escape the lure of classy white womanhood as the American wet dream.

Despite growing cultural consciousness about the sexism and racism of commercial advertisements, companies like Tommy Hilfiger continue to capitalize on the remaining power of unthinking patriotism. I chose American culture as the theme for my composition course last fall in order to teach the skill of critical thinking; I wanted students to think critically about how they are worked on by culture and produced in specific ways as Americans. Looking at an array of advertisements, I asked the students why so many use gimmicks like 'America's number one bluejeans,' 'America's favorite barbecue,' and so on. Why does this call to nationhood appeal to us as consumers? What, exactly, are we consuming? We looked at the Tommy Girl ad. The first couple of points were obvious: 'America' equals 'white.' Okay. And 'affluent.' Yes. We paused, and, not being aware of the long history of white women as icons of America, attributed the conflation of womanhood with liberty to the feminist movement (reading the link between her body and America as a reiteration of 'equality feminism'). Then the students stumped me. They noticed she wasn't smiling. Strange. She has everything a girl could want: she's beautiful, she's rich, she's white, she's American. And she's not smiling. What gives?

I feel my whiteness as a sun-blinded desert of distance
— Jane Lazarre, *Beyond the Whiteness of Whiteness*

Today I checked out an armload of books on whiteness studies from a light-skinned black woman at the university library desk. We smiled at each other politely, and I wondered what she thought as she read through the titles: *White Women, Race Matters, Beyond the Whiteness of Whiteness, The Wages of Whiteness,* and so on. Did she see me as an ally (my specious life-long hope in encounters with women of color)? Or was I just another bleeding-heart liberal with misguided notions about all of us getting along, on a mission of depthless white penance? Did she notice the titles at all? Or, more likely, was she not studying me at all? I walked out the glass library door and hurried towards my car to jot down what seemed to me a crucial question. As I reflected on my project of recuperating upper-middle-class white American womanhood as a space of antiracist and anticlassist work, I wondered a little defensively to myself, what's the difference between narcissistic navel-gazing, or 'white solipsism,' and the holy grail of cultural studies, critical self-consciousness?

It would be easy to get bogged down in this dilemma as I explore the literary and cultural history of white women as resistant emblems of America.[3] I take Ruth Frankenberg's warning seriously: 'Much work remains to be done in actually making visible and undermining white culture's ties to domination. This is perhaps a more urgent priority than looking for the 'good' aspects of white people's heritage.'[4] I stand cautiously between Frankenberg's warning above and her fleeting gesture towards hope: 'This book views white women's lives as sites both for the reproduction of racism and for challenges to it.'[5] In fact I feel somewhat crushed between her criticism of white women as suffering 'lacunae in perception' when it comes to their own racialness and her reduction of much self-aware whiteness to 'an act of backlash.'[6] In her later edited volume, *Displacing Whiteness*, Frankenberg creates room for a third option: 'in examining white self-namings one must further distinguish — although the separation is not always hard and fast — between assertions of white supremacism or superiority and critical self-examinations of whiteness.'[7] Recognizing our central place in representations of the American status quo is a first step beyond the blinding 'whiteness of whiteness,' where we may acknowledge the limits and distortions of American literary history while salvaging its spirit of rebellion.

'[I]t is in principle possible to disaffiliate,' argues Marilynne Frye; we 'are not doomed to dominance by logic or nature.'[8] Frye describes the awakening that comes with perceiving whiteness as socially constructed, and instead of seeking 'equality' with white men, which to her means wanting 'our own firsthand participation in racial dominance,' she 'give[s] [her]self the injunction to stop being White.'[9] While I follow her point, which she makes by discussing the way she has asked the men in her life to stop being 'men,' to stop living unconsciously according to culturally sanctioned masculinity, the language she uses does not work for me. Instead of telling myself and others 'to stop being White,' I would rather rewrite the concept of 'white culture' to include dissident whites and truly democratic movement. I am taken with Frankenberg's emphasis on '[w]hiteness as process,' for when whiteness is seen as something one does, one can decide to 'do' whiteness differently.[10] Given this performative definition, I argue that if culture is written primarily on white women's bodies, then white women have the unique opportunity to wear it wrong and thus bear a revolutionary message.

I align myself with Joanne Frye in her theorization of reading as *the* political arena of literature:

> For, as I see it, the fullest participation of the novel in feminist change derives from the reader, especially the woman reader, who might find through the reading of novels the growing edge of her own humanity, extending beyond available roles and categories and into a renewed future. As she learns from female characters new ways to interpret her own and other women's experiences, she helps to reshape the culture's understanding of women and participates in the feminist alteration of human experience.[11]

I would distinguish, though, among the ways feminist readers might 'reshape the culture's understanding of women.' The resisting reader (Judith Fetterley's formulation, which has become near-ubiquitous in readings of the American canon) perceives only the sexism, racism, and classism in canonical texts.. I propose instead the *reader of resistance*, who perceives characters' social disruptiveness and their authors' intentional and unintentional deployment of them to critique dominant culture. Lisa Heldke advocates 'traitorous identities' for women in privileged social positions, 'identities that betray and resist the systems of domination that overprivilege them.'[12]   Reading for resistance is one way white women can be traitorous, studying the ways middle-class white American women — who are interpellated, no questions asked, into conventional national stories of self and other — work out a contingent loyalty to the noble parts of American culture, yet resist its exploitive dimensions. I am interested, as part of this politicized reading, not only in revealing white middle-class overprivilege, but in revealing the *constraints* of white middle-class overprivilege — how it coerces, estranges, encloses. In addition to mapping out misrepresentations of people of color in literature by white Americans, then, critics might locate textual moments that lend themselves to coalition with Americans of color through a common, if differential, narrative of social justice.

In the following sections, I examine two paradigmatic texts that conflate America with middle-class white femininity: the Statue of Liberty and Henry James' *Daisy Miller*. I will be seeking within these texts their latent *narratives of disaffiliation*. I consider this project to be part of a third wave feminist literary criticism, an approach that asks, what does this text have to offer a project of multi-racial, economic, and feminist social change, rather than how does this text stand in my way? As a complement to more explicit antiracist work by white American women such as Adrienne Rich and Minnie Bruce Pratt, readings of white American women in literature and culture can amplify moments when characters rub abrasively against their representational duties. With this goal in mind, I propose readings that underscore the 'uppitiness' of white women positioned to represent America, celebrating the ways women keep getting up off the page and walking out on their representational duties. These counternarratives of the American woman, instead of being characterized by passivity, homogeneity, and patriarchal/patriotic duty, model for real live white women how to get out from under that ubiquitous icon. How to turn it over.

The Statue of Liberty is not a Pretty Girl

'Now fully saturated by a century of collective fantasy,' writes Lauren Berlant, 'the "Lady" provides an exemplary study in how the fantasy-work of the National Symbolic has worked to produce and to mobilize American citizens.'[13] 'National Symbolic' is Berlant's term for the conceptual space in which a nation comes to mean certain things through a tangle of images and agendas. Central to this space is the linking of 'regulation to desire.'[14] In other words, citizens learn to fantasize about their national identities in ways that serve the national agenda (so femininity gets linked with white motherhood, for instance, and masculinity with missile-shaped aggression). The line between what we think we want and what we are required to do as American women is blurred in this space.

The statue is an icon of American femininity characterized by stillness and silence, openness and nurture. The erotics of this icon work their magic on the men that climb all over her body doing repairs. Berlant describes men falling in love with her like another Pygmalion while working on the molds of the ribs, kissing her man-size lips, and brashly taking her off her pedestal, asserting, 'for a fee she is open to all for entry and exploration from below.'[15] Berlant presses this point to draw out the web of meanings that entangle women in the American National Symbolic: 'The construction of the national genitalia of our national prostitute reminds us that the National Symbolic is there for *use*, for exploitation, to construct a subjective dependency on what look like the *a priori* structures of power. It would not be too strong to say that the political deployment of the feminine icon has a pornographic structure.'[16] Poised at the border of the United States, the Statue of Liberty is herself a border, a hymen through which America is entered. She opens herself to throngs of immigrants and Americans, all seeking freedom up her skirt. We find ourselves attracted to her, journeying to Staten Island year after year, our American mecca. In a framework wherein 'the female body of the American National Symbolic eternally desires to be relieved of desire, to be passive and available for service, to contribute to the polis by being and needing where it needs her to be,' the lived white female body of American culture finds herself called upon to self-identify with the nation's reproductive needs.[17] Whores of culture, all of us, our personal, social, and sexual desires become obscured by this 'larger' duty. Berlant asserts, 'when the body of the woman is employed symbolically to regulate or represent the field of national fantasy, her positive "agency" lies solely in her availability to be narrativized — controlled...by her circulation within a story.'[18] My question is, can we break the oppressive pattern of this circulation? Can we change the story?

Susan Gubar addresses the problematic race of the Statue. Referring to a painting titled 'We Came to America,' featuring a black statue of Liberty, she writes, 'An America symbolized by a white Liberty white-washes the devastating past her dark double memorializes.'[19] This race change makes apparent a Black feminist oppositional stance towards American national mythology; I wonder what a white oppositional stance might look like. In Sarah Banet-Weiser's study of the Miss America pageant as a site of ambiguous feminine national representations, she indicates that white opposition to racist and classist national imagery is clearly lacking: adding women of color to the mix of beauty pageant contestants 'allows white consumers to believe that they are enacting tolerance without the messy problems of actually redistributing resources or living the effects of affirmative action. Thus the ironic, unintended effect that characterizes the realm of representation becomes one in which white Americans feel more tolerant than ever, even as they continue to live in an increasingly segregated nation.'[20] The need for critical white engagements with national representation is obscured by the rhetoric of diversity in the pageant, a microcosm of America's conservative politics.

Irish poet Eavan Boland, in her disobedient nationalist narrative *Object Lessons: The Life of the Woman and the Poet in Our Time*, writes 'Once the idea of a nation influences the perception of a woman, then that woman is suddenly and inevitably simplified.... She becomes the passive projection of a national idea.'[21] In this light, Miss Liberty is white master not only to women of color, but to white women as well — a corseting ideal we can choose to serve, or not.

Daisy Miller: Class Hero, Race Traitor

Henry James' 1878 novella *Daisy Miller* caused an uproar among American women. They protested this representation of them as indecorous and gauche. I wonder if this negative reaction stemmed in part from recognition, or fear of finally being found out, as if Daisy were their communal alter-ego, unconstrained by fears of ruined reputations, let loose across the pond. Daisy flies in the face of 'good womanhood,' her story a declaration of ideological guerilla warfare in which the machinery of manners and 'classy' behavior is laid bare in all its ugly elitism, patriarchy, and white supremacism. This is a story about how white Western culture works — and how a girl can bring it to a stop in one small corner of the world, at least long enough for her readers to recognize this culture as constructed, and to be stirred towards alternative constructions.

Rebecca Aanerud asserts, 'In film as well as literature race need not be an issue in order for it to be a relevant component.'[22]   I model much of my interpretation of *Daisy Miller* on Aanerud's reading of Kate Chopin's *The Awakening*, broadening the scope of my feminist analysis to include the multiple facets of my heroine's identity. Aanerud writes, 'Instead of reading Edna's whiteness as incidental to her womanhood, I see it as inextricably tied to the construction of the feminine gender (understood especially as motherhood) and female sexuality (understood as Edna's desire), and *I am interested in her struggle to find a space outside those constructions.*'[23]   Daisy's whiteness, highlighted by the shade of her parasol throughout the text and personified in her name, is one of the more resounding unspoken subtexts of her rebellion and her culture's reactions to it. Specifically, her race loyalty is called into question by her affiliation with the dark Italian, Giovanelli. Stopped in the public square by Mrs. Walker, she is forced to make a choice to go with Giovanelli or return to her own kind. Following an inner sense of democratic justice, she goes with Giovanelli as she has promised and severs her ties with 'nice' society. In this scene (which I take to be the most important set of exchanges in the novella), Daisy embodies the noble spirit of the American Adam, yet excises his historical race, gender, and class bias.

Aanerud reminds the reader that 'while Edna's position in the gender hierarchy is constraining, this constraint is offset by her position in the race and class hierarchies'; this is significantly less so for Daisy (as part of the *nouveau riche*) who must at every moment provide evidence of belonging lest she slip back down the social ladder.[24]   Yet this social tension too easily disappears into one-dimensional gender analyses for me not to note Aanerud's warning that '[r]eading Edna as simply a woman, unraced and universal, erases the degree to which not only her whiteness but also her class position and her heterosexuality have everything to do with her frustration, her awakening, and her death.'[25] The fallen woman motif here reveals itself as more than a problem of misogyny, more than criticism of the fact of a woman fucking — that's just one dot among many that might be connected — it's about *whom* she fucks and whether their social status will buoy her up or allow her to fall. Indeed, fallen womanhood represents not only the suppression of female sexuality, but also the strict boundaries of class and race within which 'good' women must remain. Daisy's transgression lies partly in her unwillingness to perform properly as the American girl. Her improprieties mark her as an outsider while casting doubt on traditional social institutions from the superficial promenade to the bedrock of marriage.

The text surrounds Daisy with markers of precarious social class. The name Miller, for instance, links her with the working class, those who work with their hands to earn their wages. Even the name Daisy, as many critics note, suggests she is common and uncultivated. Patricia Crick's notes to the 1986 Penguin edition tell us that Daisy's diction betrays her lesser pedigree.[26] When Daisy proposes to take a late afternoon walk unattended, and then with the questionably motivated Giovanelli, Mrs. Walker's exclamation — 'I don't think it's safe, my dear' — refers to something more than the Roman Fever about which they are ostensibly speaking.[27]   It is not 'safe' to ignore the rules of polite society if one wishes to remain within that society. Thus, racism, classism, and sexism become coded as benevolent caretaking. When Mrs. Walker calls Daisy to her carriage, the coercive edge of benevolence emerges. Mrs. Walker chides Daisy for not acting according to 'custom' and threatens 'You are old enough, dear Miss Miller, to be talked about.'[28]   Mrs. Walker's pressure increases as Daisy continues to defy her authority. She ominously calls Daisy 'a very reckless girl' and makes 'an imperious claim' on Winterbourne to leave Daisy to her rabble and join her instead in the carriage (an image evoking the machinery of social class, directing and restricting one's movements unnaturally). Daisy dismisses Mrs. Walker with panache: '"I never heard anything so stiff! If this is improper, Mrs Walker," she pursued, "then I am all improper, and you must give me up."'[29]

Winterbourne, as the person through whose viewpoint we perceive the story, previously reflected on his aunt's 'disclosures' about Daisy's family and personal life, concluding, 'Evidently she was rather wild.'[30]   Indeed, her wildness — the moments in the text where Daisy acts 'improper'— marks a refusal of the very social rules that result in such labels. The strength of character some women gain from being cast as outsiders underlies Daisy's moral integrity.   In a recent exploration of the 'slut phenomenon' in contemporary society (the use of the 'slut' label as a means of policing girls according to conventional American ideals of femininity), Leora Tanenbaum marks a similar shift in perspective: 'These girls flaunt a proud, rebellious persona. Their attitude is: Why not flee the suffocation of conformity? Why not show everyone that being "good" is a farce?'[31]   This point stands to reason, according to feminist epistemology:

> [M]embers of oppressed groups have fewer interests in ignorance about the social   order and fewer reasons to invest in maintaining or justifying the status quo than do dominant groups. They have less to lose by distancing themselves from the social order; thus, the perspective from their lives can more easily generate fresh and critical analyses.[32]

Daisy strikes many critics as unconscious of whatever social criticism her actions might deploy. Edward Wagenknecht writes, 'Daisy does not really defy society but only disregards it, and if there is an element of heroism involved in carrying personal independence to such lengths, her behavior is … too spontaneous to permit the reader to posit any calculated choice or predetermination.'[33]   This view fits seamlessly with the typology of white women in literature created by Vron Ware, who identifies three white female types: the good, the bad, and the foolhardy. The good represents a character who is spiritually opposed to all injustice but is powerless. The bad represents 'the uncomplicated attitude of the wife' who enjoys imperialist trappings and disdains 'natives' and colonial settings. The foolhardy has feminist inclinations signified by her unwillingness to conform; however, she is thoroughly naive about the privileged position she occupies.[34]

Daisy comes closest to fitting the 'foolhardy' type, but 'thoroughly naïve' may overstate things. Indeed, I find many reasons to believe she is conscious of her cultural work. One indicator is her sarcasm: ' "Gracious me!" Daisy exclaimed, "I don't want to do anything improper."'[35] I hear these words in a Vivien-Leigh-as-Scarlett-O'Hara voice, dripping sweet but sharply pointed. Her awareness of social interactions as performance offers another indicator: 'if Mr Winterbourne were as polite *as he pretends* he would offer to walk with me!'[36] Further, she recognizes the hair-splitting distinctions within her social class; demanding to know why Winterbourne visited Mrs. Walker and not her, Daisy says, 'You knew her at Geneva. She told me so. Well, you knew me at Vevey. That's just as good.'[37] She has already quickly determined, despite Winterbourne's indirection, that his aunt, Mrs. Costello, does not wish to know her. While Daisy does not articulate the class barriers that underlie this rejection, she seems conscious of ideology behind the social slight. Daisy asks rhetorically, 'Why should she want to know me?,' indicating comprehension if not acceptance of the social order.[38] The specter of class permeability motivates her culture's strict policing of the female body; her rejection of their discipline complicates the meaning of upper-middle-class femininity and disrupts the narrative of middle-class, white, American women as passive emblems of America.

Marilynne Frye speculates on the racial basis for restrictions on white women's sexuality, proposing that what can seem to be pure sexism is also a form of racism, as white men, perhaps unconsciously, enforce these rules in service of propagating the race; in this light, 'our pursuit of our liberation...is, whether or not we so intend, disloyal to Whiteness.'[39] Winterbourne's evaluations of Giovanelli reveal this implicit racism: 'You should sometimes listen to a gentleman — the right one.'[40] Crick draws the reader's attention to the nosegay in the Italian's buttonhole, pointing out that 'in James's novels, an overexuberant button-hole is the sign of someone who is not quite a gentleman.'[41] This careful differentiation pits white men against less-white men, gentleman against the 'not quite gentleman.'[42] Giovanelli tries to be classy and white, but he fails, an illustration of Frankenberg's argument that whiteness is 'made rather than...self-evident.'[43] Winterbourne illustrates that whiteness is something you do, something produced consciously through a process of elimination and policed from within. Daisy is only white to the degree that she performs her whiteness, that is, to the degree that she remains race- and class-loyal in the company she keeps. 'He is not a gentleman,' thinks Winterbourne, 'only a clever imitation of one.' 'He is a music-master, or a penny-a-liner, or a third-rate artist' — these epithets denigrate Giovanelli's economic class; according to Crick, they mean 'a freelance journalist or author paid by the line, i.e. not one of any great importance.'[44] Winterbourne is disappointed in Daisy's 'not knowing the difference between a spurious gentleman and a real one'; perhaps the truth is that Daisy does know the difference, and she knows this 'difference' doesn't make any difference, at least not to her.[45]   Her opacity (conveyed through Winterbourne's oft-quoted description of Daisy as 'an inscrutable combination of audacity and innocence') can be attributed, then, to Winterbourne's inability to comprehend a life lived outside the dominant social order.[46]   Whereas Daisy's carefully chosen wardrobe creates a facade of respectability, her manner of speaking and loose behavior create fissures of class and race contamination. She is cast as *the* American girl, yet her *faux pas* suggest this icon is inherently flawed, inherently mongrelized.

Heldke's concept of the traitorous identity recurs to me here: 'As I learn more about the way that white racism has constructed the world and my understandings of it, and as that learning comes increasingly to inform the way I live in the world, I become an "unreliable" white person who cannot be trusted by other whites to "act appropriately."'[47]   Positing Daisy as an unreliable white person, I would echo Shelley Fisher-Fishkin's paradigm-shifting question for American literary studies — is Huck black? — with the related inquiry, is Daisy white trash?   Frankenberg tells us that ' "white trash" as a concept actually marks the borders of whiteness.'[48] Indeed, Daisy 'trashes' white culture, blurring its crisp outlines with her unruly desire.   Her working class sensibility and attraction to dark 'foreigners' make her the nineteenth-century parallel of many young white women in my rural Southern home town who have in recent years been dating cross-racially—anathema to this unofficially segregrated community.   Like Daisy, these girls — marked by their association with black men as 'trashy' — betray this town's aspiration to whiteness with their refusal to police their sexuality inside class and race boundaries.   They refuse, as does Daisy, the passive, silent position of civic emblem and ideological tool.

Conclusion

'Remember who you are,' my grandfather tells me as I walk to my car at the end of every visit home.   I think to myself, 'and who would that be?' even though I know what he means.   He means: behave yourself.   Act like a lady. Keep your legs crossed.   All the lessons he taught me as a little girl, the same ones I saw him pass on to my new baby niece last month.   Contrary to his advice, I work on not remembering who I am, disremembering the white, propertied identity that would blind me to the damage I do to others — and the damage I do to myself — by performing this race and class 'appropriately.'   Or maybe I remember who I am all too carefully, more carefully than he would have me do.   When I hear him speak those words, I feel pulled into a system of domination that suppresses my sexuality, limits my gender identity, even as it gives me race and class privilege. And when I feel that pull, I tug back, trying to disaffiliate, to stay conscious and critical of where I am positioned in the world. As a reader, I look for other 'responsible traitors' as role models, integrating antiracist and anticlassist work with feminist literary criticism and establishing a method of analysis open not only to the failures of American literature but also its moments of radical insight.

Notes

[1] See Mario Klarer, 'Woman and Arcadia: The Impact of Ancient Utopian Thought on the Early Image of America,' *Journal of American Studies* 27 (1993): 1-17, for feminine representations of America, and bell hooks, *Feminist Theory from Margin to Center*, 2nd ed., (Cambridge, MA: South End Press, 2000), for a discussion of feminism as primarily white and middle-class.

[2] I take this phrase from Adrienne Rich's poem 'An Old House in America' in *Adrienne Rich's Poetry and Prose: Poems, Prose, Reviews, and Criticism*, Norton Critical Edition (New York: Norton, 1993).

[3] Susan Gubar's 'What Ails Feminism,' *Critical Inquiry* 24 (1999): 878-902, addresses the paralysis of many critics in the face of being commanded by women of color to address race in literary criticism and being told simultaneously that we are utterly unequipped to do so. Robyn Weigman's response in 'What Ails Feminist Criticism? A Second Opinion,' *Critical Inquiry* 25 (1999): 363-79, accuses Gubar of 'crafting whiteness as an injured identity' (376). This exchange represents the largely unspoken but palpable tension between critics over who has the right to write race.

[4] Ruth Frankenberg, *White Women, Race Matters: The Social Construction of Whiteness*. (Minneapolis: University of Minnesota Press, 1993), 232.

[5] Frankenberg, 1.

[6] Frankenberg, 9 and 232.

[7] Frankenberg, 4-5.

[8] Marilynne Frye, 'On Being White: Thinking Toward a Feminist Understanding of Race and Race Supremacy' in *The Politics of Reality: Essays in Feminist Theory* (Freedom, CA: Crossing, 1983), 118.

[9] Frye, 125 and 127.

[10] Frankenberg, 4.

[11] Joanne Frye, *Living Stories, Telling Lives: Women and the Novel in Contemporary Experience*, Women and Culture Series (Ann Arbor: University of Michigan Press, 1986), 191.

[12] Lisa Heldke, 'On Being a Responsible Traitor: A Primer' in *Daring to Be Good: Essays in Feminist Ethico-Politics*, Thinking Gender Series, eds. Bat-Ami Bar On and Ann Ferguson (New York: Routledge, 1998), 90.

[13] Lauren Berlant, *The Anatomy of National Fantasy: Hawthorne, Utopia, and Everyday Life* (Chicago: University of Chicago Press, 1991), 22.

[14] Berlant, 5.

[15] Berlant, 27.

[16] Ibid.

[17] Berlant, 25-26.

[18] Berlant, 28.

[19] Susan Gubar, *Critical Condition: Feminism at the Turn of the Century* (New York: Columbia University Press, 2000), 23.

[20] Sarah Banet-Weiser, *The Most Beautiful Girl in the World: Beauty Pageants and National Identity* (Berkeley: University of California Press, 1999), 20.

[21] Eavan Boland, *Object Lessons: The Life of the Woman and the Poet in Our Time* (New York: Norton, 1995), 136.

[22] Rebecca Aanerud, 'Fictions of Whiteness: Speaking the Names of Whiteness in U.S. Literature,' in Frankenberg, 36.

[23] Aanerud, 'Fictions,' 39.

[24] Aanerud, 'Fictions,' 42.

[25] Aanerud, 'Fictions,' 43.

[26] Henry James, *Daisy Miller*, eds. Geoffrey Moore and Patricia Crick (New York: Penguin, 1986), 121.

[27] James, 85.

[28] James, 92.

[29] James, 93.

[30] James, 63.

[31] Leora Tanenbaum, *Slut! Growing Up Female with a Bad Reputation* (New York: Seven Stories, 1999), 41.

[32] Sandra Harding, *Whose Science? Whose Knowledge? Thinking from Women's Lives* (Ithaca, NY: Cornell University Press, 1991), 126.

[33] Edward Wagenknecht, *Eve and Henry James: Portraits of Women and Girls in His Fiction.* (Norman: University of Oklahoma Press, 1978), 8.

[34] Cited in Aanerud, 'Fictions,' 53.

[35] James, 86.

[36] James, 86, my italics.

[37] James, 87.

[38] James, 66-7.

[39] Frye, 'On Being White,' 126.

[40] James, 88.

[41] James, 124.

[42] Frankenberg cites David Roediger for his scholarship on social class and the production of the white race.

[43] Frankenberg, 11.

[44] James, 89 and 124.

[45] James, 89.

[46] James, 90.

[47] Heldke, 94.

[48] Frankenberg, 13.

6 Bodies Political and Social: Royal Widows in Renaissance Ceremonial

Elizabeth McCartney

This essay examines the history of political government, public discourse, and state ceremonial during the French Wars of Religion (1560-1610). Of special interest to the author is how contemporaries articulated the precepts of moral and divine law that supported the authority of the widowed queen and regent, Catherine de Médicis, for more than forty years. By charting the interplay between sites of culture evident in ceremonial assemblies and sights of women as devotional focii, the author reevaluates modern literature of queenship that asserts a rigorous severance of the conceptual and social powers of state and domestic government. This study of the natural, affective elements of political discourse suggests that — to the contrary — contemporaries embraced the topoi of devotion as a means of protecting the legitimacy of female rule well into the seventeenth century.

Recent studies of the French Renaissance monarchy accord little recognition to the public celebration of a queen's jurisdiction to govern France. Modern accounts of ceremonial and public law develop a typology of rulership based on the symbolism of ritual displays of power associated exclusively with a king's body. The principal tenets of this political culture are supported with reference to the historical doctrine of Salic law, treated as a canon of legal practice supporting male-right to govern France, and the modern theoretical construct of the 'King's Two Bodies,' examined as a constitutional metaphor for seminal history.[1] To summarize recent argument, French lawyers, between *circa* 1300 and 1750, developed a repressive marital-rights regime by 'presenting female incapacity as a dictate of natural law.'[2] The thesis progresses to a set of conclusions *ex hypothosi* about the history of France, the function of royal ceremonial, and the legal rights of women (including queens.)

Yet the question central to the vitality of the French state — contemporary perceptions of the legitimacy of a queen's role as wife and mother to king and polity — suggests a gendered history at odds with the current model. This essay explores how contemporaries envisaged the political culture of regency government as a codified system of guardianship (*tutela*) that assured each queen's conjugal rights as wife and widow.[3]   Of special interest is the political authority of Queen Catherine de Médicis, regent of France, *circa* 1549 to 1588. Although her tenure in power coincided with the most dramatic episodes of the French Reformation, those who owed obedience to Catherine considered royal marriage as a political estate with a singular capacity for preserving the polity and institutions of early modern France.

When, in 1549, Catherine de Médicis was crowned queen of France, the legal principles and moral precepts supporting the legitimacy of regency government had long been incorporated into official histories. A decisive stage was reached during the early fourteenth century, when the Capetian royal house began to falter and the Valois dynasty was eventually elevated to the crown. To protect the element of kinship requisite in hereditary monarchies, successive kings issued legislation protecting the privileges and immunities enjoyed by queens in their capacities as wives and mothers. The effect of these decrees was to consolidate the relationship between family and state, ultimately to establish royal marriage as a principal tenet of French political culture. One of the most influential publicists to examine the conjugal basis of distaff prerogative was Durand de Champagne, a cleric at the court of Philippe IV and Jeanne of Navarre.   Durand, writing in 1300 of contemporary political concerns, supported an unqualified interpretation of queenship as an office ('l'estat royal'): as Philippe IV was king and father to his subjects, Jeanne was queen and mother.   Under the rubric 'The Ten Commandments of Good Government,' he included the solemn responsibility enjoined on each queen to protect life, property, and resources of the Church.[4] With reference to the *Book of Job*, the cleric also reminded his honored queen that acts of political reconciliation were regenerative qualities of government associated with the humanity and royalty of Jesus. At birth, all individuals were endowed with qualities of spiritual renewal that supported the life of the body politic. Later jurists envisaged the connection between the royal household and government as a system of kinship predicated on the overarching legal principle of *tutela*.[5] Precepts of positive law were consistently enveloped with political meanings; but in drawing comparisons between the legal principles of private law and public law, emphasis was unfailingly given to the unique character of royal marriage. Throughout the late Middle Ages, the maternal status of the queens of France was frequently defended in a variety of sources, foremost in didactic literature explicating principles of political theory derived from the study of Aristotle, Saint Augustine, and Saint Thomas Aquinas. By the mid-fifteenth century, the familial basis of royal authority was further codified. Sir John Fortescue, writing of the Hundred Years War, argued that the legal statutes regulating royal marriage protected the legitimacy of hereditary monarchies.[6] In the early 1500s, contemporaries treated royal marriage as the impresa of a political culture that continued to flourish in part because of the interplay between site (the royal household) and sight (the public presence of royal women). The daily administration of the respective domains of Valois rule of

France and Habsburg rule over extended lands was protected under the auspices of two 'royal' widows, Marguerite of Austria and Louise of Savoy. Neither widow was an ordained queen, yet both acted in similar 'maternal' capacities as guardians of public institutions. Marguerite of Austria, the widowed aunt of the emperor Charles V, enjoyed a singular position as regent of the Netherlands. Louise of Savoy, mother of François I, king of France, was a vigilant guardian of king and realm until her death in 1531. Not even political contest over royal policies diminished contemporary interest in the moral virtue of each widow who governed with prescience and compassion. In tribute, jurist and publicist alike developed testimony of the divine grace associated with female rule as they anticipated the future history of France.[7]

The political importance of Catherine de Médicis' maternal authority was fully understood by those who planned the coronation festivities of 1549 to honor her authority as queen consort of Henri II. From the outset, the unusual qualities of this cycle of pageantry reflected two grave political concerns: Henri II's ongoing military campaign against the spread of heresy and Catherine's pending tenure as regent.[8] When, on 18-20 June, the Parisians gathered to celebrate Catherine's status as 'queen of the French,' the panoply of ceremonial prepared in her honor dramatized a richly nuanced vocabulary supporting the affective bonds of political kinship. The city of Paris was now the temporal Jerusalem, the queen of France, like her heavenly counterpart the Virgin Mary, was a 'gift' from God, sent to protect her subjects, children placed in her care.[9] The subject of royal marriage was treated as a rite (sacrament) and right (covenant) supporting the Queen's political authority.[10]

As anticipated, the sense of shared intimacy between Catherine de Médicis and her subjects proved to be meta-generational. The bond of marital devotion celebrated in 1549 transposed acts of daily observance into political obligations to obey controversial royal decrees long after Henri II's death in 1559. The subsequent drama of the Wars of Religion (*circa* 1562 to 1600) rarely encourages modern historians to consider the fundamental importance of Catherine de Médicis' position as royal mother to king and to polity. However, contrary to the impression conveyed by the canon of 'misnurture' now posited against the first Médicis queen, the outstanding characteristic of public law of the mid-sixteenth century might better be understood through study of the affective vocabulary of political discourse, which continued to envelop somatic relationships between the queen of France as widow of Henri II and her subjects as children entrusted to her care. The human character of ordained rule would prove to be the most enduring legacy of early modern political discourse.

One of the earliest testimonies to the function of royal marriage as the impresa of public law was penned by a distinguished jurist, Louis Le Roy.[11] Le Roy wrote in 1559 of the gravity of the international crisis in government, juxtaposing the ethical dilemmas testing the faith of the kings of France and Spain as each tried to negotiate the question of religious plurality. According to

Le Roy, both Henri II and Philippe II were, by virtue of their status as ordained rulers, obligated to respond to acts of inhumanity with gestures of clemency; the human passions that provoked intolerance would prove a lesser resource than the emotions inspired by an individual's contemplation of the Passion of Christ, which developed from love and piety.

Writing after Henri II's death, Le Roy continued to assert that passions were the constitutive component of lawful rule.[12]   Whereas qualities of love and charity were complementary attributes of ordained government in times of peace, tears and lament were potent expressions of devotion from those who lived according to God's will in times of civil unrest. A king's faith was the impresa of legitimate rule; if the king was still a youth, his widowed mother's tears served as the testimony of redemption for a polity unable to preserve life, property, and the surety of justice. For Le Roy, Catherine de Médicis's lament prompted by her husband's death in 1559 was the affirmation of a paternal presence supporting government during the reign of François II. Eighteen months later, the death of this fifteen-year-old king elevated the widowed Queen's grief into an element of 'state' ceremonial.

When he wrote of the death of François II in 1560, Le Roy treated the inconsolable sorrow of Catherine de Médicis as a heuristic device of early modern political theory. Discussing the accession of the ten-year-old Charles IX, second son of Henri II and Catherine, the jurist treated the topos of mourning as a motif of resurrection supporting the legitimacy of regency government on the eve of the formal outbreak of the Wars of Religion. Le Roy advised the Queen to build a mausoleum, an edifice embodying the history of French royal kingship and kinship, which would honor her maternal role in relation to king and polity.[13]   From a historical perspective, the frequency with which contemporaries urged Catherine de Médicis to erect such a mausoleum suggests a political treatment of salvation predicated on late-medieval writings of dynastic history.[14]   From a ceremonial perspective, the rituals of royal death in the mid-sixteenth century offer evidence of a parallel history to that presented by Lyndal Roper regarding Reformation Germany: bodily symbolism was the deepest religious tool available to contemporaries to negotiate the fluid boundaries between language and subjectivity.[15]

Le Roy also examined the emotive basis of political theory. Of interest were questions about the natural, legal, and political significance of royal marriage as an element of public law. First, by placing Catherine's tears within the narrative context of royal succession, he described the queen's lament as if he actually had witnessed it. For Le Roy, the salvation of Henri II was not envisaged in terms of bodily resurrection, as would later occur with regard to Henri IV in 1610, but explicated in terms of reassemblage, a 'reclothing' of flesh and soul: the full *gravitas* of royal dignity and authority that had once resided in Henri II's adult body was transferred to his widow from the moment of his death.[16]   Second, the images of Catherine's lament provided a 'sense impression' necessary for the future reconciliation of communities divided over doctrinal concerns. In 1560, as violence began to spread, the natural order of French society and state was fully posited on the religious model of marriage as a covenant protecting Catherine de Médicis' legal rights as a widow and queen of France. Finally, Le Roy revalued the bodily metaphor of French constitutional history by centering the queen's grief within the context of sempiternity associated with the Passion. Whereas the king's body, specifically Henri II's, had once symbolized the divine ordinance of French kingship, the queen's body, clothed simply in the habit of a widow, now epitomized the life cycle of the body politic.

To summarize, in one decade, rituals celebrating the legal bond of royal marriage were used to define a process of bodily renewal which ultimately extended through the four reigns of Catherine's husband and sons: Henri II (1547 to 1559), François II (1559 to 1560), Charles IX (1560 to 1574), and Henri III (1574 to 1589).[17] For a public conversant with devotional literature, Le Roy's vision of lawful rule paraphrased Scripture, the text of I *Corinthians* 13.12 and related verse pertaining to resurrection: '...we must remain in this [good] and cling to it by love, that we may enjoy the presence of that from which we are, in the absence of which we would not be at all.'[18] As the sorrow and lament of the Virgin Mary dramatized the dual nature of Jesus as man and Son, Catherine's mourning was an affirmation of the true nature of kingship: the image of her maternal suffering protected the children who ruled France and the paternal bonds of communal life.

That Le Roy wrote on the sanctity of royal marriage as he contemplated anew the diminishing vitality of the French monarchy invites, I submit, re-evaluation of modern perceptions that this institution was void of any political significance. For example, recourse to the public estate of royal marriage was especially striking in the ceremonial protocol of the representative assembly convened in 1560. Originally planned as part of a political forum to institute reforms during François II's reign, the proceedings for the Estates General were changed in tenor by the king's unexpected death. The conciliar, deliberative element appropriate to approval of royal policies ultimately took second place to the *gravitas* of celebrating royal advent and the inauguration of a minority regency in a secular assembly. Those responsible for organizing the ceremonial enthronement orchestrated protocol in order to capture the primacy of emotions surrounding Charles IX's accession. Those who witnessed the enthronement acknowledged that the political elements of *tutela* were now invoked to support a queen's jurisdiction during royal minority.

Once assembled, the delegates observed the ceremonial enthronement of the widowed queen beside her ten-year-old son. The placement of the royal dais in the center of the hall was a deliberate allusion to the 'heart' of the body politic; the use of color heightened the focus of the ceremony on the queen's presence.[19] Dressed in mourning, Catherine de Médicis was seated on a chair covered with black draperies; her feet rested on black pillows; her enthronement was framed through the placement of a black canopy behind the dais. The ceremonial protocol, evocative of Aristotelian argument pertaining to sight, treated the queen's bereavement as a coeval element of royal advent. In contrast to the somber quality of his mother's enthronement, Charles IX made his first public appearance as king of France seated on a chair complete with pillows and canopy, covered with the resplendent blue tapestries embroidered with gold *fleur-de-lis* that visually signaled the quasi-divine origins of French kingship. Separated spatially from the royal dais, those in attendance were physically incorporated into a body politic created by royal marriage, protected by royal parentage.

The correspondence between family and state was also the subject of discourse. Addressing the assembly, the chancellor of France, Michel de l'Hospital, set forth the issues of politics and religion that had recently affected the legitimacy of royal policies.[20] Next, l'Hospital affirmed Catherine de Médicis' legal rights as queen and regent: until Charles IX attained the royal age of majority, at least three years hence, the queen, as mother, would determine the full agenda of government, foremost the administration of justice. Speaking of the threat posed by religious plurality, l'Hospital did not interpret the regency government to be evidence of a diminished jurisdiction. On the contrary, the chancellor spoke with authority of the proscriptive qualities of Catherine's status as guardian of the body politic, arguing that the widowed queen personified the dual jurisdiction of the late Henri II and the reigning Charles IX. After the assembly, contemporaries wrote of their evident relief that the young heir had assumed his duties of governance; seasoned observers of royal politics noted their pleasure that Catherine de Médicis was a prescient guardian of law in this fragile stage of the body politic. Official records also reveal that allegiance between the queen and her subjects was a personal attribute enacted through intimate bonds of devotion: the oaths of obedience to royalty on the part of office-holders took place in the Queen's rooms. Even the official records of the Parlement of Paris, the ranking law court of the realm, recorded the inauguration of the regency government with reference to Catherine's maternal authority as 'mother' of the magistrates, '...la Royne nostre mère.'[21]

Perhaps the most striking observation in contemporary sources is one of omission. That both Catherine de Médicis and Charles IX appeared at the assembly without regalia suggests a realism in matters of constitutional importance at odds with the modern construct of 'The King's Two Bodies.' Whereas modern scholars bestow a solemn aura on the symbolic associations of regalia and the transcendent mysteries of state, arguably 'placing the symbol before the reality,' contemporaries revalued politics through the gestures of 'practical ambitions.'[22] From a historical perspective, the occasional display of regalia during the Wars of Religion was of lesser importance than the vision of intimacy achieved during 'ordinary' ceremonial occasions, foremost the panoply of civic and religious rituals associated with Christ's body and the symbolism of spiritual renewal.[23]

Throughout the sixteenth century, the personal attributes of piety, love, and devotion that contemporaries desired to see in the guardians of Church and State remained the central precepts supporting the restitution of individual rights within communities divided over questions of faith.[24] Acknowledgment of Catherine's supreme authority as mediator of doctrinal issues was also confirmed through expressions of affection and devotion to her as a widowed mother and queen of France.[25] The attributes of maternal love, then remorse, demonstrated by Catherine de Médicis for her own family's survival — through the loss of infant children and relatives, then the death of her husband, and ultimately her bereavement over the fate of her royal sons — was revalued by members of the polity as a sign of the triune qualities of faith, motherhood, and lament. To summarize, the sight of Catherine de Médicis, clothed in mourning since Henri II's reign, was a persistent reminder to her subjects of the acute suffering all mothers felt at the loss of family. The appeal to conscience as an element of reconciliation was enhanced by the consistent presence of the queen's body within the assembled body politic. Those who had rebelled against the authority of the royal sons of Henri II and Catherine de Médicis had, in effect, dishonored the memory of Henri II; but the presence of the widowed queen-mother, enthroned beside child kings, was the resource of rectitude that rejuvenated the bonds of kinship of community life.

The frequency with which public assemblies were convened during the 1560s also supports a generalized set of observations pertaining to the character of regency government. Regardless of the venue, ceremonial protocol honored Catherine de Médicis and Charles IX, later Henri III, above all other members of the polity. On occasions of enthronement, the physical boundaries of the royal dais symbolically demarcated the unique devotional bond between royal mother and son, while simultaneously protecting the separate origins of their jurisdiction. Catherine de Médicis was always enthroned with use of black tapestries symbolizing the element of guardianship appropriate to Catherine's status as widow and regent. Her sons were always enthroned with use of blue or burgundy, suggestive of the sempiternity of royal prerogative. The sight of royalty within the diverse communities of the body politic created a sense of reflective presence which, in turn, was interpreted by individual members of the polity through private acts of devotion associated with daily observance of family rituals. Finally, Catherine's maternal devotion to king and polity confirmed a catena of duties based on love and jurisprudence, both human and divine. Combined, these qualities required the ultimate sacrifice of obedience on the part of all members of the realm to a queen whose presence in the body politic represented the salvation of the community at large.

In political discourse, Catherine de Médicis's titles of queen, widow, royal mother, and sovereign dame were invoked by individuals who atoned for past actions through a shared language of devotion. Her petitioners addressed her from a fully gendered perspective, but not with one voice.

Catholics petitioned for protection of the sacramental basis of the French monarchy and state.[26] Protestants defended faith as a covenant with God and monarchy. Each enveloped language with images of intimacy in order to enhance the symbolic kinship between the queen and those who were entrusted to her care. Perhaps the most illuminating account of emotions attesting to the character of future politics is found in the early 1560s. Antoine of Bourbon, one of Catherine's political rivals in the regency council, wrote eloquently to her of the unsettled politico-religious contests in which he had participated. These vexations had so weakened his physical stamina that, forced to his bed, Bourbon prayed for the presence (the sight) of Catherine and Charles IX as a restorative.[27] As royal vitality was the physic requisite for a body politic increasingly weakened by violence, Bourbon's pleas were in effect those of an extended family member seeking a widow's compassion for her errant progeny.

How images of Catherine's maternal devotion influenced the subsequent history of France might be gleaned from official records, for example those of the Hôtel de la Ville in Paris, the civic institution responsible for local government. In 1563, worry over the stability of the city's government prompted these administrative officers to ask for Catherine's return to Paris in order that they might present grievance to her regarding contemporary royal policies. Addressing the queen as 'our mother' — 'Madame, qui est nostre mère'— they were anxious to preserve her full authority over all institutions.[28] In 1567, the members of this collegiate body were delighted to learn that, after a two-year absence, Catherine would again be in residence in Paris. In spite of the substantive failings of royal government in the capital city, the simple narrative account of the entry ceremony staged in her honor still conveys a sense of the profound importance of her physical presence as a royal mother. A commemorative stone was set to offer testimony of the Parisians' gratitude for Catherine's continuing role as a sovereign wife and mother (*Domina*) to three generations of kings.[29] The language of reverence, combined with the public gestures of devotion performed in Catherine's honor, invites consideration of the question most pertinent to modern research on gender: do these expressions of devotion constitute a political construction of motherhood, the sight of women in the loci of power?

The answer lies partly in theories of emotional response. The value of such contemporary witness is the personal basis of subjectivity that simultaneously breached two realms of perceptual understanding. Recourse to Passion-based spirituality inspired members of the body politic to draw analogies between their lives and that of the queen of France; and the affective response to political failure reinvigorated the royal body.[30] In this context, it is difficult to support the conclusion that, during the Wars of Religion, the French interpreted law and religion as human rights dissociated from Catherine's presence. Even the queen's most embittered critics after the 1572 massacres still described her authority and her failings in terms of family metaphor and parental obligation. The very treatise now heralded as evidence of Catherine's moral depravity, the *Discours merveilleux*, contained avowals of loyalty and devotion to a queen who enjoyed a singular legal status derived from divine ordinance: Catherine de Médicis, by virtue of marriage to Henri II, had been 'eslevée en dignité' and was enjoined by precepts of moral law to protect her subjects.[31]

That few modern historians acknowledge the meta-generational history of maternal devotion in recounting the political history of Catherine de Médicis' regency governments has diminished the richly variegated history of political discourse. By discounting the viability of a 'moral law,' the study of emotions pertaining to the queen's body is predicated on what might be termed an observance of anger: at best, the history of passion during the regencies of Catherine de Médicis is judged to be an irrational response to the violence of the late sixteenth century. Scholars adopt, perhaps unwittingly, the typology of law and ceremonial developed by Norbert Elias in his study of political regimes. Elias, writing of the unfolding history of royal absolutism over the course of several hundred years, identified the religious conflicts of the sixteenth century as a crisis of rule predicated on anger, resolved through recourse to civility and subordination to the kings of France.[32] Yet the limitations of this interpretation are worth noting. First, this reconstructed typology of early modern rulership is wholly gendered and royal: there is no positive mention of a queen's authority in the entire corpus of Elias's scholarship. Second, the history of ceremonial is codified into an apassionate — secular — corpus of premeditated symbolism: passion is neither a religious virtue, as once envisaged by Saint Thomas Aquinas, nor a political quality, as realized by Louis Le Roy. Third, much of Elias's evidence is gleaned from later sources, specifically from accounts of mid-seventeenth-century ceremonial celebrating the apotheosis of Louis XIV, a subject that invariably leads to the political failures of minority regency government. Finally, Elias celebrated royal advent, specifically the king's coronation ceremony, as the birth of political realism; in turn, he ignored death and bodily decline as elements of reality (and regeneration) in ceremonial systems.[33] The last heavily qualified argument is especially significant in the study of the history of regency government.

In a basic sense, Elias' royal paradigm severs the cultural aesthetics of mourning from the political elements of ethics necessary to appreciate a queen's authority as guardian of public law. A queen's body is thus seen as an intractable object in an expanding discourse celebrating marital affection. Consequently, the lawyers of early modern France, not the realm's queens, are judged to have been the guardians ('co-tutors') of king and polity. Yet, a history of queenship can be written to different effect. My proposed emendations include recognizing the vitality of royal marriage as a site of public law regulating royal succession and acknowledging the correspondence between the political and religious precepts of Passion-based devotion sighted in royal ceremonial. In effect, such qualification 'reassembles' the queen's body within the salvation of the body politic. As the most telling evidence supporting such a gendered history may be found in the records of the Parlement of Paris, I base the conclusion of this essay on a condensed summary of early Bourbon France as articulated in those records.

Not even the detritus of the massacres of 1572, which had profoundly demonstrated the failings of secular and religious institutions, effaced the affective elements of political discourse. In 1600, as publicists and jurists alike considered the repercussions of Henri IV's forthcoming marriage to Marie de Médicis, they continued to employ the affective language of love and devotion in two contexts, those of Marie's future status as wife and mother to kings and polity. Catherine de Médicis's accomplishments as 'queen and royal mother' were invoked by those responsible for orchestrating the marriage festivities of 1600 as a model of political excellence for the second Médicis queen. Ten years later, 14 May 1610, the assassination of Henri IV revived the drama of minority regency government, while raising questions anew about the survival of France as a fully hereditary monarchy. The next day, all ranking members in service to the crown, royal household, and civic institutions assembled in the chambers of the Parlement of Paris to proclaim the advent of Louis XIII and the minority regency government of Marie de Médicis. As recorded in the official accounts of the ceremony, contemporaries were in easier voice about Marie's status as queen and regent than we now acknowledge. In addressing the assembly, the first president of the law court, Achille de Harlay, praised Marie's natural virtues as mother to king and polity, addressing her simply as 'nôtre mère.'[34] Both official records and historical accounts of the assembly also record the queen's grief, her lament visibly displayed through the device of enthronement and the lavish use of black cloth to commemorate the transfiguration of her sovereignty from potential to actualized jurisdiction.

In a basic sense, the constitutional implications of lament were the same for the history of France in 1610 as they had been in 1559. Yet the differences in the ceremonies of enthronement between 1560 and 1610 attest to the spiritual basis of political communities in early modern Europe. In 1610, the royal dais, erected in a corner of the assembly, was placed adjacent to an image of the Crucifixion, a visual reference prompting the political community of mourners to consider the conjunction of human and divine decree that protected the widowed queen's jurisdiction as mother to son and polity. Lament left an indelible mark on the symbolism of the ceremony of inauguration: during the formal declaration of Marie de Médicis' regency government, the audience witnessed a dramatization of the mystery of human salvation and the interplay between Passion and compassion which ultimately supported the reconstruction of France as a Christian political community in post-Reformation Europe.

Notes

[1] Ernst H. Kantorowicz, *The King's Two Bodies: A Study in Mediaeval Political Theology* (Princeton, NJ: Princeton University Press, 1957), Ralph E. Giesey, *The Juristic Basis of Dynastic Right to the French Throne*. TAPS 60 (Philadelphia: American Philosophical Society, 1961). The theory of the 'King's Two Bodies' is set forth by Kantorowicz and Giesey; each emphasizes the symbolic function of body metaphor in political theory and in the history of royal ceremonial. The critical symbolism of this constitutional doctrine, which distinguishes between the sovereign's public, symbolic, political body and (his) private, physical body, includes the development of fundamental ideas regarding kingship, sovereignty, and the nation-state.

[2] Sarah Hanley, 'Social Sites of Political Practice in France: Lawsuits, Civil Rights, and the Separation of Powers in Domestic and State Government, 1500-1800,' *American Historical Review* 102 (1997): 30-2.

[3] My research and argument closely follow that of Walter Ullman who examined the political elements of the legal doctrine of *tutela*; see especially 'Calvin and the Duty of Guardians to Resist: A Further Comment,' *Journal of Ecclesiastical History* 32 (1981): 499-501. The exactly opposite argument, based on the assertion of 'corporeal ipseity,' that is the celebration of the individual in Renaissance society, is developed by Alain Boureau, 'The Sacrality of One's Own Body in the Middle Ages,' *Yale French Studies* 86 (1994): 5-17.

[4] For a recent assessment of queens' patronage, see Carla Lord, 'Jeanne d'Evreux as a Founder of Chapels: Patronage and Public Piety,' in *Women and Art in Early Modern Europe: Patrons, Collectors, and Connoisseurs*, ed. Cynthia Lawrence (University Park: Pennsylvania State University Press, 1997): 21-36. See C. Stephen Jaeger, *Ennobling Love: In Search of a Lost Sensibility* (Philadephia: University of Pennsylvania Press, 1999), *passim*, treating avowals of love and affection from a 'social constructivist' position.

[5] Claire Richter Sherman, *Imaging Aristotle: Verbal and Visual Representation in Fourteenth-Century France* (Berkeley: University of California Press, 1995): 289ff.

[6] J. H. Burns, 'Fortescue and the Political Theory of *Dominium*,' *The Historical Journal* 28 (1985): 777-98 and Gerald Harriss, 'Political Society and the Growth of Government in Late Medieval England,' *Past and Present* 138 (1993): 28-57.

[7] Alcuin Blamires, *The Case for Women in Medieval Culture* (Oxford: Clarendon Press and New York: Oxford University Press, 1997), 70-95; Giles Constable, 'A Living Past: The Historical Environment of the Middle Ages,' in *Culture and Spirituality in Medieval Europe* (Aldershot, England and Brookfield, VT: Variorum, 1996), *passim*; and I D. McFarlane, 'Religious Verse in French Neo-Latin Poetry Until the Death of Francis I and Marguerite of Navarre,' in *Humanism and Reform: The Church in Europe, England, and Scotland, 1400-1643*, ed. James Kirk (Oxford and Cambridge, MA: Blackwell Publishers, 1991), 171-86.

[8] Lawrence M. Bryant, *The King and the City in the Parisian Royal Entry Ceremony* (Geneva: Librairie Droz S.A., 1986), 54-66.

[9] François Bonnardot, ed., *Registres des délibérations du Bureau de la Ville de Paris* I, 153-85, especially 169 and 180: '...nous en rendons graces à la Magesté celeste...par sa bonté et divine clemence a faict aux Françoys si riche et precieulx don....il vous plaise recevoir de face gratieuse et benigne les affections très humbles et plus que devotes voluntez des citoyens d'icelle.'

[10] John Witte, Jr. *From Sacrament to Contract: Marriage, Religion, and Law in the Western Tradition* (Louisville, KY: Westminster John Knox Press, 1997), 94-129.

[11] Louis Le Roy, *Ad Invictissimos Potentissimósque principes Henricum II. Franc. & Philippum Hispan....*(Paris, 1559), especially 3v-6r, 10r-12v.

[12] *Idem, Ad Illustrissimam Reginam D. Cathariniam Medicem, Francisci II. ...Consolatio...*(Paris, 1560), especially 2r-6v, 11v-18v, 19r-28r.

13   Christiane Raynaud, 'Humanism and Good Government: A Burgundian Rendering of the *Romuleon* by Roberto Della Porta,' *Fifteenth-Century Studies* 24 (1998): 159-74.

14   Sheila ffolliott, 'The Ideal Queenly Patron of the Renaissance: Catherine de' Medici Defining Herself or Defined by Others?' in *Women and Art in Early Modern Europe:Patrons, Collectors, and Connoisseurs*, ed. Cynthia Lawrence (University Park, PA: Pennsylvania State Press, 1997), 99-111.

15   Lyndal Roper, *Oedipus and the Devil:Witchcraft, Sexuality, and Religion in Early Modern Europe* (London and New York: Routledge, 1994), 18-22; Berndt Hamm, 'The Urban Reformation in the Holy Roman Empire,' in *Handbook of European History, 1400-1600*, eds. Thomas A. Brady Jr., Heiko A. Oberman, and James D. Tracy, vol.2 (Leiden and New York: E.J. Brill, 1994), 193-228, especially 194; and Lynn Abrams and Elizabeth Harvey, eds., *Gender Relations in German History* (Durham, NC: Duke University Press, 1997, c. 1996), especially 5-12; R. N. Swanson, *Religion and Devotion in Europe, c.1215-c.1515* (Cambridge and New York: Cambridge University Press, 1995), 140ff.

16   The argument is adapted from Caroline Bynum, *The Resurrection of the Body in Western Christianity, 200-1336* (New York: Columbia University Press, 1995), 118-36. See also Elizabeth A. R. Brown, 'Authority, the Family, and the Dead in Late Medieval France,' *French Historical Studies* 16 (1990): 823ff.

17   Elizabeth Hallam, Jenny Hockey, and Glennys Howarth, *Beyond the Body: Death and Social Identity* (London and New York: Routledge, 1999), 20-34.

18   Jeffrey F. Hamburger, *The Rothschild Canticles* (New Haven and London: Yale University Press, 1990), 120; for the related texts, see Bynum, 120ff.

19   Derek Matravers, 'Art and the Feelings and Emotions,' *British Journal of Aesthetics* 31 (1991): 322-31.

20   Michel de l'Hospital. 'Harangue prononcée à l'ouverture de la session des États généraux à Orléans le 13 décembre,' in *Discours pour la majorité de Charles IX et trois autres discours*, ed. Robert Descimon (Paris: Imprimerie nationale, 1993), 64-93.

21   Paris, Archives Nationaux, X1a 1596 [Parlement of Paris], fol 75.

22   Alain Boureau, 'Richard Southern: A Landscape for a Portrait,' *Past and Present* 165 (1999): 218-29, at 228-29.

23   Ralph E. Giesey, 'The King Imagined,' in *The French Revolution and the Creation of Modern Political Culture*, ed. Keith Michael Baker, vol. 1 (Oxford and New York: Pergamon Press, 1987), 41-60; Robin Briggs, 'The Theatre State: Ceremony and Politics 1600-60,' *Seventeenth-Century French Studies 16* (1994): 15-32; Moshe Sluhovsky, *Patroness of Paris: Rituals of Devotion in Early Modern France* (Leiden and New York: E.J. Brill, 1998), 58ff; and David Brown, *Tradition and Imagination: Revelation and Change* (Oxford and New York: Oxford University Press, 1999), 322-33.

24   Virginia Reinburg, 'Liturgy and the Laity in Late Medieval and Reformation France,' *Sixteenth-Century Studies* 23 (1992): 526-63.

25   R. J. Knecht, *Catherine de' Medici* (London and New York: Longman, 1998), 68ff.

26   E.g., *Lettres du chevalier de [Nicolas Durande de] Villegaignon, sur les remonstrances, a la Royne mere du Roy Sa Souveraine dame* (Paris, 1561), *passim*, and Susan Broomhall, ' "In my opinion": Charlotte de Minut and Female Political Discussion in Print in Sixteenth-Century France,' *Sixteenth Century Journal* 31 (2000): 25-45.

27   Antoine de Bourbon to Catherine de' Médicis, 9 October 1560, in *Lettres d'Antoine de Bourbon et de Jehanne d'Albret*, ed M. de Rochambeau, vol. 1 (Paris: Librairie Renouard, 1887), 215-16.

28   '...èseure Madame, qui est nostre mère, vous serez très bien venuz....' in Elizabeth McCartney, 'Queens in the Cult of the French Renaissance Monarchy: Selected Studies on Public Law, Royal Ceremonial, and Political Discourse, 1484-1610' (Ph.D. diss., University of Iowa, Iowa City, 1998), vol. 1, 374-83.

29   AN, X1a 1622 [Parlement of Paris. Conseil, 1568], fols 152ff and X1a 1624, fol 299r.

30   E.g., Christopher Elwood, *The Body Broken: The Calvinist Doctrine of the Eucharist and the Symbolism of Power in Sixteenth-Century France* (New York and Oxford: Oxford University Press, 1999), 145-62.

31 *Discours merveilleux de la vie, actions et déportemens de Catherine de Médicis, roine mère...*(n.p., 1578), xxii and 2.
32 Jeroen Duindam, *Myths of Power* (Amsterdam: Amsterdam University Press, 1994), 35ff.
33 Sarah Webster Goodwin and Elisabeth Bronfen, eds., *Death and Representation* (Baltimore and London: Johns Hopkins University Press, 1993), 3-25.
34 See McCartney, vol. 2, 410-568.

7 Eroticizing Virtue: The Role of Cleopatra in Early Modern Drama

Reina Green

While it is difficult, if not impossible, to disentangle myth from history when it comes to the figure of Cleopatra, there is no question that the famous Queen of Egypt has fascinated generations ever since Plutarch described her sailing along the Cydnus dressed as the goddess of love.[1] Throughout history, she has, much like Shakespeare's Ophelia, remained a dramatic 'sight' to be envisioned and revisioned by literary and visual artists alike. These multiple representations of Cleopatra do not simply recreate the mytho-historical woman as a spectacle to be observed and objectified, but are also sites inflected by the prevailing cultural constructions of female sexuality and the roles assigned to women, roles such as wife, mother, and lover. The figure of Cleopatra, therefore, demonstrates how the spectacle of the female body, the theme which frames this second group of essays, makes visible the ruptures and incongruities present in cultural constructions of women's roles and the social constraints on female behavior. Despite the popularity of Plutarch in the early modern period and his description of Cleopatra as the ultimate seductress, it was during this time that she came to be represented as both erotic and virtuous. This essay will explore the cultural context that encouraged such a multivalent construction and offer an analysis of two dramatic portrayals of the queen, one by Mary Sidney, Countess of Pembroke, and the other by John Dryden.

To the Romans, Cleopatra may have been the terrifying 'other,' a foreign, sexually transgressive, ruling woman with political ambitions, but in the medieval period representations of her changed slightly. She was still considered the woman who caused Antony's downfall, but her threat to imperial dominion was diminished. Her desire for Antony was no longer seen as due to a lust for power but to her love for him. The pair became an exemplum of the dangers of succumbing to passion.[2] Chaucer even presents her as the epitome of faithful love.[3] The sixteenth century inherited these widely differing representations of Cleopatra, and the translation of Plutarch's *Parallel Lives of the Greeks and Romans* into French and English continued the fascination with the Queen of Egypt and spawned a large number of works devoted to her.[4] Works of this period are generally much more sympathetic to Cleopatra, and a number of factors may account for this. The excavation in 1512 of a statue believed to represent Cleopatra in death with the asps entwined around her arm appears to have elicited several sympathetic paintings of the queen.[5] Finally, the parallels, both in physical appearance and personality, between the Queen of Egypt and Elizabeth I were difficult to ignore.[6]

Despite Cleopatra's royal status, late-sixteenth- and seventeenth-century works repeatedly present her in a more domestic role. She is often depicted as Antony's faithful wife, a position that (albeit tenuously) contains her within the patriarchal family.[7] This shift in Cleopatra's representation occurs at a time when the Reformation and resulting closure of the convents left women with few alternatives to marriage. As *The Lawes Resolutions of Woemens Rights* (1632) states, 'All [women] are understood either married or to bee married and their desires are subject to their husband.'[8] This narrow view of women as wives led to a subtle change in the perception of female sexuality. Women were no longer regarded primarily as sexual temptresses who might lead men into sin; instead, they were also associated with domestic harmony and sexual constancy. Representations of Cleopatra, inflected by previous historical and literary accounts, as well as contemporary views of women, 'could not be anything but problematic in this period,' as Mary Hamer notes.[9] Even as authors depicted Cleopatra as faithful and virtuous, they could not eliminate the sexual passion with which she was associated. Indeed, an examination of Mary Sidney's *Tragedy of Antonie* (1592) and Dryden's *All for Love* (1678) suggests that these representations of Cleopatra as both virtuous *and* erotic undermine accepted societal definitions of female propriety even as they present her containment by such boundaries.

Mary Sidney's closet drama, a translation of Robert Garnier's *Marc Antoine* (1578), is the first play published in English by a woman.[10] It is frequently argued that Sidney chose Garnier's work to show support for her brother Philip's views on drama and his preference for the Senecan model as expressed in his *Defence of Poesie*.[11] However, she may have also been drawn to Garnier's political views. Six of his seven dramas focus on armed rebellion, and Sidney penned her work when the fear of civil unrest in England was very real.[12] Garnier's play may have also appealed to Sidney because of the nature of its portrayal of Cleopatra, which deviates considerably from that of his source, Amyot's translation of Plutarch.[13] Mary Ellen Lamb suggests that Sidney may have been particularly attracted by Garnier's depiction of Cleopatra's death as it presents a form of heroism that could be appropriated by women. Certainly, Sidney focuses on death in a number of her works and, while Cleopatra's death is an act of defiance against Caesar, it valorizes her wifely loyalty to Antony. She thus demonstrates her virtue while acting out her rebellion.[14]

Garnier shows Cleopatra to be constantly loyal to Antony and omits any reference to her meeting with Octavius, which is featured in all the other plays of the period.[15] Moreover, Garnier's Cleopatra sees herself as Antony's 'Espouse debonnaire!' (II.556), '[sa] femme et [son] amie' (V.1950), and calls him 'mon espous' (II.586, 588).[16] Sidney picks up on this portrayal of Cleopatra and emphasizes her faithfulness further. In her first speech, Cleopatra talks of her tie to Antony in terms of a marriage vow, recalling her 'vowed-faith' (II.154).[17] In Sidney's argument, Antony is not attracted by Cleopatra's beauty but by what she does for him, how she 'entertained him with all the exquisite delights and sumptuous pleasures,' casting Cleopatra in the domestic role of welcoming her husband home.[18] Both Garnier and Sidney reinforce their representations of Cleopatra as a good wife by showing her as a mother. However, the roles of good wife and good mother are not conflated as they often are in early modern conduct literature.[19] As Tina Krontiris notes, for Cleopatra, 'the lover's instinct is stronger than the mother's.'[20] Cleopatra's faithfulness to Antony is at the expense of her children. Nonetheless, despite her apparent rejection of her children, I suggest that Cleopatra's maternal role not only validates her bond with Antony, but also gives her the authority to reject that very same role.

At the beginning of the final act Cleopatra speaks as a dying mother, and her servants and children draw around her deathbed to hear her final words. The scene evokes Holinshed's description of Sidney's mother's death. Mary Herbert was known for her ' "godlie speeches, earnest and effectuall persuasions to all those about hir . . . yet in this hir last action and ending of her life . . . she so farre surpassed hir self . . . as the same almost amazed and astonished the heareres."'[21] Like those who attended Mary Herbert, Cleopatra's attendants hang on her every word. She first places her children in the care of their tutor, Euphron, advising him to take them away from Egypt. She then says goodbye to her children, asks divine guidance for them, and advises them to forget their noble descent and right to the throne of Egypt. As the children bid farewell, she cries, 'Ah this voice kills me. Ah, good gods, I swoon! / I can no more, I die!' (V.78-79). While Sidney's work precedes the mothers' advice books that began appearing in the early 1600s, Cleopatra's last words anticipate those of the women who claimed the authority to write by virtue of their motherhood and the possibility of imminent death.[22]

Having died well as a mother, Cleopatra is revived by her attendants, Charmion and Eras, so that she can die as Antony's faithful lover. They call upon her to 'weep over Antonie; let not/ His body be without due rites entombed' (V.89-90). The rites she offers Antony in her final death speech, however, also celebrate her sexuality:

> Poor Cleopatra, grief thy reason reaves.
> No, no, most happy in this hapless case,
> To die with thee, and dying thee embrace;
> My body joined with thine, my mouth with thine,
> My mouth, whose moisture-burning sighs have dried
> To be in one self tomb, and one self chest,
> And wrapped with thee in one self sheet to rest.
>   (V.170-76)

With these lines, sexual desire is brought to the fore as, embracing Antony's dead body, her lips on his, Cleopatra faints. Here is the sexual desire that created the children who have just quitted the scene. And here, surely, is the difficulty in portraying Cleopatra as a faithful wife and a mother. It is in these roles that she most threatens the Roman empire and any society constructed on patrilineage. As an adulteress, Cleopatra can be condemned and her children disregarded for they are without claim to any paternal legacy. Reinscribed as Antony's wife, Cleopatra and, through her, her children all have a potential claim.[23] Indeed, Octavius is particularly angered by Antony's distribution of Roman territory to Cleopatra and her children. As Octavius knows, alive, Cleopatra can be labeled an enemy to society, put into chains, and her wealth seized. When she dies as a mother and faithful wife she escapes such containment: legitimizing the relationship increases its potential to cause social disruption.

While Sidney's version of Garnier's *Marc Antoine* can be seen to support the ideological causes of her brother, it can also be seen to undermine the social order many believe it promotes. It presents an adulteress as acceptable, as a loyal wife who speaks with the authority of a mother, and it does so without apology.[24] While Sidney's work, as a closet drama, had a limited audience, its confined circulation did permit one radical difference from the publicly performed drama of the period. Margaret Hannay suggests that Sidney's play may have been read aloud on an evening at Sidney's home at Wilton, and it is conceivable that a woman may have played the role of Cleopatra.[25] The audience would not have heard the 'squeaking Cleopatra' of the public stage, a cross-dressed boy whose appearance potentially reinforced notions of Cleopatra's sexual transgressiveness while eliminating the plausibility of her role as a wife and mother.[26] Instead, they would have heard a woman, living in a society that repeatedly defined her in terms of her position as a wife and mother, express the authority granted to her as such and effectively use it to escape the societal constraints placed on her.

Although actresses had made brief and sometimes unpopular appearances on the English stage prior to 1660, they became an accepted and celebrated part of English theatrical productions after the theaters reopened that year.[27] Dressed to reveal their femaleness, actresses were as much a part of the spectacle of late-seventeenth-century theater as the new elaborate scenery. On the Restoration stage, one not only *heard* women speaking women's roles, but much more obviously, one *saw* them in women's (and men's) roles.[28] The 'stage picture' of lavishly painted scenery and carefully posed actors became a vital part of Restoration drama, and Dryden makes full use of it in *All for Love* as is apparent from his inclusion of certain highly detailed stage directions.[29] For example when Dollabella tells Cleopatra that Antony is leaving her, the stage direction reads, 'All the time of this speech, Cleop[atra] seems more and more concern'd till she sinks quite down' (IV.i.165).[30] While a reader might imagine this to be the effect of Dollabella's speech on Cleopatra and while an actress might portray it as such, Dryden's stage directions present a specific picture of Cleopatra as passively suffering and finally defeated by Dollabella's words. The directions are also precise in the final scene. In contrast to Shakespeare's Cleopatra, who applies two asps, one to her bare breast and a second to her arm, Dryden's Queen of Egypt employs a more subtle eroticism and does not bare her breast but her arm. The stage direction is exact: Cleopatra first 'holds out her Arm, and draws it back' (V.i.484). Applying the asp to her extended arm, Cleopatra must expose the inner part of her upper arm. On being bitten, she 'turns aside, and then shows her arm bloody' (489). While the display of the elegantly outstretched and exposed inner arm is most often associated with dance in the movement of *portebras*, Dryden explicitly demands this gesture as essential to the final image of Cleopatra.[31] It is an image of grace, nobility and restraint that merely hints at the intense passion that led to the deed.

Dryden's Cleopatra, dying with her arm gracefully extended, her head to one side, presents an image popular on the Restoration stage, that of seductively posed suffering.[32] It also reflects Dryden's characterization of Antony's lover: her eroticism is subtle and her love is constant. She is not Shakespeare's playful cross-dressing queen.[33] Despite Arthur Kirsch's assessment of her as 'domesticated and sentimentally self-indulgent,' and her own self-deprecating remark 'Nature meant me / A Wife — a silly, harmless, houshold Dove' (IV.i.92), she has a certain nobility that is apparent both in her confrontation with Octavia and when she prepares for her death.[34] Like Sidney's Cleopatra, she is constantly faithful to Antony, and her love is not a 'weak passion,' but 'a noble madness' (II.i.6, 17). She is a woman who chooses her partner out of love, and in defiance of political expediency. Like Sidney and Garnier, Dryden has Cleopatra reject the idea of negotiating with Octavius — not once, but twice. Even her flirtation with Dollabella, an attempt to arouse Antony's jealousy, is half-hearted. And when Antony accuses Cleopatra of unfaithfulness because of her previous liaison with Julius Caesar, she denies the charge, saying 'He first possess'd my Person; you my Love: / Caesar lov'd me; but I lov'd Antony. / If I endur'd him after, 'twas because / I judg'd it due to the first name of Men' (II.i.354-57). In other words, she has experienced a relationship founded on duty and political allegiance, and rejects such associations for one based solely on love. Cleopatra dies for love, leaving the 'dull' Octavia to perform the ritual of mourning her dead husband, for as his true soulmate, Cleopatra's spousal with Antony is knit 'with a tie too strong / For *Roman* Laws to break' (V.i.415, 417-18).

Dryden's depiction of Cleopatra as a woman who gives all for love can be said to reflect a popular theme of Restoration drama, that of the role of love in marriage. While women's ability to accept or even reject a marriage partner was limited by family allegiances and economic necessity in practice, there was growing acceptance that there should be an affective bond between marriage partners.[35] Restoration dramatists began to present unsatisfactory marriages from the wife's perspective, and to portray sympathetically women who opposed their families and chose their husbands on the grounds of affection.[36] At the same time as he presents Cleopatra as a woman who loves despite the advice of her friends, whose virtue is apparent in her ability to suffer, Dryden portrays Octavia as the abandoned wife. Although Octavia appears in Shakespeare's work, her suffering is not explored, and while Sir Charles Sedley portrays Octavia's emotional agony in his *Antony and Cleopatra* which opened only months before Dryden's own play, Dryden is the first to stage a confrontation between the two women. His decision may have been prompted by Nathaniel Lee's *The Rival Queens*, also first performed in 1677, and by the particular popularity of the actresses Rebecca Marshall and Elizabeth Boutell who frequently played rivals in love with the same man.   Unfortunately for Dryden, though, Rebecca Marshall left the King's Company shortly before the staging of *All for Love*, so that Elizabeth Boutell, who normally played the role of the mild virtuous woman opposite Marshall, was cast as Cleopatra, and Katherine Corey as Octavia.[37]

While Octavia's nobility is clearly evident, Dollabella describing her as 'neither too submissive, / Nor yet too haughty; but so just a mean, / Shows, as it ought, a Wife and *Roman* too' (III.i.268-70), her domestic position is most emphasized.[38]   When she tries to persuade Antony to return to Rome with her, she first stresses their marital relationship and her position as his wife, a role that they both define by her 'duty' (III.i.265, 317, 326).   As Antony remains unmoved by her appeal, she is forced to tell their daughters to

> pull him to me,
> And pull him to your selves, from that bad Woman.
> ...
> If he will shake you off, if he will dash you
> Against the Pavement, you must bear it, Children;
> For you are mine, and I was born to suffer.
>   (354-5, 358-60)

Melodramatic as Octavia's speech is, the spectacle of his children clinging to Antony is clearly intended to move audience sympathy as indicated by Ventidius's exclamation 'Was ever sight so moving!' (361).[39]   Dryden's comments in his preface that he did not realize 'the compassion [Octavia] mov'd to her self and children' therefore seem absurd.   He knew it 'was destructive to that which [he] reserv'd for *Anthony* and *Cleopatra;* whose mutual love being founded upon vice, must lessen the favour of the Audience to them, when Virtue and Innocence were oppress'd by it' (10.30-32, 11.1-3).   He knew that his portrayal of both Octavia and Cleopatra as suffering women would divide audience sympathy, yet he went on to explore the conflict between the two women by staging a meeting between them.

In his preface, Dryden claims that it would be 'both natural and probable, that *Octavia*, proud of her new-gain'd Conquest, would search out *Cleopatra* to triumph over her; and that Cleopatra, thus attacqu'd, was not of a spirit to shun the encounter' (11.20-23).   The two women meet as equals, for while Cleopatra is already onstage when Octavia appears, they both move simultaneously toward centre stage (III.i.415).   Their equality is also suggested in their opening banter: 'I need not ask if you are Cleopatra . . . . Nor need I ask you who you are' (416, 418).   Indeed, they not only echo each other but even finish each other's sentences.   However, they clearly define each other as rivals: according to Cleopatra, Octavia is the 'Houshold-Clog' who 'bear[s] the specious Title of a Wife' (424, 459); to Octavia, Cleopatra is 'practis'd / In that lascivious art,' and 'black endearments / That make sin pleasing' (426-27, 442-43).   Despite

Cleopatra's later attempt to write herself into the role of wife, here she is the sexually experienced woman, and this makes her a sight worth seeing according to Octavia, who moves closer to 'view nearer / That face' and 'find th'inevitable charms, that catch Mankind so sure' (435-36, 437-38). Even as Octavia examines Cleopatra's 'charms,' and suggests that the queen should 'blush to own' them (443), she also indicates that her gaze is inappropriate; she should not be looking at Cleopatra in such a manner for she should be ignorant of the charms Cleopatra possesses: 'Far be their knowledge from a *Roman* Lady, / Far from a modest Wife' (440-41). Cleopatra further emphasizes the potential transgressiveness of Octavia's gaze and the desire that prompts it when she retorts, 'You may blush, who want 'em' (443), 'want' signifying both Octavia's lack of charms and her desire to have them.

Octavia, when she moves to gaze at Cleopatra, plays onstage the position of the theater audience, for they too have come to see Cleopatra. Octavia, therefore, having garnered audience sympathy as an abandoned wife representing 'oppress'd' 'Virtue and Innocence,' now encourages the audience to identify with her as she attempts to diminish and objectify Cleopatra into a mere display of sexual charm. However, even as she encourages audience identification and sympathy, Octavia also reveals Cleopatra's appeal for both men and women. After all, the Queen of Egypt has not only captured the attention of Antony but of 'Mankind' (III.i.437). Nonetheless, Cleopatra's charms both provoke the gaze and resist definition. The spectator must 'search' for them and even then may not know them (438-39). Thus, even as Octavia attempts to assert her superiority over Cleopatra by trying to objectify her, she reveals the Queen of Egypt's own power. While being an object of the gaze can certainly limit or even countermand the female self-determination often presented in Restoration drama, Cleopatra resists such objectification here because the very charms that Octavia (and the audience) want to see are not clearly visible. [40] They are, like the eroticism of her outstretched arm at her death, subtle. Cleopatra's very opacity not only prevents her objectification by her spectators but also allows her to redefine the terms of conflict constructed by Octavia, who sees their confrontation as between a 'faithless Prostitute' (IV.i.289) and a 'modest Wife.' Instead, Cleopatra argues that the distinction is between herself as a faithful mistress and Octavia as a dutiful wife, between love and law and, on the Restoration stage, love often took precedence. [41]

In the closing scene of *All for Love*, Cleopatra's love, the love that allows her to defy Octavia's gaze and win audience sympathy, is fully realized as she prepares the spectacle of her death. As in Shakespeare's work, Dryden has Cleopatra don her crown and jewels, so that in death she might look a fitting bride for Antony. In addition, though, Dryden makes the lovers' union tangible as Cleopatra has Antony, wearing a laurel wreath and bearing his shield, seated beside her. The final image of the couple is of 'Lovers [seated] in State together, / As they were giving Laws to half Mankind' (V.i.508-09). Cleopatra, having resisted Octavia's gaze, creates her own spectacle for the audience, one that emphasizes her grace, her majesty, and her partnership with Antony. Moreover, even in death, her charms are present, though indefinable. All that can be seen is 'Th'impression of a smile' (510), not the smile itself, to indicate that 'she dy'd pleas'd with him for whom she liv'd, / And went to charm him in another World' (511-12).

Both Sidney's and Dryden's depictions of Cleopatra are potentially subversive because they allow her to escape the label of adulteress, or 'faithless prostitute' by emphasizing her constancy, a virtue not usually associated with mistresses in early modern England.[42] While Sidney can only stress Cleopatra's constancy by inscribing her as Antony's wife, Dryden emphasizes her virtue by presenting her as a loving, suffering mistress in opposition to Octavia as a dutiful, abandoned wife. In addition, Sidney presents Cleopatra as a dying mother, a role that not only authorizes her speech to her children, but also allows her to abdicate that role to die as Antony's lover. In contrast, Dryden downplays Cleopatra's motherhood. Her children do not appear on stage, and neither she nor Antony make any reference to them. Instead, Dryden draws on popular theatrical techniques of the period, the 'stage picture,' the depiction of female suffering eroticized, and the inclusion of two actresses as rivals for the same man, to elicit audience sympathy for Cleopatra as the embodiment of love in contrast to Octavia's dutifulness. Even as she is presented as an erotic spectacle of suffering, however, Dryden's Cleopatra resists the objectification associated with being a target of the gaze. Not only does Dryden imply that such a gaze may be transgressive, but also that Cleopatra has the power to both provoke and resist her spectators. Her eroticism is sufficiently apparent that she attracts their attention — a necessity in popular theater — yet subtle enough to remain undefinable to their stares. While early modern society attempted to define women as either/or: either modest wives or faithless prostitutes, mothers or lovers, both these depictions of Cleopatra, even as they reflect conditions for women in general and within the theater in specific, subvert such exclusive definitions by inscribing her as both virtuous and erotic.

Acknowledgements

I wish to acknowledge the support of the Social Sciences and Humanities Research Council of Canada and the Killam Trust in writing this essay.

Notes

[1]   Plutarch, "Antony," XXVI, *Plutarch's Lives*, trans. Bernadotte Perrin (Cambridge, MA: Harvard University Press, 1920; rpt. 1968), pp. 193-95.

[2]   For a discussion of historical representations of Cleopatra see Mary Hamer, *Signs of Cleopatra: History, Politics, Representation* (New York: Routledge, 1993); Mary Morrison, 'Some aspects of the Treatment of the Theme of Antony and Cleopatra in Tragedies of the Sixteenth Century,' *Journal of European Studies* 4 (1974): 113-25; Max Patrick, 'The

Cleopatra Theme in World Literature up to 1700' in *The Undoing of Babel: Watson Kirkconnell, The Man and his Work*, ed. J.R.C. Perkin (Toronto: McClelland and Stewart, 1975), 64-76; and Marilyn L. Williamson, *Infinite Variety: Antony and Cleopatra in Renaissance Drama and Earlier Tradition* (Mystic, Conn.: Lawrence Verry, 1974).

3   In view of the accepted medieval perception of Cleopatra as a destructive force of passion, Chaucer's depiction is probably satirical. See 'The Legend of Good Women,' ll.566-69, in *The Riverside Chaucer*, 3rd ed., ed. Larry D. Benson (Boston: Houghton Mifflin, 1987).

4   Patrick, 76, counts more than forty plays, fifteen operas, two epics, fourteen prose narratives, and countless poems written about Cleopatra between 1478 and 1697.

5   Morrison, 113. The statue is actually of Ariadne sleeping, and the asps are a snake bracelet.

6   Patrick, 64-70, notes the physical similarities between the two queens, both being fair skinned and red haired, with strong facial features. Both spoke several languages and were accomplished negotiators. They were also popular with their people, and known for using their personal charm for political gain. Both Mary Sidney and Samuel Daniel may have drawn on the similarities between Cleopatra and Elizabeth to present their works as warnings about the potential consequences of Elizabeth's passion for the Earl of Essex. See also Margaret Hannay, *Philip's Phoenix: Mary Sidney, Countess of Pembroke* (Oxford: Oxford University Press, 1990), 126-29.

7   Morrison, 120, notes that the nine tragedies published in the second half of the sixteenth century in French, English, and Italian all present Cleopatra as 'unshakeably true,' that the three Italian dramas depict her love as having 'a dignified conjugal quality.'

8   T.E., *The Lawes Resolutions of Womens Rights: or, The Lawes Provision for Woemen* (London, 1632), 6.

9   Hamer, 26.

10 Sidney's drama was first published under the title of *Antonius, a Tragoedie*, along with her translation of Phillipe de Mornay's *Discourse of Life and Death*, in 1592. A second separate edition titled *The Tragedie of Antonie* was published three years later.

11 Mary Ellen Lamb, *Gender and Authorship in the Sidney Circle* (Madison: University of Wisconsin Press, 1990), 68-71; Elaine Beilin, *Redeeming Eve: Women Writers of the English Renaissance* (Princeton: Princeton University Press, 1987), 123; Nancy Cotton, *Women Playwrights in England 1363-1750* (Lewisburg: Bucknell University Press, 1980), 29; and Hannay, *Philip's Phoenix*, 120, argue that the view of Sidney's work as determined by her brother's opinions has distorted our perception of her. However, as the title of Hannay's book indicates, it is difficult to escape identifying Sidney *and her work* with her brother.

12 For a discussion of closet drama as a tool of political discourse, see Marta Straznicky, '"Profane Stoical Paradoxes": *The Tragedie of Mariam* and Sidnean Closet Drama,' *ELR* 24, no.1 (Winter 1994): 104-34; and Nancy A. Gutierrez, 'Valuing *Mariam*: Genre Study and Feminist Analysis,' *Tulsa Studies in Women's Literature* 10 (1991): 233-51.

13 For a discussion of Garnier's use of his source see Robert Garnier, *Two Tragedies: Hippolyte and Marc Antoine*, eds. Christine M. Hill and Mary G. Morrison (London: Athlone Press, 1975), 15-19. Three tragedies based on Plutarch were written in Italian between 1541 and 1576, and Etienne Jodelle had written *Cleopatre captive* in 1552. While Sidney may not have known all of the Italian tragedies, she was fluent in French and Italian and therefore had a choice of texts for translation. See Williamson, 76-123.

14 Lamb, *Gender and Authorship*, 24, 119-31. Lamb argues that by translating works in which women assume heroic status through death Sidney removes "the sexual stain" (24) associated with women's writing. However, as Sidney's depiction of Cleopatra's final moments is remarkable for its eroticism, I do not see how in this case the "sexual stain" can be said to be eliminated.

15 Morrison, 116.

16 All quotations and line numbers are taken from *Marc Antoine* in Robert Garnier, *Two Tragedies*, 106-66. Williamson, 18, notes that Antony and Cleopatra were married in 36 BCE, a year after Antony's marriage to Octavia. Roman law recognized neither his marriage to Cleopatra nor his naming of Caesarion, her son by Julius Caesar, in his will.

17 All quotations and line numbers are taken from Mary Sidney, *The Tragedy of Antonie* in

Renaissance Drama by Women: Texts and Documents, eds. S.P. Cerasano and Marion Wynne-Davies (New York: Routledge, 1996), 19-42.

[18]   Sidney, 19.

[19]   The conflation of the roles of good wife and mother appears in *Proverbs* 31, and is promoted in several seventeenth-century conduct books. For examples, see William Gouge, *Of Domesticall Duties, Eight Treatises*, 3rd ed. (London, 1634), 282, 371, 517; and Richard Baxter, *A Christian Directory: or, a Summe of Practical Theologie, and Cases of Conscience* (London, 1673), 531-34.

[20]   Tina Krontiris, *Oppositional Voices: Women as Writers and Translators of Literature in the English Renaissance* (New York: Routledge, 1992), 71-2.

[21]   Holinshed, quoted in Hannay, 55-6, and in Lamb, *Gender and Authorship*, 122-23.

[22]   See Mary Beth Rose, 'Where Are the Mothers in Shakespeare? Options for Gender Representation in the English Renaissance,' *Shakespeare Quarterly* 42, no. 3 (Fall 1991): 291-314. For examples of mothers' advice books see Betty Travitsky, ed., *The Paradise of Women: Writings by Englishwomen of the Renaissance* (New York: Columbia University Press, 1981), 50-68.

[23]   Samuel Daniel's 1607 revision of *The Tragedie of Cleopatra*, in *The Complete Works in Verse and Prose of Samuel Daniel, Volume III*, ed. Rev. Alexander B. Grosart (London, n. pub., 1885), 1-94, a play likely prompted by Sidney herself, makes the threat posed by Cleopatra's children clear when Cesario, her son by Julius Caesar, vows to seek revenge on Rome.

[24]   Unlike many other early modern women writers and translators who remain anonymous, or who apologize for their presumption in writing, Sidney adopts the authoritative voice of those whose works she translates. Her name is boldly placed alongside the author's on the title page of the first edition of *Antonie*, and she makes no prefatory apology for publishing this work.

[25]   Hannay, 120.

[26]   For this reference, see William Shakespeare, *The Tragedy of Antony and Cleopatra*, 5.2.216, in *The Norton Shakespeare*, eds. Stephen Greenblatt et al. (New York: W.W. Norton and Co., 1997).

[27]   For discussions of why actresses were accepted on the stage at this time and not earlier see Katharine Eisaman Maus, ' "Playhouse Flesh and Blood": Sexual Ideology and the Restoration Actress,' *ELH* 46 (1979): 595-617; and Michael Shapiro, 'The Introduction of Actresses in England: Delay or Defensiveness?' in *Enacting Gender on the English Renaissance Stage*, eds. Viviana Comensoli and Anne Russell (Urbana: University of Illinois Press, 1999), 178-200. Maus, 595, notes that, in 1629, actresses appearing with a French company were hissed from the stage in London.

[28]   Deborah C. Payne, 'Reified Object or Emergent Professional? Retheorizing the Restoration Actress' in *Cultural Readings of Restoration and Eighteenth-Century English Theater*, eds. J. Douglas Canfield and Deborah C. Payne (Athens, GA: University of Georgia Press, 1995), 1-38. Payne argues that both the objectification and professionalization of actresses resulted from emphasizing the visual. Laura J. Rosenthal, 'Reading Masks: The Actress and the Spectatrix in Restoration Shakespeare' in *Broken Boundaries: Women and Feminism in Restoration Drama*, ed. Katherine M. Quinsey (Lexington, Kentucky: University Press of Kentucky, 1996), 201-18. Paradoxically, when actresses were cast as men, in 'breeches parts,' the costume often intentionally emphasized their femaleness.

[29]   For a discussion of how Dryden uses the stage picture in *All for Love* see H. Neville Davies, '*All for Love*: Text and Contexts,' *Cahiers Elisabethains* 36 (Oct 1989): 49-71.

[30]   All quotations and line numbers are taken from *All for Love* in *The Works of John Dryden*, volume XIII, ed. Maximillian E. Novak (Berkeley: University of California Press, 1984), 1-111, 363-440.

[31]   See Margaret Lamb, *Antony and Cleopatra on the English Stage* (Toronto: Associated University Presses, 1980), 37-42, for a discussion of the representation of the dying Cleopatra and the influence of Dryden's play on later stagings of Shakespeare's *Antony and Cleopatra*.

[32]   See Jean I. Marsden, 'Rape, Voyeurism, and the Restoration Stage' in *Broken Boundaries: Women and Feminism in Restoration Drama*, ed. Katherine M. Quinsey (Lexington, Kentucky: University Press of Kentucky, 1996), 185-200, especially 185-86.

[33] Many critics have examined the difference between the two Cleopatras and without exception note the fidelity and submissiveness of Dryden's characterization. See J. Douglas Canfield, *Word as Bond in English Literature from the Middle Ages to the Restoration* (Philadelphia: University of Pennsylvania Press, 1989), 240. Also see *Cleopatra*, ed. Harold Bloom (New York: Chelsea House Publishers, 1990), 15 and 29.

[34] Arthur C. Kirsch, *Dryden's Heroic Drama* (Princeton, N.J.: Princeton University Press, 1965), 131.

[35] See Lawrence Stone, *The Family, Sex and Marriage in England 1500-1800* (New York: Harper and Row, 1977) 123-24, 326-28; and Susan Staves, *Players' Scepters: Fictions of Authority in the Restoration* (Lincoln, NB: University of Nebraska Press, 1979), 189.

[36] Rosenthal, 203-4; and Staves, 131.

[37] See Elizabeth Howe, *The First English Actresses: Women and Drama 1660-1700* (New York: Cambridge University Press, 1992), 147.

[38] Kirsch, 129.

[39] The spectacle is not solely visual, however. Davies, 64, notes that the line shared by Dollabella, Octavia, the children, and Antony presents a verbal climax which is followed by Antony's embrace of his children.

[40] Rosenthal, 207.

[41] Staves, 120.

[42] Although women were characterized in multiple, shifting ways throughout the early modern period, their lack of constancy, particularly as linked to sexual appetite, was repeatedly emphasized. Mistresses, by making public their sexuality, were therefore deemed inherently subject to inconstancy. For representative writings on women's supposed vices, including inconstancy, see N. H. Keeble, ed. *The Cultural Identity of Seventeenth-Century Woman: A Reader* (New York: Routledge, 1994), 71-95.

8 Applauding Shakespeare's Ophelia in the Eighteenth Century: Sexual Desire, Politics, and the Good Woman

Susan Lamb

The author of this essay analyzes Restoration and eighteenth-century adoption of the figure of the mad Ophelia, arguing that this figure is sited at a conjunction of the histories of sexuality and women's public (and political) influence. The early realizations and uses of the mad Ophelia speak to our understanding of how conceptions of women's 'normative' sexuality developed, and prompts the reassessment of many feminist working assumptions about connections between 'free' sexual expression and 'freedom' from patriarchal oppression. More locally to eighteenth-century studies, the author shows how reinventions of the mad Ophelia are in fact one of the few sites at which Restoration and eighteenth-century writers, painters, actors, and commentators could openly display what they conceived to be 'natural' and undissembled expressions of virtuous, female heterosexual desire.

In Shakespeare's *Hamlet*, Ophelia is a young woman who loves a prince, who may or may not be loved by him, who may or may not have had sex with him, and whose male courtier relatives seek both to protect her and to use her to advance themselves. She goes mad, may or may not commit suicide, and, in most certainly dying young and in mental anguish, becomes one more item on her brother's list of grievances against Prince Hamlet. For *Hamlet*'s Elizabethan audiences, the iconography of Shakespeare's white-clad and flower-distributing madwoman, Bridget Gellert Lyons has argued, was simultaneously that of both the whore and the virgin.[1] Ophelia had, then, sexual identities that moralists of any age would argue could not inhabit the same woman at the same time. While subsequent audiences and readers may not have been as familiar with Elizabethan iconography as the Elizabethans, Ophelia's language and her story are ambiguous enough in terms of her sexual status that commentators, censors, illustrators, actors, and audiences alike have historically focused on exactly this aspect of her character and its significance. In this essay, I want to put a twist on the old question of the nature of Ophelia's sexuality, using Restoration and eighteenth-century treatments of it to look at the significance of this focus both in the period and in terms of feminist history.

Since Elaine Showalter's 1985 article on the topic, Ophelia has been singled out as a role that depends for its power on the expression of female sexual desire, and, because of this, one that acts as a weather vane for attitudes towards women's sexuality. Showalter, Edna O'Brien and Mary Floyd-Wilson implicitly argue that the more verbally Ophelia expresses her sexual longings, the more seriously the part, and — by extension — women in general, are taken.[2] For them, only a verbally explicit Ophelia expresses desire and the representation of a desiring woman indicates a healthy and admirable cultural attitude towards women. In feminist terms, then, these critics imply that the main and transhistorical value of the part to actresses, audiences, readers, and critics rests in its portrayal of women's sexuality. Showalter's and O'Brien's Restoration and eighteenth-century Ophelia is shorn of her bawdy language and played by singers (not actresses), a diminution of the part that results (in Showalter's terms) in a polite, decorous Ophelia who 'minimized the force of female sexuality.'[3]   Floyd-Wilson adopts Showalter's assumptions but, extrapolating from recent scholarship on eighteenth-century women, argues against Showalter that a 'veiled sexuality' remained despite censorship. For these feminist critics, representations of Ophelia illustrate a progressive history of women in which the amelioration of women's condition is directly indicated by how explicitly a female character can express sexual desire onstage.

How we tell our history — what in the past is important to us in the present — allows us to position ourselves, and more importantly, to map the direction of change. For a reform movement such as feminism, what history is told is therefore crucial. I have concerns about the history of women's sexuality and its significance as it has been mapped through the history of Ophelia's representation. Early Ophelias have a far different significance to women's history than they have been credited with: not only do they reveal the dark side of the assumption that open expressions of sexual desire and freedom from oppression are one and the same thing, but they demonstrate the way in which an exclusive focus on women's sexuality can in fact erase or obscure the place and influence of women in the public sphere.

In making their claims, Showalter, O'Brien, and Floyd-Wilson left long-eighteenth-century records unexamined, usually taking at face value nineteenth-century statements about earlier Ophelias. From the mid-nineteenth century, stories of Ophelia's treatment begin by dismissing long-eighteenth-century Ophelias — this essay's focus — on the grounds that no one in the period treated the part as more than an ornamental set piece for a pretty singer. The actress Helena Faucit's husband could claim in good faith that before his wife took the role in 1844, no one 'would have dreamed of asking a leading actress' to do it.[4] For much of the twentieth century, the story proper began in 1827, when the then minor actress Harriet Smithson was forced to play Ophelia with two days' notice in the first-ever English-language *Hamlet* performed in Paris.[5] Smithson had a weak singing voice and knew it. Because she viewed the part as reliant on singing, she tried (unsuccessfully) to convince several other company members to undertake Ophelia in her place, offering as inducement a week's extra salary. As matters turned out, the role made her career. Smithson's Ophelia was not innovative, but it riveted French audiences. The straw she wore in her hair as the mad Ophelia became the rage of Parisian high fashion. The composer Hector Berlioz fell in love with Ophelia and finally convinced the woman who played her to marry him.

The bewildered English press attributed the French enthusiasm for Smithson's Ophelia to a lack of judgment born of ignorance, and by all accounts Smithson's performance had a negligible impact on Ophelias in England. Nonetheless it is usually taken as the first time Ophelia was treated seriously, and therefore as the story's beginning. But Smithson's lack of influence in England, her excellent use of inherited conventions, and her initial resistance to undertaking the part might suggest a different story, one in which she concludes, rather than begins, a fascinating episode. In many respects — the straw in the hair, the use of music and miming to express the verbally inexpressible, the white dress — her performance is directly eighteenth-century in character. The English no longer paid much attention to this Ophelia, but the astonished French gave it its last and loudest hurrah. The conception of Ophelia that by 1827 could inflame Paris but had become so tired in England that serious actresses avoided the role, and the significance of understandings about Ophelia in the long eighteenth century, are the main concerns of this essay.

Although they have been ignored, the records concerning Ophelia in the long eighteenth century are in fact surprisingly generous. Not only did Ophelia repeatedly appear on stage in the century's most popular Shakespeare play, but she and characters based on her had a consistent place in the period's critical commentary, poetry, novels, illustrations and paintings. Until the end of the eighteenth century, critics and adaptors alike considered her crucial to *Hamlet* and the most prominent actresses of the age (not singers) played the part.[6] Arguably, the changes theater companies made to the script enabled Ophelia to express sexual awareness within eighteenth-century paradigms. Furthermore, signs of her desire were neither veiled nor erased by these changes, nor in the period's extra-theatrical adoptions of the Ophelia figure. Indeed, Ophelia's sexual desires were emphasized at the expense of other aspects of the part.

Period Ophelias and Ophelia figures demonstrated what most contemporaries thought normative 'good' female desire looked like when sanity and propriety no longer worked together to conceal it. If a woman was insane, her virtue did not necessarily come into question when she demonstrated sexual desire in public. Of course, there were commentators (as there are now, for that matter) who found *any* revelation of female sexual desire appalling. Nonetheless, for most, Ophelia was the model for presentations in which the sexual desires experienced by virginal, unmarried women could become available to spectators. When Ophelia is adopted or alluded to in the novel and in poetry, she exhibits a powerful, unconstrained, and virtuous (i.e. unfulfilled) heterosexual desire that is received as comforting, even reassuring in an unmarried woman. This is particularly clear when novelists such as Sarah Fielding and Laurence Sterne adopt Ophelia (as we shall see). But for now it is enough to say that Ophelia and Ophelia figures enabled writers, actresses and visual artists to showcase what for many contemporaries was a 'good' version of women's sexual desire.

The love-mad woman was a popular figure in medical literature and in works of the imagination. Roy Porter has shown that in the period's medical discourse a love-mad woman's sexual desire was not what was considered sick about her, something that changed in the nineteenth century and has become almost inconceivable in Freud's wake.[7] Experts and the public alike believed that lack of gratification rather than the desire itself caused the insanity. The circumstances commonly thought to induce love-madness included: a husband slighting a loving wife (as in the character of Belvidera in Otway's *Venice Preserv'd*); a lover deserting a loving, unwary, and now fallen woman (Alicia in Rowe's *Jane Shore*); or an acknowledged suitor's withdrawal of his declared love from a loving virgin. In the madness portrayed in works of the imagination, this last stereotype both informed and was informed by understandings about Ophelia. *This* madwoman has loved according to the strictest rules of propriety and virtue. She becomes mad when, on the brink of the relationship's socially-sanctioned sexual consummation (typically immediately before the marriage ceremony), the man becomes unavailable (having been kidnapped, killed, or believing lies against his betrothed). Since her overwhelming desire is focused on one man, most assumed that her interaction with other men could not be suspect although in any other circumstances it would be treated as damagingly sexual.

The use of these formulas is striking in much of the related literature. For instance, the popular and anonymous broadside ballad 'The Maid's Lamentation in Bedlam' describes a Bedlam maid who becomes insane when her betrothed disappears on the eve of their wedding (he is impressed into the navy). The refrain demonstrates her virtue: she sings 'I love my Love, because my Love love me.'[8] For many contemporaries, a virtuous woman only returned and did not initiate love. Luckily for this maid, the lover returns from sea, seeks her in Bedlam (a famous insane asylum in London), and, upon marrying her, 'He quickly brought her to herself...And now they live in Happiness,/ In Joy and Unity.' The moral of the ballad is the metrically clumsy 'Pretty Maidens wait with Patience,/ You that have Loves at sea,/ And love your Love if ye find ye Loves love ye.' For the balladeer, as for many contemporaries, madness is a predictable response to disappointed love that is also exemplary when the love is virtuous.

Contemporary poems and ballads about such love-mad women often explicitly (and with no irony) praise the madwomen's management of blameless sexual longings — a management that literally drives them insane. In a 1796 epigram, Samuel Bishop praises the lovesick virgin as a virtuous foil for the unmarried high society women who falsely display the benefits of marriage (that is to say, pregnancy):

> The love-sick maid, in Bedlam's cells who pines,
> Weaves a straw coronet; and a princess shines:--
> While in high life our spinster daughters ape,
> In mock protuberant bulk, a mother's shape:--
> Say, between frenzy's crown, and fashion's pad,
> Is madness prouder? or is pride more mad?[9]

In this widespread cultural fantasy, an unmarried woman's sexual desire costs her a lot — her sanity or her virtue — if she remains unmarried after it is triggered, but the desire in and of itself is not condemned. Given this context and the centrality of Shakespeare for the English during this period, it is not surprising that Ophelia functions both as an illustration of this cultural fantasy and as the figure particularly invested with it. Despite nineteenth-century claims to the contrary, for most of the period Ophelia was not regarded as an unimportant part taken only by lowly singers. Of the fifty-six women documented as playing the role in Restoration and eighteenth-century London, all had acting pretensions, and only three were primarily singers. These singers 'hogged' fifteen of the 601 documented London performances.[10] In fact, the actresses who played the part in London were the period's stellar female performers (such as Mary Betterton, Anne Bracegirdle, Kitty Clive, Peg Woffington, Susannah Cibber, Dora Jourdan, Maria Macklin, Ann Barry, Mary Robinson, Nannette Johnston, and Sarah Siddons). These actresses usually retained sole property of the role in their respective companies for over a decade and at the height of professional success and power (when they could easily have dropped less prestigious roles).[11] Until late in the eighteenth century, not only did actresses need to possess considerable status in order to play Ophelia to begin with, but typically they also kept a firm hold on the part once they had inherited it.

Actresses were not alone in recognizing the importance of Ophelia in *Hamlet* or indeed as a representative woman. While most considered Hamlet and his predicament more important on metaphysical and critical planes than Ophelia and hers, Ophelia caught the popular imagination. In poetry, for instance, she became emblematic for lost potential (as in the Ophelias of Edward Jerningham's 1806 'The Nun; or, Adaleida to her Friend' and William Shenstone's 1773 'Elegy IV. Ophelia's Urn. To Mr. G—'), and the type of the love-sick maid (the Ophelia of William Broome's 1739 'A Dialogue between a Lady and Her Looking-Glass, while she had the Green-Sickness'). She was representative of British women's virtue (the Ophelia of Daniel Bellamy's 1722 'Cantata IV. The Agreable [sic] Mistake: Or, Venus Discarded'); the example of how madness is a hidden blessing (the Ophelia of Matthew Prior's 1740 'On a Pretty Madwoman'), and a complementary pseudonym for a real woman (Joseph Mitchell's 1732 'On Ophelia' or Arthur Mainwaring's 1730 'Mainwario's Welcome to Ophelia, on his Meeting her in the Shades'). While this essay focuses on the most widespread understandings of Ophelia, how she figures in eighteenth-century poetry demonstrates that contemporaries conceived of her as broadly representative of women.

Ophelia was among Shakespeare's most popular characters, male or female, and until the end of the eighteenth century was usually considered vital to *Hamlet*'s success. For instance, the marginal commentary for the cheap and popular 1774 *Bell's Edition of Shakespeare's Plays* identified Ophelia as 'the chief support' of the fourth act, and she is one of thirty-six Shakespeare characters chosen to be depicted in the illustrative prints for Bell's volume.[12] In the century's only major reworking of *Hamlet* to bring it into line with contemporary tastes, the part bore more weight than in Shakespeare's original. As Jeffrey Lawson Lawrence Johnson has shown, in David Garrick's 1771 *Hamlet*, he significantly expanded Ophelia's part even though he shortened the last two acts from approximately two hours' playing time to approximately one half hour.[13]   Garrick's alterations underscored that Ophelia's madness arose from thwarted but virtuous sexual desire. Throughout the last act, not only does Ophelia still sing songs about valentines and lost or dead loves, but Garrick's Laertes confronts Hamlet for having led a virtuous woman to love him with no intention of following through as a gentleman should. Furthermore, in a period in which Shakespeare adaptors tended to alter Shakespeare in order that the bad be punished and the good triumph, Garrick's Ophelia, like Nahum Tate's Cordelia before her, is alive at the close of the play. His version shows no inclination to condemn Ophelia's desire.[14]

Many of Ophelia's bawdy lines were cut in staged versions of the play (including Garrick's), prompting recent critics to argue that there was a campaign to de-sexualize Ophelia because she is female.[15]   In fact, Shakespeare adaptors cut sexually explicit language in general, not just in the mouths of women. As John Mills' discussion of players' texts makes clear, most cuts to Hamlet's part 'have to do either with sexual explicitness or with lack of reverence in matters of religion.'[16]   Moreover, given the age's propensity for 'correcting' Shakespeare's 'errors,' the cuts probably had more to do with eighteenth-century ideas about the kind of language people of Hamlet's and Ophelia's social position would have used than with an attempt to make them seem asexual.   It was, after all, common practice in the eighteenth century to gentrify Shakespeare's more socially-elevated characters on the grounds that Shakespeare would have done so himself had he lived in the eighteenth century and benefited from a gentleman's polite education.

Most importantly, however, the cuts do not seem to have interfered with audiences' perception of Ophelia as displaying sexual desire. A minority of commentators attacked the staged mad Ophelia's sexual awareness; the majority applauded it. Jeremy Collier and his respondents set the pattern early. Collier, an extremist who attacked the immorality of the stage in 1698 (almost forty years after the bawdiest lines had been cut from *Hamlet*) complained of the 'Lewd' and 'unreasonable' characterization of Ophelia. The 'young Virgin Ophelia,' he laments, loses her modesty when she goes insane. This is a problem because '[t]o represent [women] without [modesty] is to make Monsters of them, and throw them out of their Kind.' Without irony, he likens Ophelia to Euripides' Phaedra whose 'Frensy is not Lewd; She keeps her Modesty even after She has lost her Wits.'[17] He suggests that since Shakespeare 'was resolv'd to drown the Lady like a Kitten, he should have set her a-swiming [sic] a little sooner. To keep her alive only to sully her Reputation, and discover the Rankness of her Breath, was very Cruel.'[18]

Floyd-Wilson cites Collier to support her claim that a disturbing 'veiled sexuality' remained despite censorship, serving to 'transform the character [Ophelia] into a passive object of desire.'[19] But Collier is specific — for him it is not the audience who desire Ophelia but Ophelia herself who is unfortunately sexual. Moreover, he is not in his commentary taking the position that he is uncovering something hidden, but rather that he is putting into proper perspective something he thinks everyone sees. Collier's complaint indicates that for him and his contemporaries, sexually explicit language was not the only way a woman might express sexual desire. He, like scattered later commentators in the long eighteenth century, was deeply appalled by the spectacle of female desire he saw in Ophelia.

Collier's attack on the stage articulated a minority opinion that had proponents throughout the long eighteenth century. Public expressions of this opinion provoked spirited defences of the stage and, like Collier's attack, succeeded neither in closing the theaters nor in transforming them into venues that offered only those shows that unambiguously promoted and modeled moral perfection. Fortunately for us, diatribes such as Collier's goaded contemporaries into articulating viewpoints so common as to have otherwise remained unvoiced. James Drake wrote to defend Ophelia's open sexuality from Collier's 'deprav'd' 'Uproar.' After arguing that Ophelia's love represents an act of filial and patriotic virtue, Drake counters Collier's attack on Ophelia's 'monstrous ... immodesty' by claiming that the desires her madness reveals are natural and transhistorical:

> But Children and Mad Folks tell truth, they say, and [Collier] seems to discover thro [Ophelia's] Frenzy what she wou'd be at. She was troubled for the loss of a Sweet-heart and the breaking off her Match, Poor Soul. Not unlikely. Yet this was no Novelty in the days of our Fore-fathers; if [Collier] pleases to consult the Record, he will find even in the days of *Sophocles* Maids had an itching the same way, and longed to know what was what before they died.[20]

Ophelia's madness reveals something in her that Drake takes as innocent and expected, and that disgusts Collier as monstrous. Both identify this 'something' as sexual in nature.

Even if the cuts to Ophelia's bawdy language in the theater *had* interfered with an occasional audience member's perception of her as sexual (as suggested by critics such as Showalter), there was clearly no such interference when readers responded to the full-text Ophelia. What was then a new phenomenon — Shakespeare adulation — was signalled by the first wave of those who dreamed of producing or reading the 'complete' and authoritative *Hamlet*. Multiple scholarly editions of Shakespeare's works appeared in the eighteenth century and were eagerly consumed by the public.[21] Furthermore (and somewhat atypically for the period), not only was *Hamlet* usually cut rather than substantially rewritten for staging, but in the long line of popular players' texts, the unperformed sections were carefully indicated, usually by quotation marks.[22] Therefore, although the stage versions cut large portions of the full text (as is still standard practice), in print every word remained sacred. Yet the openly sexual Ophelia of the written *Hamlet* did not prompt readers to see her as 'immodest' or lacking in virtue. In his comments on his scholarly (and unexpurgated) edition of *Hamlet*, for instance, the famously ethical Samuel Johnson described Ophelia as 'the young, the beautiful, the harmless, and the pious.'[23] For him, as for many contemporaries, her bawdiness did not undermine her innocence.

Shakespeare fans, therefore, did not encounter only the expurgated Ophelia of the theater. Full texts of *Hamlet* were widely available and avidly read. That actresses did not deliver Ophelia's bawdiest lines on the stage is true — but they were to be imagined doing so by readers of the popular scholarly editions or players' texts. Since much of the theater audience would have read *Hamlet*, the bawdiness of the textual Ophelia would have added a layer to the mad scenes played on stage, as would the very fact that the character was played by actresses, perceived by many as equivalent to prostitutes.[24] The cuts made by theater companies and writers to Ophelia's explicitly sexual speech and song for the purpose of staging the play did not block audiences' appreciation of her as a woman whose love had a strong enough erotic component to madden her.

A visual record of Ophelia became available in the second half of the eighteenth century. Imagined Ophelias are particularly telling because they did not reflect an actual actress impersonating Ophelia, but an ideal. Two of the most widely distributed of these images — a souvenir print commemorating Garrick's Shakespeare Jubilee, and a print after Benjamin West's 1789 painting of the mad scene for Boydell's Shakespeare Gallery — are startling if one expects prettiness and decorum in Ophelia. The first memorializes a famous episode in the development of Bardolotry. The eminently respected and respectable actor, writer, and theater manager David Garrick envisioned, organized and publicized a three-day festival at Stratford-upon-Avon celebrating Shakespeare as a national hero. Mounted in 1769, the Shakespeare Jubilee included balls, masquerades, dedications, a horse race, and fireworks, and culminated in Garrick's reading (to elaborate musical accompaniment) of his elegant ode to the Bard. Given the nature and expense of the entertainment, only the well-heeled could afford to go. No Shakespeare play was performed.[25] In the popular souvenir print of this festival, Ophelia joins other well-known Shakespearean characters paying homage to Garrick. A gentlemanly Garrick stands under a bust of Shakespeare as his living representative (Fig. 8.1).

For the print's commemorative purposes, Ophelia worked wonderfully: her straw, flowers, loose hair, dishevelled white dress, and trademark 'frenzied' expression distinguished her unequivocally from other popular Shakespearean heroines such as Desdemona or Cordelia. Ophelia stares boldly at the viewer of the print, her hair loose, and her dishevelled and shape-revealing bodice baring one breast. Her loose hair and dishevelled clothing suggested iconographically a victimized (usually raped) woman or a woman of sexual abandon. The single bared or almost bared breast appeared in eroticized images of the Magdalen, images of the Madonna Lactans and in portraits of royal mistresses. To a viewer ignorant of Ophelia's significance in Shakespeare and unfamiliar with contemporary perceptions of female madness, Ophelia here appears as a whore enticing the men encircling her, or as an innocent victim pleading for mercy from them.

While this figure is openly sexualized, the very fact that its original viewers would have known the woman to be Ophelia rescued it from indecency. This contextualized decency is amplified by the further context of Garrick's own decorum. Garrick was renowned for his gentlemanly propriety, and the event the print commemorates had not the slightest whiff of subversiveness. Furthermore, Hamlet's advice to the players — 'o'erstep not the bounds of modesty' — serves as a caption for the image. Text and image together imply that Garrick fulfills Shakespeare's dictates about naturalistic acting and that his versions of Shakespeare are impeccably acceptable. This Ophelia is mainstream, and although she springs from a culture that profoundly eroticized the female breast, her bared breast could suggest her sexual desire without drawing into question her modesty. The print's effectiveness presupposes understandings about Ophelia that prevent the image from being read as lewd despite the visual indicators to the contrary. While they do not prevent Ophelia from being represented and viewed here as both the object and subject of sexual desire, they do tend to mediate and mitigate the monolithic categorization of this sexually charged image of an abandoned young woman as 'bad' or 'immodest.'

Benjamin West painted Ophelia's mad scene (Fig. 8.2) for the wealthy print seller John Boydell's Shakespeare Gallery. As Garrick had intended of his Shakespeare Jubilee, Boydell meant the Gallery to celebrate Shakespeare as *the* national poet. He believed that Shakespeare's plays would offer ideal subjects for a venture that he openly planned as a profitable and patriotic encouragement of native history painting (then the most prestigious painting genre). Artists such as West painted for the Gallery, where the public could view the works. Boydell hoped to market prints after the paintings to recoup his initial outlay plus some. Paintings in the Gallery were to portray what particularly popular and dramatic Shakespeare scenes might look like had they really taken place. For about ten years the Gallery was a place of fashionable resort.[26]

Although painters were freed in this enterprise from the limitations placed on performers of Shakespeare in the theater, they remained under the influence of widely held perceptions about characters and scenes. This context, like that of the Jubilee souvenir print, may have led West to paint an Ophelia who is not revisionist. While her movement is stylized, this bug-eyed and flailing Ophelia is anything but ornamentally pretty, restrained, and decorous. Her clothing reveals her figure, her hair is loose, and her feet are bare. Once again, the image demonstrates a split between concrete visual content (indicating Ophelia's abandon) and the viewer's knowledge, a knowledge that blocks the display from indicating a lack of virtue. The Jubilee and Boydell Ophelias followed precedents on stage. As in the images of Ophelia that were made up, a white dress and loose hair were *de rigueur*. So was unusually revealing clothing, as demonstrated by a print dated 1787 of an unidentified actress playing Ophelia (Fig. 8.3). She runs before classical columns, holding straw in one hand, and flowers in the other. Her clothing is loose, shape-revealing, flowing and bares more of her body than was fashionable.

These last two images overlapped, however, with the growing dominance of a mode of interpreting Ophelia that cast her as a model for women to emulate instead of as a kind of everywoman. This understanding of the character stressed Ophelia's prettiness, musicality, passivity, and ornamentality. An early instance of this shift can be seen in Bell's 1775 edition of Shakespeare, an expurgated version new to the publishing scene. The format (a cheap octavo) banked on a wide market. It explicitly broke with tradition in printing only the most decent and inoffensive stage versions of Shakespeare's texts. (It did not, in other words, provide the text that had been cut in performance, as was previously customary.) The edition's print of Jane Lessingham as Ophelia shows the minor actress in a rigorously corseted and petticoated dress decorated with garlands, a delighted smile on her face. Despite its depiction of the then conventional stage attributes (the basket, the wild and loose hair, the white dress, the flowers), this image was not meant to present a mainstream Ophelia, but one of whom even a Collier could approve. If one did not know differently from the context and the subtitle, this Ophelia could easily represent an aristocratic shepherdess in a pastoral poem (Fig. 8.4).

Bell's image marked a rising trend. By the beginning of the nineteenth century, Ophelia *was* played by singers and minor actresses, and criticism began to emerge that deployed Shakespeare's heroines as models for female behaviour, not as reflections of it.[27] In the visual record, Ophelias become passively pretty women. The viewer knows they are mad from the reactions of others in the images (Laertes, Gertrude, Claudius) or the knowledge that a loose-haired woman in white with flowers, and labelled 'Ophelia' is mad by convention. For audiences and readers, the character of Ophelia was flattened out and, perhaps as a result of this flattening or perhaps because she was not an unambiguous model for female behaviour under stress, de-emphasized. In other words, the widespread conception of how to understand Ophelia shifted, even though, as Smithson's Ophelia demonstrates, the conventions of playing the part remained much the same. By the mid-nineteenth century, the cultural memory of the earlier Ophelias had faded.

I mentioned above that the eighteenth-century conception of Ophelia showcased sexual desire at the expense of other aspects of the character. This is easily demonstrated by looking at how the novelists Sarah Fielding and Laurence Sterne employed Ophelia figures. Fielding demonstrated by means of the Ophelia figure what virtue would look like without the perversions of custom or the knowledge of vice. The orphaned heroine of her 1760 novel *The History of Ophelia* is brought up in the wilds of Wales by an aunt who educates her and keeps her from contact with other people. Her aunt was

> desirous not to lessen my Innocence and Simplicity while she dispelled my Ignorance, [and so she] gave me no Account of the Manners and Customs of a People with whom she hoped I should never have any Intercourse. The Books she had brought into *Wales* were chiefly Books of Divinity, and such Histories as served to enlarge and instruct the Mind of the Reader, without informing him of the existence of Vices, which a pure Imagination, untaught by Observation and Experience, cannot represent to itself.[28]

Lord Dorchester comes upon the household by accident, falls in love with Ophelia and kidnaps her. He places her in compromising situations (such as living with him openly) and revels in the open ('natural') affection she shows for him. Ophelia herself does not know (being 'natural') that she should dissemble any attachments to unmarried men who are not acknowledged suitors.

Dorchester means, of course, to have Ophelia as his mistress. He makes his own task difficult. Assuming Ophelia would wish to avoid vice should she discover what it is, Dorchester tries to lead her into vice without her knowledge. Cataloguing these attempts enables Fielding to show the reactions of a natural woman to flattery, fine clothing, money, the opera, Shakespeare's history plays (which according to Fielding have no vice represented in them), and various pleasure spots. Given a different education, Ophelia's behaviour and open affection for Dorchester would be improper in the extreme for a woman of virtue. In other, contemporary novels, a heroine engaged in such activities with a man, not her relation, is typically destined for prostitution, Newgate Prison, and transportation to the colonies. If, on the other hand, the heroine is knowingly virtuous, the narrative becomes one of resistance (Samuel Richardson's tragic *Clarissa*, for instance). Fielding implicitly acknowledges both narratives in a multitude of passages such as that in which Ophelia reflects that 'A Woman sensible of the Dangers attending her Situation, might, perhaps, have taken Alarm frequently, when I saw no Cause for Fear; thus far my Ignorance was convenient to his Design, who wanted to engage my heart entirely, before I could suspect him.'[29] Fielding presents Ophelia as the exception to both paradigmatic narratives because she is naturally virtuous and Dorchester is not naturally vicious. Dorchester eventually marries Ophelia.

The connection between Fielding's and Shakespeare's Ophelias may not be immediately apparent, but naming in eighteenth-century fictional narratives is, of course, a significant indicator of character. Fielding's work depends on widespread understandings of the Ophelia figure. Shakespeare's Ophelia had licence to show longings and affections not usually sanctioned in a woman who wanted to be understood as virtuous, and Fielding built her novel on that foundation. She uses her Ophelia figure to explore what is and is not 'natural' in the public behaviour of a virtuous woman. It is natural to desire the society of one man, and that, in itself, is not a vice.

Similarly, when Laurence Sterne's tourist Yorick encounters in France a love-mad woman named Maria, the dynamics of the encounter are predicated on what Ophelia could be to an eighteenth-century audience. As he had already done with Yorick, Sterne took Ophelia off the stage and out of the grave and incorporated her into a tourist script. Maria first appears in *Tristram Shandy* when a travelling Tristram is startled by 'the sweetest notes I ever heard.' These are played on a pipe by a beautiful young woman who went mad when her marriage banns were forbidden. In *A Sentimental Journey*, Yorick seeks out Maria because 'The story [Tristram Shandy] had told of that disorder'd maid affect'd me not a little in the reading... .'[30] He finds Maria with her pipe and a dog, and, like the stage Ophelia, loose haired, dressed in white, mad, and musical. Yorick and she cry together, and Yorick alternately wipes her tears and his with his handkerchief. She washes Yorick's tear-steeped handkerchief, lays it to dry on her bosom ('twill do me good,' Maria says).[31] The intimacy and exchange of bodily fluids in this scene is remarkable for an eighteenth-century novel, but, in Maria, Sterne appropriated one of the few figures available to him whose sexual openness was typically read as innocent and praiseworthy. Maria's overwhelming desire for the man she was to marry legitimates her madness, and her madness, in turn, legitimates a display of suggestive activity and desire impossible for a virtuous, chaste, and sane woman. Maria's still active desire for her fiancé is neither criticized nor suppressed — her madness releases her from the decorum that proscribed open expressions of what contemporaries could consider a natural, healthy, and legitimate sexuality.

That many period narratives about 'good' women revolve around the difficulties encountered in maintaining the reputation or the reality of virtue should not be taken as a sign of discomfort with female sexuality. Such narratives center on the problems inherent in the public management of desire in communally acceptable forms, including the problems of insuring that desire is directed towards widely sanctioned objects (husbands, for instance). These works concern themselves with inappropriate behaviour or the appearance of it; if they censure anything it is bad personal or public management of desire and its indicators, not the desire in and of itself. The narratives do not aim to reveal what 'natural' heterosexual desire looks like but how it should best be shaped for public consumption and private use.

In Ophelia and Ophelia figures, however, writers, painters, and actresses were released from this paradigm. Ophelia enabled what the period thought to be natural, virtuous, and virginal desire in a woman to be visible to spectators. But what was left out when contemporaries employed Ophelia and Ophelia figures is also significant. Fielding transformed Ophelia into an orphan with no friends and only an impoverished aunt as a relative, and Sterne transformed her into a French peasant. Shakespeare's Ophelia is a member of the royal court, her brother is politically powerful enough to threaten a King's position, and her father is the King's chief counsellor. The courtly and powerfully-connected Ophelia's mad language and song potentially threatens the security of the state. Fielding's and Sterne's Ophelia figures, on the other hand, harbor no dangerously unfixed sexual, political, or economic desires, and no social position that would make their actions and speech dangerous to the state or to family fortunes.

Eighteenth-century readers, writers, performers, painters, audiences and critics focused on Ophelia's sexual desire and suppressed the political, familial, and social ramifications of the original character's madness. I strongly suspect that the focus from the eighteenth century to the present on Ophelia's management of her sexuality has served to turn discussion from exactly those aspects of the role that are literally deleted from eighteenth-century performances and borrowings of Ophelia-figures such as Sarah Fielding's and Laurence Sterne's. It is not women's sexual desire but the place of women in the social and political web that is problematic. Ophelia's position as the daughter of a powerful courtier, the lover of the Prince who kills her father, the sister of a man with considerable political power, and as a woman whose speech in madness has political implications for her hearers is lost in what has become a long-term focus on her sexuality. We like to think of openly expressed female desire as subversive of patriarchy. Yet in the eighteenth-century Ophelia, we have a strong example of how female sexual desire can be put to the service of a male-dominated culture with some ease — how such a culture can indeed crave demonstrations of sexual desire in women, especially when such demonstrations block recognition of the political, social, and economic dimensions of women's lives.

Notes

[1]   Bridget Gellert Lyons, 'The Iconography of Ophelia,' *English Literary History* 44 (1977): 60-74. I delivered an early version of my essay at the 1997 Annual Meeting of the Group for Early Modern Cultural Studies and thank the participants for their suggestions.

[2]   Elaine Showalter, 'Representing Ophelia: Women, Madness, and the Responsibility of Feminist Criticism,' in *Shakespeare and the Question of Theory*, eds. Patricia Parker and Geoffrey Hartman (London and New York: Methuen, 1985): 77-94; *The Female Malady: Women, Madness, and English Culture, 1830-1980* (1985; New York: Penguin Books, 1987); Ellen J. O'Brien, 'Ophelia's Mad Scene and the Stage Tradition,' in *Shakespeare and the Arts*, eds. Cecile Williamson Cary and Henry S. Limouze (Washington D.C.: University Press of America, Inc., 1982): 109-125; Mary Floyd-Wilson, 'Ophelia and Femininity in the Eighteenth Century: "Dangerous Conjectures in Ill-Breeding Minds,"' *Women's Studies* 21 (1992): 397-409.

[3]   Showalter, 'Representing Ophelia,' 82. Cf. *The Female Malady*, 11.

[4]   Sir Theodore Martin, *Helena Faucit (Lady Martin)* (London: William Blackwood and Sons, 1900): 131.

[5]   See Peter Raby, *'Fair Ophelia': A Life of Harriet Smithson Berlioz* (Cambridge: Cambridge University Press, 1982), esp. 63-8.

[6]   For *Hamlet's* performances in London, see Charles Beecher Hogan, *Shakespeare in the Theater, 1701-1800* (Oxford: Clarendon Press, 1952-1957) and W. Van Lennep, et. al. *The London Stage, 1660-1800: A Calendar of Plays, Entertainments & Afterpieces Together with Casts, Box-Receipts and Contemporary Comment* (Carbondale: Southern Illinois University Press, 1960-1969). For fast access to *Hamlet* criticism, see Brian Vickers (ed.), *Shakespeare: The Critical Heritage, 1623-1800* (London and Boston: Routledge and Kegan Paul, 1974-1981). A quick search of the *English Short Title Catalogue* and the Chadwyck-Healey databases located over fifty eighteenth-century poems using Ophelia, a fraction of those extant. Some of the novels and illustrations are discussed below.

[7]   'Love, Sex, and Madness in Eighteenth-Century England,' *Social Research* 53, no. 2 (1986): 211-42.

[8]   [London?], [1775?]. (Houghton Library, 25242.61F* 39v).

[9]   Samuel Bishop, 'Epigram CCXXII,' in *The Poetical Works*, vol. 2 (London: 1796): 321.

[10] Charlotte Brent Pinto (once in 1760 at Covent Garden); Elizabeth Billington (once in 1790 at Covent Garden); and Martha Frances Caroline Poole (thirteen times between 1793 and 1794 at Covent Garden). Information compiled from Hogan and the *London Stage*.

[11] E.g. Susanna Mountfort played it from 1705-1717; Hester Booth, 1717-1733; Elizabeth Vincent, 1732-1762; Kitty Clive, 1735-1753; Susannah Cibber 1749-1765; Maria Macklin 1755-1773.

[12] *Hamlet. Prince of Denmark. A Tragedy*. In *The Plays of David Garrick*, Vol. 4, eds. Harry William Pedicord and Frederick Louis Bergmann (Carbondale and Edwardsville: Southern Illinois University Press, 1980).

[13] 'Sweeping up Shakespeare's "Rubbish": Garrick's Condensation of Acts IV & V of *Hamlet*,' *Eighteenth-Century Life* 8, no. 3 (1983): 18.

[14] *Hamlet. Prince of Denmark. A Tragedy*. In *The Plays of David Garrick*, Vol. 4, eds. Harry William Pedicord and Frederick Louis Bergmann (Carbondale and Edwardsville: Southern Illinois University Press, 1980).

[15] Showalter, Floyd-Wilson, and O'Brien each interpret the cuts in this manner.

[16] *Hamlet on Stage: The Great Tradition* (Westport: Greenwood Press, 1985): 19.

[17] In Euripides' *Hippolytus* Phaedra is lovesick for her step-son Hippolytus. Her maid tells him this and Phaedra witnesses him react with horror. She kills herself, leaving a note on her body accusing him of rape. Her husband Theseus finds it, curses his son, and the son dies. Collier's praise of Phaedra as modest is therefore extraordinary.

[18] *A Short View of the Immorality and Profaneness of the English Stage: A Critical Edition*, ed. Benjamin Hellinger (New York: Garland Publishing, Inc., 1987): 18.

[19] Floyd-Wilson, 403.

[20] *The Antient and Modern Stages Survey'd. Or, Mr. Collier's View of the Immorality and Profaneness of the English Stage Set in a True Light...* (London, 1699): 297.

[21] These were produced by Alexander Pope, Samuel Johnson, William Warburton, Lewis Theobald, Nicholas Rowe and others.

[22] For the London theaters alone, versions of players' texts for *Hamlet* appeared in 1676, 1703, 1718, 1751, 1774, and 1800. Each typically received multiple printings.

[23] Notes on *Hamlet* (1765), in *The Yale Edition of the Works of Samuel Johnson*, Vol. 8, ed. Arthur Sherbo (New Haven and London: Yale University Press, 1968): 1011.

[24] See Kristina Straub, *Sexual Suspects: Eighteenth-Century Players and Sexual Ideology* (Princeton: Princeton University Press, 1992), esp.89-126; Katherine Eisaman Maus, '"Playhouse Flesh and Blood": Sexual Ideology and the Restoration Actress,' *English Literary History* 46 (1979): 595-617.

[25] For details, see Johanne M. Stochholm, *Garrick's Folly: The Shakespeare Jubilee of 1769 at Stratford and Drury Lane* (London: Methuen, 1964) and Michael Dobson, *The Making of the National Poet: Shakespeare, Adaptation and Authorship, 1660-1769* (Oxford: Clarendon Press, 1992).

[26] See Winifred H. Friedman, *Boydell's Shakespeare Gallery* (New York: Garland Publishing Inc., 1976).

[27] See for instance Anna Brownell Jameson's immensely popular *Characteristics of Women* (1832), later titled *Shakespeare's Heroines*.

[28] Sarah Fielding, *The History of Ophelia*, vol. 1 (London, 1760): 12.

[29] Fielding, 79.

[30] Laurence Sterne, *A Sentimental Journey* (1768; reprint, edited by Gardiner D. Stout, Jr., Berkeley and Los Angeles: University of California Press, 1967): 269.

[31] Sterne, 273.

Figure 8.1   Isaac Taylor, 'O'er step not the modesty of Nature.' Engraving, 1769.

*Figure 8.2   Francis Legat, after Benjamin West, Hamlet. Act IV. Scene v. Elsinore —
King, Queen, Laertes, Ophelia, & c. Engraving, 1802.*

Figure 8.3   *Bartolozzi and Madan, Unidentified actress as Ophelia. Engraving, 1787.*

Figure 8.4   *Unidentified artist, 'There's Rue for you.' Mrs. Lessingham in the*
                  Character of OPHELIA. Engraving, 1774.

9 Mother(s) of Invention: Prostitute-Actresses and Late Nineteenth-Century Bengali Theater

Sudipto Chatterjee

This essay uses the analytical tools that have come to characterize Performance Studies — a disciplinary field that has gained in importance over the last twenty years — to consider the history of the theater of colonial Bengal in British India during the final years of the nineteenth century. In doing so, the essay builds its theoretical framework from the apparatus of more recognizable disciplines like history, sociology, psychology, feminism, queer studies and cultural studies. The subject is that of prostitute-actresses, women who performed on the late-Victorian Bengali stage. The essay sketches the story of how these women came to be actresses and what the profession did for them vis-à-vis what they did for their "new" profession. The essay locates in the issues surrounding these women a site, a negotiating table where concerns and anxieties that rocked the late-nineteenth-century Bengali society at large surface and intersect.

> A woman's garb covers me from tip to toe.
> Inside, made of stone,
> A hardened heart alone
> Can stone ever be molten by tear's ebb and flow?
> ~ *Binodinī Dāsī*[1]

Calcutta, 1873. Yet another theater company, called the Bengal Theatre, was established in the city in the footsteps of the National Theatre. The two main figures behind it were Śarat Candra Ghoṣ (1834-1880) and Bihārīlāl Caṭṭopādhyāy (1840-1901), both members of the rich *bābu* community, the intelligentsia of Calcutta. The theater was built 'in imitation of Mrs. Lewis' Lyceum Theatre [an American-owned English theater] at Chowringhee.'[2] But the Bengal Theatre's intention was more than just that of creating a permanent Western-style stage for Bengali theater. Ghoṣ and Caṭṭopādhyāy convened a special all-male group of advisors, including leading intellectuals, civil servants, Saṅskṛt pundits and social reformers of Bengal, to decide whether it was 'proper' to introduce (prostitutes as) actresses on the Bengali stage. In the select group were the poet-playwright Michael Madhusūdan Datta, the inventor of the Bengali blank verse and author of the first Western-style original play, and Īśwarcandra Bidyāsāgar, one of the social reformers who had spearheaded the movement against child marriage for women and in favor of the legalization of widow remarriage. While Datta wholeheartedly endorsed the idea of women appearing on stage, Bidyāsāgar resigned to protest the committee's decision to allow prostitutes on stage. Ultimately, four women were brought into the company from the 'red-light' districts of Calcutta.

The decision rubbed the Bengali intelligentsia, the *bābu* community, the wrong way. The *bābu* sensibility, too, had itself grown to embrace a larger constituency. It now included the fast growing middle class within its moral, if not economic, compass, overarching the *bhadralok* category or gentlemen class that comprised both the rich and not-so-rich (but) educated gentry. So much so, that now the appelations *bābu* and *bhadralok* had become practically interchangeable.[3]   The controversies surrounding the prostitute-actresses affected the entire *bhadralok* class, generating discussion in the press, with mounting disapproval. But the disapproval was not uncontested. The most vocal antagonists were the movers and shakers of the Bengali stage, who argued well against the conservative press and noted the contradictions inherent in their objections. An early historian of the Bengali stage cites Giriś Candra Ghoṣ (1844-1912), the leading director-playwright working with the Bengal Theatre's rival company, the National Theatre, who argued first that

> Europe can boast of many chaste housewives who are in the acting profession, but that's not the case in most instances. There aren't many distinctions drawn between ballet dancers and lowly prostitutes. Nonetheless, if we are to talk about the [European] theaters, discerning members of the audience there do not despise the theater seeing prostitutes on stage.[4]

Elaborating on the same point, Giriś Ghoṣ exposed an inherent contradiction among his *bābu* or *bhadralok* critics. The same *bābu*s who were routinely entertained by *bāijis* — female dancers and singers who were often prostitutes — and many of whom also kept mistresses, now opposed permitting prostitutes on the stage. What so distinguished the stage? Giriś Ghoṣ overlooked (at least in this article) the fact that the theater was not simply performance *for* the *bābu*s; it was also *by* and *of* the *bābu*s. Allowing prostitutes on the stage would involve 'respectable' men in consorting with 'unrespectable' women as co-professionals. It was one thing to witness, but quite another to participate. The theater had been celebrated for a long time as a 'playground' of moral instruction, an instrument of social change and improvement. The entrance of prostitutes onto its stages would sully its edifying function. The theater was meant to advertise, announce, argue for, and elicit social change, but was not generally thought of as an active participant in acts of change themselves.

However, Giriś Ghoṣ argued, the social reality of the theater as a profession and industry that employed and sustained those who worked in it discredited that idealistic function. The reality was that those who worked in the theater had to survive as professionals and eke out livings by relying on their vocation to pay their bills. The introduction of actresses weighed heavily in the theater's viability as an industry.

Ghoṣ' contemporary Amṛtalāl Basu (1853-1929), also a leading actor and comedic playwright, offered another line of reasoning. He built his case on two arguments — first, the boys who had been playing the female parts would soon grow up, become physically unsuitable to portray female roles, and refuse to act; and second, the scarcity of good plays that had caused the theaters to settle for music-dominated, operatic plays made the introduction of actresses essential to box-office success. The first reason, thus, was characterized as internal, the second as external to the theater itself. The theaters saw both an administrative as well as a commercial advantage in introducing actresses to the stage. Morality had become a lesser issue for them.

The social controversy regarding actresses raged well beyond 1873. Even as late as 1877, *Āryadarśan*, a leading Bengali journal, published an article that offered more support for prostitute-actresses.[5] One of the first justifications was culled from the orientalist past. The author argued that this was not the first time actresses had participated in the history of Indian performance. He referred his readers to the time of the Bharata-muni, the fabled author of the ancient Sanskṛt theatrical treatise *Nātyaśāstra*.[6] When the white Europeans were no more than cave dwellers, the author contended, veritable *apsarā*s (heavenly nymphs) would descend to perform for Bharata, trained personally by him. The *apsarā*s had even been called upon to perform episodes from the ancient Indian epic *Rāmāyaṇa* at the behest of its author, the sage Vālmikī. It was widely known, the author claimed, that these same *apsarā*s were also prostitutes. If such a practice had not been acceptable to the ancients, why would they have allowed it to tarnish a text as holy as the *Rāmāyaṇa*? The prostitutes were, after all, entertainers of a kind, well-versed in the art of pleasing men, which better equipped them for the theater than housewives. Would it not be safer, the author proclaimed, to leave the business of entertainment in the hands of entertainers than to display housewives before the public or doll up young boys as females?

The author next argued the effectiveness of verisimilitude in acting — the appropriateness of the sexes each playing their own on stage. Until 'respectable' women were sufficiently capable of performing, would it not be appropriate to hold up a mirror to nature as best one could, the moral question of putting prostitutes on stage notwithstanding? Bidyābhūṣaṇ then proceeded to the most classic appropriative argument to have augmented the debate, connecting it with social movements that had advanced the cause of female liberation in nineteenth-century Bengal. By allowing prostitutes on stage, he argued, Bengali theater actually undertook a great social service. It allowed lowly women a way out of their despicable lives by providing them with the opportunity to find atonement in the practice of art. The final argument came as an apology for the institution and practice of prostitution itself. The author claimed that the *bābu*s who would frequent prostitutes' quarters at the end of the week for want of other cheap entertainment would now turn to the theater, since their paid paramours would now be adorning the stages. This would divert them from carnal lust and lure them to the world of aesthetic pleasures.

This debate posited a series of interrelated concerns that were very much linked with the general discourse of change and self-fashioning that permeated the lives of the intelligentsia in nineteenth-century Bengal. At the level of internal orientation, western-style Bengali theater required actresses to uphold the virtues of realism it was inheriting from the European theaters and to establish the credibility of being their capable counterpart. At a commercial level, Bengali theater was obliged to bring actresses to the stage to sustain it not only as a site of pleasure, but also as a site of desire for the male gaze. The prostitute-actresses on stage would enable the *bhadralok* to engage voyeuristically with their bodies.

Interestingly, when some of the very same prostitute-actresses who had aroused suspicions were called upon to play male roles, especially those of divine characters displaying feminine characteristics, no eyebrows were raised. On the contrary, the performances were always lauded with exceptional praise. When, in 1884, Binodinî (1863-1941), one of the most celebrated actresses to have appeared on the Bengali stage, played the title role in Giriś Ghoṣ' play *Caitanyalîla,* dramatizing the life and times of the medieval *Baiṣñab* Bhakti cult leader Nimāi Caitanya, a British officer commented that '[t]he poor girl who played Chaitanya may belong to the class of unfortunates..., but while on the scene she throws herself [into the role] so ardently that one sees the Vaishnava saint before him.'[7]

Six years later, however, Giriś Ghoṣ repudiated the success of *Caitanyalîlā* and its sequel in a curious betrayal of his own actions as playwright and director that bespeaks a generalized discomfort with the idea of genders crossed, made material in Binodinî's transvestism. He wrote:

> [W]hen *Caitanyalîlā* was performed, although the renowned actress in male costume enraptured the hearts of the perceptive audience, although a number of honest men forgot her low social status and wanted to touch her feet, although the audiences shouted the name of Kṛṣña in tumultuous unison with her, the acting was still never quite manly. [...] This feminine adumbration would have been a contrariety if the religious heart of the Hindu [audience] had not intervened.[8]

The virtuosic achievement of Binodinî's performance was treacherously lost in the inversion Ghoṣ made by assigning the credit to the receptivity of his religiously zealous audience. The question, however, remains, why then did Giriś Ghoṣ cast Binodinî in the role? Were there no male actors in his theater company, Star — one of the most prestigious and resourceful public theaters of the time — who could have performed the role with equal aplomb? This was not a stray incident. Ghoṣ had cast Binodinî in a male role at least three times before. But Ghoṣ seems to have been ready to fall with his casting choice, leaving it unexplained, and even to admit a generic weakness in his writing and characterization in order to vindicate the failure of the idea that, ironically, was his own to start with. Ghoṣ ascribed the 'failure' of the female (to portray the male) to nature itself, to the accoutrements of theatrical 'naturalism.' Instead of rationalizing his own casting decision, Ghoṣ invoked the illustrative story of the Victorian actress Sarah Bernhardt's attempt to play Hamlet in French. He recounted that the Europeans, too, despite commending the virtuosity of the attempt and with due regard for the actress, had objected to the offense against 'naturalism.' The operative notion for Ghoṣ, then, was that of 'naturalism,' and anything short of it was to be regarded as 'unnatural.'

But the big question is still left unanswered — why was Ghoṣ subverting his own directorial choice in casting an actress in male roles? Perhaps it was the sheer novelty of the choice and the attraction of the commercial prospects it held that originally prompted Ghoṣ's actions. Or perhaps, in the case of *Caitanyalīlā* at least, it was the traditional *baisñab* view that the saintly Caitanya, in spite of his anatomical maleness, was figuratively feminine because he romanced the male figure of Lord Kṛṣña in his devotion, and was supposed to have appeared with feminine physical attributes. The conjectures will remain conjectures, but what is certain is that Giriś Ghoṣ now used the very same logic he had used elsewhere to castigate male actors playing female roles to invite females to the stage and then prohibit them from playing male characters.

Beyond the caprices of male sexual desires and colonial commerce lay two overarching ideological constructs that continued to justify the project. First, the redemptive element in orientalist perceptions of a high Hindu culture of the past, ideologically at least, set the Hindu intelligentsia of nineteenth-century Bengal on a par with their British masters and helped to salve the wounds of colonial ignominy. Secondly, the utilitarian tradition of social work upstaged the privilegentsia as the builders and vanguards of a new (however Utopian) egalitarian society. On the one hand, the idea of accordance with the *apsarās*' ancient practice of performing for the sages constituted at a symbolic level the *bābu*s as the new sages. Yet on the other, the idea of performing social service to redeem the disenfranchised privileged the *bābu*s as the agents of social progress. These 'sagified' *bābu*s would thus rescue the prostitute-*apsarā*s from a lowly life, the same lowly life, however, sponsored (hence perpetuated) by a great many of the upper class *bābu*s at other times. The lines of gender politics, the power dynamics between the sexes, stand out quite clearly in this. It was the male, always already the male, who determined where the female, especially the morally-outcast female, should or would stand.

Moreover, it should be noted also that all plays produced by the Bengali public theaters were written by male authors.   Darśan Caudhurî, a contemporary historian of Bengali theater, discusses Giriś Ghoṣ' portrayal of female characters in his plays.[9] He argues that Ghoṣ would take into account the limitations of the female members of his company when writing their parts and make them 'easier' to play than those played by male character actors. As a result, Caudhurî argues, Ghoṣ' male characters were intentionally more complex than the females, the assumption being that his 'actors' were more capable of handling stronger, more complex emotions than his 'actresses.' According to Caudhurî, this is most evident in the fact that the best female characters in Ghoṣ' plays were invariably the heroines of his mythological and historical plays in which characterization, in general, was thinner in psychological complexity than in his social plays, whose subjects were closer to contemporary reality. Caudhurî's argument, thus, relies on the assumption that 'the uneducated actresses of the period were simply not capable of rendering subtle impersonations' in general, because 'any performance of a domestic lady would require rare talents of character portrayal.'[10]   But was it really a simple lack of talent that stopped Ghoṣ from giving his actresses fuller characters to play? What 'rare talents of characterization' would be needed for portraying contemporary women that would be less essential in depicting mythical nymphs and historical heroines? Giriś Ghoṣ used a special meter he had created himself for the resonant verse of his mythological and historical plays, venerated in Bengali literature as the 'Gairiś' meter. Were the sparsely trained, uneducated actresses truly more capable of mouthing the heavy 'Gairiś ' lines than the more colloquial dialogue of Ghoṣ' social plays, modeled as they were on everyday speech?

Darśan Caudhurî does not answer this basic question.   Rather, he focuses — derivatively — on the inherent histrionic quality, the melodramatic potentialities of the ponderous 'Gairiś' of Ghoṣ' mythical/heroical women. Caudhurî deems this histrionicity 'easier' to perform than the colloquial, familiar roles of domestic women. In fact, in driving home his point, Caudhurî singles out the one stock role that he claims prostitute-actresses could play with ease — the hysterical madwoman. This stock character would often appear in Ghoṣ' social plays as a theatrical device for providing a symbolic metatext that propelled and highlighted the thematic issues of the plays. The raw, hysterical abandon of the loose-haired madwoman whetted the imagination of male gazers in the audience while, at the same time, distilling clemency from the middle class audience, both male and female. The madwoman was usually shown as having turned mad due to social or familial injustice. There is an objective correlative between the character of the madwoman and the prostitute-actress playing her — they are united in their sufferings. And charged as they were with melodramatic excesses the audience loved, they were effective stage devices that kept the audience riveted.

Ghoṣ's view of women, however sympathetic, and whether unwittingly or otherwise, was always sited at the crux of sexual politics and informed by gender hierarchies and the power structure of a patriarchal society. While his portrayals of historical heroines and mythical goddesses were packed with concessions for the fairer/weaker sex, the real-life women in the social plays are martyred mothers or daughters, vamps or temptresses, or mad. In short, Ghoṣ' women tend to be either too good, or no good at all. They are all too easy to read. If it was his progressive ideas that made his women characters 'good,' it was the same 'goodness' that rendered the same progressive program somewhat duplicitous. The plays, even in their apparent glorification of the female, were not doing much to alter the patriarchal perception of the feminine, if not pandering directly to it.

Arguably, Ghoṣ' (or for that matter, any nineteenth-century Bengali male playwright's) problem with female characterization may have been located in a symbolic shame generated by the interface between prostitute-actresses and domestic women of the *bābu* society. The identification of the characters on stage (women of the *bābu*'s household) and the women playing them (prostitute-actresses) would be a potentially dangerous (identity) liaison for the nineteenth-century *bābu*-playwright. Socially outcast women could well play women with whom audiences could not identify at home, and playwrights would willingly submit to the onerous undertaking of coaching their 'uneducated' tongues in order to have them speak the formal 'educated' lines of the mythical/historical plays. But they could not *be* (even in staged reality) the familiar, domesticated women. These 'outcaste' women could really only play cast out madwomen, or heroines cast away from the present by myth and history. They could not be fleshed out. They could not get 'real.' The only reality available to them was that of 'unreal' staged portrayals of mythical/historical women or 'real' domestic women — (vainly) glorious in suffering or martyrdom, or plainly mad. Effectively, the repertoire of characters made available by male playwrights to the prostitute-actresses worked mostly — indirectly and otherwise — to subvert the very liberation from their 'lowly' profession that the theater business had offered them. The prostitute-actress indeed, as we shall see later, could represent even the Mother Nation (as in the case of the nationalist pantomimes that were commonplace in the public theaters) but not the mother or mother-to-be at home. It was unspeakably dangerous to allow the 'home-breaker' prostitute-actress, whose social role was to entertain the *bābu*s and lure them out of their homes, to portray the 'homemaker' on stage. It comes as no surprise, then, that Giriś Ghoṣ wrote many more historical and mythological plays than social dramas.

Partha Chatterjee, in *The Nation and Its Fragments*, casts women within a binary bind that straddles the hemispheres of the home and the world.[11] He argues that the patriarchal nationalism of the Hindu *bābu* customized the position of the female in the Bengali society of the nineteenth century to fulfill the agenda of nationalism. While the men made 'innumerable surrenders' in the materialistic domain of the colonial capitalist market, women were educated in order that they uphold all that stood for 'spirituality and pureness of heart.' Having reconstructed this narrative through close examination of four 'supposedly self-revelatory' autobiographical texts by women that allow him to trace the 'genealogy of the nationalist construct of the "new woman,"' Chatterjee introduces into his lineup the autobiography of Binodinî.[12] Chatterjee's purpose here seems to be to point out the parametric variables of appropriation possible within the matrix of social order in the ideology of nationalism. Binodinî, in Chatterjee's sequence, is all that the others are not in terms of social location.

Binodinî's is a case of betrayal at several levels — in her professional career as well as in her personal life. She had believed in giving herself to the theater as redemption from a life of prostitution. Yet when her theater required it, she agreed to sell herself to a rich non-Bengali patron, Gurmukh Rāy, who had agreed upon that condition to support the sickly theater company with which she was associated. She had joined the public theater at the young age of ten, but her theatrical profession could/did not prevent her from taking on the profession she had inherited by birth. She had to sell her body. Binodinî's life as a prostitute-actress is recounted with such painful intensity in her autobiography (first published in 1912) that extensive citations do not seem unwarranted.[13]

> The young gentleman who had given me shelter was yet unmarried [when Binodinî met him], but he had just married a few months ago and misbehaved with me on a few occasions on account of the insobriety that so characterizes the well-to-do youth.[14] It saddened me a great deal. It made me think that God has given me the strength to earn my own living, and if with physical labor I can support myself and my family, I would put myself out of misery and not have to sin any further by selling my body. If with my help a theater can be built, then I could live off it for the rest of my life. It was at this time that the late Gurmukh   Rāy was busy with the project of building the "Star Theatre." I heard this from our actors, and it so happened that the gentleman with whom I had lived had gone somewhere far away on some business. In the meantime, the actors started insisting, "Help us in any way you can to establish a theatre [of our own]." I was certainly not averse to doing theatre, but the idea of having to leave someone unfairly to go to someone else troubled me. But on the other side were the ardent entreaties of my theater friends! I was in a double bind. Giriś-*bābu* was telling me that theater was my ladder of self-improvement. That the success of the education he had imparted could only be realized in me. That theater could bring a world of honor and respect. My fantasies were puffing up in all this turmoil. My theater friends would not stop

imploring, and I, too, was realizing that a new theater could indeed come into being if I really wanted it to happen. But I couldn't forget the youth with whom I had lived, either! However, in time, his absence and the presence of my friends, their ardent exhortations, pushed me towards theater. [...] I decided to go for the theater! And why not? These people with whom I have lived like siblings, they, who have a perpetual hold on me, are right as well. If my action would lead to the founding of the theater, we would live forever like brothers and sisters. My resolve consolidated, and by giving myself to Gurmukh Rāy, I built the theatre. [....] But this change took a toll on me, as well as on the theater people. For when the young gentleman found out I had moved in with someone else and was determined to be in the theater for good, he started, be it in anger or obstinacy, to try and obstruct me in various ways. And they weren't very easy obstacles! He brought armed fighters from his *jamidāri* estate and surrounded my house; Gurmukh-*bābu* sent for hoodlums, too. The police got involved and there was a lot of trouble. Even my life was endangered.[15]

Binodinî's former lover appeared one night in her bedroom with a sword and first threatened, then attempted to kill her. Binodinî finally managed to dissuade him. After this, she was obliged to flee Calcutta and live in hiding for a couple of months, waiting for the storm to blow over. In the meantime, Gurmukh Rāy, in a desperate bid to extricate himself from the situation (even at the cost of giving up Binodinî), offered Binodinî a huge sum of 50,000 rupees as compensation, which she declined. Binodinî's colleagues became very nervous at Gurmukh Rāy's efforts and pleaded with her not to accept his offer, though 'all their attempts were really quite unnecessary. I had decided upon the theater. I would never proffer myself to [Gurmukh Rāy] unless he built the theater house.'[16] Binodinî's involvement in the project could not be justified by mere material gain. Her dedication to this dream was total and she was willing to do whatever was needed of her. Her repayment was that

> [w]hen the theater was ready, everyone told me, "This theater house will be linked to your name. Your name will remain long after you are gone.... [T]his theater will be called the 'B' Theatre." This excited my euphoria even further. But when it came to brass tacks they fell back on their promise — I do not know why. Until the moment the theater was registered, I had known that it would be named after my name! The day they went and registered it, when everything was a done deal, with just a few weeks before opening, I asked them in haste what the new name of the theater was going to be, and [they] answered happily, "The Star." The news hurt me so much that I had to sit down and could not speak for two whole minutes. Finally, I controlled myself and said, "Good!"[17]

Binodinī swallowed the insult and continued to work. But in three and a half years the situation at the Star became unbearable for reasons that Binodinī was loathe to explain in her memoirs. She gave up the stage in 1887 at the ripe old age of twenty-three, her career having spanned a meager thirteen years.

The next betrayal that shook Binodinī's life after the end of her career in the theater was the premature death of her only child, her daughter Śakuntalā , who was only thirteen when she died in 1903. Then Gurmukh, who loved Binodinī, had stood by her through thick and through thin, and had promised her a lifetime's economic security, failed to fulfill his promise when he died in 1912, ending a thirty-one-year-long relationship. Gurmukh's 'real' family spurned Binodinī and denied her any kind of inheritance. The final betrayal came in Binodinī's guru Giriś Ghoṣ' inability to speak the truth about her life in his foreword to her autobiography. The foreword was written in very 'safe' language and did not even attempt to address the reasons for Binodinī's untimely departure from the public theater. Binodinī complained to Ghoṣ upon reading the piece, asking him to speak out, and he promised to rewrite it. He died before he could do so.

Binodinī's life story exemplifies the betrayals prostitute-actresses suffered at the hands of the society at large as well as at those of their associates in the theater, their self-proclaimed 'rescuers.' First-hand knowledge of a brighter, freer world, of creativity and enlightenment, and yet, a concomitant prohibition against the enjoyment of its fruits typifies the tragedy of Bengali prostitute-actresses' experience of the nineteenth and early twentieth centuries. They could be and were given the roles of queens, princesses, and mythical/historical heroines, and every conceivable position of social grace, but only on the illusory stage. The stage whetted their appetite, but never satisfied it. It raised their expectations only to dash them with grim disillusionment. The stage, the society, the nation could accommodate and ideologically emancipate only their images and their corporeal presences, their bodies-on-stage, but never honor their spirits, their aspirations or desires, or undo the political gendering of their bodies on the social margin. Binodinī had to make a gift of her body to a man in order to make possible the creation of a new theater that would eventually cast her out when she had served its purpose. This is not merely a symbolic action in a larger social spectacle, but a personal tragedy of great proportion, and ultimately a palpable cut to the humanist ideology of the colonial nation-state.

The notion that, for all practical purposes, nationalism entails an infinite 'capacity to appropriate dissenting and marginal voices' is clearly visible in the way in which the nationalist agenda in nineteenth-century Bengali theater utilized the figure of the woman, the Goddess/Mother, to serve its purpose through elevation, then negation and, finally, evacuation of it.[18] The idea of the nation as the Mother had already gained currency in nationalist discourse in the last quarter of the nineteenth century, in literature and in the general political rhetoric, drawing both from European paradigms and from notions of the mother goddess in Hindu mythology. But with the admission of prostitute-actresses into Bengali theater, the idea of the woman-nation found a certain corporeality as a site of cultural performance that it had lacked in the realm of ideas. Ironically, the female body of the prostitute-actress could/would now physicalize the idea of the Mother Nation. More ironically still, these Mother(s) of invention who served the needs of the nation were women/actresses without the right, societally-speaking, to raise families and be 'proper' mothers. (Binodinī's lover's death left her penniless, without legal recourse to his inheritance and the rights of legal widowhood or motherhood.) But then these very same actresses were the only palpable representations of the imagined figure of the Mother Nation. These very same women paraded on the stage as the exalted female figures at whom audiences came to gaze. After all, to see ('Mother India') was to believe (in her)! As a logical corollary, then, it was this very staged Motherhood which denied them through its social impossibility the motherhood of which they were biologically capable. These women, thus, could be gazed at but not identified with. Even on stage, they were as far from home as they were within the class structure of nineteenth-century Calcutta — disenfranchized, marginalized, subaltern.

The question arises once again how lowly prostitutes could be acceptable as Mother Nation, Hindu goddesses, and (even) male saints (as in the case of Binodinī's portrayal of Caitanya)? It was, perhaps, the fact that the historical or mythological romance that enveloped these exalted female characters inoculated them against the morally infectious truth of prostitution. That the actresses were actually prostitutes did not in any way impinge upon how they were received by the *bhadralok* audiences. As I argued earlier, the inherent ethereality of goddesses and heroines was far enough from the reality of the home (and homemakers) that the male *bhadralok* audience might turn the other way and view it outside the context of the primal profession of the prostitute-actresses. It was acceptable as long as prostitutes were not representing the real women in their homes to whom the *bābu*s returned at the end of each day. We can now add to Partha Chatterjee's binary vision of the 'home' and the 'world' of the Bengali respectable (*sambhrānta*) *bhadralok,* a second binary within the larger group of Bengali women situated at the very intersection of the first, segregating women as 'private' (*bhadramahilā*) and 'public' (*bārāṅganā*/prostitute), the wife and the mistress. These two could never meet within the larger moral schema of the *bhadralok bābu,* although they could touch the two extremes of the *bābu*'s world, as long as there was no actual interface between the two. And in this, we return to the question of verisimilitude. Stage realism was an acceptable mode of representation insofar as it did not propose something that hit home with the force of a major epistemic rupture. Prostitutes, allowed to enter mainstream sociocultural activity from the margins of bourgeois society, threatened to undermine the social cohesion the Bengali *bhadralok* held so dear to his heart. But the winds of commerce had blown down part of the protective wall that fortified the *bābu*'s social world.   Prostitutes had to be allowed in.   Once admitted, however, begrudgingly or otherwise, they could not then be allowed further ingress into the innermost sanctum of that world, namely the domain of the home that enshrined feminine domesticity and kept the woman 'manageable.' It was necessity that had made it possible to reinvent prostitutes as actresses, but no further invention could justify their playing the *bhadramahilā*.   This final mimesis, which would allow a prostitute to become a housewife, perhaps suggested an even more dangerous, unspeakable alterity, an inversion — the fearful possibility that a housewife could in reality become a prostitute.   The *bhadralok* sensibility could not possibly accommodate the idea of prostitutes representing their *bhadramahilā*s.   The two worlds — private and public — had to be kept apart.   The emergence of prostitutes on the nineteenth-century Bengali stage had posited itself abjectively (I am appropriating Julia Kristeva's mediated use of the term) in relation to *bābu*-society and its moral fabric, initially and if only for a moment, as a possible threat of violence that had to be somehow managed, contained and purged.[19]   And when the extensive debate over this 'abject' innovation came to a concluded acceptance, when the idea of the prostitute-actress became normative, the crisis had been averted, managed, contained.   The 'abject' figure of the prostitute-actress had been used by the predominantly male theater community, even if without explicit agendas, to remedy a larger abjectivity to which the theater community itself was subject. But the public theater's so-called ennobling rescue act of delivering the prostitute-actresses from an ignoble life was at its best an act of deception.   It was couched in the vested interests of the male-dominated theater industry to gain commercial as well as ideological advantage.   Although it gave some of them education and fame, the theater had done little more for the prostitute-actresses than turning them into actress-prostitutes.   This is clearly and repeatedly evidenced in their autobiographies, which bespoke the success of this deceptive sticks-and-carrots strategy of management/containment that has been identified as the 'betrayal' of patriarchal nationalism.   The betrayal Binodinī had experienced when she was denied a theater in her name is then effectively quite the same as that of the elevation and the concomitant rarefaction of the female figure on the stage of nationalism.   Thus, in a reversal of the time-worn adage, the mother here had become the necessity of invention.

Notes

All translations are mine, unless otherwise noted.

[1]   Binodinī Dāsī (1863-1941) was one of the greatest actresses to have adorned the Bengali stage.   These lines are from a poem, Anutāp ('Repentance'), from the collection entitled *Bāsanā* (1896).   Binodinī and her role in Bengali theater are discussed extensively in this essay.

2   Sushil Mukherjee, *The Story of the Calcutta Theatres* (Calcutta: K P Bagchi & Company, 1982), 51.
3   This collapsing of the two appellations meant that any educated Bengali with a certain cultural refinement could now be called a *bābu*, whether rich or poor.   This was a reflection of the changing economic order, the rise of an educated and professional middle class.   The *bābu* epithet had moved from being an economic denominator to becoming a a cultural one.   In this essay, I have used *bhadralok* and *bābu* somewhat interchangeably. The issue, however, does get more problematic with the theatre practitioners who were called *bābu*s as well, since they belonged to the educated 'comprador' middle class as well, but contradicted *bābu* values in many fundamental ways.   But the irony of how close the theatre practitioners were, in reality, to the seat of *bābu* morality, despite their progressive and liberal attitudes regarding the use of prostitute-actresses on the Bengali stage, is also interesting to note.
4   Kiran Candra Datta, *Baṅgīya Nātyaśālār Itihās* [The History of the Bengali Theatre] (Calcutta: Paścim Baṅga Nātya Akādemi, 1996), 160.
5   Jogendranāth Bidyābhuṣan '*Mañce Bārāṅganā* [Prostitutes on Stage],' *Āryadarśan* 4, no. 5 (Calcutta, 1877).
6   A Saṅskṛt treatise on theatre and dance, ascribed to Bharata Muni, was probably composed in the third century BCE.   However, the manuscript that is used today can only be dated back to the seventh or eighth century CE.
7   Dasi, 158.   The *Baisñab*s (Saṅskṛt *Vaisñava*) represent a sub-faith within the Hindu belief system.   The *Baisñab*s are followers of the sixteenth century saint Śrī Caitanya (known as Nimāi before he attained sainthood).   Caitanya (1486-1534) believed that both the male and female godheads — *prakṛti* and *puruṣ* — resided within the human body.   His *sā dhanā* (endeavor, devotional practice) was to reach that combined ineffable spirit.
8   Giriś Candra Ghos, *Giriś Racanābalī*, ed. Debīpada Bhaṭṭācārya, vol. 3 (Calcutta: Sāhitya Saṅgsad, 1972), 820-21.
9   Darśan Caudhurī, *Uniś Śataker Nātyabiṣay* [Topics in Nineteenth Century Theatre] (Calcutta: Pustak Bipani, 1985).
10 Caudhuri, 101.
11 Partha Chatterjee, *The Nation and Its Fragments: Colonial and Postcolonial Histories* (Princeton, NJ: Princeton University Press, 1993).
12 Partha Chatterjee, 151.
13 A full English translation of Binodinī's memoirs, *Binodini Dasi: My Story and My Life as an Actress* (New Delhi: Kali for Women Press, 1998), by Rimli Bhattacharya is available in print. However, for the purpose of this essay, I have chosen to use my own translations (made before Bhattacharya's book became available).
14 'Given me shelter' is, of course, a euphemism for 'kept me as mistress.'
15 Dāsī, 39-41.
16 Dāsī, 43.
17 Dāsī, 44-5.
18 P. Chatterjee, 156.
19 According to Julia Kristeva, the abject is an agency of disruption that stands between the formation of subjectivity and its dependence on objects to fashion itself.   The abject 'disturbs identities, systems and orders.   Something that does not respect limits, positions, rules.   The in-between, the ambiguous, the mixed up.'   See Julia Kristeva, *The Kristeva Reader*, ed. Toril Moi (New York: Columbia University Press, 1986), 12.

10 'Art' for Men, 'Manners' for Women: How Women Transformed the Tea Ceremony in Modern Japan

Etsuko Kato

This essay investigates how an historical and cultural discourse associated with the tea ceremony and its visual presentation, and focusing on women's mastery of manners, has uniquely sited women within modern Japanese society. Analyzing discourses from around the turn of the twentieth century through the post-World War II period, the author claims that the notion of the tea ceremony as embodied for women in 'manners' is a product of nationalism from the late nineteenth century. In its relation to another notion of the tea ceremony emerging during the same period — as 'art' for men — the 'manners' discourse typifies man-woman, mind-body, public-domestic and Western-Japanese dichotomies of the era. The essay argues further that women are not only passively sited within the context of socially-dictated manners through the tea ceremony, but that it also enables them to actively situate themselves and their performances within the gaze of the general public: to (re-)create their own unique, social space.

In Japan and abroad, the tea ceremony is closely associated with women's culture. Indeed, more than 90 percent of the 2.6 million tea ceremony practitioners in Japan are women.[1] When asked why they study the tea ceremony, Japanese women offer responses such as: 'because it would be a shame if I didn't know how to have tea and a sweet when invited' or 'because I should be a little more *shitoyaka* [graceful and feminine].' These women see the tea ceremony as a means of acquiring fluency in traditional manners, and in fact, in modern Japan, the tea ceremony is widely considered an appropriate training ground for young women.

This association of the tea ceremony with women's manners is a late development in the history of *chanoyu* or *sadô*, the 'Way of Tea.' Created in the sixteenth century and developed during the feudal era, the tea ceremony had been practiced almost exclusively by men. It was only at the end of the feudal era in the late nineteenth century that the tea ceremony was opened to women, and even thereafter, men continued to practice the tea ceremony. That is, there is no innate relationship between the tea ceremony and a feminine ideal. When and why did this association come about?

This question can be answered by examining two popular discourses from the Meiji Era (1868-1912) centering on the tea ceremony, which emerged in the context of gender roles prescribed by specific movements during this era, namely westernization and nationalism.[2]   The first discourse, concerning the notion that the tea ceremony was 'a means of acquiring manners,' was fostered by female educators. This stands in contrast to the discourse in which the nationalistic male intellectual elite engaged during the same period, viewing the tea ceremony as 'art' equivalent to Western art. These two discourses reflect the differing social roles women and men of the era were expected to play: those of guardians of traditional culture in domestic space and promoters of westernization in public space, respectively.

One can argue that the tea ceremony is innately a means of acquiring manners, though this is not its *only*, or even primary, function.[3] It is built around strict rules of body movement called *temae*. *Temae* govern every act and posture of a practitioner, even to the movement and position of a single finger. For example, when one is scooping powdered green tea from the container, one's back should be straight, both elbows akimbo, and the fingers of the hand holding the scoop should be centered on the handle. In addition, *temae* include various body movements that are not directly related to making tea. When entering the room, for example, the host opens the sliding door, bows to the guests, and steps into the room in a certain posture. Then s/he enters the room in a prescribed manner: the feet glide silently over the tatami mats, the toes slightly raised occasionally, carefully avoiding the edges of the mats.

It is widely accepted today that the very germ of *temae* was sown by wealthy merchants in the sixteenth century, during the Warring States period (1467-1568), when they established the ceremony itself. Merchants initiated the practice of making tea in the presence of guests, and, in addition, constructed small rooms exclusively for gathering over tea, where the host and his guests sat close to each other. This performance-like tea-making in a confined space is supposed to have led to the development of refined body movements, which were later formalized as *temae*.[4] Thus, the birth of the tea ceremony is synonymous with the birth of *temae*.

The practice of the tea ceremony soon spread to the *samurai*. Both merchants and *samurai* used the tea ceremony for multiple purposes: as opportunities to socialize, for business discussions (or battle strategy), and to demonstrate their dignity in a public setting. Since neither of these groups belonged to the aristocracy, it can be assumed that a crucial motive for their practice of the tea ceremony was a desire to acquire refined manners, thereby achieving elevated status.

By the middle of the Edo period (1603-1867), there had been a dramatic increase in tea ceremony practitioners, especially among the merchant class, and *temae* were further elaborated and systematized. Although a large and wealthy middle class had been established during this period of peaceful rule, merchants remained at the bottom of the government-sanctioned, warrior-centric class system. These social restrictions made cultural activities such as the tea ceremony, flower arrangement (*ikebana*), calligraphy, and traditional music and dance especially attractive to the merchants; through these activities they could bypass their lowly status by gaining esteem sometimes superceding that of people more elevated in the social hierarchy.[5]

In the case of the tea ceremony, achievement depended first of all on the acquisition of *temae*. As so many merchants were eager to learn *temae*, the Sen family, descendants of the sixteenth-century merchant considered to be the founder of the tea ceremony, restructured the pedagogical methods previously used in teaching the practice of the tea ceremony; they selected old *temae* and created new *temae*, establishing drills for pupils to follow.[6] These drills were expanded by the head of the Sen family in the aftermath of the feudal era, post 1867.[7]

Let us now turn to the question of when and why the tea ceremony as a means of acquiring manners became so closely associated with women. During the feudal era, opportunities for women to participate in the tea ceremony were severely limited.[8] Some aristocratic women, female servants for high-ranking samurai, and *tayû* (professional entertainers for high-class men) were among those few women who are supposed to have practiced the tea ceremony in the middle of the Edo period.[9] This is not surprising given that a warrior-centered society had dominated since the early twelfth century; even if non-warriors shared in certain aspects of the culture, it was difficult for women to insert themselves into what was clearly male territory.

In the late Edo period, however, some upper-middle-class young women studied the tea ceremony at temples, many of which served as schools for commoners, or with private tutors.[10] Often taught by female teachers, the tea ceremony by and for women began to develop as a genre in its own right. Although women's tea ceremony did not have official discourses (at least no texts survive), one can assume that it was opened to young women to teach them the manners associated with femininity and domesticity, in keeping with prevailing notions of woman's role as a compliant wife and daughter-in-law for her husband and his parents. Such ideals of femininity and domesticity are clearly delineated in *Onna daigaku* (The Great Learning For Women), a manual of ethics and proper behavior supposedly written in the middle of the Edo period and used for young women's education at home or at temple-schools.[11] The manual instructs its readers to '[sew], and prepare meals for your parents-in-law. Fold clothes, sweep the floor, raise children and clean yourself for your husband. Stay at home. You shall not go out casually.'[12]

After the Meiji Restoration ended the shogunate, the new government (1868-1912) promoted the modernization and westernization of Japan.[13]

Consequently, traditional Japanese culture, including the tea ceremony, came to be despised as obsolete and ineffectual, and suffered a great loss of practitioners. Women's tea ceremony, however, was introduced into official 'etiquette' (*sahô*) courses in some girls' schools established in the aftermath of the 1872 Education Law.[14]   The founders of the girls' schools were often female educators, as were the teachers of the tea ceremony at the schools. It is true that women's education did not actually take hold for the first three decades of the post-feudal period.[15]   It is also true that the majority of etiquette courses taught at the girls' schools did not include study of the tea ceremony.[16] Yet the documentation of some schools' efforts indicates that *temae* gained official status as etiquette, especially for women, in the new institutions of the Meiji era.

In Kyoto prefecture in 1872, the year the local government tried unsuccessfully to levy an 'amusement tax' on the Sen family,[17] the tea ceremony was introduced to the curriculum of a newly founded girls' school that later became a school run by the prefecture.[18]   The principal of the school was a female educator, Nîjima Yaeko, and the teacher of the tea ceremony course was Shinjôin, the mother of the headmaster of the Sen family school.[19] To compensate for the great loss of (male) pupils after the Meiji Restoration, the Sen family had opened its doors to women.

More than a few girls' schools followed this pattern over the next decades. In some cases the tea ceremony was a substitute for an etiquette course, as happened at the Atomi-Gakuen Girls' School in Tokyo, while in other cases it was incorporated into the etiquette course. At Kazoku Jogakkô in Tokyo, the tea ceremony was juxtaposed with *ryûrei* (propriety sitting on Western chairs), *zarei* (propriety sitting on tatami mats), and flower arrangement, under the general course title of 'learning propriety' (*shûrei*).[20]

That the educators valued the tea ceremony as a cultivator of 'manners' is clearly articulated in the following statement by Atomi Kakei, who founded Atomi-Gakuen Girls' School in 1875: 'These days girls' schools teach manners, which pupils do not seem to utilize in their daily lives. I think the tea ceremony is better than manners.' She attributes this idea to her belief that tea ceremony practitioners know where in the room to sit as guests, how to sit, and how to manage utensils properly.[21]   Okuda Shôzô, a male educator and the principal of Seikei Girls' High School in Tokyo around 1920, realized his long-time wish 'to educate young women with Zen Buddhism and the tea ceremony.' In his book *Chami* (Tea taste), he claimed that the tea ceremony should refine the mind 'through learning the correct way of hosting guests and of conducting harmonious conversation.'[22]   Here it seems that his objective of educating young women in the practice of the tea ceremony was to teach them to be proper hostesses.

These discourses contrast with another popular discourse relating to the tea ceremony promulgated by the intellectual elite around the turn of the century. The new nationalism that emerged following Japan's victories in the

Sino-Japanese War (1894-1895) and the Russo-Japanese War (1904-1905) led to the championing of traditional culture as art, equal in stature to Western art. One of the earliest examples of this trend was the internationally acclaimed educator Nitobe Inazo's reference to the tea ceremony as 'fine art' in his 1899 English book on *bushido* or the ethical code of the ruling *samurai* class.[23] Nitobe's discussion of the tea ceremony in this wider context was followed by discussion specifically devoted to the tea ceremony itself by Okakura Kakuzo, an art critic and curator at the Boston Museum of Fine Arts. In *The Book of Tea* published in English in 1906, Okakura not only defined the tea ceremony as 'a religion of aestheticism' and 'a cult founded on the adoration of the beautiful,' but also devoted a chapter to 'Art Appreciation,' describing the tea ceremony as one example of art within that chapter.[24] At that time, 'art' (*geijutsu*) itself was a concept newly imported from the West.[25]

In Japan, *The Book of Tea* had a great influence on the intellectual elite, fostering the perception of the tea ceremony in general as art, and tea utensils specifically as works of art.[26] In 1929, the year that the Japanese translation of *The Book of Tea* appeared, Takahashi Tatsuo, an academic, defined the tea ceremony as a 'synthetic art of utensils (*dôgu no sôgô geijutsu*).'[27] He suggested that tea utensils were 'works of fine art' (*bijutsuteki sakuhin*), and that the tea ceremony, which coordinated and utilized these works of fine art, was therefore itself art.

The idea that tea utensils were works of art was echoed by many of the new industrialists. In the years following the Meiji Restoration, when traditional Japanese culture had lost its everyday currency, these businessmen had collected antiques, including tea utensils. For these collectors, tea utensils, although sold at low prices immediately after the Restoration, symbolized the wealth of the feudal regime and functioned as emblems of their owners' new social standing in the modern era.[28] In response to growing public criticism of their extravagant lifestyle, some industrialists defended their antique collecting as a means of protecting Japanese 'art' from Western collectors.[29]

The discourse characterizing the tea ceremony as art was maintained among men but not among women. In the same way, the discourse characterizing the tea ceremony as manners was maintained among women but was not adopted by men. I claim that there were three reasons for this gender-based dichotomous acceptance of the two discourses.

First, if the tea ceremony constituted art because tea utensils were deemed to be works of art, only men had the economic power to acquire these works of art, while women continued to be socially and economically subservient to men. According to the 1898 Meiji Civil Law, which established a patriarchal state based on husband-centered households, the wife had no jurisdiction over her own property. As *Minpô seigi*, a commentary on the Civil Law's first draft, put it, '[t]he husband's rights are to rule the whole economy of the household. The wife's property affects her husband, her children, and the household's rise and fall. Therefore the wife's property is to be managed [by the husband].'[30] In addition, the government slogan of 'good wife and wise mother' (*ryôsai kenbo*) encouraged women to marry and fulfill this ideal.[31] Thus, subject to both the husband-centered law and a national discourse emphasizing marriage and motherhood as the fulfillment of feminine ideals, women in the Meiji period were unlikely to have the economic power necessary to purchase and appreciate works of art.[32]

The second reason can be sought in the gender-based dichotomy that developed in this period between the public/western/masculine and the domestic/ Japanese/ feminine. On the national level, when westernization took place, public space was the first domain to be westernized, while domestic space was the last. A textbook of manners used at a girls' high school in 1937, seven decades after the Meiji Restoration, still presented a picture of a woman in kimono, sitting on tatami, bending slightly, handing gloves to a man in a western suit standing in the doorway. The picture delivered a clear message: public space, into which the man is about to enter, is western space, while inside the house, where the woman remains in kimono sitting on tatami, is Japanese space. And as men became promoters of westernization, that which was designated as 'public' and 'western' came to be associated with masculinity. 'Art,' a concept newly imported from the West, was considered part of this masculine realm. That which was considered 'domestic' and Japanese was associated with the feminine realm.

Furthermore, with the rise of nationalism, men were urged to 'publicly' champion Japanese culture on the international level using Western concepts in general as intellectual weapons in a manner analogous to the use of Western armaments in international wars. Meanwhile, women were expected to guard the nation's culture 'domestically' in two senses: within the homeland as well as within the household. As repeatedly maintained in ethics (*shûshin*) textbooks used in girls' high schools from the late nineteenth to the early twentieth century, societal expectations dictated that 'Men's place is out (*soto*), women's place is in (*uchi*).' One textbook published in 1907 expanded this principle to the international level: 'For women's duty is to manage *uchi*, those who are not the master of the household should rarely go out to interact with others, *let alone with foreigners*.'[33] In the same textbook, discussing the necessity of fighting against foreign countries 'in an emergency,' the author claims: 'although women cannot join the war like men...they can fulfill their duty by managing the household...removing all the worries about domestic matters from their husbands' minds....'[34] Clearly, the gender-based dichotomous acceptance of the discourses regarding the tea ceremony was dictated by the social roles played by men and women on both national and international levels. The tea ceremony for men was defined as 'art' in Japan's strategic rivalry with the West, whereas the tea ceremony for women was associated with domesticity and daily activities.

The third reason for the development of these two separate discourses can be located in the widely accepted dichotomy between 'mind,' associated with men, and 'body,' associated with women, that scholars such as Susan Bordo trace in Western intellectual history as well.[35]   Although the Meiji government educated women, the overriding purpose in doing so was to make them good housekeepers. Therefore, the school curriculum for girls included domestic training, while boys not only lacked such training but instead had more hours of abstract studies such as math or natural science.[36] Moreover, prior to the Meiji Restoration, women were taught that they were intellectually inferior to men and that their designated role was that of bearing children.[37] In this milieu, it is not unnatural that the majority of the intellectual elite at the turn of the twentieth century, as well as female students themselves, believed that women could not, need not, and should not rationally or metaphysically understand the tea ceremony because reason was designated a male domain. Rather, the refinement of movement and practical manners were deemed much more beneficial to women in their future roles in the home.

As outlined above, the discourse centering on the tea ceremony that characterized it as a means of acquiring manners for women developed in response to trends of westernization and nationalism in late-nineteenth and early-twentieth-century Japan. Women's engagement in the tea ceremony, however, was not merely a case of passive acceptance. In fact, the active nature of their involvement from the Meiji era to the present has been demonstrated by their growing dominance of the teaching profession over this period.

According to the records of Urasenke, one of the branches of the Sen family, women made up a third of the participants in the summer seminar held by the family in 1913 to teach *temae* at the advanced level; in 1920, the ratio increased to one half. The decision by the Sen family in 1914 that the seminar should award the license for teaching the tea ceremony to any woman wishing to teach it at girls' high schools must have increased the number of female participants.[38] Another factor that may have contributed to this increase is that teaching the tea ceremony became socially accepted as a women's occupation around this time, especially for war widows.[39] In any case, the number of female tea ceremony practitioners is supposed to have surpassed that of male practitioners in the early twentieth century. By mid-century, the number of women participating in the tea ceremony, both as pupils and as teachers, overwhelmed that of men. According to the son of a high-ranking tea ceremony teacher in Tokyo, interviewed in 1998, twenty-nine of the thirty pupils his father taught immediately prior to World War II, all teachers themselves, were women.

The transmission of 'manners' from woman to woman implies a certain empowerment of women. As Jorge Arditi suggests regarding American women's etiquette literature which came to be written by women themselves in the late nineteenth century, 'the group defined as "other" [gave] expression to its own, however constructed, specificities within the newly opened space.'[40] Embedded in these male-female, public-domestic, (economically) dominant-subservient, and mind-body dichotomies, the reproduction of set movements gives women the power to control and possess, to some degree, their own bodies. In addition, as teachers, women are enabled to assert authority over other women and to acquire economic power from the income generated through tuition fees.

The '*temae* as women's manners' discourse continued to attract women even after World War II, despite the decline in government promotion of westernization and nationalism. In the postwar era, the (male) intellectual elite created a new discourse focused on the tea ceremony: that the tea ceremony was a 'synthetic cultural system' (*sôgô bunka taikei*) and that '*temae* as manners' was only one of many aspects of the tea ceremony.[41] Nonetheless, '*temae* as women's manners' has continued to be perpetuated by and for women, as is typified by a series of etiquette books for women written by a female tea ceremony teacher from the Sen family, Shiotsuki Yaeko. Shiotsuki's 1973 textbook, for example, *Wakai-hito no tame no sadô no hon* (The book of the tea ceremony for young people), shows abundant pictures of young women in kimono, but none of young men. In the introduction, titled "*Nichijô seikatsu ni ikiru chanoyu no sahô*" (Manners of the tea ceremony in daily life), she writes, 'When you visit somebody's home ... you may sometimes notice the serenity...and elegance of movement of the hostess.... Am I favoring my position too much if I conclude that such an attitude reflects, without exception, her mastery of the tea ceremony?' Thus, the '*temae* as women's manners' discourse coexists with other discourses that discursively and tangibly inform the practices of Japanese women today.

Acknowledgements

I am grateful to Professor Tanaka Hidetaka for detailed bibliographic information, and to Meg Taylor for her useful suggestions.

Notes

All translations are mine, unless otherwise noted.

[1]   According to the 1996 survey by the Statistics Bureau of Management and Coordination Agency, 2,365,000 (a little more than 90 percent) of 2,626,000 tea ceremony practitioners are women. Although these figures do not represent the total number of tea ceremony practitioners, the male-female ratio of this subset reflects the overall situation to a great extent. Obtaining accurate data on tea ceremony practitioners is difficult for two reasons. First, there are several schools of tea ceremony, each with its own licensing system. Despite this, many practice the tea ceremony without such licenses while licensed teachers are not necessarily active practitioners. Second, as is typical of all the traditional arts in Japan, the tea ceremony schools maintain a certain level of secrecy and do not publish data on their practitioners.

[2]   Westernization as a movement involved the introduction into Japanese society of political,

3   judicial, economic, and educational systems from the West. See note 13 below.
    That the tea ceremony is not only a means for refining manners but also, and more essentially, a means of *discipline* will be established in my dissertation, *Body-Representing the Past: Japanese Women and the Tea Ceremony after World War II* (forthcoming).

4   Isao Kumakura, *Chanoyu no rekishi: Sen Rikyû made* (The history of the tea ceremony to Sen Rikyû) (Tokyo: Asahi Shimbunsha, 1990), 222; Sen'o Tanaka, *Cha no bi: Nihonjin ni totte 'cha' wa naze bi na no ka?* (Beauty of tea: Why is the tea ceremony beauty for the Japanese?) (Tokyo: Asahi Sonorama, 1976), 184-86.

5   Matsunosuke Nishiyama, *Iemoto no kenkyû* (Studies on the *iemoto*) (Tokyo: Yoshikawa Kôbunkan, 1952, 1982), 135, 141, 468, 519.

6   Nishiyama, *Iemoto no kenkyû*, 429-32. While little is known of these methods prior to the restructuring carried out by the Sen family, it is thought that the selection of *temae* taught was left to the discretion of each teacher.

7   Isao Kumakura, *Kindai sadô-shi no kenkyû* (Study of the history of the tea ceremony in modern times) (Tokyo: Nihon Hôsô Shuppankai, 1980), 114-16.

8   The scarcity of philological findings prior to 1868 on tea ceremony practice by women suggests, along with the marginality of the topic in the studies of the tea ceremony, that women did not officially participate in the tea ceremony. According to Yabunouchi school records, only twenty-five of its 1,578 recruits between 1802 and 1879 were women; if we limit the question only to the Edo period (that is, before 1868), the number of female recruits was only fifteen of 1,384 (Matsunosuke Nishiyama, *Iemoto monogatari* [The tale of the *iemoto*] [Tokyo: Shuei-shuppan, 1971], 353). In the mid-eighteenth century, Fuhaku, the head of a tea ceremony school, forbade women to attend the tea ceremony in his five prohibitions (Nishiyama, *Iemoto no kenkyû*, 400-1).

9   Nishiyama 1998, personal communication; Machiko Kagotani, *Josei to chanoyu* (Women and the tea ceremony) (Kyoto: Tankôsha, 1985).

10   Kagotani, 176, 209; Haruo Shirane and Tomi Suzuki, eds., *Sôzô sareta koten* (The invented classics) (Tokyo: Shinyôsha, 1999), 410.

11   Shizuko Koyama, *Ryôsai kenbo to iu kihan* (Standards of 'the good wife and wise mother') (Tokyo: Keisô Shobô, 1991), 19.

12   Hokudo Hirahara, ed. *Shinchû: Onna-daigaku* (The Great Learning for women) (Kyoto: Bunka-jihôsha, 1943), 26.

13   The Meiji Restoration was a time of drastic social change, during which political power passed from the shogun back to the emperor, the feudal rank system was banned, and the new government sought to create a nation-state to compete with the West. The Meiji government introduced political, judicial, economic, and educational systems from the West under the slogan of *wakon yâsai*, 'Japanese spirit, Western knowledge.'

14   Before the 1868 Meiji Restoration, education varied greatly according to class and gender. The 1872 Education Law, however, declared the necessity of education regardless of gender or former feudal rank. Yet girls' education continued to emphasize domestic training, as it had in the feudal era.

15   In 1892, twenty years after the enactment of the Education Law, only 37 percent of girls attended elementary schools, as opposed to 72 percent of boys. It was after 1899 that women's education was promoted on the state level as befitting future wives and mothers (Koyama, 41-2).

16   In the Meiji era, the term *sahô* (etiquette) usually referred to the manners associated with Ogasawara, a venerable samurai family that was recognized as a model of propriety by the shogunate. 'Ogasawara's Manners,' introduced to girls' schools after the Meiji Restoration, however, were often in fact the invention of Edo townspeople (*Ogasawara-ryû reihô* [Ogasawara's manners] website, 1999, available at http:// www.ogasawararyu-reihou.gr.jp).

17   The head (*iemoto*) of Urasenke submitted a written protest to the Kyoto government in which he argued that the tea ceremony inculcated Confucian values and was therefore beneficial to society and not merely 'entertainment' (Kumakura, *Kindai sadô-shi no*

kenkyû, 114-16).

18   Kumakura, *Kindai sadô-shi no kenkyû*, 116; Hiroichi Tsutsui, '*Kindai no josei chajin*' (Modern female tea masters), in *Kindai no sukisha: zoku chajin-den* (Modern tea lovers, second series). Special Issue, No. 23 (Kyoto: Tankôsha, 1997), 104.

19   Tsutsui, 104.

20   Kumakura, *Kindai sadô-shi no kenkyû*, 298-304. The association of the tea ceremony with domesticity in general is exemplified by the curriculum of Kyôritsu Joshi Shokugyô Gakkô in Tokyo, which included the tea ceremony with cooking and sewing under the name of 'domestic training program.'

21   Kumakura, *Kindai sadô-shi no kenkyû*, 299-300.

22   Kumakura, *Kindai sadô-shi no kenkyû*, 303.

23   Inazo Nitobe, *Bushido: The Soul of Japan* (1899; reprint, New York: Putnam, 1905), 57. Nitobe's reference to the tea ceremony as 'art,' which is often overshadowed by references to Okakura's book published seven years later, is noted in Hidetaka Tanaka, '*Sadô no kigôka to Shôwa yo-nen*' (The tea ceremony as a sign and the fourth year of Showa), *Tokugawa Rinsei-shi Kenkyûjo, Kenkyû kiyô* 26 (March 1992): 200; and by the same author in '*Sadô bunkaron no kôzô*' (Cultural theories on the tea ceremony), in *Sadô-gaku taikei* (Studies on the tea ceremony), vol. 1, edited by Sen Sôshitsu. (Kyoto: Tankôsha, 1999), 139-40, 142.

24   Kakuzo Okakura, *The Book of Tea* (1906; reprint, Tokyo: Charles E. Tuttle, 1956), 3.

25   The earlier meaning of the word *geijutsu* included 'studies' (*gakugei*) and 'skills in aesthetic activities or entertainment' (*gijutsu*). In the Meiji era, *geijutsu* came to be used as the translation for 'art' in the Western sense, that is, creative work or its principles (Noriaki Kitazawa, *Me no shinden:"Bijutsu" juyô hen'yô-shi nôto* [The temple for eyes: The history of introducing 'art'], Tokyo: Bijutsu Shuppan, 1989, 146-7; Tanaka, '*Sadô bunkaron no kôzô*,' 151).

26   Tanaka (*Sadô no kigôka to Shôwa yo-nen*) discusses this theme thoroughly.

27   Tanaka, '*Sadô bunkaron no kôzô*,' 148.

28   Kumakura, *Kindai sadô-shi no kenkyû*, 164, 193, 247.

29   Christine M.E. Guth, *Art, Tea, and Industry: Masuda Takashi and the Mitsui Circle* (Princeton: Princeton University Press, 1993), 161-2; Tanaka '*Sadô bunkaron no kôzô*,' 142-3.

30   Noriyo Hayakawa, *Kindai tennôsei kokka to jendâ* (Modern imperialist state and gender) (Tokyo: Aoki Shoten, 1998), 157.

31   'Good wife and wise mother' was officially promulgated by the Ministry of Education in 1899. The objective of the slogan was to promote the education of women as future wives and mothers who would contribute to the state by supporting their husbands and raising future citizens. (Koyama, 45-7, 49.) The slogan was both a product and a promotion of nationalism.

32   The Meiji Civil Law was replaced by new democratic laws only in 1947.

33   Tetsujiro Inoue, *Teisei: joshi shûshin kyôkasho* (Ethics textbook for girls), vol. 3 (1907) in *Kôtô jogakkô shiryô shûsei* (Collected materials on girls' high school), vol. 10 (Tokyo: Ozorasha, 1989), 67; emphasis added.

34   Inoue, 18.

35   Susan Bordo, *Unbearable Weight: Feminism, Western Culture, and the Body* (Berkeley: University of California Press, 1993), 2-5.

36   See the comparison between the 1901 national regulations for girls' and boys' secondary schools in Koyama, 50-1.

37   *Onna daigaku*, for example, argues, 'For women are more stupid than men, they do not know how to manage the things before their very eyes' and 'Women who do not bear children should leave their husbands. This is because marriage should bring offspring who succeed [the family]' (Hokudo Hirahara, 29, 12).

38   Kumakura, *Kindai sadô-shi no kenkyû*, 303.

39   Matsunosuke Nishiyama, *Iemoto no kenkyû*, 146.

40   Jorge Arditi, 'The Feminization of Etiquette Literature: Foucault, Mechanisms of Social

Change, and the Paradoxes of Empowerment,' *Sociological Perspectives* 39, no. 3 (1996): 431.

41 The 'synthetic cultural system' discourse was introduced by Hisamatsu Shin'ichi, a professor of Buddhist philosophy, in 1947 (Shin'ichi Hisamatsu, *'Sadô-bunka no seikaku* [Characteristics of the culture of the tea ceremony] [1947; reprint in *Sadô no tetsugaku* (Philosophy of the tea ceremony), ed. Jikai Fujiyoshi (Tokyo: Kodan-sha, 1987)], 52).

PART III

Si(gh)ting the Woman as Cultural Resource

11 Portrait Medals of Vittoria Colonna: Representing the Learned Woman

Marjorie Och

In the following pages, the author explores ways in which a particular type of portrait image — the portrait medal — offered more than a genre of self presentation to the Renaissance men and women, in particular, who situated themselves within their cultures by its means. This essay argues that the portrait medal provided a forum wherein its subject might speak through a language of symbols and texts. This visual and literary language was recognizable to both public and private audiences, and was seen and read while the woman was, herself, absent. As described here, such portrait images literally created an environment for women humanists through an iconography firmly siting the female subject within the traditionally male humanist paradigm.

The end of the fifteenth century witnessed a proliferation of small, privately commissioned medals that carried portraits of both men and women.[1] Along with the portrait, each medal was inscribed with a brief and often cryptic text and image referring to the person whose face was portrayed. Women were described according to their family positions as daughters or wives, or were celebrated for their beauty and virtues. For men, however, medals referred to their public positions, occupations, and honors; for example, many of these medals depicted the Renaissance humanist in his classicizing setting and garb. It was into this largely male domain that learned women began to make an appearance. As objects that could stand in for a woman's actual presence, medals were powerful emblems in the creation of an audience, both male and female, for women humanists. The intricate familial and social relationships that existed between the persons depicted and the various audiences addressed by the medals highlights the humanist community created through the documented exchange of medals. I will consider here how portrait medals of a particular literary woman, Vittoria Colonna (circa 1490-1547), poet, Catholic reformer, friend and confidant of Michelangelo, functioned within this humanist context (figs. 1-2, 4-5).[2] Colonna's iconography, placed within contemporary visual and literary traditions, may be read to discover how this woman, and perhaps others, defined and placed herself within the larger community of (male) humanists.

The low cost of commissioning these small objects relative to that of other works (painted portraits, for example), perhaps helped to make medals far more accessible to a greater number of individuals, particularly to women whose financial independence in the sixteenth century was seldom secure. Indeed, the number of early-sixteenth-century medals representing women suggests that they did find this art especially responsive to their increasing presence in the world of letters. With respect to their relative economy, medals were similar to printed books, which were now far less expensive to produce or purchase than were manuscripts. Medals resembled printed books in another manner — in the possibility they presented of making numerous impressions of one image or text. Furthermore, it is likely that both media — medals and early printed books — shared the same humanist audience. And this context, I believe, offers a key to understanding how the portrait medal was used by Vittoria Colonna.

There are a number of issues to be explored concerning the portrait medals of Colonna. Here I will focus on the visual and literary traditions within which this sitter actively placed herself and was placed by artists. An examination of these medals within these traditions allows for an interpretation of what defined Colonna's visual appearance for her sixteenth-century humanist audience. Moreover, it is important to consider what personal characteristics of an individual, actual or imagined, enable his or her depicted likeness to be recognized by various audiences.

There are at least six different medal types representing two distinct periods in Colonna's life, the time between her marriage in 1509 and the death of her husband in 1525, and the period between the death of her husband and her own death in 1547. Although they remain undated and unattributed to any artist or workshop, on the basis of style and iconography, I believe that all of these medals may be dated to the period from around 1510 to the early 1540s. They are small objects, all roughly two inches in diameter, intended for a close, private examination, and they function as personal self-expressions laden with material for an iconographical study.[3] These medals are, I believe, among the most personal works of art that can be associated with Colonna. Traditionally, none of the medals depicting Colonna is thought to have been commissioned by her, perhaps because scholars have concentrated on Colonna's literary and religious activities while regarding her involvement in the visual arts as limited to her relationship with Michelangelo.[4] However, the iconographic parallels among Colonna's medals, her life, and her poetry suggest that the medals may be considered as much a product of her thought and agency as her poetry.[5] The medals allow access to an individual who was highly placed within Roman noble families of the early sixteenth century, whose marriage alliance with a Neapolitan family brought her politically onto the international stage, and whose early interests in Catholic reform were known to every pro- and anti-reformer within the papal curia.

These images may be referred to as secure identifications of Colonna not because they necessarily present a verifiable likeness, but because of their self-declarations as likenesses through the inscriptions surrounding Colonna's profile on each of them.[6]   Are we to understand these portraits as 'true likenesses?' Probably not — they are either too idealized or too abbreviated. For her sixteenth-century audience, recognition of these images as portrait evocations was possible because of the combined effects of Colonna's personal iconography and imagery from established visual and literary sources to which the medals made reference. As portraits, they depended upon visual and literary traditions familiar to both artist and humanist communities, and these traditions defined the sitter's appearance and made recognition possible.

In what is perhaps the earliest of the medals, Vittoria and her husband, Ferrante Francesco d'Avalos, are depicted on the obverse and verso (Fig. 11.1a). Vittoria is draped in classicizing dress, one breast exposed, with hair styled all'antica; to the right of her forehead is a star. Ferrante appears as a warrior, helmeted and wearing a breastplate. The Latin inscriptions translate as follows: 'Vittoria Colonna d'Avalos,' and 'Ferrante Francesco d'Avalos, Marchese of Pescara, Great Commander.' A second medal carries a similar profile of Colonna paired with classicizing elements that probably refer to her husband's military exploits; this obverse is decorated with a laurel-like wreath surrounding the figures (Fig. 11.1b).   In the center is a trophy, at left, a crowned, female allegorical figure, a possible reference to the Holy Roman Empire, and at right, a winged Victory holding a shield and a cross.[7]   In spirit, these are similar to their ancient Roman sources, such as coins pairing the bust of a woman with military trophies from a conquered province, or the pairing of emperor and empress. A third medal carries a profile almost identical to that in the first two, but differs in the looser depiction of the hair, in the accentuation of the distinctive topknot, the covering of Colonna's breasts, and the absence of a star at her forehead; the verso is blank (Fig. 11.2).

These medals may be read, in part, as biographical accounts. After their marriage in 1509, Ferrante became a celebrated military leader in the Imperial army of Charles V, and the medals may have been presented to the Emperor at the time of this service. Vittoria became the focus of the court at Ischia, where she and Ferrante had lived for several years with his aunts. The Ischian court was renowned for its literary and artistic patronage; Vittoria, however, was more than patron, she was a poet, and became increasingly devoted to this art. Her poetry of this early period focused on her love for Ferrante, whom she glorified as husband, lover, and military hero. The capture and imprisonment of her husband and of her father, Fabrizio Colonna, in 1512, after the Battle of Ravenna, resulted in a literary outpouring from Vittoria, the *Epistola a Ferrante Francesco D'Avalos suo consorte nella rota di Ravenna.*[8] The work inaugurated a theme reiterated in Colonna's poetry and prose for many years, the glorification of her husband. The Epistola begins with a lament, and develops into a dialogue between Colonna, the suffering wife, and her absent lover.[9]   These early medals represent the first stage of Colonna's public presentation, and on the basis of their iconography may be dated to between 1510 and 1525. The iconography symbolizes Colonna as she was known to her contemporaries prior to her husband's death: that is, as the wife of a military hero, evoking the image of an Amazon with her bared breast, and as a poet.

The representation of Colonna as poet that we have here is more symbol than portrait. In the fifteenth and sixteenth centuries, numerous medals of poets were struck. Overwhelmingly, they commemorate male poets who are shown wearing laurel crowns, the attribute of the poet.[10]   This attribute was not utilized here. Indeed, to depict a female poet in the early sixteenth century was artistically problematic — there was no visual pattern for an artist to follow. For the depiction of Colonna, this artist solved the problem by turning to the most famous painting of poets of the early sixteenth century, Raphael's 'Parnassus' of around 1510 in the Stanza della Segnatura of the Vatican: specifically, to the figure of Sappho, immediately to the left of the window opening (Fig. 11.3). The poet Sappho is the only female figure on Parnassus crowned with laurel; to secure her identity, however, Raphael painted her holding in her left hand a scroll on which her name is inscribed. She was the only poet he pictured with such a name card, as though it had been difficult, even for Raphael, to visualize a female poet, and for his audience to recognize one.[11]   Both Sappho , as portrayed by Raphael , and Colonna, by her medallist, are shown in profile, with bodies turned toward the viewer, and both are depicted wearing the topknot of hair. Colonna, however, is not shown wearing a laurel wreath, although she wears what appears to be a braid, as if to draw our attention to the absence of laurel.

It is simple enough for an artist, in this case the medallist, to fashion a sitter, such as Colonna, after a famous image of a female poet. Certainly, Raphael's frescoes in the Stanze were well known, and their motifs easily accessible. But was this a case of mere visual borrowing? This reference to Raphael's Sappho was, rather, an acknowledgment of Colonna's literary indebtedness, which defined her appearance and asserted her status as a poet. This visual connection is supported by contemporary literary references to Colonna on Ischia as Sappho on Parnassus.

Colonna's reputation as both a poet and a literary patron was well established by 1519 when the poet Girolamo Britonio (born before 1491 to circa 1549) praised her style. Britonio made the further claim that Colonna's poetry had come 'from Parnassus,' a possible allusion to her mountainous island home of Ischia to which poets from throughout Italy were invited.[12]   In a sonnet of the same period, though published some years later, Pietro Gravina (circa 1453-1528) referred to Colonna's court at Ischia as a new Parnassus.[13] The connection between Vittoria Colonna and Sappho was made by Ludovico

Beccadelli even more strongly the year Colonna died. In his lament on the death of Pietro Bembo, who also died in 1547, Beccadelli described Colonna as another Sappho.[14] Indeed, Colonna's place among the poets and muses on Parnassus was one which she, herself, had initiated in her early sonnets treating the amorous exploits of Apollo and other gods.

The year 1525 marked a dramatic shift in Colonna's life, and we can see this shift in the medals. At the age of thirty-five, she became a widow, and a widow she remained until her death twenty-two years later, in 1547. Colonna's grief was so great that she desired to take the veil and enter a convent, though ultimately forbidden to do so by a decree of Pope Clement VII.[15] From around 1526 until around 1534, Colonna spent most of her time in Naples or Ischia within the d'Avalos court. Letters from this period suggest that she was an active member of court with an interest in architectural and charitable projects.[16] Indeed, her life from this point on was directed by her religious fervor. Christian themes came to dominate her poetry, but true to sixteenth-century Christian humanism and to her earlier literary interests, this was a Christianity infused with variations of classical tales. She completed a body of work referred to today as the 'Secular Sonnets.'[17] Here, Colonna presented herself as a lover separated from her beloved by the physical world. This separation caused her suffering, but through her suffering she realized that she would ultimately be reunited with her beloved, a theme she explored in the Epistola of 1512.[18] Such Neoplatonism informed not only her poetry but her visual iconography, as well.

There are two medal types that recall these years. Each depicts Colonna wearing the traditional widow's veil. In one, Colonna is shown wearing a simple dress and veil (Fig. 11.4a). The verso is inscribed with the story of the devoted, star-crossed lovers Pyramus and Thisbe, the Romeo and Juliet of classical mythology.[19] In both stories, the union of true lovers is possible only through the death of both, an allusion to Vittoria's longed-for reunion with Ferrante. The inscription on the Pyramus and Thisbe medal, which translates as 'Vittoria Colonna d'Avalos, Marchesa of Pescara,' further connects Colonna to her husband through his title.[20] This inscription paired with the Pyramus and Thisbe legend emphasizes Colonna's role as wife in mourning. This medal parallels, as well, the desire she expressed in her poetry for her own death, and her longing to be reunited with Ferrante.[21]

The second of these medals shows Colonna wearing a slightly more elaborate costume (Fig. 11.4b). Here, Colonna's portrait is surrounded by the words 'D Victoria Columna.' No aristocratic title is included in this inscription, nor is there any reference to Colonna's husband except through her characterization as a widow. The image on the reverse, framed by a laurel wreath, shows the phoenix rising from flames toward the sun, a Neoplatonic reference to the soul transcending the mortal world of suffering. This combination of phoenix, inscription, and laurel wreath suggests a reference to

Colonna the poet; the 'D' in the inscription may be an abbreviation for 'Diva' or 'Divina,' referring to Colonna's literary accomplishments.[22]

In her poetry from around 1530, Colonna gave voice to her new self, even comparing her present thoughts about death and salvation with her concerns of earlier days. She even wrote of turning her back on Parnassus, for it was no longer her home.[23] This turning away from Parnassus is apparent in the iconography of her medals. The later medals marked a second stage in the visual fashioning of Colonna's public self, and referred to her new status as a widow. With this event, Colonna's visual and literary iconography shifted from poet on Parnassus to pious widow. To find a visual vocabulary for the depiction of a widow posed no artistic problem — a veil similar to that of contemporary nuns could signal to the viewer the woman's marital status. Furthermore, there were readily available contemporary medallic portraits of such women. Colonna's medals showing her as a widow are similar to Giancristoforo Romano's 1507 medal of Isabella of Aragon, the widow of Giangaleazzo Maria Sforza.[24] These portrait medals are characterized by a truncated bust-length profile portrait of a woman in modest contemporary dress; both women wear the widow's veil. The costume assures recognition of Colonna as the dutiful wife and faithful widow.

From around 1534 until her death, Colonna spent a great deal of time in Rome, and it is likely that yet another medal dates from this period (fig. 5). Colonna's return to her own family is represented here in the emblematic column, the symbol of the Colonna. The column is superimposed upon a tree whose roots and leaves are depicted in detail; the enigmatic Latin inscription, 'Huic animus similis,' translates as 'a soul similar to this one,' suggesting to the humanist viewer a likeness of mind between the viewer and Colonna, whose spirit is evoked by the column sprouting what may be a laurel tree.[25] The 1530s and 1540s were difficult years for the Colonna in Rome. The family's involvement in the 1526 attack on the city and in the Sack of the following year, as well as their strained relations with Pope Paul III Farnese, resulted in their political weakening at this time. Their properties in and around the city were confiscated by the papacy, and from 1541 the family was exiled from Rome. Vittoria Colonna, whose periodic visits to the city throughout this time can be documented, worked to build and maintain a Colonna presence in Rome through her patronage of religious orders.[26] It is likely that this medal represents Vittoria's efforts to stand in for the Colonna in Rome.

Colonna's medals exhibit a passion, both literary and visual, for references to the ancient world. Indeed, they are strong evidence that she was inspired by antiquity in the type of object she commissioned. The poet medals are especially similar to their ancient Roman sources in their pairing of the portraits of wife and husband, or of a portrait with a symbolic image; even with regard to size they are similar to their ancient prototypes. Furthermore, the all'antica quality of the Colonna/Sappho medals suggests that they were directly inspired by ancient examples, and were thus intended to be part of a medallic *uomini famosi* of contemporary persons.[27]

When viewed as part of early sixteenth-century courtly and humanist life, the medals suggest something of Colonna's interest in self-representation. All are symbolic of her commitment to the humanist tradition of which her poetry partakes. If Colonna accepted her role as a poet from Parnassus, as suggested in her poetry and in that of her contemporaries, her appearance on a medal all'antica , as Sappho, suggests that she may well have considered herself within the humanist tradition of the recovery of ancient texts, perhaps even in the aspiration that proliferated among her learned contemporaries to surpass the achievements of antiquity. Indeed, the early medals may even participate in the sixteenth-century debate concerning language and style. In Roman humanist circles, 'Vittoria Colonna as Raphael's Sappho' would have had special resonance. As Martha McCrory has shown in her studies of the collecting interests of the Medici Grand Dukes, ancient coins and medals were valued as both commentary on and clarification of ancient texts.[28] 'Vittoria Colonna as Sappho' may have directed viewers and readers not only to a particular understanding of Colonna, but to an understanding of Sappho through Colonna.

While none of the medals depicting Colonna have been attributed to her patronage, references they contain to Colonna's life and poetry suggest that the medals were products of her agency. Indeed, Colonna's own reference in her poetry to Parnassus rather than to Lesbos, a Parnassus here associated with Sappho rather than with Apollo, indicates that Colonna identified herself as a woman among men, even projecting her work and image into the male domain of humanism. The widow medals, too, parallel what is known of Colonna's life after 1525: her relationship to her deceased husband is alluded to through the classical story of Pyramus and Thisbe, and her own salvation is depicted through the neoplatonic metaphor of the phoenix.[29] Finally, her courageous return to the Colonna household in Rome is celebrated in what must have been a most unwelcome sign to opponents, the symbolic column, which here daringly asserts a Colonna d'Avalos, and hence imperial, presence with its beckoning to 'a soul similar to this one.' Indeed, it seems unlikely that someone other than Vittoria Colonna herself would have commissioned multiple copies of at least six different medals, all of which have been shown here to be such personal expressions. Documentary evidence for Colonna's patronage appears in her correspondence.

On 25 July 1532, Pietro Bembo responded to a letter from Colonna. Although Colonna's letter no longer survives, its contents can be gleaned from Bembo's response. He wrote that he wished to satisfy Colonna's desire for his 'imagine dipinta,' his 'painted likeness.' In fact, he had already thought of giving her a medal of him, but this had been left unfinished at the death of the artist he had commissioned to produce it. Bembo added that he would like her portrait in return.[30] On 2 July 1533, Bembo again wrote to Colonna thanking her for the 'imagine' she had sent him.[31] Bembo declared that this 'caro dono' ('precious gift') did not seem to be 'una figura dipinta,' so similar was it to Colonna herself.[32] It was Colonna who had initiated this exchange of portraits. The gift of portraits among friends was not uncommon in humanist circles, and the surprising number of Colonna's medals that survives suggests that they found a receptive audience. Such gifts were similar in purpose to letter-writing and to the exchange of sonnets, as significant tokens of friendship and physical manifestations of this bond. In this regard, Colonna may be seen as having participated in what Sir John Pope-Hennessey described as a humanist 'cult of friendship' that emphasized such exchanges.[33]

It is possible to detect something of the power of portraiture for Colonna and her contemporaries in Francisco de Hollanda's *Four Dialogues on Painting*.[34] Here, Hollanda records Colonna's comments on portraiture.

> "And what of the way in which [painting] makes present to us...noble deeds.... It transmits memory of the living to those who come after them.... And not only does the noble art of painting do all this but it sets before our eyes the likeness of any great man, whom on account of his deeds we desire to see and know; and likewise, the beauty of an unknown woman many leagues distant.... It prolongs for many years the life of one who dies, since his painted likeness remains; it consoles the widow, who sees the portrait of her dead husband daily before her; and the orphan children, when they grow up, are glad to have the presence and likeness of their father and are afraid to shame him."
> Here, the Signora Marchesa paused, almost in tears....[35]

According to Hollanda's account, a 'painted likeness,' and we might add the portrait medal, is a visual experience for the soul, the mind, and the heart. Here, a portrait assists the viewer with more than memory, it becomes an experience and creates a community for individuals separated by time and distance.

In these examples, 'likeness to subject' may be assessed more in relation to the subject's activity than to the depiction of the subject's physical features. Whether Colonna actually resembled any of the depicted women on the medals was less important than the fact that her audience, her humanist community, would have recognized her through her placement within specific pictorial and literary traditions that defined her occupations — as wife and widow, poet and humanist. Fame was important to Vittoria Colonna, and apparently so was the way in which that fame was manifested.

What do these medals really mean? What purpose did they serve? Their size and Janus-like quality require that they be held and looked at very closely, and those with versos are touched and turned. This emphasizes their private nature, as though they were meditations meaningful to but a few persons. Colonna's public for these was a very select group of friends — humanist friends who exchanged letters, sonnets, and portraits.   In this respect, medals were similar in purpose to letter-writing — they presented the recipient with something of oneself, in this case, an image of one's likeness, even a self-commentary.   But I would like to suggest that, in a more public arena, these medals quite literally stood in for Colonna — they represented Colonna in the public and predominantly male world of humanism.   While it was clearly Colonna's writings that created her reputation as a poet, Catholic reformer, and humanist, it was the medals, her symbolic portraits, that projected her presence into this public sphere.

Notes

1. On Renaissance medals, see Cornelius von Fabriczy, *Medals of the Italian Renaissance*, trans. Mrs. Gustavus W. Hamilton (London: Duckworth and Co., 1904); Sir George Francis Hill, *Medals of the Italian Renaissance* (Oxford: Clarendon Press, 1920); and especially Stephen K. Scher et al., *The Currency of Fame: Portrait Medals of the Renaissance* (New York: Harry N. Abrams, Inc., 1994).

2. The medals are most legible in engravings from a nineteenth-century publication of Colonna's poetry. Pietro Ercole Visconti, *Le rime di Vittoria Colonna corrette su i testi a penna pubblicate con la vita della medesima* (Rome: Salviucci, 1840).

3. For a brief discussion of the medals see Sylvia Ferino-Pagden, 'Vittoria Colonna im Portrait,' in *Vittoria Colonna, Dichterin und Muse Michelangelos*, ed. Sylvia Ferino-Pagden (Vienna: Kunsthistorisches Museum and Skira, 1997), 108-47.

4. Colonna's presence in art history is dominated by speculation about her friendship with Michelangelo. However, this friendship occurred in the final decade of Colonna's life, that is, from around 1536. The years before 1536 have, until recently, been almost entirely ignored by art historians, suggesting that Colonna's interests in the arts were not noteworthy until she met Michelangelo.

5. For a discussion of the interrelationship between Colonna's life and poetry, see Marcia Weston Brown, 'Vittoria Colonna, Gaspara Stampa and Louise Labé: Their Contribution to the Development of the Renaissance Sonnet' (Ph.D. diss., New York University, 1991).

6. There are numerous references to these images as true portraits in nineteenth- and twentieth-century literature on Colonna. Michael Hirst has referred to a medal in Vienna as 'the finest record of Vittoria Colonna,' and has used this as the image against which to compare painted portraits that have been associated with Colonna. Michael Hirst, *Sebastiano del Piombo* (Oxford: Oxford University Press, 1981), 117, n. 119. Colonna's medals are not alone in being used as a mirror of true appearance. The dependence on medals as evidence of a sitter's likeness is a notion that was strongly advocated in the Renaissance. Ancient coins and contemporary medals were collected in the sixteenth century as a source of historical portraiture. Coins and medals continue to be collected and studied by twentieth-century scholars who insist on the mimetic veracity of medals. See J. Graham Pollard, 'The Italian Renaissance Medal: Collecting and Connoisseurship,' in *Italian Medals*, 161-69, for a brief history of major collections and collectors' interests.

7. Sir George F. Hill calls the seated female figure 'Italy.' He has identified the head on the shield carried by the Victory as that of Medusa. See his *A Corpus of Italian Medals of the Renaissance before Cellini*, vol. 1 (London: British Museum, 1930), 299; see also vol. 2, pl. 192, no. 1154.

8. Written in 1512, the *Epistola* was first published in 1536 in Fabricio Luna's *Vocabulario di cinque mila vocabuli toschi*, Naples.

9. Both the lament and dialogue forms are traditional to classical literature and Petrarchan verse, the foundation of Colonna's humanist education. See Dennis J. McAuliffe, 'Vittoria

Colonna, Her Formative Years (1492-1525) as a Basis for an Analysis of Her Poetry' (Ph.D. diss., New York University, 1978), 59-61.

[10] See the illustrations in George F. Hill and Graham Pollard, *Renaissance Medals from the Samuel H. Kress Collection at the National Gallery of Art* (London: Phaidon Press, 1967), numbers 299, 300, and 301. On portraits of Dante and Boccaccio, see Victoria Kirkham, 'Portraits of Boccaccio: Renaissance Portraits,' in *Boccaccio visualizzato II*, ed. Vittore Branca (Florence: Sansoni Editore, 1987), 284-305; see also Jonathan Nelson, 'Dante Portraits in Sixteenth-Century Florence,' *Gazette des Beaux-Arts* 120 (1992): 59-77.

[11] In Raphael's drawing for the figure of Sappho (British Museum, London), the poet is not wearing a laurel wreath, which may suggest that this drawing, or a similar drawing, may have been a source for Colonna's medallist. See D. A. Brown, *Raphael and America* (Washington, D. C.: National Gallery of Art, 1983), 172, pl. 16.

[12] Girolamo Britonio di Sicignano, *Opera Volgare, intitolata Gelosia del Sole* (Naples: Sigismondo Mair, 1519).

[13] Girolamo Britonio, *Opera* (Venice: Sessa, 1531).

[14] Quoted in Ermanno Ferrero and Giuseppe Müller, *Carteggio* (Turin: Ermanno Loescher, 1892), 367.

[15] Alfred Reumont, *Vittoria Colonna, fede, vita e poesia nel secolo XVI*, eds. Giuseppe Müller and Ermanno Ferrero (Turin: Ermanno Loescher, 1892), 88-9.

[16] See the letter from Pope Clement VII of 5 May 1526, permitting Colonna to build and decorate a chapel within the Naples *palazzo*; Ferrero and Müller, *Carteggio*, XXVII, 38-9. See also P. Igino da Alatri, 'Fede e opere nella vita di Vittoria Colonna,' *L'Italia Francescana* 21 (1946): 207-18.

[17] See the edition of Vittoria Colonna's *Rime* compiled by Alan Bullock (Rome and Bari: G. Laterza, 1982).

[18] See McAuliffe.

[19] Ovid, *The Metamorphoses*, trans. Horace Gregory (New York: Mentor, 1960), Book 4, 113-16.

[20] Colonna continued to sign her name to letters and documents as 'Marchesa di Pescara'; even after her death, it was as 'Marchesa di Pescara' that she was known.

[21] McAuliffe, 59-68.

[22] The epithet 'Divine' was given to artists as early as 1282. See the sources cited by David Cast, 'Liberty : Virtue : Honor : A Comment on the Position of the Visual Arts in the Renaissance,' *Yale Italian Studies* 1 (1977): 394-5, n. 33. DIVA or DIVUS is not uncommon on sixteenth-century medals.

[23] 'Although my chaste love for a long time held / my soul desirous of fame, living like a serpent / in my breast, now, weeping, my soul languishes, / turned toward the Lord from whom comes its cure. / May those holy nails henceforth be my quills, / may the precious blood be my undiluted ink, / the sacred, bloodless body be my writing paper, / so that I may inscribe, within, what he suffered. / It is useless to invoke Parnassus or Delos here, / for I aspire to other water, to other mountains / tend, where human foot does not climb by itself. / That Sun who illuminates the elements and the sky, / I pray that, when he reveals his clear fountain, / He offers me drink equal to my great thirst.' Translation in Joseph Gibaldi, 'Child, Woman, and Poet: Vittoria Colonna,' in *Women Writers of the Renaissance and Reformation*, ed. Katharina M. Wilson (Athens and London: The University of Georgia Press, 1987), 39.

[24] This medal is in the Kunsthistorisches Museum, Vienna. For illustrations, see Hill and Pollard, Appendix, numbers 73a and 77.

[25] Sir George F. Hill has called the tree a 'laurel branch'; see Hill, *Corpus*, 299.

[26] Marjorie Och, 'Vittoria Colonna: Art Patronage and Religious Reform in Sixteenth-Century Rome' (PhD diss., Bryn Mawr College, 1993).

[27] Even the abridged arm and torso present Colonna as if an ancient statue, reminiscent of a contemporary medal of Bramante. I am indebted to Eunice Howe for bringing this comparison to my attention. See Luke Syson in Scher et al., cat. no. 33.

[28] Martha A. McCrory, 'Domenico Compagni: Roman Medallist and Antiquities Dealer of the Cinquecento,' in Pollard, *Italian Medals*, 115-29.

[29] See especially McAuliffe, 7-58.

[30] Ferrero and Müller, *Carteggio*, LII, 79-81.

[31] Ferrero and Müller, *Carteggio*, LVIII, 88.

[32] There are further references to portraits of Colonna and of others that she gave as gifts to her friends. Giovanni Guidiccioni (1500-1541), Bishop of Fossombrone, expected to receive Colonna's portrait; see the reference in Ferrero and Müller, *Carteggio*, 378, to Guidiccioni's *Lettere* (Venice, 1780), 146. This letter is translated in Domenico Campanari, *Ritratto di Vittoria Colonna, Marchesa di Pescara, dipinto da Michelangelo Buonarotti, illustrato e posseduto da Domenico Campanari*, trans. Henrietta Bowles (London: P. Rolandi and C. Molini, 1850), 9.

[33] Pope-Hennessey identified a 'cult of friendship' in the correspondence of Erasmus, Sir Thomas More, and Petrus Aegidius. Sir John Pope-Hennessey, *The Portrait in the Renaissance*, (Princeton, NJ: Princeton University Press, 1963), 92-6.

[34] The reliability of Hollanda's account of Colonna's conversations with Michelangelo in 1538-39 is an important and necessary question to consider, but not the issue here. Colonna's comments, as recorded by Hollanda, may be taken as characteristic of her time, place, and status.

[35] Francisco de Hollanda, *Four Dialogues*, trans. Aubrey F. G. Bell (Lisbon, 1548; Oxford: Oxford University Press, 1928), 25-6.

Figure 11.1a   (Top) Italian, Medal of Vittoria Colonna (recto; left) and Ferrante
Francesco d'Avalos (verso; right).   16th century.

Figure 11.1b   (Bottom) Italian, Medal of Vittoria Colonna (recto; left) with classicizing
military trophies (verso; right). 16th century.

Figure 11.2   Italian, Medal of Vittoria Colonna. 16th century.

Figure 11.3   *Raphael, Parnassus (detail). Fresco, 1511. Stanza della Segnatura, Vatican Palace.*

Figure 11.4a   *(Top) Italian, Medal of Vittoria Colonna (recto; left) with Pyramus and Thisbe (verso; right). 16ᵗʰ century.*

Figure 11.4b   *(Bottom) Italian, Medal of Vittoria Colonna (recto; left) with phoenix (verso; right). 16ᵗʰ century.*

Figure 11.5   *Italian, Medal of Vittoria Colonna (recto; left) with column and tree (verso; right). 16ᵗʰ century.*

12 Si(gh)ting the Mistress of the House: Anne Clifford and Architectural Space

Elizabeth V. Chew

Using architectural patronage and autobiographical writing, Anne Clifford consciously made herself both a site and a 'sight' of culture. Because she was forced to wait for forty years to assume her position as head of the Clifford estates in northern England, she chose architectural patronage, specifically the renovation and publicly- staged reuse of six medieval castles, as a means through which to create visible signs of her control. At the same time, she maintained extensive written records of her activities, through which she valorized and minutely described her own achievements in refurbishing and reoccupying the centuries-old family residences. Using Clifford's writings and her own examinations of the architectural plans, the author of this essay shows that by reclaiming and inhabiting a site while exhaustively documenting her actions therein, Clifford asserted a female place in the family's dynastic tradition, thereby reshaping it for her own benefit.

Anne Clifford (1590-1676) — Dowager Countess of Dorset, Pembroke, and Montgomery, Baroness Clifford, Westmorland and Vesey, hereditary high sheriff of the county of Westmorland, and Lady of the Honor of Skipton in Craven — spent the last thirty-three of her eighty-six years as a substantial landowner in the counties of Westmorland and Yorkshire in northwestern England and as the heiress to one of the great northern English dynasties of the Middle Ages (Fig. 12.1).[1] An ardent architectural patron and family historian, she restored and inhabited six ancestral Norman castles (Appleby, Brougham, Brough, Pendragon, Skipton, and Barden), renovated numerous churches, and erected public buildings and commemorative and funerary monuments. These achievements of her old age, however, were hard-won. Upon his death in 1605, Clifford's father, George, third Earl of Cumberland, disinherited her, despite the jurisdiction of an entail (dating from the reign of Edward VI) that protected female heirs and despite the fact that she was his only surviving child.

From the time of her father's death in 1605, when she was fifteen, until 1643, Clifford — first with her mother, Margaret Russell Clifford, Countess of

Cumberland, and later alone — fought persistently in all the legal channels open to her for the restoration of the inheritance.[2] In her quest, she operated independently of her two prominent husbands, Richard Sackville, third Earl of Dorset (married 1609-24), and Philip Herbert, fourth Earl of Pembroke (married 1630-50), and vociferously rejected their efforts and those of King James I to convince her to acquiesce to unfavorable legal decisions. She finally achieved victory through attrition, inheriting the property in 1643 at age fifty-three when her first cousin, to whom the properties had passed, died without a male heir. In 1649, at the end of the Civil War, Clifford left the Earl of Pembroke, from whom she was already estranged, and moved north to her ancestral lands. She remained there until her death in 1676.[3]

This essay examines Clifford's use of her restored medieval castles. It demonstrates that the architecture of the castles and her autobiographical writings about them reveal her fierce determination to bind herself and her progeny to the legacy of her eminent family. As an heiress who had fought long to assume her lands, as a major architectural patron, and as an aristocratic woman reusing medieval houses in the middle of the seventeenth century, Clifford understood her houses as both family monuments and viable domestic spaces in which she performed her long-coveted role of head of the family. I will show that by simultaneously assuming the roles of participant and observer — by occupying a house while exhaustively documenting her actions therein — Clifford asserted her place in the family's dynastic tradition and reshaped it for her own benefit. In her houses, the floor plans that traditionally functioned to place visitors in a position of deference to the master of the house also demonstrated to her circle and to Clifford herself that she was mistress.

This investigation will show that Clifford's actions as an architectural patron alter our picture of early modern domestic architecture in Britain and its uses. In a society in which architectural success entailed competition with one's social peers and superiors to build the largest, grandest, or most innovative house, Clifford eschewed all contemporary models for claiming distinction. She chose instead to be consciously anachronistic, adapting medieval buildings because of their importance as witnesses to past glories of the house of Clifford or to specific events in her own life. In looking to the medieval past instead of to current fashion to inform the present and future, Clifford alters our perception of the available options for producing spaces that had resonance for seventeenth-century patrons and audiences.[4]

The Writings

Anne Clifford is better known today as an autobiographical writer than as a litigant or architectural patron. Her works comprise one of the most extensive existing bodies of writing by an early modern Englishwoman. In addition to a number of letters, three different genres of works survive: personal diaries, condensed yearly chronicles, and family histories. Lady Cumberland, Clifford's mother, began the family histories by collecting family genealogy as evidence for Anne's rights to her father's properties. Clifford eventually hired professional scribes to produce multiple copies of her massive three-volume compilation of this material entitled *The Great Books of the Clifford Family*. Each set included family genealogies going back to the twelfth century, lives of her parents, and an autobiography from her conception to the year 1650, written or dictated in 1652-3.[5] Clifford believed that she and her mother had proved her claims to the family titles and properties through painstaking genealogical research; the *Great Books* were intended to present and preserve the evidence.

Katherine Acheson's deductions about the relationships among the different types of texts suggest the extent to which Clifford consciously strove to document her place in her family's history and to preserve her version of that story for posterity.[6] Acheson speculates that Clifford initially kept diaries and from them generated the annual chronicles, condensed summaries of the highlights of her year, later putting away or even discarding the diaries. She then used the chronicles as the basis for her autobiography. Clifford's texts should be understood as vehicles consciously created to transmit the story of her victories and achievements to the next generation, while placing them in the context of the family history.

Like her texts, Clifford's buildings were also intended to remain when she was dead as testaments to the glories of the Clifford family and to her specific achievements as a self-made female landowner. The 1650-75 chronicles contain rich and heretofore under-utilized references to architecture and to her building projects in the north, particularly to her specific use and understanding of her houses. The chronicles make it clear that architectural space enabled Clifford to both understand and manipulate her position. Viewing her writing and building endeavors as parallel activities, I will consider how Clifford produced a space, both narrative and concrete, for herself and her achievements.[7]

Assuming Her Northern Estates

Clifford's six castles would have signified to her, in the seventeenth century, a glorious era in her family's past. Castles had been built in England since the ninth century, but the Norman invasion of 1066 resulted in widespread construction as the Normans strove to hold their new territory.[8] Among the line of strongholds established along the Eden Valley were the oldest castles of Clifford's inheritance, Appleby and Brough, first built early in the twelfth century and granted by King John to her ancestor Robert de Vipont in 1204.[9]

When Clifford assumed the role of keeper of her castles, she inherited complex physical and social structures in varying states of repair, which were, and for centuries had been, domestic forts, venerable residences, and the administrative and cultural centers of the surrounding areas (Fig. 12.2).[10] The new role involved far more for Clifford than just legal ownership; it meant inhabiting the structures, touring them regularly, and maintaining and improving them by repairing the damage of time and war.

It is obvious that her architectural heritage was of the utmost importance to her, for almost as soon as she arrived in the north in July 1649, Clifford began an ambitious program of building and renovation at the castles, and also at local churches and other civic buildings. Clifford's efforts created habitable domiciles for herself and her successors out of structures that had been neglected, in some cases for centuries. In taking on a series of restoration projects of such magnitude, she was not merely behaving as her uncle and father, as Earls of Cumberland, had before her, but radically reclaiming, improving, and reinhabiting ancient properties for herself.

She first mentioned her ongoing building work in her yearly chronicle for 1650, emphasizing the 'disorder' of her properties and the pleasure she obtained from improving matters:

> I enjoyed my selfe in Building and Reparacons at Skipton and Barden Tower, and in Causeing the Boundaries to be ridden, and my Howses kept in my severall Manners in Craven, and in those kind of Countrie Affairs about my estate. Which I found in extreme Disorder by reason it had bene so long kept from mee, from the death of my Father till this time, and by occasion of the late Civil Warres in England.[11]

The riding of the boundaries in particular would have been an overt statement of her assumption of control over the 'disorderly' situation. In 1651 she began repairs at Appleby and Brougham Castles 'to make them habitable as I could, though Brougham was verie ruinous.'[12] She also asserted early on her understanding of *noblesse oblige* by establishing her own charitable institution and continuing one founded by her mother; she constructed St. Anne's Hospital, a women's almshouse at Appleby, and maintained an almshouse erected by her mother at Beamsley in Yorkshire.[13]

Clifford continued her building and restoration for twelve years, noting in her chronicles her works at a number of castles, churches, and civic buildings including the Church of St. Lawrence in Appleby, where she commissioned funerary monuments for her mother and herself in order to insure that they would persevere in the memories of the local inhabitants. Clifford's steward Gabriel Vincent oversaw her building works, residing at whichever castle was currently under repair. The account books indicate that Clifford maintained a heavy personal involvement, down to her examination and approval of all expenditures on building.[14] George Sedgwick, Clifford's secretary from 1652 to 1668, estimated that she spent the great sum of £40,000 on building projects.[15]

'The Lands of Mine Inheritance'

In her annual chronicles for 1650-75, Clifford explicitly connected her use of her houses with her role as the sole heir, propagator, and historian of her distinguished family. She meticulously recorded how much time she spent at each of her residences, the exact dates and sequences of her movements between them, visits from her two daughters and many grandchildren and great-grandchildren, how much time had elapsed since the visitor's last visit, which house she occupied when family births, deaths, and marriages occurred, and which events in the lives of her parents had also taken place at those houses. She also recorded her building and renovation activities, both familial and charitable, and her civic duty of hosting the judges for the annual assizes at Appleby.

Clifford's words suggest that she saw quite specific connections among her own life; her land and houses, as the physical and material aspects of her inheritance; the history of her family, with which she was intimately familiar; and the promise of its continuance in the hands of her progeny. Beyond the security of her titles and the knowledge that she had claimed her properties and made the dwellings habitable again, it was extremely important for her to experience the estates physically and in relation both to past events and to living family members and future descendants. She did this by spatially connecting her occupation of the castles with past events in the history of the family and with time spent in the castles earlier in her life, and by seeing and enjoying her family on her estates. She strove to create links between her existence in Westmorland and Craven and her families' in London and elsewhere.[16]

Moving Around

In addition to her preoccupation with the movements and lodgings of her offspring, Clifford carefully documented her own. The transfer of her household from one residence to another, undertaken two or three times a year, became an event of particular ritual significance to Clifford. For the last nine and a half years of her life, beginning in 1666, she described her procession through architectural spaces during these moves as thoroughly as she did her overland journeys between the castles, and in a manner which implies that the particular rooms and their sequences bore great and growing consequence.[17] These writings provide the most complete evidence of the connections Clifford understood among physical spaces, their meanings for the past and future of her family, and her assumption of control of them.

Between April 1666 and October 1675 Clifford described twenty-one moves among her six homes. These household moves were large undertakings, redolent of medieval practice. An account book entry for an earlier move from Brougham to Appleby in August 1665 gives an idea of the size of her train. She paid inhabitants of Brougham and surrounding hamlets for carriage of four wagons, twenty-six carts drawn with two horses, and five single carts; inhabitants of Appleby for fourteen cart loads; and inhabitants near Appleby for seven cartloads.[18] She was accompanied on each move by a large retinue that she referred to as her 'family,' comprised of her household staff and groups of local gentry, other neighbors, and tenants; she would dismiss anyone not residing with her upon her safe entry of the house that was her destination.[19]

In adopting an essentially nomadic existence in Westmorland and Craven, Clifford emulated her medieval ancestors whose proprietorship of the family estates had figured so prominently in her own struggle for control. Her method of dividing her time among all of her houses also confirms Mark Girouard's characterization of the medieval household on the move as 'a tortoise without a shell.'[20]   As shells, Clifford's six houses stood empty upon her assuming the family mantle, bearing certain fixed characteristics and redolent of past occupants, but ready to be filled and directed to meet the needs of the present. After her departure from Barden Tower in July 1667, Clifford chose to avoid the longer journey to Craven and to limit her traveling to the country around her four more closely spaced houses in Westmorland, since by 1667 she was seventy-seven years old. In the following discussion, I will concentrate on Appleby Castle, for which Clifford provided the most detail.

Appleby Castle and Rituals of Ownership

Perhaps because of its antiquity in structure and in terms of Clifford family history, Appleby Castle was particularly well suited as a setting in which Anne Clifford might enact her role as landowner. Her writings include repeated, almost ritual expressions of that belief, showing that site and space, but not furnishings or other interior embellishments, comprised a visual manifestation of ownership and control. This is in direct contrast to the writings of another seventeenth-century Englishwoman who wrote about architecture, the tourist Celia Fiennes, who, in journal entries about visits to numerous castles and stately homes throughout England from 1682 to around 1712, noted not architectural spaces but their ornamentations, features more traditionally seen as 'womanly' concerns. Where Clifford focused on sequences of named rooms, Fiennes the tourist recorded family portraits, velvet upholstery, and painted wainscoting.[21]   When she visited Dover Castle, of comparable age and structure to Clifford's houses, Fiennes again noted its lack of contents, the 'spoyl'd' character of the place, with 'the floores taken up and the wainscoting pulled down.'[22]   Although Fiennes and Clifford recorded their observations about buildings for distinctly different reasons, it seems clear that Clifford would never have shared Fiennes' interests in interiors.

Appleby Castle, a curtain-wall castle with a keep that Clifford referred to as 'ye most auncient seat of myne inheritance,' is located to the southeast of the town of Appleby, the Westmorland county-seat, on a steep cliff over the River Eden (Fig. 12.3).[23]   Appleby's development from a twelfth-century defensive structure to an early modern residence conforms to that of other similar houses, such as Langley Castle (Northumberland). [24]   With Clifford's restorations, Appleby's four-story Norman keep, no longer needed for defensive purposes, became additional lodgings, while the curtain wall continued to shelter the domestic range at its east end.   On the interior of the domestic block, suites of rooms seem to have been arranged both horizontally along the curtain wall and vertically in the towers.

In October 1669 Clifford moved from Appleby to Brough.   She described her movements as she left Appleby Castle: 'Coming out of my own chamber there I pass'd through the great chamber and went into the Chappell and through the Hall, took my litter at the Hall Door in the Court, so passing through the Towne of Appleby over the Bridge and Sandford Moore, went through Warcop Towne into the sayd Brough Castle.'[25]   Such descriptions recur regularly throughout the period 1666 to 1675.   In early August of 1670, Clifford moved her household back to Appleby from Pendragon, where she had moved from Brough in May.   In her summary of her activities of that year, she recorded her route as she left Pendragon and entered Appleby:

> So as we now went within sight of Wharton Hall, Brough Castle, and Harley Castle and through Wateby and Soulby and over Soul by Mask to my said Castle of Appleby safe and well (I thank God) where I alighted in the Court and came through the Hall, the Chapel, the Great Chamber, the Withdrawing Room (in every of which places I stayed a while to see them) and so up into my owne chamber in it where I formerly used to lie, and where I had not been since the 19th of October last.[26]

Clifford's description highlights the processional aspect of her movement, both through the house, and from town to town.   She describes the much shorter distance from the Great Chamber to the adjacent Chapel in the same way that she does the one between the towns of Waitby and Soulby, implying that she understood the household spaces to have a geographical significance.

In October 1670, when she left Appleby for Brougham Castle, some eleven miles distant, Clifford noted carefully her reverse movement through the rooms of Appleby and her overland route to Brougham:

> And the 14th of October, being Friday, about 9 or 10 a clock
> in the forenoon after I had lain in Appleby Castle ever since
> the 3rd of August last, that I came from Pendragon Castle
> thither, did I remove with my family from thence, coming
> through the Withdrawing Chamber and great chamber into
> the Chapel for a while, and so through the Hall, took my litter
> at the Hall door in the Court, in which I rid through the
> Towne of Appleby, over the Bridge and so through
> Crackenthorp, Kirby Thure, Temple Sowerby, Woodshide
> and by the Hartshorn Tree (which I look'd on for a while). I
> came safe and well I thank God into my Castle of Brougham
> in the same Countie about 3 a clock in the afternoon.[27]

Returning to Appleby from Brougham in August 1671, she passed through the towns of Temple Sowerby, Kirkby Thore, and Crackenthorpe, over the bridge, through the town of Appleby, and then 'went through ye Hall up into ye Chappell for a while and into the great chamber and so up ye greene staires and through ye Withdrawing Chamber into my owne chamber where I formerly used to lye and where I had not been since the sayd 14th October last, until now.'[28]

Her description of her return to Appleby in July 1673 is one of the most specific about the two staircases this journey involved. She 'came through the Hall and upstairs to ye Chappell, and great chamber, and from thence up ye green stairs and through ye Withdrawing Room into my owne chamber....'[29] Departing again for Pendragon in March 1674 she 'came down through the Withdrawing Chamber, great chamber and Hall into ye Court, where I went into my Horslitter....'[30]

The sequence of rooms described by Clifford at Appleby conforms to seventeenth-century expectations of progression through a great house, from the Great Hall to the bedchamber of the most important apartment.[31] The major difference in Clifford's case was the gender of the chief occupant. Through her processions, Clifford both demonstrated and documented her control of all of these spaces.

The residential part of Appleby Castle through which Clifford recorded the route of her processions dates from the fifteenth century and lies at the east side of the castle's curtain wall, away from the keep. Only the eastern portion of the current L-shaped structure existed in Clifford's time.[32] Plans of the currently existing structure published by the Royal Commission on Historical Monuments of England in 1936, examined in tandem with Clifford's descriptions of her routes, enable the speculative location of ground and first floor rooms during Clifford's tenure (Fig. 12.4). Clifford's writings indicate that upon arriving at Appleby each time she left her horse litter in the courtyard and entered the building through the Great Hall. She says that she then proceeded up some stairs, through the Chapel, and into the Great Chamber in the northeast tower. Next she climbed the 'green stairs' to the Withdrawing Room on a higher floor in the tower before her own chamber, which may have been either on the same level as the Withdrawing Room or above it. The 'Green Chamber,' where she reported being carried after fainting during a departure in January 1673, was located under the Withdrawing Room, as she tells us elsewhere in the chronicles, and thus was likely between the Great Chamber and the Green Stairs.[33]

Clifford's repeated descriptions of her entrances and exits at Appleby indicate her consciousness that her particular route from the door of the Great Hall to the bedchamber of the principal apartment identified her as the owner of the house. Having been mistress of two great houses — Knole in Kent where she lived with the Earl of Dorset and Wilton House in Wiltshire where she lived as Countess of Pembroke — as well as being familiar with every other house she occupied during her childhood, marriages, and first widowhood, Clifford would have understood how one's progression through a house related to one's status and gender. Clifford furthermore would have had a very good understanding of the number of rooms required in the house of a person of her stature, how large or small those rooms should be, and in what sequence the rooms should be arranged.

In the early modern period, the social choreography that aristocratic houses functioned to contain required very particular spatial delineations, based on rank and gender.[34] Every location on an estate and room in a house bore a particular specification as to who was or was not allowed to be there. Only the lord would have had unfettered access to every part of the house. Clifford entered Appleby Castle from the courtyard into the Great Hall, as had lords and their important visitors since the establishment of household ritual in the Middle Ages.[35] The Great Hall served as point of contact between the head of household and the house's public functions of entertainment and hospitality. There in the Middle Ages the lord and family would have sat for meals on a raised dais in view of all. The next room, the Great Chamber, through which Clifford's own rooms were located, was on the second floor above the dais end of the ground-floor Hall.[36] The Great Chamber evolved between the thirteenth and seventeenth centuries from a dining room for the lord once he stopped eating in the Hall into a private dining and reception room near the most important apartment in the house. Only a small portion of those received in the hall would have proceeded to the Great Chamber.[37] The important ceremonial processional route up a staircase from the Hall to the Great Chamber offered the head of household the opportunity to display to visitors fashionable or impressive interiors.

From the Great Chamber, Clifford gained access to her own apartment, which included a withdrawing room and bedchamber, and may have also included a closet.[38] Once again, access from the Great Chamber to the withdrawing room would have been limited to the (usually) male owner of the house and his selected following or important visitors. The principal apartment belonged to the head of the household, and by carefully controlling access to its innermost reaches, the owner could use the plan to place anyone else in a position of deference or subordination.

As a female head of household, Clifford occupied an unconventional and potentially transgressive position. Attaining this position had cost her much time, money, and trouble. As she had resisted being disinherited by her father and opposed by the king, Clifford again attempted to create her own position in which she could wield power and gain access to spaces usually reserved for men. Clifford's writings capture and document her processions through the house and her attainment of the spatial position of the owner in the central apartment. Like the processions themselves and the rooms through which they wove, her documents also proved to Clifford and to her retinue that she had assumed her rightful place. Clifford saw architecture not merely as a container for her actions, but as a crucial participant in her performance of the role of head of household.

For Clifford, it would seem, the re-assumption of her property upon each arrival was carried out both visually and spatially, as she reconnected with chambers resonant with family significance in a floor plan in which her own room was the ultimate destination. During her walk from the hall to the lord's bedchamber — her bedchamber — her clearest and strongest connections to her property and her very identity are spatially reasserted, under the gaze of her retinue and her own documentary impulse. She understood her position at Appleby through place, not through possessions. In leaving such extensive documentation of her movements at Appleby, she showed how use of the architectural plan constructed, demonstrated, and satisfied a female owner's sense of possession, connection, and power.

Acknowledgements

I would like to thank Helen Hills, Barbara Harris, and Carolyn Allmendinger for their invaluable comments on previous versions of this essay.

Notes

[1]   Clifford's lands were located in the modern-day counties of Cumbria and North Yorkshire.

[2]   Margaret Russell Clifford, Countess of Cumberland (1560-1616), was the youngest daughter of Francis Russell, 2nd Earl of Bedford, in whose household George Clifford had grown up.

[3]   Pembroke died in 1650.

[4]   Although she has not specifically discussed Clifford's writings about her use of architecture, Alice T. Friedman has argued that Clifford's choice of traditional styles in both architecture and painting distanced her from her contemporaries and 'conjur[ed] up an image of hereditary privilege in which the role of patriarch could be played by a woman.' See 'Constructing an Identity in Prose, Plaster and Paint: Lady Anne Clifford as Writer and Patron of the Arts,' in *Albion's Classicism: The Visual Arts in Britain, 1550-*

1660, ed. Lucy Gent (New Haven and London: Yale University Press, 1995) and 'Wife in the English Country House: Gender and the Meaning of Style in Early Modern England,' in *Women and Art in Early Modern Europe: Patrons, Collectors, and Connoisseurs*, ed. Cynthia Lawrence (University Park: Pennsylvania State University Press, 1997).

5   Three sets of *The Great Books* are still extant, two in the Cumbria Record Office, Kendal, and one in a private collection. For an excellent summary of all of Clifford's writings and the surviving manuscripts, see Katherine O. Acheson, ed., *The Diary of Anne Clifford 1616-1619: A Critical Edition* (New York and London: Garland, 1995), 14-29. The full title of the autobiography is *A Summary of the Records and a true memorial of the life of me the Lady Anne Clifford, who by birth being sole daughter and heir to my illustrious father, George Clifford, the 3rd Earl of Cumberland, by his virtuous wife Margaret Russell my mother, in right descent from him, and his long continued noble ancestors the Veteriponts, Cliffords, and Veseys, Baroness Clifford, Westmorland and Vesey, High Sheriffess of Westmorland, and Lady of the Honor of Skypton in Craven was by my first marriage Countess Dowager of Dorsett and by my second marriage Countess Dowager of Pembroke and Montgomery.* In *Writing Women in Jacobean England* (Cambridge, MA: Harvard University Press, 1993), Barbara Kiefer Lewalski misleadingly abbreviates the title of the autobiography as 'Life of Me,' which gives the document an anachronistically individualistic and modern sound, while Clifford's text is in keeping with the early modern concern for dynasty as the key to a sense of self. A 1737 copy of the autobiography, lives of her parents, and part of the genealogy is to be found in Harleian Mss. 6177 in the British Library and was published by J. P. Gilson as *Lives of the Lady Anne Clifford, Countess of Dorset, Pembroke, and Montogmery (1590-1676) and of Her Parents, Summarized by Herself* (London: The Roxburghe Club, 1916).

6   Acheson, 16-17. Acheson corrects previous editors and scholars who have failed to draw the important distinctions among Clifford's various types of writings.

7   For a fuller discussion of this entire topic, see Elizabeth V. Chew, 'Female Art Patronage and Collecting in Seventeenth-Century Britain' (Ph.D. diss., University of North Carolina, Chapel Hill, 2000), 35-110.

8   N. J. G. Pounds, *The Medieval Castle in England and Wales: A Social and Political History* (Cambridge: Cambridge University Press, 1990), 6-7.

9   Pounds, 43-4. See also W. Douglas Simpson, 'The Town and Castle of Appleby: A Morphological Study,' *Transactions of the Cumberland and Westmorland Antiquarian and Archaeological Society* [*CWAAS*] n.s., 49 (1949): 120 and Martin Holdgate, *A History of Appleby* (Appleby: Dalesman Books, 1982), 14-5. The Eden Valley is a strip of lowland between the Lake District and the Pennine mountains where Clifford's Westmorland castles are located.

10   Appleby, Brough, Brougham, and Pendragon are in Westmorland, part of modern-day Cumbria. Skipton and Barden are in the deanery of Craven, in the West Riding of Yorkshire.

11   D. J. H. Clifford, ed., *The Diaries of Lady Anne Clifford*, (Stroud, Gloucestershire: Sutton Publishing, 1990), 106 [hereafter *Diaries*].

12   *Diaries*, 110.

13   *Diaries*, 110, 116. On St. Anne's Hospital at Appleby, see E. Alexander Heelis, 'St. Anne's Hospital at Appleby,' *CWAAS* n.s., 9 (1909): 192-7. As Lena Orlin noted in her response to the session 'Women and Art in Early Modern Britain' at the North American Conference on British Studies, Colorado Springs, Colorado, October 16, 1998, almshouses are an important area for further investigation of women's building.

14   *Diaries*, 130, 138; Cumbria Record Office (CRO), Kendal, WD/Hoth/A988/17.

15   Sedgwick's now lost memoir is published in Joseph Nicolson and Richard Burn, *The History and Antiquities of the Counties of Westmorland and Cumberland* (London: W. Strachan and T. Cadell, 1777), 300.

16   Katharine Hodgkin discusses what she calls the 'land/family link' very briefly in 'The Diary of Anne Clifford: A Study of Class and Gender in the Seventeenth Century,'

History Workshop 19 (Spring 1985): 157-8, but does not consider the implications for
material culture of Clifford's extreme preoccupation with family, land, and space.

[17] Before April 1666, Clifford describes her moves in far less detail, only noting which
chamber she slept in, but not describing her routes through houses. See *Diaries*, 105-79.

[18] CRO, Kendal, WD/Hoth/A988/17. When she moved to Brough on 22 November 1665,
she paid for two wagon loads and twenty-three cartloads.

[19] For example, in her move from Appleby to Brougham on 14 October 1670, Clifford states
that she had been accompanied 'by several of the Gentrys of the Countie and my
Neighbors and Tenants both of Appleby, Brougham, and Penrith.' *Diaries*, 205.

[20] Mark Girouard, *Life in the English Country House: A Social and Architectural History*
(New Haven and London: Yale University Press, 1978), 14.

[21] Christopher Morris, ed., *The Illustrated Journeys of Celia Fiennes, 1685-c. 1712* (London
& Sydney: MacDonald & Co., 1982), 38.

[22] Morris, 122. In the late 1690s Fiennes visited the vicinity of Appleby and Kendal and
toured Lowther Hall, home of Clifford relatives, but did not visit any of Clifford's houses.
Clifford's only reference to interior furnishings in the chronicles comes in a brief 1666
account of a fire in a bedchamber at Brough. *Diaries*, 180.

[23] *Diaries*, 100. For a description of the location of the castle, see Simpson, 118. In a
curtain-wall castle, the buildings were enclosed by a stone wall, usually with defensive
towers at certain intervals. For a discussion of the development of castle architecture, see
N. J. G. Pounds, *The Medieval Castle in England and Wales: A Social and Political
History* (Cambridge: Cambridge University Press, 1990).

[24] Girouard, 66-7.

[25] *Diaries*, 200.

[26] *Diaries*, 204.

[27] *Diaries*, 205.

[28] *Diaries*, 209.

[29] *Diaries*, 219.

[30] *Diaries*, 221.

[31] Girouard, 40-59. Peter Thornton discusses the plan from the perspective of its use, in
Seventeenth-Century Interior Decoration in England, France & Holland (New Haven and
London: Yale University Press, 1978), 55-63. For discussion of the 'social geography of
the great house,' see also Felicity Heal, *Hospitality in Early Modern England* (Oxford:
Clarendon Press, 1990), 29-30.

[32] The existing façade of this block was added in 1686-88 by Clifford's grandson Thomas
Tufton, fourth Earl of Thanet, with stone brought from Brougham. Royal Commission on
Historical Monuments, England, *An Inventory of the Historical Monuments in
Westmorland* (London: His Majesty's Stationery Office, 1936), 8.

[33] The fainting episode is detailed in *Diaries*, 217. She describes the Green Chamber this
way in an earlier entry, in *Diaries*, 197.

[34] Most discussions of this issue to date have concentrated on social class or rank rather than
gender. See H. M. Baillie, 'Etiquette and the Planning of the State Apartments in Baroque
Palaces,' *Archaeologia* (1967): 169-99; Girouard; Thornton; Heal. Alice T. Friedman
considers the relationships between gender and the architectural plan in 'Architecture,
Authority, and the Female Gaze: Planning and Representation in the Early Modern
Country House,' *Assemblage* 18 (1992): 41-61. Patricia Waddy's work on Rome provides
a methodological model for consideration of the degree to which the roles of early modern
women and the architectural spaces they occupied shaped and reinforced one another. See
Waddy, *Seventeenth-Century Roman Palaces: Use and the Art of the Plan* (Cambridge,
MA: M.I.T. Press, 1990).

[35] Girouard, 53.

[36] Girouard, 51-2. At Appleby, the kitchens were located to the south of the Great Hall, so
the screens would have been at the south and the dais at the north.

[37] For the Great Chamber, see Girouard, 88-94.

[38] For the withdrawing room, see Girouard, 94-100.

Figure 12.1   *Unidentified artist after Sir Peter Lely, Anne Clifford, Countess of Pembroke. Oil on canvas, circa early 1670s.*

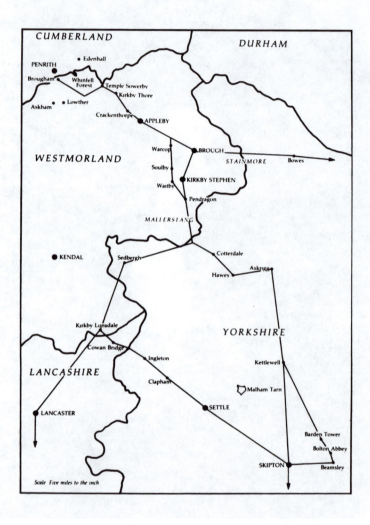

Figure 12.2   Map showing locations of Anne Clifford's castles and the routes she traveled between them.

Figure 12.3   Aerial view of Appleby Castle.

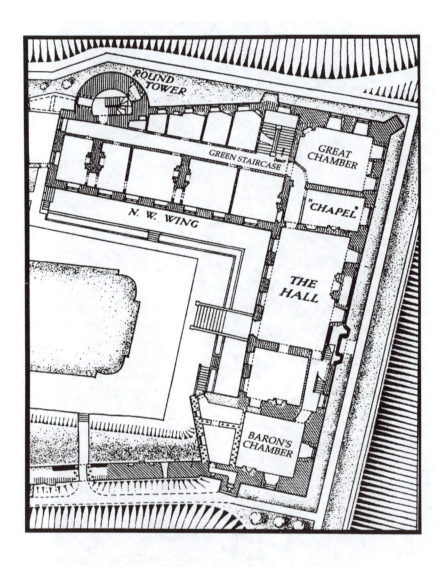

Figure 12.4   Speculative plan of Appleby Castle, circa 1670.

13 The 'Wild Woman' in the Culture of the Polish-Lithuanian Commonwealth

Lynn Lubamersky

The image of the wild woman was constructed in Polish culture from the sixteenth to the eighteenth century to provide a model of heroic, noble womanhood that would help perpetuate the power of the nobility to control the social, cultural, and economic life of the Commonwealth. The wild woman archetype situated noblewomen as Amazons: women warriors, hunters, and political strong women who possessed exceptional powers enabling them to hunt wild animals, lead armies in uprisings, and act heroically. Analyzing the memoirs, diaries, songs, and poetry of this period, the author concludes that the noblemen of the Polish-Lithuanian Commonwealth promoted the wild woman archetype as a cultural site of the unifying myth of the "Sarmatian" origin of the nobility. The archetype was rooted in a specific, visible reality — women were sighted hunting, commanding, and displaying heroism — though their achievements were framed by men. The author characterizes the wild woman archetype not as a misogynistic discourse meant to marginalize strong women who might challenge patriarchal authority, but rather as one aspect of an ideology underlining the bravery, exceptional nature, and strength of the nobility of the Polish-Lithuanian Commonwealth.

The figure of the wild woman appears in the literature, music, and other cultural forms of the Polish-Lithuanian Commonwealth, one of the largest states extant in Europe from 1385-1793, stretching from the Baltic Sea in the north to the Black Sea in the south, and incorporating many nationalities within its borders. The wild woman has been inappropriately likened by some scholars to the virago, the emblem of a misogynistic discourse that worked to marginalize strong or unconventional women, but the function of the wild woman and that of the virago were dissimilar. The elites of the Commonwealth developed a cultural outlook in which an ethos of rugged individualism was cultivated to encourage the nobility to settle and defend the eastern borderlands. In the image of the wild woman, one sees the construction of a female archetype who breeches boundaries of propriety and tradition but who is above all a heroine.

European observers of the Polish-Lithuanian Commonwealth often remarked upon the degree of freedom enjoyed by the nobility. One critical observer in 1778 called the Commonwealth a state of anarchy in which the privileged noble few enjoyed complete freedom over the subjugated majority.[1] In the "frontier" eastern borderlands of the Commonwealth such as present-day Belarus and Ukraine (a name which literally means 'at the edge'), the Polish nobility, constituting less than ten percent of the population, held power. Although this was a patriarchal society, Polish noblewomen were not excluded from aristocratic privileges. As the noble nation was such a small one, and the territory of the Commonwealth so vast, all hands were needed for such a small minority to assert its control over such a large territory.

The image of the wild woman, especially as she appeared in the sixteenth to eighteenth centuries, represented one element of the power structure that allowed the nobility to perpetuate its control of the social, cultural, and economic life of the Commonwealth. The nobility retained power precisely because it was deemed exceptional. The wild woman was constituted as a noblewoman, and therefore as exceptional among women. She was also a kind of Amazon, who could bend a horseshoe with her bare hands, who fearlessly hunted wild boar and bears, led uprisings against Turkish and Tsarist armies, and acted heroically without the protection of men.[2] Toward the end of the eighteenth century, her image was transformed into that of the Spartan Mother, who molded the citizens of the nation and trained them to fight to regain their now-lost freedom. Polish national consciousness was dominated during the Commonwealth by the nobility and its culture; therefore it is important to examine how this integrating mythology constructed the image of the wild woman.

This article will draw upon and analyze some of the published — and unpublished — memoirs, diaries, and songs that refer to the wild woman from the sixteenth to the eighteenth century.

The Wild Woman Archetype in Poland and Europe

According to Tiffany and Adams, 'Women, the archetype of what men are not... appear in various roles as Amazons, virgins, and matriarchs. The wild woman represents a projection of civilized men's imaginations.'[3]

The wild woman archetype conveys recurring themes centering on the nature of women in Western thought. In Poland, a genre of literature exists that describes unique women who are perceived to behave like men and conform to the wild woman archetype. Lorence-Kot reflects upon one object of the genre:

> Whether as (eastern) border she-wolves, who donned armor
> to protect their possessions against marauding Tartars... these
> women exercised power.... Some like Anna (née Grabianka)
> Raciborska forged out into the world (into political life)...She
> was admired and feared. Had she been less powerful she
> would have been called a "*Herod Baba*" (meaning bossy and

unfeminine.) The singularity of women like Raciborska stemmed from their encroachment on male preserves. While they astounded, they were praised only to the extent that they did not challenge male supremacy...[4]

In Poland-Lithuania then, a model existed for strong women. Even as women who conformed to this model were both admired and feared for their power, the model supported patriarchal authority, rather than undermining it.

Strong women both in Poland and in early modern Europe as a whole were sometimes labeled viragoes. The word 'virago' was first used popularly in Renaissance Italy to describe a type of Amazon, and had positive connotations, implying a lady of beauty who, in extremity, was the equal of or superior to men. The term was used to characterize huntresses and noblewomen, but it evolved over time to indicate women who had gained some degree of distinction through their mastery of arts and letters. In Restoration England, the nature of the virago was debated, some holding that the virago was patriotic, brave, and beautiful, others that she was unacceptable in her vulgarity and aggressiveness.[5] This debate took a rather negative turn, with the term 'virago' often used interchangably with that of '*hic mulier*' or 'man-woman.' One of the features attributed to the 'masculine woman' in late sixteenth- to early seventeenth-century England was that she was characterized as wearing man-tailored clothing, a presumed trend widely satirized by moralists, chroniclers, and even playwrights of the time. The woman who appropriated men's clothing styles could be villified as a usurper of male supremacy.[6] William Prynne's 1628 Puritan diatribe against 'masculine' women comprehensively gathered and reiterated the epithets of abuse in common usage at the time. Prynne commented that

> ...our Immodest, Impudent and *mannish Viragoes*, or audacious *Men-Women* [who] doe unnaturally clip and cut their Haire...as if *they were really transformed and transubstatiated into Males, by a stupendious metamorphosis*...our audacious, brazen-faced, shameless (if not unchaste, and whorish), English Hermaphrodites, or Man-Women Monsters....[7]

Prynne chastised the 'men-women' of seventeenth-century England for cutting their hair short, wearing men's clothing, and thereby attempting to transform themselves into men. Such behavior was deemed audacious and shameless, and women who engaged in it were worthy of condemnation. 'Men-women' were deemed 'whores' because they violated conventional standards of femininity in various aspects of their public and private behavior, and therefore called into question their chastity.

The wild woman archetype of the Polish-Lithuanian Commonwealth did not generally incorporate cross-dressing activities, nor did it cast aspersions on female honor, chastity, or sexual propriety. While early modern Poland-Lithuania is replete with examples of misogynistic satire and polemic, they occur outside of the wild woman discourse. Some examples of anti-feminist and misogynistic discourse in Polish literature include the Marcin Belski's satirical '*Sejm niewieści*' (Women's Parliament) of 1566, the anonymous '*Sejm białogłowski*' (Women's Parliament) of 1617, the numerous poems of Wacław Potocki in the seventeenth century, and Ignacy Krasicki's satirical '*Żona Modna*' (The Modern Wife) of the late eighteenth century.

The Wild Woman Archetype as Part of 'Sarmatian' Ideology

In the 1569 Union of Lublin, Poland and Lithuania were formally unified as a single republic. From the time of this unification, the nobility developed and began to promulgate the originary myth of Sarmatism. According to this myth, the nobility came not of the same Slavic stock as the peasantry, but instead were the descendants of the Sarmatians (sometimes spelled Sauromatians), a warrior people who had inhabited the fertile, vast, black-soiled steppe that ran from the Black Sea to Central Asia, having swept through South-Eastern Europe in the sixth century.[8] According to Sarmatism, the nobility of the Polish-Lithuanian Commonwealth was of a different race than the peasantry, and was alone entitled to the rights of citizenship and conceived as constituting the political nation. Sarmatism was a unifying myth created by a multi-ethnic nobility and developed into an all-embracing ideology from the sixteenth to the eighteenth century.

Jan Kochanowski (1530-1584), a Polish poet educated at Padua, told the history of Poland-Lithuania through the prism of Sarmatism. Kochanowski's history of the Slavs began with the Amazons who landed in Scythia, then migrated toward the north and founded the two Sarmatias (Poland and Russia).[9] Kochanowski's poem, '*Orpheus Sarmaticus*,' cautioned the Poles that their country was in danger, and he issued a call to arms:

> And you, Sarmatian, when suddenly you have found yourself
>   amid so many arms and arrows, you stand petrified as if
>   seized by a dose of old age.
> Do you believe these are only dreams?
> Yet, you do not possess towns surrounded by strong walls, or
>   inaccessible fortresses on high rocks, or rivers flowing
>   under old ramparts
> Or anything serving men to defend their lives. Today the only hope is the
>   hand armed with a sword.[10]

Sarmatism reminded the nobility of its mythic ancient glory that would be revived in modern militaristic virtues. These ancient examples of their Sarmatian forefathers would inspire the modern 'Sarmatian' nation, or the nobility of the Polish-Lithuanian Commonwealth, to take up the sword.

Many of the classically educated nobles had read chronicles that recorded the feats of the Sarmatian tribe and its successes against ancient armies. Polyaenus, in his *Strategies of War*, told of the heroism of the Sarmatian queen Amage, who declared war, stationed garrisons of soldiers, and defeated invaders.[11] It is difficult to know what proportion of the nobility read Polyaenus or any of the other ancient chroniclers who noted the bellicose prowesss of Sarmatian queens. It is possible that they might have read Herodotus' accounts of the Sarmatians and their customs. According to Herodotus, the Sarmatian tribe was the product of intermarriage between the Scythians and the Amazons. He described their customs in great detail:

> The women of Sauromatae... observed their ancient customs, frequently hunting on horseback with their husbands, sometimes unaccompanied; in war taking the field; and wearing the very same dress as the men... Marriage-law lays it down that no girl shall wed until she has killed a man in battle. Sometimes it happens that a woman dies unmarried at an advanced age, having never been able to in her whole lifetime.[12]

The Sarmatian people were real, of course, and not just the invention of a Renaissance-inspired imagination. Fifty ancient burial mounds near the town of Pokrovka, Russia, recently excavated, reveal the skeletons of women buried with weapons, in mounds known to have been used by the Sarmatians. Some of the women were apparently priestesses, some women warriors, while others appear to have been warrior-priestesses.[13]

The nobility of the Polish-Lithuanian Commonwealth linked its mythic origins to those of the real Sarmatian tribe. In my view, it is clear that the modern, noble 'Sarmatians' wished to find parallels between themselves and the ancient Sarmatians. The modern 'Sarmatians' wished to perpetuate the myth of common origins with the ancient Sarmatians by stressing the customs, traditions and practices that they shared with their supposed ancient ancestors. One means of perpetuating that myth was to cultivate the image of the wild woman, the modern 'Sarmatian' noblewoman of the Polish-Lithuanian Commonwealth, who would be a brave warrior and a huntress on the model of her Sarmatian ancestors.

Examples of the Wild Woman: The Woman Warrior and the Political Boss, or 'Strong woman'

In Polish history, the wild woman appears most frequently as a woman warrior, defending the nation either as a soldier or as a general in battle. This woman warrior was either a noblewoman who would take up arms to defend her castle and estate or a noble huntress who exhibited strength and prowess in the hunt, part of daily life among the nobility and an essential aspect of the noble ethos. Another instance of the wild woman archetype occurs in the 'strongwoman,' representing the fact that some Commonwealth noblewomen held so much political power that they were regarded as political bosses, or female 'strongmen.'

The Woman Warrior

The first feminist history of women in Poland, written by Łucja Charewiczowa, detailed the achievements of the women warriors of the seventeenth century. Charewiczowa's work chronicled the heroic and very real achievements of noblewomen who defended their estates and their country from foreign invasion. Charewiczowa described the battles of Teofilia Chmielecka against the Tatars, of Helena Niemerzycowa against the Tatars, and of Anna Dorota Chrzanowska against the Turks.[14] Chrzanowska's bravery and skill as a commander gained her fame in her own time and legendary status in Polish history.[15]

In both Polish and Slavic folk songs sung during the early modern period (1500-1800), one finds the theme of the warrior noblewoman or the princess who leads soldiers into battle to defeat the invading enemy. The folk song 'The Warrior Princess of Poland' recounted the king's laments that he had no male heir to fight for him. He was surprised to find that his youngest daughter bravely took up the challenge and laid waste to enemy territory, leading soldiers into battle and killing three hundred Turks single-handedly.

> When the king came to old age
> Bitterly he wept with rage
> 'Though I have fair daughters three
> I've no son to fight for me.'
>
> Then he called the oldest one
> 'Come, my child, fight as a son.'
> 'No, my father, I'll not go
> Never can I fight the foe.'
>
> Then he called the second one
> 'Come my child, fight as a son.'
> 'No, my father, I'll not go
> Never can I fight the foe.'
>
> Then he called the smallest one
> Though he thought her weak and young
> 'Come, my child, do you agree
> To go forth and fight for me?'
>
> 'Yes, my father, I will go
> I fear neither pain nor foe
> Brave my heart and strong my hand
> I'll lay waste the foeman's land.'
>
> She led soldiers to the fray
> Bravely did they fight that day
> By her mighty sword did fall
> Full three hundred Turks in all.[16]

The warrior princess was portrayed in positive terms; the song emphasized her bravery, her gifted leadership, and her talent in battle. It underlined the fact that even women could prove fearless, overcoming the liabilities of physical weakness and youth, should they be called upon to protect their homeland. The figure of the warrior princess buttressed noble authority by presenting this princess as a heroic model to be emulated. The song underlined the nature of the royal family as the true defenders of the nation. The legend of the warrior princess was preserved in memory by the peasants themselves through their folk song, and was therefore an effective device for asserting throughout the various segments of Commonwealth society the primacy of the noble house and the exceptional nature of those who ruled.

Another Polish version of this song was sung in Nowy Sącz, in Southern Poland, as well as in the Eastern borderlands of the Commonwealth. In this version, 'A Girl in War,' the heroine was not a princess, but a noblewoman. The song recounted that a nobleman asked his two elder daughters to wage war on his behalf, but they refused to do so. The two claimed to be too soft-hearted to kill, while the youngest daughter claimed that she was hard-hearted and would kill each one (of the invaders). The villagers mourned this daughter's (anticipated) loss as she rode off into battle: '...As they saddled up her horse, all of the peasants wept, / As she mounted her horse, the whole village wept, / But as she went into battle, she killed three hundred Prussians.'[17] Although the narrative underlying 'A Girl in War' resembles that of 'The Warrior Princess,' there are subtle and important differences between the two songs. Both support the notion, via the figure of the youngest daughter that the exceptional noblewoman would rise to the occasion and fight, and would act heroically. The two versions differ primarily in the degree to which their heroines serve as models, and in the scope of their activity. 'A Girl in War,' recounting that the entire village wept as the young daughter went to battle, emphasizes that sending a woman to war is an occasion for mourning, and thus not behavior to be wholeheartedly emulated. The heroine of 'The Warrior Princess' exercises command over other soldiers as well as attaining personal glory, while the heroine of 'A Girl in War' is said not to command, only to have, herself, killed three hundred Prussians. The scope of her activity is limited to personal heroism; the woman warrior here does not serve as the inspirational military leader offered by 'The Warrior Princess.'[18]

In the climate of violence created by both foreign invasion and civil conflict in seventeenth-century Poland, residents were expected to defend themselves, and a lone woman was at a disadvantage. Wives and daughters on the front often defended their castles or manors by arming themselves, in the absence of any male figures to protect them.[19] Jan Chryzostom Pasek (1636-1701), the 'purest example of a Sarmatian nobleman,' wrote a memoir of his experiences in the army of the Commonwealth.[20] Pasek related somewhat disparagingly that a widow living in the eastern borderlands in the year 1662 had stood by as her estate was looted by Polish troops. In contrast, he approvingly described noblewomen who defended their castles, and were able to capably manage their estates by themselves. Pasek wrote about the noblewoman Olędzka, the Lady Castellan of Zakroczym who held an estate at

Strzała, a village near the town of Siedlce. Olędzka managed her affairs independently because her husband was 'touched in the head. That's why they lived apart from each other, having borne only one daughter. He ruled over his estates, she over hers; and each kept a separate court and staff of servants.'[21] She must have managed the estate competently, because it had a surplus bountiful enough to garrison Pasek's troops. Pasek wrote that during the period that his troops remained under her roof, she supplied the men with abundant provisions, twelve ladies-in-waiting to serve them, music, dancing, card-playing, and exotic delicacies for them to eat.[22]

Pasek sympathetically portrayed another noblewoman, Pani Sułkowska, whose property was occupied and damaged by royal troops in the civil war of 1665. In accordance with Polish noble tradition, undeterred by regal authority and unafraid to air her grievances against the crown, Sułkowska greeted King Jan Kazimierz with a stream of vitriolic epithets as he passed by. Pasek recorded her words as follows:

> Oh just God! if ever you sent diverse plagues to punish evil and unjust kings, extortionists, assailants, shedders of innocent human blood, show Your justice today over our king, Jan Kazimierz. Let thunderbolts smite him from a clear sky, let the earth eat him up alive, let not the first bullet miss him, let him endure all those plagues which You sent the Pharaoh, for all these same wrongs, which we, his miserable people, and the whole Kingdom are suffering!...[He concludes,] Such a bold dame she was; having given the King a piece of her mind.[23]

Not only did Sułkowska go unpunished for her impertinence, she was reimbursed for more than the value of her loss by the King. Her behavior recalls the tradition of the wild woman, figured as speaking her mind boldly and doing as she pleased. Sułkowska's example also exemplified the tradition of noble independence from royal authority. The monarchy of Poland-Lithuania was an elective one, and the nobility constantly asserted and emphasized the ideal of their complete independence from the King's power. By mocking, insulting, cursing, and berating the king, Sułkowska was therefore neither rebelling against nor overturning authority. Rather, she was viewed as upholding noble authority and independence as a bold dame should.

The Huntress

The nobleman Krzysztof Zawisza (1666-1721) related in his memoirs the notion that by having exposed his daughters to danger, he might have strengthened them. He recounted having taken his daughters with him on the daily hunt, and their having joined him on a hunting trip to Ruthenia (in present-day Ukraine) in the spring of 1719, during which he 'killed eleven bears, almost all of them by my own hand and gun, and from two (bears) on I was afraid, most of all for my daughters, the amazons, for exposing them to such danger.'[24] Zawisza explicitly characterized his daughters as amazons, having raised them to be as amazons, showing no fear of wild animals, able to ride on the daily hunt with the men, and to defend themselves from danger. To raise one's daughters according to the model of the amazon was not an uncommon strategy in this time and place; girls were often taught to hunt, to shoot, and even to wield a sword.[25]

The Politically Powerful Woman as Political Boss or 'Strong woman'

Within the ideology of the wild woman archetype, women who were politically powerful were sometimes characterized figuratively as having great physical strength as well. Marcin Matuszewicz (1714-1773), a politician and nobleman who wrote voluminous memoirs, described the great power of Helena Ogińska (1700-1792), 'a lady of beauty, wisdom, and great strength, who could bend a crowbar into a horseshoe.'[26] Helena Ogińska was a *de facto* diplomat recognized and paid 10,000 rubles for her services by the Court of Tsarina Anna in St. Petersburg in 1731. The reputedly beautiful and intelligent woman was frequently received by Tsarina Anna as an unofficial representative of the Saxon King August II.[27] Matuszewicz was prone to hyperbole in his oratory, but such exaggeration as he displays in describing Ogińska is uncharacteristic of his memoirs, which he wrote with the stated intention of enabling his progeny to benefit from his own life experience. From this, I would conclude that he intended to inform his children about the realities of life, rather than to spin tall tales of women with superhuman strength. Ogińska's role as political 'strongwoman' was thus metaphorically translated by Matuszewicz into actual physical strength, characterized as one of her virtues, along with femininity, beauty, and wisdom.

Aristocratic women wielded considerable political power in the Polish-Lithuanian Commonwealth of the eighteenth century.[28] The first time noblewomen self-consciously gathered together to rally around a political and military cause appears to have been in connection with the Confederation of Bar (1768-1772). The Confederation of Bar was an armed struggle with the stated aim of ridding Poland of Russian influence and domination, but also intended to undo the progressive reforms undertaken by the unpopular king of Poland, Stanisław August Poniatowski. Noblewomen were so prominent on both the reformist and the conservative sides of the conflict that even contemporaries spoke scornfully of the conflict as a 'squabble among women.'[29]

After Poland was partitioned in 1796 by the absolutistic powers of Russia, Prussia, and Austria, reform-minded people in Polish society came to believe that women, as Piotrów-Ennker has articulated it, 'in their dual role as mothers and citizens, would have to counteract the danger of lost national identity by a new focus on children's upbringing.'[30] Polish women would keep the national fires burning by instilling in their children a sense of national consciousness and national mission. Such commitment could even extend to supporting insurgencies and to rearing their children to take up arms to fight for the independence of Poland. The figure of Izabela Czartoryska (1671-1758) can stand for many noblewomen who, through the traditional activity of patronage of educational and cultural institutions became politically engaged in restoring the Polish state and preserving the Polish nation. In just one instance of Czartoryska's work, she provided a forum for talented artists and writers of the day. The Czartoryski Palace at Puławy became a center of cultural life, and its theater was the site of many premieres. Czartoryska commissioned a play called '*Matka Spartanka*' or 'The Spartan Mother.'[31] In the eighteenth-century rendering of Spartan virtues, the Spartan mother would inculcate martial virtues in her children and inspire them to fight victoriously for their state or to die trying.

Other women did not just simply support male insurrectionists as Czartoryska did, but carried on the tradition of armed struggle themselves. The female warrior-heroine was personified in the nineteenth century by Emilia Plater, who, in her determination to drive the Russians out of Lithuania, raised a regiment of volunteers and fought in the anti-Russian insurrection. On account of her bravery, action, and leadership, Plater became a national heroine, memorialized in histories and in poetry.[32]

Conclusion

The wild woman discourse cultivated in the Polish-Lithuanian Commonwealth is distinct from that of the 'masculine woman' or the virago of sixteenth- and seventeenth-century English satire, in that it was created by men to sustain the image of strong and exceptional noblewomen, rather than to deride supposedly transgressive women for their potential to challenge the existing class and gender order. The archetypal wild woman did not find her way into Polish satire because she was held up as a model to be emulated rather than as an example to be satirized and marginalized. Articulated largely in noblemen's memoirs and in folk songs that taught the peasantry about the exceptional nature of the Sarmatian noblewomen who ruled them, the wild woman's embodiment of the virtues of strength and heroism functioned as a mechanism for reenforcing the prerogative of the nobility to rule by virtue of their nature as an exceptional group, descended from the ancient Sarmatian warriors.

Notes

[1]   William Coxe, *Travels in Poland and Russia* (London, 1802; reprint, New York: Arno, 1970), 13.

[2]   In invoking the term 'amazon,' I concur with Abby Wettan Kleinbaum's definition of the term in *The War Against the Amazons* (New York: New Press, 1983), 1: 'The Amazon is a dream that men created, an image of a superlative female that men constructed to flatter themselves.' Kleinbaum traces the Amazon archetype in Western culture over the past three milennia.

[3]   Sharon W. Tiffany and Kathleen J. Adams, *The Wild Woman: An Inquiry into the Anthropology of an Idea* (Rochester, Vermont: Schenkman Books, 1985), xi.

[4]   Bogna Lorence-Kot, *Child-Rearing and Reform: A Study of the Nobility in Eighteenth-Century Poland* (Westport, Connecticut: Greenwood Press, 1985), 61.

5 Jessica Amanda Salmonson, *The Encyclopedia of Amazons* (New York: Paragon House, 1991), 262.
6 Susan C. Shapiro, 'Amazons, Hermaphrodites, and Plain Monsters: The "Masculine" Woman in English Satire and Social Criticism from 1580-1640,' *Atlantis* 13, no. 1 (1987): 66.
7 Shapiro, 70.
8 Adam Zamoyski, *The Polish Way* (New York, Toronto: Franklin Watts, 1988), 107.
9 Czesław Miłosz, *The History of Polish Literature*, 2nd ed. (Berkeley and Los Angeles, CA: University of California Press, 1983), 63.
10 Miłosz, 75.
11 Salmonson, 7.
12 Herodotus, 'History,' George Rawlinson, trans. in *The Internet Classics Archive* available from 150. Internet; accessed June 1, 2000.
13 Jeannine Davis-Kimball, 'Warrior Women of the Eurasian Steppes,' in *Archaeology Magazine* 50, no. 1 (January/February 1997): 45-8.
14 Łucja Charewiczowa, *Kobieta w dawnej Polsce* (Women in Old Poland) (Lwów: Państwowe Wydawnictwo Książek we Lwowie, 1938), 38.
15 Zbigniew Kuchowicz, *Úywoty niepospolitych kobiet Polskiego baroku* (Lives of Exceptional Women of the Polish Baroque) (Łódź: Wydawnictwo Towarzystwa Krzewienia Kulty Świeckiej Łódź, 1989), 91.
16 Salmonson, 266.
17 Author's English translation of a Polish version of '*Dziewczyna na wojnie*' (A girl in war); see *Polska epoka ludowa* (Poland during the era of the people), ed. Stanisław Czernik (Wrocław: Biblioteka Narodowa: Seria I, nr. 176, 1958), 275-6.
18 I wish to thank Dr. Robert Rothstein of the University of Massachusetts, who provided the Polish translation of the song.
19 Alexandre Wolowski, *La vie quotidienne en Pologne au 17ème siècle.* (Daily Life in Poland in the 17th Century) (Paris: Éditions Hachette, 1976), 322.
20 Miłosz, 143.
21 Jan Chryzostom Pasek, *Memoirs of the Polish Baroque*, trans. Catherine Leach (Berkeley and Los Angeles, California: University of California Press, 1981), 57.
22 Pasek, 55-6.
23 Pasek, 179-80.
24 Krzysztof Zawisza, *Pamiętniki* (Memoirs), ed. Julian Bartoszewicz (Warsaw: Nakładem Jana Zawiszy, potomka Wojewody, 1862), 171.
25 Władysław Łoziński, *Úycie Polskie w dawnych wiekach* (Polish life in past centuries), 2nd ed. (Lwòw: H. Altenberg, 1908), 207-8.
26 Marcin Matuszewicz, *Diariusz Życia Mego* (Diary of My Life), vol. 1 (Warsaw: PWN, 1986), 315.
27 Zofia Zielińńska, 'Helena z Ogińskich Ogińska,' in *Polska Słownik Biograficzny* (Polish biographical dictionary), (Wrocław: Ossolineum, 1986): 593.
28 Lynn Lubamersky, 'Women and Political Patronage in the Politics of the Polish-Lithuanian Commonwealth,' *The Polish Review* XLIV, no. 3 (1999): 269-85.
29 Bianka Piotrów-Ennker, 'Women in Polish Society: A Historical Introduction,' in *Women in Polish Society*, eds. Bianka Piotrów-Ennker and Rudolf Jaworski. (Boulder, Colorado: East European Monographs, 1992), 9.
30 Piotrów-Ennker, 17.
31 Miłosz, 187.
32 Halina Filipowicz, 'The Daughters of Emilia Plater,' in *Engendering Slavic Literatures*, eds. Pamela Chester and Sibelan Forrester (Bloomington, Indiana: Indiana University Press), 34.

14 'At the end of the Walk by Madam Mazarines Lodgings': Si(gh)ting the Transgressive Woman in Accounts of the Restoration Court

Susan Shifrin

This essay considers the cases of two so-called 'women of quality' resident at the Restoration Court of Charles II of England during the latter half of the seventeenth century: one a duchess by heredity, the other by royal appointment. The author explores how these women and their 'private quarters' — as both the subjects and instigators of extensive written commentary and visual iconographies — were configured as the literal and rhetorical sites of political action and social and cultural creation.

Following the death of King Charles II of England in 1685, the noted diarist John Evelyn remarked, 'I am never to forget the unexpressable luxury, & prophanesse, gaming, & all dissolution...which...I was witnesse of; the King, sitting & toying with his concubines Portsmouth, Cleaveland, & Mazarine....'[1] Subject to his mistresses even in death, Charles had been lampooned during his reign as hopelessly submissive to, and emasculated by, the manipulations of the women with whom he surrounded himself. Evelyn's distasteful memorial to the King represented a pervasive perception of corruption perpetrated at the Restoration Court by Charles's mistresses and their cabals.

I will focus in this brief essay on accounts of two of these women, the Duchess Mazarin (1646-1699) and the Duchess of Portsmouth (1649-1734), that paint them as transgressive in their natures and in the power they wielded over their monarch and his affairs of state. I will pay particular attention in considering these accounts to the rhetorical 'si(gh)ting' of these women and their residences as repositories of illicit behavior and power.

Mazarin, the most widely-remarked of the nieces of the French court's Cardinal Mazarin, was conceived as notorious across the Continent and described by Evelyn himself as a 'famous beauty and errant Lady.' Prior to setting foot on English soil in 1675, she had abandoned her marriage and children, penned memoirs that sought to convey a truth contrary to that published by her estranged husband, and carried on multiple notorious liaisons in the public eye, repeatedly transgressing the accepted bounds of the 'normative woman,' to use Peter Stallybrass's phrase, set forth in contemporary commentaries.[2] A bilingual coffee-house burlesque marked her arrival in England with warnings of the political upheaval it was likely to cause, emphasizing the already heightened level of exasperation with Charles's subordination to his mistresses.

> *1st Coffist.* Indeed the arrival and reception of this Duchess at Court does afford matter for politic reflections.

> *3rd Coffist.* I have heard this matter variously discoursed of already. Some say, that the nation, already too sensible of the amorous excesses of their Prince, may be more inflamed by such an accession of great expense that way as this appears likely to prove. Besides, her great beauty, quality and adroitness, of which there is so great a character in print, seem to furnish occasion for apprehending a greater power in her over the King, if once he come to love her, than any other of his mistresses have had.

> *4th Coffist.* They are fools, in my opinion, who fear that.... I think it much more honourable for Great Britain to have its monarch subdued by a famous Roman dame, than by an obscure damsel of Little Britain....[3]

(This last was a reference to Charles's mistress reigning at the time of Mazarin's arrival, Louise de Kéroualle, whom he had first encountered in 1671 in the retinue of his sister, and to whom he granted the title of Duchess of Portsmouth in 1673.) Likened in this same *Coffee-House Conversation* (as well as in other contemporary commentaries) to a 'new Queen of the Amazons,' Mazarin was also portrayed in both paint and verse as the goddess Diana, destroyer of Actaeon, and as a latter-day Cleopatra, subjugator of two Roman rulers. The historical paradigm of Cleopatra as transgressor and destroyer constructed by Augustan poets and sustained by Dante, Boccaccio and Spenser, rendered hapless the warrior Antony, who, made effeminate and incapable by the 'lustful and avaricious' Cleopatra, was led to neglect 'The whole world's rule for Cleopatra's sight, / Such wondrous power hath women's fair aspect / To captive men, and make them all the world reject.'[4] Shakespeare's Cleopatra subjugated Antony, 'put my tires [attire] and mantles on him, whilst / I wore his sword Philippan.'[5] Later seventeenth-century adaptations of the story of Antony and Cleopatra, such as Dryden's *All For Love...* and Sedley's *Antony and Cleopatra...*, appropriated both those aspects of the narrative that construed Cleopatra as a transgressor of gender boundaries, ranging into the territories given exclusively to male prerogative, and those that constituted the men she had subjugated as emasculated — 'unmanned' — by her transgressions.

During much of his reign, Charles II was perceived by many at Court as having fallen victim to the Cleopatras of his own time. Samuel Pepys recorded in his *Diary* the influential roles played by the mistresses of both the King and the Duke of York in directing the politics of the Court and of the country, and bewailed 'the horrid effeminacy of the King,...[who] hath taken ten times more care and pains making friends between [his mistresses] when they have fallen out, than ever he did to save his kingdom.... [He] ...adheres to no man, but this day delivers himself up to this and the next to that, to the ruin of himself and business. ...[He] is at the command of any woman like a slave.'[6]

A portrait of Mazarin as 'Cleopatra with the pearl,' painted in Italy during the early 1670s and recently re-attributed to the Flemish portrait painter Ferdinand-Jacob Voet, served as an iconographical precedent for several other portraits of her that appear to have found their way into English collections during her lifetime or shortly thereafter (Fig. 14.1).[7] These portraits pictured their sitter in the same legendary moment as did the original: a significant, determinant moment from the familiar narrative related by Pliny in which Cleopatra, in order to fulfill a boast made to Antony that she would hold a banquet costing in excess of 10,000,000 sesterces, dissolved her pearl ear-ring in vinegar and drank it. As re-presentations of this narrative moment, the portraits of Mazarin emblematized an act of scandalous extravagance self-consciously generated by the whim of a powerful woman. They could be viewed as signifying Cleopatra/Mazarin's conquest of her own male consort by a notorious act of bravura and extravagance (indeed, her consort is obliterated from the tableau of the canvas).

Letters of the French ambassadors, among others at the Restoration Court, confirm that Mazarin was viewed in the political arena much as her portraits 'in the character of Cleopatra' would have suggested: as a procurer of patriarchal disarray, her very body the site of political upheaval.[8] In April of 1676, the Marquis de Ruvigny cautioned his successor as the French Ambassador Extraordinary to England that

> The arrival of the Duchess Mazarin provoked a great stir and provided a new focus of attention at [the English] Court. The King of England appeared moved by her beauty, and although their liaison has been conducted until now with a degree of secrecy, it appears that this nascent passion will take precedence in the heart of this prince. His Majesty [the French king] will have all the more interest in [observing]...what the intentions of this Duchess are with regard to him....[9]

A letter from Ruvigny's successor, Monsieur de Courtin, written to the French king Louis XIV two months later, noted that the damage to French interests wrought by the anti-French sentiments of Charles's highest ministers would be dangerously compounded by a failure on the part of the French themselves to appease his new mistress:

> We have discussed with [the King of England]...the Cabals that have been organized to join forces with Madame de Mazarin. He firmly assured us that he will not allow them to win him over: but she is beautiful, he speaks with her more readily than with anyone else when he chances to meet her. All those about him speak of nothing but her merits. It will be very difficult for him to resist the temptation for long, and [meanwhile], it will be a dangerous thing to have to combat both the [King's] minister and his mistress at the same time.[10]

Finally, in a letter of August 1676 to the French Secretary of Foreign Affairs, Courtin urged his reader,

> You know better than I that the whole of the English nation is full of animosity against France, that the Lord Treasurer, he who of all the ministers is the most ascendant in the esteem of the King of England, affects the same sentiments....It only remains for us to have turned against us the person who occupies the greater part of the heart of this Prince. ...[It] is most perilous to allow to fall into a condition of want a lady who has as great resources at her disposal as Madam Mazarin may have here.[11]

Mazarin was not by any means the only woman at the Restoration Court viewed by her contemporaries as a latter-day Cleopatra. Richard Braverman has recently proposed that Sedley's version of *Antony and Cleopatra* served overtly and was popularly understood as a political vehicle for the anti-French views of the opposition faction at court: that the play clearly delineated analogies between Charles's and Antony's privileging of lovemaking over soldiering, Louis' and Augustus' consuming ambitions for empire, and the Duchess of Portsmouth's and Cleopatra's ensnarement and disenfranchisement of their unwitting lovers.[12] Sedley, Braverman posits, wrote his play as a means of warning that 'a fatal attraction [for the Duchess of Portsmouth/Cleopatra] might cost [Charles/Antony] his empire' and cede England's sovereignty to that of Louis' France. Braverman offers as evidence of the popular perception of analogy between the political roles played by Louise de Kéroualle and Cleopatra several satirical verses published under the rubric of *Poems On Affairs of State*.... One of these poems, titled 'To Be Written Under the Dutchess of Portsmouth's Picture' (Fig. 14.2), encapsulated the range of powers — from prepossessing to villainous — attributed to Cleopatra by the seventeenth century. The second verse of the poem, in particular, makes clear the likenesses drawn between the Queen of Egypt and her perceived counterpart at the Restoration Court, the 'she' of the poem: 'Oh that she'ad liv'd in Cleopatra's Age, / And not in ours, to fill us all with Rage! / To see Great Britain thus by her betray'd, / And Ch–es, who once was great, a Beggar made. / Of such a Theme no Poet sure will boast, / That would have stole the Pearl that then was lost....'[13]

I have written in detail elsewhere regarding the significance of this poem both for seventeenth-century appropriations of the mythology constructed around Cleopatra and for their particular application to representations of women at the Restoration Court.[14] Clearly, such works bespeak an antipathy towards the amorous and political liaison between Charles and his foreign mistress, commonly believed to be a spy for the French and an active agent for a French and English alliance. Like the Cleopatra with whom she was compared, the Duchess of Portsmouth was widely perceived as having seduced her royal lover into the foreign enemy's camp by seducing him into her bed. She was condemned, like his other mistresses, for having distracted him from the affairs of state by means of the affairs of his bedchamber, to have depleted his treasury through her extravagant tastes and thus to have indebted him to the will of his French cousin. The papers of the French ambassadors provide corroboration, once again, that Charles' foreign mistresses were perceived on both sides of the Channel as figurative and literal sites of political negotiation. Many communications written to Louis XIV by his representatives in England during Charles II's rule give accounts to the French king of meetings — whether impromptu or arranged, ostensibly social functions or overtly political assignations — held 'chez Madame de Portsmouth.' In September 1676, for instance, Courtin wrote to Louis, regarding the news of the lifting of the siege of Maestricht,

> The letters from France and Flanders had not yet arrived yesterday evening. Along with the rest of the ministers of the Confederation, I waited...in the place where the Queen of Great Britain meets with her circle, to see if the King had received any news. [This] morning at nine o'clock, His Majesty...sent [for me]....I found him chez Madame de Portsmouth, where she told me...that she did not wish me to learn from anyone else [first] that the siege of Maestricht had been lifted....[15]

And in October 1684, the then ambassador M. de Barrillon wrote to the French king,'Madame de Portsmouth...sent for me to come to her chamber yesterday and told me that the King of England had spoken with her about the [latest] intelligence he had received from Holland....'[16] Indeed, Barrillon's letters to France reveal that, in the ultimate demonstration of her roles as a repository of political intelligence and as an underminer of the nationalist integrity of the English state, Portsmouth made known to him as Charles was dying that the English king had secretly converted to Catholicism. According to Barrillon's account, it was through the offices of Portsmouth, who urged him to solicit the assistance of the Duke of York in attending to 'the conscience of the King' that the English king received last rites from a Catholic priest. Having apparently refused the ministrations of a Protestant priest, the English king was reported by Barrillon to have avowed his Catholicism in the presence of the Catholic priest summoned by the King's brother to his bedside following Portsmouth's intervention. Once again, Portsmouth's own apartments are reported to have served as the setting for this crucial exchange of information between her and Barrillon.

I have suggested that allusions to the private apartments of the Duchess of Portsmouth — to her equivalent of Cleopatra's barge on the river Cydnus, perhaps, or more viscerally, to her 'private quarters,' as we might call them — served in the rhetoric of ambassadorial dispatches during the 1670s and 1680s to constitute the Duchess of Portsmouth as a literal and figurative site at the crux of amorous and political intrigue. What might be called this trope of 'si(gh)ting' was applied in a somewhat different context to Mazarin.

The Comtesse d'Aulnoy, a contemporary and French compatriot of Mazarin, is remembered largely as the author of numerous fairytales still read to this day. One of her most well-known works aside from her fairytales — her *Mémoires de la Cour d'Angleterre* of 1695 — appears to have represented to the bulk of her eighteenth- and nineteenth-century readers an entrée into the intrigues and eccentricities of the English court by means of the reports of a discerning traveller whose authority was beyond question due to her adoption within her text of the literary convention of claiming first-hand experience.[17] D'Aulnoy's *Memoirs of the English Court* establishes its credentials as an account of 'the most agreeable Adventures, and private Intreagues of the Court of England' through recourse to several of the English court's most notorious participants in such intrigues. The author/narrator claims early on in the text the privilege of acquaintance with these court players, enjoining her readers to approve her authority by acknowledging the celebrity of her acquaintances and the privileged information her knowledge of them transmits to her:

> You, who are not unacquainted with the Dutchess of Mazarine, must allow her to have Charms, that render her the most agreeable of her Sex, which made her House the Rendezvous of all the Men of wit and Quality, and the Scene of all the News of the Town, of Gaming, Entertainments, and all manner of Diversions....[18]

Having cited the ubiquitous Mme. Mazarin as one of her entrées to English society in the dedicatory letter to the *Mémoires*, d'Aulnoy returns again to Mazarin in her capacity as a linchpin of the notorious liaisons, feverish gaming, and high society machinations that colored virtually all characterizations of the Restoration Court of Charles II, in *The Unknown Lady's Pacquet of Letters*... printed with the English translation of the above *Mémoires*. In an account of a supposedly infamous series of trysts between an ill-fated gentleman who teeters between affluence and disrepute, and the mysterious woman of quality who supposedly subsidizes him until he can no longer resist the desire to uncover her identity, the putative author of the *Pacquet of Letters...* uses as a repetitive signpost for the location of the couple's illicit assignations Mazarin's residence, famous itself as the site of reputable and disreputable assignations alike: '[she] charg'd him to attend the next Night...at the Rail that goes into St. James's Park, at the end of the Walk by Madam Mazarines Lodgings'; and then '...ordring him to stay...for a quarter of an Hour, she struck, unseen by him, into Madam Mazarine's, where her Chair and People waited...'; and finally 'We took Coach at St. James's Gate, and I set him home at his own Lodgings ...for fear he should return and ask what Ladies were at Madam Mazarine's....'[19]

In these passages, d'Aulnoy makes strategic use of what I have called the trope of 'si(gh)ting.' Troping Mazarin, an icon of notoriety at the Restoration Court, d'Aulnoy draws on her readers' familiarity with the woman, the mythology of her transgressions, and the notoriousness of her 'private quarters' to imbue with the credibility of a 'true story' the narrative as a whole, pegged as it is on particular details associated with Mazarin's life at the English court.

Translated from the arena of public and diplomatic commentary, which sited women such as Mazarin and Portsmouth in the halls of political power; to that of painterly figuring, which enabled sitter-patrons Mazarin and Portsmouth to situate themselves and be 'sighted' by others as latter-day types for historical and mythological women associated with the mastery of womanly and manly virtues alike; and finally, to that of literary conceit, which sited them as accomplices in accounting for the myths of the royal courts, 'si(gh)ting' the transgressive woman thus became for chroniclers like d'Aulnoy not only a means of establishing rhetorically their own places within the politics of the Restoration Court, but more than that, a mechanism for establishing the credibility of rhetoric itself.

Acknowledgements

Earlier versions of this essay were presented at annual meetings of the Group for Early Modern Cultural Studies and the American Society for Eighteenth-Century Studies. I am grateful to my colleagues at both those meetings for their responses, and wish to thank in particular John H. O'Neill for his close reading and suggestions for revision of the conclusion of the essay.

Notes

[1] *The Diary of John Evelyn*, ed. E.S. De Beer (Oxford: Clarendon Press, 1955), vol. 4, 413-4.

[2] Peter Stallybrass, 'Patriarchal Territories: The Body Enclosed' in *Rewriting the Renaissance: The Discourses of Sexual Difference in Early Modern Europe*, eds. Margaret W. Ferguson, Maureen Quilligan, and Nancy Vickers (Chicago and London: The Univerity of Chicago Press, 1986), 123-42.

[3] Translated in *Public Records Office Calendar of State Papers, Domestic*, March 1675-Feb 1676, 474.

[4] Edmund Spenser, *The Faerie Queene*, Book V, viii, cited in Lucy Hughes-Hallett, *Cleopatra: Histories, Dreams and Distortions* (London: Bloomsbury, 1990).

[5] William Shakespeare, *The Tragedy of Antony and Cleopatra*, ed. Barbara Everett, Signet Classic Shakespeare Series (London and New York: Penguin Books, 1988), II.v. ll. 21-23.

[6] Entries dated 24 June and 27 July 1667 in *The Diary of Samuel Pepys*, eds. R.C. Latham and W. Matthews (Berkeley and Los Angeles: University of California Press, 1970-83), vol. 8, 288 and 356.

[7] See Susan Shifrin, ' "A Copy of my Countenance": Biography, Iconography, and Likeness in the Portraits of the Duchess Mazarin and Her Circle' (Ph.D. diss, Bryn Mawr College, 1998), 99-101 and 271-6, for a discussion of this and related portraits, as well as of the artist's work. See also Francesco Petrucci, 'Monsù Ferdinando ritrattista. Note su Jacob Ferdinand Voet (1639-1700?),' *Storia dell'arte* 84 (1995): 283-306 and Petrucci, 'Gaulli, Maratta e Voet: Nuove Attribuzioni,' *Fima Antiquari Arte Viva* 9 (1996): 54-64.

[8] The portrait is described as 'in the character of Cleopatra' in an eighteenth-century inventory, British Museum MSS: Althorp Papers L15, *Catalogue of the Pictures at Althorpe and Wimbledon belonging to the late Honble Mr Spencer*, 1746.

[9] Public Record Office, Kew, 31/3/132, 138. Baschet transcriptions from the Archives des affaires Etrangères, Angleterre. My translation from the French:
'...L'Arrivée de la Duchesse Mazarin cause une grande et nouvelle attention en ceste Cour. Le Roy d'Angleterre a paru touché de sa beauté, et bien que ceste affaire se conduise jusques à ceste heure àvec assez de secret, il y a apparence que ceste passion naissante prendra la première place dans le coeur de ce Prince. Sa Majesté aura d'aultant plus d'intérest que le Sieur Courtin observra quelles seront les intentions de ceste Duchesse à son esgard....'

[10] PRO 31/3/132, 178-80. My translation from the French:
'...Nous sommes mesme entrez avec luy sur les Cabales qu'on fait pour l'engager avec Madame de Mazarin. Il nous a fort asseurez qu'il ne se laisseroit pas gâgner: mais ell est belle, il luy parle plus volontiers qu'à personne quand il la rencontre en son chemin: Tous ce qui est auprez de luy ne s'entretient que de son mérite: Il sera fort difficille qu'il se défende longtemps contre la tentation, et pour lors ce seroit une chose dangereuse d'avoir à combattre le Ministre et la Maistresse tout à la fois....'

[11] Thomas Osborne, Duke of Leeds and Earl of Danby was Lord Treasurer at the time that Courtin wrote his letter. PRO 31/3/133, 256.

[12] Richard Braverman, *Plots and Counterplots: Sexual politics and the body politic in English literature, 1660-1730*, Cambridge Studies in Eighteenth-Century English Literature and Thought 18 (Cambridge: Cambridge University Press, 1993), 134-52.

[13] *Poems On Affairs of State: From the Time of Oliver Cromwell, to the Abdication of K. James the Second* (London: 1716); vol. 3, 118.

[14] See Shifrin, op. cit., 85-9. For a related discussion of the relevance of Cleopatra iconography in Restoration portraits of women, see Shifrin, 'Undress, Cross-Dressing, and the Transgression of Gender in Restoration Portraits of Women' in *Fantasy and Fashion: Essays on the History of Costume*, eds. Mary Leahy and James Tanis (Bryn Mawr, PA: Bryn Mawr College Library, 1996), 105-18.

[15]   PRO 31/3/133, 282. My translation from the French:
'Les lettres de France et de Flandres n'arrivèrent point hier au soir: je fus, aussi bien que tous les Ministres des Confedérez, j'usques à onze heures, dans le lieu où la Reine de la Grande Bretagne tient la Cercle, pour sçavoir si le Roy ne recevroit point de nouvelles. Hier au matin [sic], sur les neuf heures, sa Majesté Britannique m'envoya guérir. Je la fus trouver chez Madame de Portsmouth, où elle me dit avec un visage riant qui faisoit assez connoistre sa joye, qu'elle ne vouloit point que j'apprisse par un autre que la siège de Maëstrick estoit levé....'

[16]   PRO, 31/3/135, 348. My translation from the French:
'Madame de Portsmouth que a esté assez mal d'une colique depuis deux jours, me fit hier entrer dans sa chambre et me dist que le Roy d'Angleterre luy avait parlé sur les nouvelles qu'il a receues de Hollande....'

[17]   *The Mémoires des la cour d'Angleterre* open with such an affirmation of first-hand knowledge, in which the author/narrator writes to her dedicatee, 'The Time I spent in London, and the Intimacy I had with the Dutchess of Richmond and my Lady Harvey, furnish'd me with the Opportunity of being acquainted with the most agreeable Adventures, and private Intreagues of the Court of England.'

[18]   Countess of Dunois [Madame d'Aulnoy], *Memoirs of the court of England...To Which is Added, The Lady's Pacquet of Letters, Taken from her by a French Privateer in her Passage to Holland...,* Eng. translation, (London: B. Bragg, 1707), 1-2.

[19]   [D'Aulnoy], Memoirs...To Which is Added, The Lady's Pacquet of Letters...,

Figure 14.1   *Attributed to Jacob-Ferdinand Voet (previously attributed to Sir Godfrey Kneller), Duchess Mazarin, 'in the character of Cleopatra.' Oil on canvas, circa 1670.*

Figure 14.2   *Pierre Mignard, Louise de Kéroualle, Duchess of Portsmouth.*
                   Oil on canvas, 1682.

PART IV

The Female Voice as the Site of Cultural Authority

15 'Why do you call me to teach the court?: Anne Hutchinson and the Making of Cultural Authority

Ross J. Pudaloff

Anne Hutchinson was tried, convicted and exiled by the male political and religious elite of Massachusetts Bay. Civil and church trials sought to establish a hegemonic discourse by gaining her assent to their interpretations of Bible, commonwealth and gender. Hutchinson's refusal to so agree and her brilliant disputation forced her judges to silence her. Their failure made exile, the removal of her voice from public discourse, a necessity. Silencing was more than punishment for speaking; it solicited what it punished: a woman as speaking subject. Anne Hutchinson is the site of culture because she was silenced. She is the site of cultural authority because she spoke. The two apparently exclusive roles cannot be separated. Condemned and celebrated, Anne Hutchinson illustrates how discourse and technologies of power produce resistance, how a dominant culture is contingent on its 'others,' and how the subject of power gains agency through her appropriation and revision of discourse.

Anne Hutchinson's fame derives, initially at least, from her leadership of a group known as the Antinomians in a religious dispute in Massachusetts Bay Colony between 1636 and 1638. Insofar as formal theology seldom plays a central role in histories of the formation of American culture, the meaning of the event is often translated into other terms, in particular readings that privilege her as the avatar of feminism and doctrines of individual liberty. Despite the wide variety of readings, they all employ a historical narrative governed by the figure of chiasmus. The triumph of Anne Hutchinson reverses the judgments of exile and excommunication passed upon her at the time. Convicted for violating gendered norms by appearing on the public stage, her value for later generations depends upon an agreement between those that convicted her and those that praise her that she appropriated a masculine identity by entering discourse.

Regardless of the specific historical narrative, Anne Hutchinson has become the most famous colonial woman for later generations of Americans, serving as an inspiration especially for latter-day feminism and as a 'founding

mother.'   The combination suggests her value derives from a link between
gender and her entry as a woman into the public realm.   No two items better
indicate her status as a public figure and the inevitably ironic uses to which
history has put her than the re-evaluation by the institutions that condemned
her.   Church and state have long since honored the woman they punished.
They have done so in ways that combine the idea of Anne Hutchinson as a
public figure with representations that construct her identity in terms of
feminine interiority.

The church had placed, in 1904, a commemorative tablet that ends with
an internal quotation from John Winthrop, governor of the Massachusetts Bay
Colony and her most inveterate opponent.   It reads: 'A "breeder of heresies / Of
ready wit and bold spirit" / She was a persuasive advocate of / the right of
Independent Judgement.'[1]   Even as Winthrop's judgment has been overturned,
his words, especially the phrase 'breeder of heresies,' set the precedent for the
link between gender and ideas.   Similarly, in 1920, coincident with the
ratification of women's suffrage, a statue of Anne Hutchinson with a daughter
by her side and a Bible in her hand was placed at the Massachusetts State
House.   It describes Anne Hutchinson as a 'courageous exponent of civil
liberty and religious toleration.'[2]   History has been able to have its cake and eat
it too.   As Amy Schrager Lang notes, this version of Hutchinson 'as a
farsighted visionary and heroic mother requires, of course, the elision of the
very history that made her famous, but the elision of that history highlights the
tension between heretic and mother.'[3]   The tension between 'heretic' and
'mother' is perhaps greater for Lang than for those who have memorialized
Hutchinson.   The monuments indicate that Anne Hutchinson's identity as a
public and thus masculinized figure is contingent upon her representation as a
feminized one.   Wrong as he undoubtedly has come to seem to later
generations, Winthrop's words continue to govern discourse by linking public
and masculine with private and feminine.   The Anne Hutchinson remade by
American history is a figure who overcomes the tension.   She issues forth what
is already present within her; citizens become her children.

Her interiority as the source of meaning and value for a nation she
never imagined elides the fact that it was her identity as a woman that impeded
her conviction and punishment by state and church.   Her judges accepted the
distinction between thought and act.   She could be convicted only for behavior.
Only behavior, which included speech, could justify, if not draw, the
punishment of exile upon her.   Insofar as she acted (that is, spoke) in public
and as a public person, Anne Hutchinson threatened the order of the colony.
Thus the church and state attempted to put her back in the gendered role of a
woman, not merely to silence her — though that was crucial — but to make her
and others accept that what she did could only be understood as a violation of
gender norms.

The statue and the plaque, to say nothing of a multitude of biographies,
justify themselves by disputing not so much the correctness of the verdicts as

the logic of gendered separation that undergirded them. I argue here, *pace* the professional historians, that the amateurs have got it right.[4] The trials of Anne Hutchinson, intended to enforce the distinctions of public — masculinity and action — from private — femininity and thought — undid the divisions they intended to reassert. History as chiasmus is not imposed by later generations but rather was present from the start. The state and church trials began the process of creating the figure who initiates American freedom. The trials produced crime and criminal. Winthrop, who directed events more than any other man, knew that he was inciting deeds to punish Anne Hutchinson for those deeds. Revisions of sequence and chronology between the transcripts and his later history of events attempted to obscure his and others' complicity in the crime.

****

The Antinomian Controversy culminated in two trials, one religious, which excommunicated her and the other civil, which exiled her. While it would be foolhardy to reduce the Antinomian Controversy to any one set of terms, it is fair to say that the two sides fundamentally disagreed upon the reliability and efficacy of human signifiers to represent internal realities. The dispute was about whether representation itself, as present in behavior and language, could be trusted. Anne Hutchinson and her supporters said no; neither human means nor Biblical law guaranteed reliable statements about the internal state of the believer. The elders and magistrates disagreed. Aware that the structure of representation was itself endangered, whether of that of governors for governed, men for women, ministers for the laity, or upper class for lower class, they said that God had provided reliable human means to demonstrate the existence of saving faith.

Put somewhat differently, Anne Hutchinson was accused of acting as if she could speak for herself; unwilling to be represented, doubting indeed that representation could accurately convey any internal truth, she spoke for herself rather than let others speak for her. Anne Hutchinson was put on trial to punish her for speaking in public. According to the Reverend Hugh Peters, 'you have rather bine a Husband than a wife and a preacher rather than a Hearer; and a Magistrate rather than a Subject.'[5] Yet the trial solicited, even demanded, the public discourse and identity that defined the crime.

If we ask why the General Court allowed her to act as a public figure, the answer goes beyond the Puritans' commitment to consensual approval. It goes to the fundamental issues of the Antinomian controversy and to questions about the reliability and validity of representation that they entailed. In a sense, the controversy begins and ends with two errors, as he understood them, that John Winthrop identifies the first time he mentions Mrs. Hutchinson in his journal: '1. that the person of the Holy Ghost dwells in a justified person. 2. That no sanctification can help to evidence to us our justification.'[6] The first claims a radically new identity for the believer. The second makes this self unknowable by others. I focus on the second here as it pertains to the long running debate, central to the emergence of Protestantism, of the relation between faith and works and thus that between internal reality and outward sign.

Her judges provided Anne Hutchinson with a public identity because, insofar as they were willing to argue that works might in fact evidence faith, sanctification demonstrate justification — the very positions Anne Hutchinson disputed — they needed to demonstrate that human works could sift truth from falsity, innocence from guilt and orthodoxy from heresy. A kind interpretation would call attention to their consistency and to their apparent willingness to leave a way back for Anne Hutchinson insofar as her participation in dialogue with the elders implicated a community of beliefs and interests on both sides of the dispute. A less kind interpretation would say they forced her to play by their rules and on their field. But they paid a price, if at the time not so great a one as she did, for this victory. If she accepted their assumptions about the role of humans, to say nothing of the rule of men, in finding truth, she also was given, so to speak, an honorary masculinity not only in being allowed to speak but in being allowed to discover truth through human endeavor. If that was ironic and it was because she denied the efficacy of human agency as well as that of works and sanctification, the irony cut against the elders as well as against her.

As the tablet and statue suggest, gender matters in the case of Anne Hutchinson. As a speaking subject, one who possessed a masculinized identity, she threatened social order and stability. Yet Anne Hutchinson's identity as a public (that is, masculinized) figure was constructed within and by the application of legal procedures whose purpose was to silence her. A further irony is that, if it were not that the trial demanded she speak, we would not have her words at all. Rather oddly for a Puritan, Anne Hutchinson apparently did not put her thoughts into writing. The historical record contains not even the slightest suggestion that she ever wrote a diary, a spiritual autobiography, a treatise or an apologia. All the words we believe are hers came in response to the charges against her and were recorded by her adversaries.

The political and religious elite of Massachusetts Bay tried Anne Hutchinson for the crime of speaking in public. In a world in which conversation referred both to language and to conduct, to speak was to act, language was behavior. In his later (1644) history of the affair, *A Short Story of the Rise, reign, and ruine of the Antinomians, Familists & Libertines*, John Winthrop apparently revised the trial transcript to make the point that it was public behavior rather than internally-held beliefs that led to trial and conviction.[7] He quotes Anne Hutchinson as asking, 'Do you ask mee upon point of conscience?' To which he claims to have replied, 'No, your conscience you may keep to your self,' and told her it was her 'practise' for which she was on trial.[8] The trial transcript, however, tells a different story. In it, Winthrop tells Anne Hutchinson, in response to her claim that she is being persecuted for a 'matter of conscience' that 'Your conscience you must keep or it must be kept for you.'[9] The difference is clear. Certainly in A Short Story, Winthrop had an eye toward a British audience likely to be sensitive to persecution for matters of conscience. But more is at stake. Focusing on 'practise' defines the crime as acting in public, acting, in short, like a man. My point here (though not later) is not that Winthrop lied. Rather, he defined Hutchinson's crime as a violation of the identity appropriate for her as a private (that is, feminized) person.

Winthrop may not have initially appreciated that putting her on trial demanded that the crime be repeated. On the one hand, that replication served to condemn her. On the other, however, it not only permitted but demanded that Anne Hutchinson become a speaking subject. The trial provided a legitimated position from which she could speak. The contradiction quickly became obvious to all. It served the Court's interest to punish her for 'practise.' But to do so, she had to do what she was accused of in the first place. The process and its participants demanded that she speak at the time and place in and at which she was condemned as unnatural, heretical and treasonous because she had spoken. She recognized this double and contradictory demand when she asked her judges '[d]o you think it not lawful for me to teach women and why do you call me to teach the court?'[10] Anne Hutchinson saw the opportunity; whether she saw the trap is not so clear. In any event, she took full advantage of the legal processes to equalize (albeit temporarily) the relationship between her judges and herself by insisting that her accusers be compelled to take the oath before their testimony could be heard.

Ironies abound because Anne Hutchinson and her accusers each stake out positions that they could maintain only by speaking from within the discourse of their opponent. In her case, having denied the efficacy of words and works, she relied upon them to equalize power relations in the courtroom. In their case, having claimed it was not her conscience but her practice that brought her to the bar, she was given the right to practice the crime of which she had been accused in order that she might be convicted.

Winthrop's language suggests that the trial granted Anne Hutchinson the very public self for which he claimed she was being tried. In remarks prefatory to his report of the trial, Winthrop states that the trial's purpose was to convict 'this woman who was the root of all these troubles.'[11] Isolating Anne Hutchinson was, of course, good strategy then and in the later report for the British audience. By casting her as an eccentric, he denied, incorrectly, that any fundamental differences existed within the colony or Puritanism.[12]

Immediately following, however, he indicates that getting at the root was at cross-purposes with the claim that her crime was her practice. The trial's purpose was for her 'to be rooted out of her station.'[13] A slippage in meaning appears between the two statements. Winthrop first implies that, now that the branches and trunk have been dealt with, only the root remains. But his extension of the figure adds another dimension to rooting Anne Hutchinson out. She must not merely be uprooted from the garden of commonwealth and church; or rather, in order for Anne Hutchinson to be so uprooted, she must first be uprooted from 'her station,' which first and last is defined by her gender. His verb form is critical: she was 'to be rooted,' the act performed not by her but by others. They, not she, would place her in the public realm.

The court forced Anne Hutchinson into the position of the criminal, out of her station. The crime and its remedy were identical. Accused of violating gendered norms for women by asserting a public identity, the only way to condemn Anne Hutchinson was to force her to act as she was accused.[14] The obvious glee with which her claims of immediate revelation were greeted has long been noted. For the court, it was best that 'her owne mouth should deliver her into the power of the Court, as guilty of that which all suspected her for, but were not furnished with proofe sufficient to proceed against her.'[15] Not noted has been how the trial — as trial — put her in the position of a speaking subject who could make the claims for which she would be punished.

Winthrop describes both her confession and crime as 'bottomless revelations,' and stresses that to accept such claims made her and others 'not subject to control.'[16] In so doing, he shows how he accepts the argument against reliance on representation intellectually even as he rejects it practically. Interpretive control cannot be justified; it must be imposed and maintained. The relation is cause and effect. The court needed to have Anne Hutchinson speak. It authorized her to speak to condemn her for speaking. Hence Winthrop's glee that she condemned herself out of her mouth even as the court solicited that speech.

But if the court had its way and thus undid itself, so did Anne Hutchinson as the matter of swearing oaths makes clear. The initial clash over whether she had been called to account for her conscience or to teach the court already indicates how the trial authorized Anne Hutchinson as a speaking subject, thus producing the criminality it claimed to punish. But if Anne Hutchinson perceived the equation of being called to account and to teach, Winthrop's denial does not admit any recognition on his part. Neither Winthrop nor Hutchinson, at this point at least, acknowledged the irony that accepting the opportunity to speak essentially doomed her. Moreover, after this moment, the rest of the first day of the trial proceeded as if, having expressed her sarcasm, Anne Hutchinson did not quite realize or accept the opportunity. She characterized herself on the first day as a private individual, not a teacher, but an unfairly accused person who had done nothing wrong, who had followed the rules governing behavior, especially those of gender. First, she claimed Biblical sanction for her meetings. In doing so, she claimed orthodoxy in following the 'law,' but necessarily gave the law an authoritative epistemological status in determining truth, the position she otherwise contested. Second, she denied that she had stated the ministers preached a covenant of works but insofar as she had come close to saying that, she claimed that her previous conversations had been private.[17]   That is, she attempted to draw a line between public and private, accepting and trying to use against him Winthrop's distinction between 'conscience' and 'practise.'

To accept the law and the public/private distinction, however, only put her at a greater disadvantage, all the more so since she was in the clearly anomalous position of claiming publicly to have acted only privately. On the second day of the trial, she reversed course and acted as a public figure. She requested that the ministers testifying against her be sworn.[18] In a trial full of dramatic moments, none is more so — and none presented more difficulty — than Anne Hutchinson's request/demand that the ministers be sworn before their testimony was accepted by the court. This moment epitomizes the fluid discourse in which both sides found themselves taking each other's position. Her request seems reasonable enough to latter day observers, hardly anything to excite comment. Indeed, the debate over swearing the ministers has not been discussed heretofore in the voluminous secondary literature.

The second day had begun with Winthrop apparently attempting to summarize the evidence against her; his intention seems to have been to wrap matters up. At this point, Mrs. Hutchinson stopped disputing the memories of the ministers about her statements to them. Up to this point, she had claimed Biblical precedent, itself ironic in that she was appealing to law when she, herself, was skeptical about law. Now she shifted ground and entered the public realm, taking on a masculine persona. She took full advantage of the formal structure of a trial with its two opposing sides. Rather than quarrel with Winthrop's summary, she cast doubt on its legal status. She argued that '[t]he ministers come in their own cause. Now the Lord hath said that an oath is the end of all controversy; though there be a sufficient number of witnesses yet they are not according to the word, therefore I desire they make speak upon oath.'[19] Winthrop's response denies this is a trial: 'it is not in this case as in case of a jury.'[20]   His language acknowledges that a trial authorizes Anne Hutchinson to speak, granting her a formal equality with witnesses against her, even or especially when those witnesses are the most prestigious individuals in the colony.

Several important points are at issue. First, in seeking to have the ministers sworn, Anne Hutchinson was suggesting that their testimony was inherently no more credible than hers. If less dramatically than in her initial question whether she was called to 'teach' the court, she here more effectively equalized relations between magistrate and citizen, male and female, and minister and layperson. But in doing so, Anne Hutchinson also betrayed the position she took on works and representation by seeming to assent that outward representations, in this case an oath, could accurately signify inner truths. Contrarily, Winthrop clearly recognized that, insofar as this was a trial, the very hierarchy she was accused of violating had to be put, so to speak, in brackets if the outcome were to have legitimacy. Hence his denial that this was in fact 'as in case of a jury.' This was clearly not a strong argument, since Anne Hutchinson's appeal was to a formal equality between accuser and accused regardless of the presence of a jury. Finally, and apparently at a loss, Winthrop stated that the decision would be up to the Court and left matters conditionally: 'If they be satisfied they have sufficient matter to proceed.'[21] She was not to be put off and continued pressing for an oath, finally arguing that '[i]f they accuse me I desire it may be upon oath.'[22]

The importance of this matter is easily seen in that the court turned its exclusive attention to what seemed a purely technical matter. In rapid order, Simon Bradstreet, Richard Brown, Increase Nowell, John Endicot, Israel Stoughton, Hugh Peters, John Wilson, Roger Harlakenden, Zechariah Symmes, Townsend Bishop, John Coggeshall, William Colburn, Thomas Shepard, Thomas Weld, Thomas Leverett, Thomas Dudley and John Eliot, some several times, joined Winthrop in what was by far the single occasion during which the greatest number of individuals spoke.[23] The dispute remained unresolved and was temporarily put off by Dudley's suggestion that Hutchinson's witnesses be called.   Magistrates and elders knew to be sworn would imply Anne Hutchinson's equality with them. It was not until after Anne Hutchinson had made her notorious claim of immediate revelation, which served in the eyes of the court to convict her, that the ministers were sworn. And that only occurred because Stoughton objected to censure as irregular because 'she hath not been formally convicted upon oath as others are by witnesses.'[24] Since there is no doubt that he regarded her as guilty and deserving of punishment, it is clear that swearing was not a mere technicality. To appease him and who knows how many others, three ministers, Weld, Eliot and Peters were sworn and a sort of truncated trial occurred that enabled the court to proceed to sentencing. The court, upholding the validity of representation itself, could hardly refuse to engage in signifying acts.

Further evidence of how sensitive the matter was can be gleaned from Winthrop's account in *A Short Story*. Whereas the trial transcript made clear the ministers' reluctance to take the oath and the circumstances under which they finally did so — in effect when the trial was over — Winthrop misrepresented the sequence. Having mentioned Hutchinson's request, he noted that the Court saw no need and had the ministers sworn only that 'all mouths might be stopped.'[25] This dramatically collapsed the time and energy on this debate: it occupies less than a page in *A Short Story* whereas, in the transcript, eighteen pages separated her first request that the ministers take an oath from the moment at which they did so. Even more crucially, Winthrop's narrative reversed the relation between her conviction and the oath. In the trial transcript, it was only after she was convicted and thus reduced to an inferior position that her accusers would swear the oath. But in *A Short Story*, the oath had an almost magical effect. It was immediately followed by her claims of revelation, as if one produced the other. In this narrative, works have efficacy.

Representation is both true and powerful. Winthrop rewrote history in order to prove that signs do tell the truth; indeed, they compel it.

****

The same concept pervades latter-day representations of Anne Hutchinson. Her fame, her monumentalization by later generations, depends on the faith in representation(s) her opponents were offering. She has become a true sign, whether that truth is individualism, freedom, the rights of women, freedom of speech, and so on. How she came to do that is a long and complex story. Here I concentrate not on what later generations have done but rather on how she herself participated in giving to representation a legitimacy and authority that she otherwise denied.

To put the matter somewhat differently: the Antinomian Controversy was a debate over the reliability of signs and representations and thus a linguistic as well as theological debate.[26] The linguistic debate becomes visible in the position held by Antinomians, their 'refusal to see any visible signs as efficacious,' itself a consequence of 'a radical distrust of signs' in and of themselves.[27] For Anne Hutchinson, the point of one's justification was that it escaped the realm of representation and mediation, which by their very nature could never promise any assurance. Her epistemological certainty was predicated on its incapacity to be expressed in signs. One felt the presence of the Lord in a manner that representation could not convey. Her brother-in-law and ally, the Reverend John Wheelwright, insisted on this distinction: 'therefore when the Lord is pleased to convert any soule unto him, he revealeth not to him some worke, and from that worke, carrieth him to Christ, but there is nothing revealed but Christ, when Christ is lifted up, he draweth all to him, that belongeth to the election of grace.'[28]   From this perspective, Antinomianism in Massachusetts Bay is the inevitable result of Protestantism's mistrust and rejection of mediating institutions (whether church, apostolic tradition, even the language of the Bible itself). It was only a matter of when, not if, the crisis would occur.

The rejection of representation also entailed, in Hutchinson's eyes and those of her opponents, an escape from the (sinful) self, a phrase that calls attention once again to elements both sides shared. We are familiar with the idea of being born again; perhaps not as easily perceived is the destabilizing and disorienting effect of that self on a society, especially a society committed to stability and hierarchy. Such radical transformations of identity threatened the complex model of the organic body politic most famously articulated in John Winthrop's 'A Modell of Christian Charity.' In the ultimate list of eighty-two theological errors, the ministers included the belief that 'to comfort my conscience…from former experience of God's grace in mee, is not a way of grace' as a necessary consequence of Antinomian thought.[29] David D. Hall notes that this confutation 'contains, in brief, the position of Shepard, Bulkeley, and the orthodox ministers on assurance' because the saint 'could take comfort from his "conversation," his constant walk with God.'[30] The self was defined as the continuity of one's 'conversation.' One's entry into language is one's acceptance of the self already available, discursively prescribed and constructed. Describing the self as 'conversation,' however, imagines individuals as speaking subjects, something impossible for 'members' of the body politic in Winthrop's sermon.

Personal identity thus was central to representation. To imagine a person as undergoing radical shifts in interiority inevitably suggested that the publicly known self was always already a misrepresentation, that it could be no other than that. Like the statistical concept of reliability, representation guarantees not truth but continuity. From Anne Hutchinson's point of view, however, the experience of grace radically reinvented the self. When John Wheelwright, in his fast day sermon, used the phrase, 'Jesus Christ, with whom we are made one,' he threatened the order of the colony because that implied a new identity beyond society's control.[31] All forms of representation, whether of child by parent, citizen by magistrate, subject by ruler, servant by master or woman by man, worked only if they continued through time.

Requiring Anne Hutchinson to represent herself convicted as it authorized her. Winthrop's response to her question whether she had been called to teach the court manifests his desire that she accept the already existing form of representation as identity. He demanded that she 'lay open yourself.'[32] The sexual politics implicate all other forms of authority. Moreover, his demand inscribes the self within a structure of representation and defines her crime as misrepresentation. But for Hutchinson, any representation was already a misrepresentation. She would have understood, even as she condemned, the uses to which we have put her.

Notes

[1]   Quoted in Elaine C Huber, *Women and the Authority of Inspiration: A Reexamination of Two Prophetic Movements From a Contemporary Feminist Perspective* (Lanham, MD and London: University Press of America, 1985), 122.

[2]   Quoted in Amy Schrager Lang, *Prophetic Woman: Anne Hutchinson and the Problem of Dissent in the Literature of New England* (Berkeley, Los Angeles, London: University of California Press, 1987), 215.

[3]   Lang, 216.

[4]   In 'A Radically Different Voice: Gender and Language in the Trials of Anne Hutchinson,' *Early American Literature* 25 (1990): 253-70, Lad Tobin argues gender has not been accorded its rightful primary place in the commentary. He ignores, however, the enormous body of 'popular' (i.e., not scholarly) literature and memorials that foreground gender.

[5]   David D. Hall, ed., *The Antinomian Controversy, 1636-38: A Documentary History*, 2nd ed. (Durham and London: Duke University Press, 1990), 383.

[6]   James Kendall Hosmer, ed., *Winthrop's Journal: 'History of New England,' 1630-1649*, vol. 1 (New York: Barnes and Noble, 1946), 195.

7 There is no evidence to indicate when Winthrop compiled the documents and wrote the history. Nor do we know anything, as Hall indicates, about the book's transmission to England though its relevance to disputes there is clear. See Hall, 200.

8 Hall, 266.

9 Hall, 312.

10 Hall, 315.

11 Hall, 265.

12 On the fundamental divisions within Puritanism between what she labels the 'Intellectual Fathers' and the 'Spiritual Brethren,' see Janice Knight, *Orthodoxies in Massachusetts: Rereading American Puritanism* (Cambridge, MA and London: Harvard University Press, 1994).

13 Hall, 265.

14 Typically, and certainly not incorrectly, previous commentators have focused on Ann Hutchinson's crime as one of violating gender norms and ignored the ways in which she was solicited to violate them by the court. See, for example, Amy Schrager Lang's summary comment that 'the ministers of the seventeenth century recalled Hutchinson to her role as woman,' op. cit., 88.

15 Hall, 274.

16 Ibid.

17 Hall, 318-9.

18 Hall, 270.

19 Hall, 327.

20 Ibid.

21 Ibid.

22 Ibid.

23 Hall, 327-32.

24 Hall, 345.

25 Hall, 271.

26 Hall writes, 'the rhetoric of the controversy is the reality' (xiii). On language, see Patricia J. Caldwell, 'The Antinomian Language Controversy,' *Harvard Theological Review* 69 (1976): 345-67; Ross J. Pudaloff, 'Sign and Subject: Antinomianism in Massachusetts Bay,' *Semiotica* 54 (1985): 147-63; and Anne Kibbey, *The Interpretation of Material Shapes in Puritanism: A Study of Rhetoric, Prejudice, and Violence* (Cambridge: Cambridge University Press, 1986).

27 Both quotes are from Amy Schrager Lang. The first is found on 26; the second, which occurs in her discussion of the Great Awakening, is on 102.

28 Hall, 161.

29 Hall, 234.

30 Hall, 235n.

31 Hall, 160.

32 Hall, 315.

16 A Criticism of Contradiction: Anna Leticia Barbauld and the 'Problem' of Nineteenth-Century Women's Writing

Robin DeRosa

For a female voice to be deemed a site of cultural authority, critics generally require that voice to be, as the editor of this volume writes in the Introduction, 'authentic and potent.' Of course, these terms are far from transparent, and they shift dramatically from one historical moment to another. In the case of nineteenth-century writer Anna Leticia Barbauld, the terms are particularly vexed, as she works so often with paradox and contradiction. As this essay will show, while critics condemn her for failing to be an authentic woman or a powerful voice for what a woman should be, Barbauld slyly writes her way to authority by inverting the very notion of what it means to be a woman writer in the first place.

To the vast majority of both nineteenth- and twentieth-century literary critics, Anna Leticia Barbauld has not been woman enough. John Wilson Croker, famous for his skewering attack on 'Eighteen Hundred and Eleven' in the Tory *Quarterly Review* in 1812, wrote, 'We had hoped...that the empire might have been saved without the interference of a lady-author...An irresistible impulse of public duty...[has] induced [Mrs. Barbauld] to dash down her shagreen spectacles and her knitting needles, and to sally forth.'[1] Barbauld was attacked for the 'traitorous' quality of the poem, as interpreted by many critics of the time who felt that it was akin to a crime against the nation to predict the fall of Britain, especially during the tenuous years of Napoleon's encroachment. But what Croker's criticism displays is the way that many critiques of Barbauld's material — especially her poetry — counted as her greatest crime her failure to uphold the appearance of the docile, domestic woman of the private home space. This, of course, is not particularly surprising, since women authors of the nineteenth century constantly found themselves at odds with social custom from the very first moments that they picked up their pens to write. What is interesting, and perhaps surprising, however, is the way that today's critics replicate the charge against Barbauld that she is not woman enough. In the last five years, since Barbauld has been 'recovered' and placed (tenuously) into the academy's revised Romantic canon, critics have found fault with her failure to stand up for women's rights in any kind of consistent or explicit way. This is, admittedly, an inversion of Croker's accusation against her, but nineteenth- and twentieth-century critics share an impulse to fix Barbauld on the political spectrum, and to somehow make her gender identity continuous and compatible with her written material.

No recent critics of whom I am aware have intended to belittle Barbauld and her work. In general, today's critics tend to want to 'rescue' Barbauld from her own conservatism, demonstrating how she should rightfully be recognized as one of the mothers of British Romanticism. But these accolades are tempered by a wistful disappointment that Barbauld could not quite live up to the image that critics currently create for women writers from the Wollstonecraftian era. Marlon Ross, in a chapter relevantly entitled 'The Birth of a Tradition: Making Cultural Space for Feminine Poetry,' writes, 'The limits of Barbauld's feminism are also the limits of her poetics. A woman who cannot grant women absolute equal rights with men also cannot grant them the right to write freely from the dictates of their own desire.'[2] Embedded in this critique is an assumption that desire is somehow outside political strictures, and that women who do not transcend social boundaries around gender roles will not be able to write authentically. In the final sentences of a section on Wollstonecraft and Barbauld in *The Muses of Resistance*, Donna Landry praises Barbauld's recognition of the importance of women's work; but a moment later, she concludes, 'The boldness of such a recognition cannot be sustained. Barbauld's text remains marked by contradictions that she shares with other women writers.'[3] Here, the contradictions that mark the text ('The Rights of Woman'), even though they are understandable and explainable, are the endpoint of the discussion. William Keach, who has been instrumental in situating Barbauld in the revised Romantic canon, is sensitive to the precarious position of women writers during the period. Specifically, he is interested in what he calls the status of 'double dissent,' in which dissenting women such as Barbauld are encouraged to think of themselves as the spiritual equals of men within their religion, and yet are expected to subordinate themselves just the same to the men in their lives (fathers, brothers, ministers, etc.). Despite noting this complex positionality, Keach, like Ross, finds fault with Barbauld: 'The limits of Barbauld's position of 'double dissent' are evident throughout 'The Right of Woman' [sic]: her own active participation in the public sphere of political as well as literary discourse, based again and again on an appeal to 'common' human nature and universal human rights, falters when faced with the prospect of breaking from middle-class norms of gender.'[4]

My intention is not to argue that Ross and Keach are uniformly wrong in their critique of Barbauld's complicated relationship to feminism, but I do think it important to consider the emphasis here. If so many critics are so keen to note the complex of competing personal and political circumstances that subsume the writing of women from the Romantic period, why are they not interested in reading that contradiction within women's texts? In other words, Ross and Keach attempt to resolve the paradox of the conservative woman writer by explaining away her traditional values as failures, limits, stumbles in her otherwise groundbreaking career. I do not want to dispute that gender inflects women's writing; quite conversely, I am suggesting that we must not be so quick to fix women such as Barbauld (and this paradigm could of course be extended to other women writers of the period such as Hannah More and Felicia Hemans) to particular points on any historical-political spectrum, but we must instead allow the contradictions in their lives and work to signify in new and sometimes unstable ways. In 'Women Readers, Women Writers,' Stuart Curran discusses nineteenth-century women writers who earned a good living from writing that extolled traditional values. 'Rather than see inconsistency, or worse, hypocrisy in such attitudes,' he writes, 'we should perhaps recognize the priority of the enveloping cultural contradictions within which these figures labored.'[5] Though many critics have delineated the qualities of these contradictions, none have extended these contradictions into a theory of reading that can offer productive interpretations of the works of these women writers. The aim of this essay is to use the self-contradiction inherent in the work of Anna Barbauld to sketch a new, nonjudgmental, complex vision of 'conservative' Romantic women writers.

Barbauld's essay 'Against Inconsistency in Our Expectations' starts with a plea: 'As most of the unhappiness in the world arises rather from disappointed desires than from positive evil, it is of utmost consequence to attain just notions of the laws and order of the universe, that we may not vex ourselves with fruitless wishes, or give way to groundless and unreasonable discontent.'[6] This statement characterizes the Mrs. Barbauld that critics — of both the nineteenth and twentieth centuries — have known and loved to discuss: committed to order, to social position, to good cheer, to the idea that there are, in fact, 'just laws' which, when learned and memorized, can guide humanity on its course to heightened morality and civility. But a small contradiction, one that grows throughout the essay as a whole, begins to emerge. There is (mostly) no positive evil, and yet there are laws and order. This is a quintessentially Barbauldian maneuver, in which that which masks as the most fixed, stable, regulatory truth is in fact revealed to be fluctuating, man-made, temporal, etc. 'Consider this world as a great mart of commerce,' she writes, 'where...riches, ease, tranquility, fame, integrity, [and] knowledge' are our 'commodities.'[7] On the one hand, this certainly suggests an ordered world comprised of purchasable values, but on the other, it associates lofty, meritorious notions such as integrity and fame with products that can be acquired by essentially vulgar people. In fact, she suggests that a 'mean, dirty fellow' isn't unlikely to be wealthy: 'Not in the least. He made himself a mean, dirty fellow for that very end.'[8] But the essay isn't just a simple attack on the seedy ladder climbers in high society. It goes farther than that, suggesting that the premise that social laws derive from self-evident and organic truths belies the discontinuity between inner worth and outer worth, indeed between the inner and outer in general, underlying those very laws.

'Nature,' Barbauld writes, 'is much more frugal than to heap together all manner of shining qualities in one glaring mass. Like a judicious painter, she endeavors to preserve a certain unity of style and coloring in her pieces.'[9] Here, Nature exists through a metaphor in which she is compared to a human; the idea that the world is a man-made market economy and not a divinely inspired Pope-ian universe is strengthened. In addition, the equation of Nature and the 'judicious painter' de-naturalizes the natural itself, invoking not a spontaneous and wild divine energy but a cultured and cautious human artificer. 'There are combinations of moral qualities which never can take place but in idea,' Barbauld writes, suggesting that the urge to merge conflicting dreams can always only be literary (for what is an idea if it is not, like language, the sign or representation of a thing that is separate from itself?). But this is where she fully reveals her paradox. Though the thrust of the essay is undoubtedly conservative in that it does, on one level, provide a matrix upon which human beings can grid themselves into classes, occupations, genders, it also simultaneously reveals that grid to be artificial, culturally constructed, and enticingly transgressable.

In 'On Female Studies,' an essay written as a series of letters to a young woman friend, Barbauld treads a thin line between an argument in favor of women's rationality, and one that supports the view of women as primarily sentimental creatures. 'From books, from conversation, from learned instructors,' she writes, 'she will gather the flower of every science; and her mind, in assimilating everything to itself, will adorn it with new graces.'[10] The flower-gathering metaphor would have struck a chord with her contemporaries, as botany was one of the few sciences in which women were encouraged to participate. And the diction of 'adorning' and 'grace' also suggests a female-appropriate activity, related to decorating, ornamentation, and holy virtue. But embedded in this traditional word choice is an untraditional message, for botany is *not* the science (or at least not the *only* science) being discussed here, nor is this a tract about women's dress or women's moral fiber. Instead, the diction cloaks a remarkable vision of female education. Indeed, the essay suggests that women, rational creatures, should have access to science, history, etc., but it also suggests that such subjects, when learned by women, will be fundamentally altered. On one level, this asserts that the truths of science are produced by the mind, and, more significantly, are malleable and impermanent (and in post-Enlightenment Britain, this would have been an unsettling claim from anyone, let alone a woman). On another level, it asserts that science is not an essentially masculine discipline, and that it can and will be feminized by women who study it. This does not necessarily endorse an essentializing concept of separate spheres; Barbauld's attention to the way that external truth and gendered disciplines are constructed by human minds instead suggests that such separate spheres are infinitely permeable, and anything but distinct.

In the conclusion to this essay, Barbauld again cloaks a potentially radical revisioning of 'truth,' 'gender,' and 'order' in traditional, conservative rhetoric. 'The modesty which prevents [the learned woman] from an unnecessary display of what she knows,' she writes, 'will cause it to be supposed that her knowledge is deeper than in reality it is: as when the landscape is seen through the veil of a mist, the bounds of the horizon are hid.'[11] For all of its self-contradictions, this is a nearly dizzying passage. The 'modesty' that prevents women from appearing too learned is partially the social stricture that quietly asserts that proper nineteenth-century women were not supposed to be well-educated in certain fields. And yet, Barbauld claims, by hiding her education, a woman can actually appear even more educated than she actually is, which certainly violates the limits and boundaries set up around women's proper fields of study (morality, *belles lettres,* botany, etc.). Barbauld demonstrates how women can use the very limits that bind them as the vehicles that carry them out of their feminine spheres. The veil of modesty is in this scenario that which fully unveils the woman as a scholar. In her study of Barbauld's poetry, Laura Mandell notes what she calls the 'contradictory potential' of Barbauld's use of personification, in that it can both 'serve and subvert ideological mystification.'[12] This is, I would argue, precisely the potential that characterizes her prose writing in general.

Though I have so far been primarily concerned with Barbauld's oft-ignored prose writings, the themes I am addressing can be found throughout her poetry as well. In 'To a Lady, with some painted Flowers,' Barbauld confuses the natural and the artificial:

> Flowers to the fair: To you these flowers I bring,
> And strive to greet you with an earlier spring.
> Flowers sweet, and gay, and delicate like you;
> Emblems of innocence, and beauty too.[13]

As the title tells us, the flowers are painted, but this leaves much still to be determined. Is the narrator bringing a painting of flowers to a real lady, or is the lady part of the painting as well? The flowers are, like the lady, sweet, gay, and delicate, but could the 'too' in the third verse suggest that, *like the lady,* the flowers are *emblems* of beauty and innocence? The flowers, 'born for pleasure and delight alone,' are chillingly similar to the woman, as both emerge as representations for something else. 'Nor blush, my fair,' the poem concludes, 'to own you copy these; / Your best, your sweetest empire is to please.'[14] Here, the woman is a copy of the flowers, inverting the traditional metaphor that would place the flowers as vehicle to the woman's tenor. But as we know, the flowers themselves are copies of *real* flowers. In a sense, Barbauld jostles the very notion of priority or originality, opting instead to paint a world where artifice inhabits even the most natural of spaces: the woman's body and the poem. The flowers are called 'lovely without art,' which rings ironic for, of course, the flowers *are* art, that is, painted. If the poem reinscribes a feminine stereotype, all flowers, grace, and ornament, it also deconstructs such a stereotype by revealing its artificial core. The allusion to women's 'empire' in the final line catches the spirit of the Barbauldian paradox: through a self-conscious interrogation of the mechanisms that confine women to their feminine graces, women can become powerful. The paradox does not relieve women's oppression by inverting the male-female power differential, nor does it step outside of its confining culture; instead, it parodically plays with the constructedness of the social order, revealing its instability, its unnaturalness, and its arbitrary 'nature.'

This paradox seems particularly evident in 'The Rights of Woman,' a poem that has troubled many twentieth-century feminists. It is most often read as an anti-Wollstonecraftian response to the woman question, and a pointed attack on Wollstonecraft herself, who had attacked 'To a Lady, with some painted Flowers' in the *Vindication*. Though Wollstonecraft and Barbauld were noted allies on a number of political platforms, William McCarthy and Elizabeth Kraft have this to say about 'The Rights of Woman': 'It need not be read as representing ALB's considered judgment on women's rights; rather, it is an outburst of anger at Wollstonecraft.'[15] In order to preserve Barbauld's feminist potential, McCarthy and Kraft feel impelled to treat Barbauld's only poem which explicitly addresses women's rights as a mere 'outburst of anger' by an insulted lady. I cannot, of course, discount the possibility that Barbauld was peeved at Wollstonecraft, but I think it quite likely that there is more going on in this complicated poem. The poem certainly advocates that woman 'resume thy native empire o'er the breast,' suggesting that she is most adept at ruling the sentimental, emotional side of the world. And yet, the poem also constantly calls attention to how women achieve their femininity, their access to special emotional powers: not through a biological assignment of gendered characteristics but through an elaborate system of performance and ornamentation. 'Go forth arrayed in panoply divine,' Barbauld writes, 'That angel pureness which admits no stain.'[16] Is the pureness intrinsic to the woman, or has she arrayed herself in that, as well? And though the pureness *admits* of no stain, is this perhaps a cover for what is, underneath, slightly imperfect or marred? 'Gird thyself with grace,' the poem continues, again suggesting that the most natural of feminine qualities not only has to be put on, but that it must be put on like the armor of a knight. 'Thou mayest command, but never canst be free,' may suggest, as many readers understand, that women should abandon their unladylike quest for dominance and power, but it might also suggest that hierarchy in general always inscribes a binary opposition which holds captive both of its poles. As opposing elements in the poem are aligned (as in the girding of the grace), Barbauld melts the binaristic system itself; the loss of separate rights, while admittedly a potential setback for nineteenth-century women on the cusp of a major feminist uprising, is less a disappointing failure than a caution to feminists that demanding rights and demanding freedom are not, in fact, the same thing.

Even more popular than 'The Rights of Woman,' 'Washing-Day' is certainly the Barbauld poem which is most anthologized today. Critic Anne Mellor has suggested that Barbauld's celebration of the value of the quotidian, of daily domestic duties and social involvements, helped to turn British literature as a whole towards a national literary taste that favored domestic life and matrimonial happiness.[17] Though Mellor is passingly interested in what she calls Barbauld's 'study of narratology,' revealed in the poet's groundbreaking outlining of omniscient, first person, and epistolary styles, she does not significantly relate the celebration of the everyday with the self-conscious attention to style in Barbauld's texts. 'Washing-Day,' I would argue, is as concerned with connecting the role of poetry to domestic labor as it is with investing washing day with epic importance. The poem's opening, which takes up the question of the poem's meter, claims that the gossipy domestic muses speak in 'slip-shod measure,' which belies the near-perfect iambic-pentameter of 'Washing-Day.' This is the first quiet suggestion that this poem and its subject, while masking as the banal and the daily, are in fact worthy of the formal literary tradition that it is often said by critics to 'mock.' In fact, the poem enters into a complex dialectic; on the one hand, it mocks itself and its subject through hyperbolic comparisons (of a housewife on washing day and Guatzimozin roasting on burning coals), but on the other hand, its own form recalls the epic form of *Paradise Lost,* casting the washing day into a pre-eighteenth-century-epic context. In other words, it is impossible to know whether the form is ironic here, since its ironies are potentially relieved by the very form that creates them.

As the lonely male character wanders onto the scene of the poem, he receives a cold reception from both the washing and 'Washing-Day': 'Crossing lines / Shall mar thy musings, as the wet cold sheet / Flaps in thy face abrupt.../ Looks, blank at best, and stinted courtesy shall he receive.'[18] The diction here ('lines,' 'sheet,' 'blank') refers *both* to the wash and to lines of poetry, written upon blank sheets, or written, as this poem is, in blank verse. The wash and the poem are both inaccessible to men, and they are positioned as an obstacle to his pure musings. I would suggest that this is a radical departure from what is conventionally called 'British Romanticism,' in that poetry is revealed not to be a connection to the inner landscape of man's mind or soul, but to the exterior world of object, of domestic labor. Lines cross and looks are blank; indeed the poem is confusing to the musing, self-indulgent mind. The poem only makes sense, is only readable, when the reader's identity is subsumed by the physical presence of the laundry. When the crossed lines are clotheslines and the blank looks are simple signs of the washers' annoyance, then the reader can avoid the insult of being slapped in the face, like the male character. That the male character is called 'thee' intensifies the poem's delicious game of cat and mouse with the reader; we must outwit the poem's interpellation in order to turn 'thee' and 'thy' into 'friend,' 'he,' and, finally, 'the unlucky guest.'

The final lines of the poem return again to the question of the connection between washing and the poem about washing: 'Then should I sit me down, and ponder much / Why washings were. Sometimes thro' hollow bole / Of pipe amused be blew, and sent aloft / The floating bubbles, little dreaming then / To see, Mongolfier, thy silken ball / Ride buoyant thro' the clouds – so near approach / The sports of children and the toils of men. / Earth, air, and sky, and ocean, hath its bubbles, / And verse is one of them – this most of all.'[19]   Elizabeth Kraft argues that this finale demonstrates how the imagination can transcend the domestic context.[20]   This seems likely, but I think it only part of the significance of these rich and complex lines. First of all, the young girl who witnesses the chaos of washing day becomes the grown-up narrator who remembers sitting down to ponder why washings were. This retrospective is set against the metaphor of Mongolfier's (for Montgolfier's) balloon, which can only be made by the elder of the two (yet single) narrative perspectives. What strikes me as compelling here is that the bubble precedes the balloon in the poem's narrative sequence, and that the balloon is cast as that which is like a bubble (it 'so near approach[es] / The sports of children'). A tension exists between the priority of the bubble and its attendant status as 'original' or 'ideal,' and the ensuing fruition of the bubble's potential in the rise of the silken ball. Barbauld disrupts the order between tenor and vehicle, pitting chronological time (the priority of the bubble) against human history (the triumph of the balloon). By taking the historical triumph of the balloon and casting it as an attempt to achieve a kind of bubble-hood, Barbauld disrupts rational conceptions of progress, associated here with both the science of aviation and the literary-esque 'dreaming' of the male muser, instead investing the original object with significance. Metaphors generally depend on a detachment from thing-ness, an imprecise discursive maneuver in which an original morphs into something else, while still retaining its own discrete identity.   But Barbauld, by playing with the very concepts of priority, chronology, and progress changes metaphor from a move to the figurative into a move toward the literal.

By calling verse a 'bubble,' Barbauld does not mean that verse is frivolous or childish. Instead, I think she takes poetry itself and transforms it from a discourse on the egotistical sublime into an incarnation of the quotidian; this is not merely a shift in subject matter, but a formal, stylistic shift as well. For Barbauld, 'Washing-Day' is a poem which thematizes its own struggle to transform parody and metaphor into both an inversion of meaning (washing is *not* being 'mocked' in this mock-heroic epic; bubbles do *not* strive to be balloons in this poem's comparison) and an investigation of poetry's forms and devices. In this sense, to say that 'Washing-Day' is a poem about daily life is true, but we can also extend this argument, saying that the poem is about the quotidian quality of poetry itself. Consider, as well, that washing day is part of a domestic routine of maintaining order in the household, and yet, simultaneously, it is the day, as the poem demonstrates, during which that same household is thrust into chaos. The poem suggests that the very stuff of order, order itself, even, carries the seed of its own undoing. Barbauld has it both ways here, conforming to proper themes for women poets and strengthening the separate sphere that contains women's roles while also rebelling against these very themes and revealing the constructedness of the supposedly natural condition of gender.

Barbauld's 'Eighteen Hundred and Eleven,' a poem for which she was attacked during her time because of its 'treasonous' overtones, makes a similar claim about order: 'Fairest flowers expand but to decay; / The worm is in thy core, thy glories pass away; / Arts, arms and wealth destroy the fruits they bring.'[21] The poem is concerned with Britain's corruption in the years of the Napoleonic wars, and Barbauld, who ultimately seems to end the poem by throwing in the towel on Britain and turning to America for regenerative hope, was condemned by period critics for injecting doubt into what was supposed to have been an era of seamless nationalism. But 'fairest flowers,' though here a clear allusion to Britain, might also be the ornaments and signs that define women in culture; Barbauld suggests that such trappings make women what they are, as well as ensure the ensuing demise of the same women. The worm in the core is both an allusion to Satan, merged as he is with Eve's purity, and masculinity, which as femininity's opposite is also inextricably part of the 'feminine's' definition. In other words, if we look at the poem in the context not of the Napoleonic wars but of Barbauld's literary works as a whole, we can trace the development of a paradox in which the status quo is revealed to be transient and corrupt even at the height of its invisibility or naturalness.

'Thy world, Columbus, shall be free,' the poem ends. But does this suggest that America will somehow be freed from the worm in the flower dilemma? Isn't America raised here as precisely the 'fairest flower?' It, too, will have its fall, as all systems must. Far from being a fatalist, though, Barbauld instead suggests that hope is possible and appropriate, for as systems fail, new opportunities arise which, though culturally produced and eminently fallible, can resituate the human mind into a context that feels freer and more comfortable. Critic Sarah Robbins, who writes on Barbauld's many children's tales, says of Barbauld's moralizing fables, 'Barbauld's texts assume that becoming cultured is essential to being truly human.'[22] Robbins characterizes becoming cultured as learning proper, civilized codes of behavior, but I would argue that for Barbauld, these kinds of efforts to mold the wild child into the perfect English citizen are, ironically, the kinds of efforts which characterize the human compulsion to control anxiety through the building of systems, orders, and identities. In this sense, then, culture and natural 'humanness' are opposites *and* inseparably continuous. 'America' is not a land apart from culture, but a symbol of the human compulsion to dismantle and rebuild temporal social orders.

In his article, 'We Hoped the *Woman* Was Going to Appear,' William McCarthy describes Barbauld's unhappiness with the status of women, suggesting that her use of idealization in her so-called 'pattern' poems (or 'character' poems) is her 'usual form of psychic defense — compensatory fantasy.'[23]   This sets up Barbauld's view of gender as that which must be escaped — in a kind of delusional way — through poetry.   I would argue that her fantasy does not compensate for a 'real,' unsolvable problem, but makes concrete interventions into the characterization of the 'real.'   Just as she predicts the fall of her country in 'Eighteen Hundred and Eleven,' Barbauld's texts envision the most solid of systems as deeply flawed already, and these flaws are illuminated, rather than eliminated, in her fantastic works.   In 'Romanticism and the Colonization of the Feminine,' Alan Richardson notes the appropriation of a feminine sensibility by soul-searching male Romantic writers such as Wordsworth and Shelley.   He wonders (somewhat facetiously, no doubt), 'Why didn't [women writers of the time] simply claim these characteristics as, after all, their own and become (or create) Romantic heroines in their own right?'[24]   Anna Barbauld's texts offer a strong set of responses to such a question.   First, her work takes issue with the 'after all,' since Barbauld more often than not challenges the naturalizing assumptions that comprise the foundation of separate spheres rhetoric.   Second, her work is consistently occupied with the slippage, demonstrated here by Richardson, between the heroine/the story or poem and the writer/her textual production. Though Richardson seems unaware of the meatiness of this slip, Barbauld continually asks how her work is related to its repercussions in the real world. Today's critics have been quick to embrace Barbauld as a kind of missing link between Enlightenment rationality and Victorian self-improvement, and they have praised her, too, for her groundbreaking efforts in opening Romantic writing to the woman's voice.   But in both cases, critics have tried to explain away her conservatism as a maternal relic of the good domestic teacher or as an odd, inexplicable accompaniment to her feminism.   Instead, I think it time that we recognize that Barbauld herself was interested in the paradoxes which inhabit much of her work, and that she has thematized over and over again the tricky situation of speaking out against the master in the master's own language.

Notes

[1]   William McCarthy and Elizabeth Kraft, eds., *The Poems of Anna Leticia Barbauld* (Athens: The University of Georgia Press, 1994), 310.

[2]   Marlon Ross, *The Contours of Masculine Desire: Romanticism and the Rise of Women's Poetry* (New York: Oxford University Press, 1989), 217.

[3]   Donna Landry, *The Muses of Resistance: Laboring-Class Women's Poetry in Britain, 1739-1796* (Cambridge: Cambridge University Press, 1990), 273.

[4]   William Keach, 'Barbauld, Romanticism, and the Survival of Dissent,' in *Romanticism and Gender*, ed. Anne K. Mellor (New York: Routledge, 1993), 56.

[5]   Stuart Curran, 'Women readers, women writers,' in *The Cambridge Companion to British Romanticism*, ed. Stuart Curran. (Cambridge: Cambridge University Press, 1993), 190.

[6] Grace A. Ellis, *A Selection from the Poems and Prose Writings of Mrs. Anna Læticia Barbauld* (Boston: James R. Osgood and Company, 1874), 234.

[7] Ellis, 235-6.

[8] Ellis, 238.

[9] Ellis, 242.

[10] Ellis, 286.

[11] Ellis, 286-7.

[12] Laura Mandell, "'Those Limbs Disjointed of Gigantic Power": Barbauld's Personifications and the (Mis)Attribution of Political Agency,' *Studies in Romanticism* 37, no. 4 (1998): 27-41.

[13] McCarthy and Kraft, 77.

[14] McCarthy and Kraft, 77.

[15] McCarthy and Kraft, 289.

[16] McCarthy and Kraft, 121.

[17] Anne K. Mellor, 'A Criticism of Their Own: Romantic Women Literary Critics,' in *Questioning Romanticism*, ed. John Beer (Baltimore: The Johns Hopkins University Press, 1995) 32, 36.

[18] McCarthy and Kraft, 134.

[19] McCarthy and Kraft, 135.

[20] Elizabeth Kraft, 'Anna Letitia Barbauld's "Washing-Day" and the Montgolfier Balloon,' *Literature & History* 4, no. 2 (1995): 33.

[21] McCarthy and Kraft, 160.

[22] Sarah Robbins, '*Lessons for Children* and Teaching Mothers: Mrs. Barbauld's Primer for the Textual Construction of Middle-Class Domestic Pedagogy,' *The Lion and the Unicorn* 17, no. 2 (1993): 139.

[23] William McCarthy, 'We Hoped the *Woman* Was Going to Appear: Repression, Desire, and Gender in Anna Letitia Barbauld's Early Poems,' in *Romantic Women Writers: Voices and Countervoices*, eds. Paula R. Feldman and Theresa M. Kelly. (Hanover: University Press of New England, 1995), 134.

[24] Alan Richardson, 'Romanticism and the Colonization of the Feminine,' in *Romanticism and Feminism*, ed. Anne K. Mellor. (Bloomington: Indiana University Press, 1988), 21.

17 Silent at the Wall: Women in Israeli Remembrance Day Ceremonies

Kristine Peleg

This essay explores ways in which women silent at the Western Wall in Jerusalem during the annual Remembrance Day ceremony signify a culture of limitations. Orthodox, religious Judaism prohibits the sound of women's voices at this holy, national, symbolic site. The author argues that women who participate in this ceremony, which is intended to encompass and incorporate, play a silent and complicit role that accentuates their own invisibility. She further investigates how the sight on other, non-ceremonial occasions, of a non-complicit group of women designated as the 'Women of the Wall,' insisting on their right to pray as they see fit, sounds a powerfully disruptive voice at this normally uncontested national site.

Remembrance Day ceremonies in Israel reflect a country that has faced wars of survival in almost every decade of its existence. The national service takes place in Jerusalem, at the Western Wall, one day before the Israeli Independence Day celebration. Despite deep divisions within Israeli society, Remembrance Day ceremonies reflect a common religious denominator and unified security aspirations. Conflicts are papered over in the pursuit of a unified approach to this reflection upon the loss of human life. To the extent that women have always had a limited participatory role in organized Judaism, the Remembrance Day services are no exception. The course of the development of this ceremony indicates an early willingness on the part of the state to circumvent the religious constraints excluding the active participation of women — until the Western Wall was selected as the venue for the ceremony. Since that time, the ceremony has further rigidified and the role of women has become prescribed silence. Disagreements over religion, state security, and the roles of women in Israeli society are simply set aside for the duration of the ceremony. They return to the agenda even as soon as the Independence Day celebrations the next day. The exclusion and silencing of women remains virtually unnoticed and remarkably unchallenged.

I hope to demonstrate in this essay that the selection of the Wall as the venue for these services has determined who will participate in them and what types of participation are deemed acceptable. The role given to women, or the lack thereof, is the primary focus of my study, though it should be said that the fact of the Wall as venue works to exclude other citizens of Israel as well. Perhaps documentation of these exclusions will contribute to a general refocusing on the overall limits of the Remembrance Day observances.

One barometer of the powerful constraints imposed by religious authorities on ceremonies at the Western Wall is the impact that a group of women known as the 'Women of the Wall' has had on public awareness. In examining the roles of women overall in the Remembrance Day ceremony, I will consider the approach of this group to prayer and their ongoing attempts to broaden women's participation in religious ceremony, which have clarified a nominally social taboo and made it visible for what it really is: a religious prohibition that has taken on the force of law. Recent Supreme Court rulings in favor of the 'Women of the Wall' have provoked the drafting of legislation that proposes a seven–year prison sentence for any woman convicted of praying in a prohibited manner at the Wall. While the 'Women of the Wall' are not proposing a change in the Remembrance Day services themselves, their activities focus attention on the limitations of government policies that do inform those services.

While one might assume that such holidays accurately reflect women's level of participation in Israeli society as a whole, and while women in Israeli society are, to a certain extent, marginalized politically and economically, there are no formal legislative barriers to their participation. Women have representation, minimal as it is, in the Knesset (the national, elective, legislative body) and in other political, economic and social forums. Thus, it is the normative element of holiday engineering that will be crucial to this study: not the reflection of what is, but rather the promotion of specific visions of society. I would suggest that there is no innocent, unintentional component of holidays as they are constructed in Israel. Each element is carefully considered in and of itself, and in view of its symbolic value. The selection of the Western Wall as the location for the central, national commemoration of Remembrance Day observances ensures, in a sense, that women will never be welcome as full participants, as the taboo against women's speech at the Wall is strong enough to prohibit even a (female) Knesset member from speaking during an official ceremony taking place in its shadow.

Edward Said has written that 'we can best understand language by making discourse visible not as a historical task, but as a political one. The model ought then to be a strategic and not finally a linguistic one.'[1] Non-participation and not-speaking become political mechanisms when they cease to be background and become foreground. Women's passive participation and silence in the ceremonies can be analyzed for their relationship to the values of the society, or at least to the values of those preparing the holiday programs.

Holiday Engineering as a Normative Tool

Holidays such as the Israeli Remembrance Day mirror to those observing them two crucial reflections: that of the so-called reality, a coalescence of the values of those producing the public events that comprise holiday observances; and secondly, the reflection of the vision of the society as it might be. I will suggest that by examining the intentional aspect of the organization of holidays, we can better see the role they play in creating consensus and reinforcing current political realities.

Edward Shils has described a concept crucial to the so-called reflected reality, that of the central value system of the society: 'The center, or the center zone, is a phenomenon of the realm of values and beliefs, which govern the society...The center is also a phenomenon of the realm of action. It is a structure of activities, of roles and persons, within the network of institutions. It is in these roles that the values and beliefs which are central are embodied and propounded.'[2] Shils adds that the elites of the society, 'by their very possession of authority, attribute to themselves an essential affinity with the sacred elements of the society, of which they regard themselves as the custodians.'[3]

The orchestration of holiday celebrations can be seen as a particularly efficient means by which these 'custodians' are able to promote their values to broad constituencies. According to Don Handelman, 'public events are phenomenally valid forms that mediate persons into collective abstractions, by inducing action, knowledge and experience through these self same forms.'[4] He describes holidays as conveying 'well-honed' messages in a way that day–to–day living does not and cannot. More specifically, as Handelman and Katz describe the combination of Remembrance Day and Independence Day ceremonies, '[each] ceremony is one in which this nation-state, through official agencies, intentionally presents something of its self-understood purposes, and their foundations, aspirations, and apprehensions. Each ceremony presents a version of moral and social order that contrasts with the other. Each version, suitable to its occasion, stands on its own, valid in and of itself.'[5] There are no deviations, the content is controlled by the organizers of the ceremony: 'It may be likened to a mirror held up to reflect versions of the organization of society that are intended by the makers of the occasion.'[6]

The discourse of holiday organization on a national scale indeed must reflect the priorities of the governing elites, with symbols and rituals developed to serve specific purposes. Foucault's comments on the intersections of forbidden and ritualized speech are helpful in elucidating the particular discursive field of Israeli Remembrance Day ceremonies: 'In the taboo on the object of speech, and the ritual of the speaking subject, we have the play of...prohibitions which intersect, reinforce or compensate for each other, forming a complex grid which changes constantly... the grid is tightest [at] sexuality and politics.'[7] The discussion of Remembrance Day ceremonies includes these issues: the production and control of the ceremony, the struggle, or lack thereof, for mastery over venue, and the consequential exclusions of women as active participants. Furthermore, the notions of ritual and the exclusive right to speak intersect at the crux of the ceremony.

The emphasis on ritual and symbol in the development of the Remembrance Day ceremony further underscores that ceremonies are not random constructs, but clearly thought out and forceful in their messages. The symbolic value of public events endures beyond their immediate occurrence, as Handelman describes: 'The features of the public event indicate that it points beyond itself: in other words, it is symbolic of something outside itself. Public events are locations of the dense presence and the high production of symbols.'[8] The symbols to which Handelman refers serve as connectors between present and absent, the absent readily evoked by the dedicated, agreed-upon symbols. He suggests that 'cultural information makes sense best when imparted through occasions that are set up to do this kind of coded, communicative work.'[9] The issue, within the context of this essay, is that some of the messages seem to work so thoroughly that the process of decoding them becomes worse than subversive, it may be seen by some to approach betrayal in that any diversion from the sacrifice and bereavement memorialized in the Remembrance Day ceremony would be considered inappropriate. Thus, the deconstruction of the silencing of women at the wall not as an inconsequential or insignificant by-product of ceremony in general, but rather as an integral part of that coded communication constructed to realize specific intentions is considered a kind of communicative work inappropriate to this day and these services.

Holiday engineering constitutes the event or ceremony as necessarily fulfilling diverse functions. It connects participants with society. Furthermore, the holiday ceremony creates consensus where it does not ordinarily exist. This is especially true in the Remembrance Day ceremonies, in which conflicts tend to be integrated or absorbed if they manage to surface at all. Perhaps the lack of overt conflict apparent regarding women's ability to speak in the course of the ceremony implies that its engineers have already, successfully limited the conflict by permitting the small passive role allocated to women. This returns us to the dual function of the ceremonies — to reflect the reality, to project the vision. The question I wish to raise here is to what extent women's limited role in the Remembrance Day services is the reflection of the reality, and to what extent a vision of the future of the society?

Israeli Remembrance Day Ceremonies

The hour is night. At the siren's moan, the ceremony begins. The plaza is in semi-darkness, the Wall lit. All stand at attention, gazing towards this illumination. The spatial focus is the Memorial-Heroism Beacon, in a small rectangular

enclosure located just outside the fenced off prayer area...
The beacon itself is encased in a squared cone, made of
dressed stones that evoke those of the Wall. Within the
enclosure stands an honor guard of four young soldiers. The
flagpole, the national flag at half-mast, is aligned linearly
with the beacon, between the enclosure and the prayer area.
Facing the enclosure, standing at a marker on the ground is
the President of the State. He is flanked by two high-ranking
officers, one of whom is the Chief-of-Staff of the Israeli
Defense Forces. Well behind these three stand invited
members of the bereaved families and behind them, to the
borders of the plaza, other spectators. On the northern side of
the plaza are two small rostra, that of invited speakers and
that of the announcer. On the southern side, a large honor
guard closes off and completes the rectilinear space of the
ceremony.[10]

The Handelman-Katz description of the Remembrance Day ceremony
emphasizes the details and symbols packed literally into a very small space,
both in terms of time and in terms of physical presence. The text records the
ceremony's extreme deliberateness. Neither the organizers of the event nor its
recorders have neglected any presence integral to their conception or
perception of the event. If something is missing from this picture, it is
intentionally so. In the following pages, I will, myself, describe this ceremony
on several levels: first, its symbolic components and contents; secondly, a
characterization of its participants; and finally, the literally discursive segment
of the ceremony. I will follow this with a short historic overview detailing the
interplay between state and religion that culminated in 1969 in the selection of
the Western Wall as the venue for the ceremony. Finally, I will examine the
relationship between the wall as venue and women's participation in the
ceremony.

Both the symbols and the rhetoric of the Remembrance Day services
deliver the messages of the ceremony. The ceremony centers on the unity of
the nation, the 're-membering' of the dead as part of the community, and the
encompassing of one symbol by another until evoking only the outer
encasement is adequate to evoke the totality of content.[11] The siren invokes
unity symbolically, joining the immediate participants with the rest of the
country. The 're-membering' of the dead into the national community through
the lighting of the flame, the moments of silence, and then through the spoken
contents of the services, is the beginning of the process of encompassing. This
ceremony works to include those who are no longer physically present,
utilizing 'markers of presence' such as the siren and the flame to encompass
those who have died. Thus encompassment works effectively by encoding in
symbols the full message of absent members' continued presence in the
community. In addition, the symbols are nested, 'president, memorial flame,
flag and Wall,' with each symbol encompassing all of the messages of the

previous symbols.[12] The Wall, as the ultimate symbol in this progression, thus becomes the densest and most meaning-laden of all.

The nature of those who participate in the ceremony conveys its strong emphasis on the nuclear (Jewish) family. Israel is not a state exclusively inhabited by Jews, but this ceremony, with its symbolic roots in Judaism — as the role of the Wall and the religious content of the services make plain — excludes other people who are also citizens of Israel. The nuclear family is another structure within Israeli society that does not necessarily include all of the members of the family of Israel, and in this ceremony its rigid structure is absolute. As Handelman and Katz describe it, 'the atmosphere of familism is implicated in the lighting of the memorial flame. The fire is lit by the President, who structurally is something of a father-figure in this nation-state. He is aided by a bereaved mother or war widow.'[13] The family icon is completed by the inclusion of a young female soldier escort as emblem of the daughter or sister, and a young male honor guard as emblem of son or brother. The ceremonial roles played by these markers of familial presence invoke mourning for the past while simultaneously envisioning the potential for procreating the future.[14]

The spoken segment of the ceremony also follows rigid patterns. Each element is formatted with attention to content, form, and the patterns formed by alternating between speakers representing civilian and military authorities. These spoken elements amount to six discursive acts, including speeches given by the President and the Chief of Staff, readings by the civilian and the Israeli Defense Forces (IDF) rabbis, and recitations by the bereaved father and the IDF cantor.[15] In the concentration of attention on who is reading what segment, and in what order and ranking the readings are presented, those excluded from speaking do not, in general, receive mention in accounts of these services. Such accounts examine the flow of the verbal discourse, parse the division of segments, and describe the divisions of authority and control implicit in each segment and subdivision of segments, and all along secular/religious and military/civilian axes. The fact that women are not speaking is generally neglected. The balance of power is clearly analyzed, but only among those whose power is represented in this discourse. Those absent from the discourse only receive notice when the focus shifts to their silence.

Historically, there have been different approaches to past Remembrance Day ceremonies. They have always had a religious focus, and as women historically have been excluded from a substantial degree of participation in Jewish religious ceremonies, they have been excluded from many of these ceremonies as well. However, Remembrance Day ceremonies have not always been held under the physical jurisdiction of the religious (as they are now, in their location at the Western Wall). Remembrance Day ceremonies were less centralized in the past. There were national radio broadcasts unifying the country at specific hours, much as the sirens continue to do now. The influence of deliberate holiday engineering on these occasions became obvious as early as 1952, when a 'program of home observance' was broadcast as a result of consultations between the Defense Ministry and the Cultural Council's committee on 'evolving characteristic patterns of national life.'[16]

Religious symbols were integral to the early ceremonies. In 1949, a shofar (a ram's horn used in religious ceremonies) was blown to symbolize a cry to the heavens. By 1951, some of the familiar components were already in place: flags were lowered and beacons lit in local ceremonies. In addition, the writing of a new 'Sefer Torah' (Book of the Bible) was begun, and in 1954 the final verse was inscribed by President Ben-Zvi, also at a Remembrance Day ceremony.[17] Certainly, women's participation in such traditions as the donning of the prayer shawl or in writing those last few words, would have been proscribed regardless of the venue. And ceremony participants in 1953 clearly aspired to siting the Remembrance Day observations at the Wall when at Mt. Zion [in Jerusalem], the lighters of the candles ended the ceremony by 'looking in the direction of the Western Wall [and saying] in a single voice: "Next year in Jerusalem undivided."'[18]

Thus, I do not wish to minimize the religious motivations intrinsic to Remembrance Day ceremonies, with their inherently Jewish traditions, but rather, simply to note the ways in which the state was once more flexible than it is now in integrating religious, secular, and military components within the occasion of Remembrance Day, and allowing no one sector to govern *a priori* content or terms of participation. This flexibility was evident in the degree to which the state experimented with the elements of timing, content, and participation. In 1955, women were reported to have taken part in the local ceremonies, with Mrs. Golda Meyerson the chief government spokesperson in the city of Rehovot services.[19] In 1956, the Public Council for the Remembrance of the Fallen 'issued two versions of a memorial prayer for members of the IDF who lost their lives. One is a traditional *yizkor* (memorial) prayer, while the other does not mention the Deity, but calls on the people of Israel to remember its fallen heroes.'[20] The last real deviation from the currently acceptable model of Remembrance Day ceremonies occurred in 1974, when Independence Day was separated from Memorial Day by a half day. By 1975, the ceremonies had reverted to their former pattern.

The Wall

The Western Wall stands in the enclosed Old City of Jerusalem, facing the Jewish Quarter. Under Jordanian jurisdiction and inaccessible to Israelis from 1948, after the Six Day War in 1967, the Wall became the symbol of the completion of the unification of Jerusalem. Before Israel achieved statehood in 1948, the area surrounding the Wall had been an Arab neighborhood and did not arouse the same nationalist passion as it has since its transformation into a national monument. The Wall is considered holy to the Jewish people, thought to be part of the Second Temple destroyed by the Romans in 70 CE.[21] This connection is considered one of the underpinnings of the legitimacy of the current state (even while the authenticity of the Wall as part of the Second Temple is debated by modern archeologists). The Wall was a religious symbol in the past and has developed into a nationalist passion. After the Six Day War, the immediate neighborhood streets facing the Wall were cleared to build a plaza which fell under the jurisdiction of the Ministry of Religious Affairs. Now the Wall has become a powerful common denominator, the focus not only of the religious, but also of the secular, the civilian and the military, as well as of international Diaspora Judaism and the nationalist forces in Israel.

The Wall works so convincingly on such a widely disparate population, and in a way that no other symbol has been able to, that the contradictions underlying its potency are difficult to discern. The Wall was not a component of the secular Zionist imagination and yet it moves even some of the most secular Israelis, who after all, share a Jewish identity that preceded the State. Handelman and Katz write that 'the Zionist vision ... was one in which all Jews of the world would move to the Jewish State to become its citizenry. At the end of this process, state and nation would become coterminous, but the authority of the Zionist state would encompass and subsume its citizens, the people.'[22] The question arises today, which authority is subsuming and which is being subsumed? The religious ministry is not often overruled. This is not necessarily as a result of popular consensus but usually of the political strength of the crucial few religious ministers influential in the coalition-building politics of Israel. The transition from civil jurisdiction to religious authority and ownership can be seen in events such as that which occurred when Chaika Grossman, a member of the Knesset, was prevented from speaking at the closing ceremony of the Gathering of Jewish Holocaust Survivors held at the Western Wall in 1981 solely because of her gender.

The Women

As I have discussed, the nature of women's participation in Remembrance Day ceremonies has changed over the history of the State. Earlier ceremonies integrated women at both the local and the national levels. Since the Wall has become the exclusive venue of the central state ceremony, the role of women in the ceremony has been reduced to that of bearing the flame to the President that enables him to light the beacon. There is also an escort of female soldiers. Both of these roles are silent and usually anonymous.

The anonymity of these participants could be interpreted as the means by which the entire population of bereaved widows or mothers can be represented, much as the anonymity of the father reading the *Kaddish* (prayer of bereavement) might more effectively represent the general population of bereaved fathers. Without particulars, the symbol remains intact, undisturbed by the attributes of unique personality. The roles of the bereaved woman and man are not equal, however, within the scope of the ceremony. The transfer of the flame is a passive role, one that declares the woman's presence without allowing her to actively express her grief. Even as the young women soldiers symbolize the potential for continuity, their role in realizing that continuity will be passive. They will be expected to contribute as vessels of procreation, and then to remain silent once again when the roles of widow or mother fall upon them. The women who function in the ceremonies in passive anonymity experience a lack of symmetry with their male counterparts. In general, featured speakers —- those actively taking part in the ceremonies — whether they are granted the freedom to compose their own words or only recite part of a traditional prayer, are identified by name. Speaking is rendered by this naming an active, identifiable mode of participation, in contrast to the passive, anonymous, silent mode to which women's participation is relegated.

Reports in the *Jerusalem Post* describing Remembrance Day ceremonies spanning more than twenty years confirm this lack of symmetry. I have analyzed each report to recover what I have termed the male and female participants' 'representational possibilities,' which I have characterized as follows: invisible — that is, entirely missing from the report of the ceremony; anonymous — mentioned as having been participants but unnamed; and named — not only mentioned, but referred to by name.[23] The breakdown from this sampling revealed that in eight instances, women could be characterized as 'invisible,' in eight, as 'anonymous,' and in five instances, as 'named.' In the same sampling, men were found to be 'invisible' or 'anonymous' in six instances and 'named' in nine. These statistics demonstrate that men had an almost equal chance of being named as they did of being invisible or anonymous, and nearly twice the chance of being named as did women. Women had a more than three to one chance of being invisible or anonymous than they had of being named. Perhaps it is the nature of reporting that anyone who speaks in a program must be identified, while flame-passing remains in the shadows. The speakers are described, their roles outlined, the content of their presentations elaborated upon. These participants have content and not only form. They are part of the discourse on a different level than their silent counterparts.

'Women of the Wall'

In 1989, 'a women's prayer meeting at the Western Wall...ended in a near riot, with worshippers from the men's side of the partition separating the sexes shouting abuse and hurling chairs at the women.'[24] The women had been careful not to recite prayers that traditionally can be said only with a male *minyan* (ten men in prayer), but they had opened a Torah scroll, which Orthodox religious Jews contend only men should handle and from which only men should read aloud. The police did not respond to the women's complaints of the men's violence against them. In the months that followed, the women were warned by the police that they were considered a 'threat to public safety' and could be arrested.[25] They were dispersed with tear gas and the Religious Affairs Ministry contended that it was not obliged to provide protection to these women. Their prayer meetings were violated again in the following months and the women were kicked and punched by onlookers. The mayor of Jerusalem asked them to refrain from their meetings. The women appealed to the High Court of Justice, which granted the religious authorities six months to 'show cause why the women should not be allowed to read the Torah and wear prayer shawls at the Wall.'[26] Extensions were issued repeatedly. Only recently, in May 2000, did the Supreme Court rule that women must be allowed to pray at the Western Wall, their activities to lawfully include 'reading aloud from the Torah.'[27] A bill was drafted in the Knesset within a week of the ruling that would impose a seven-year prison sentence on any woman reading aloud from the Torah at the Western Wall.[28]

One of the aspects of these women's prayer meetings deemed most unacceptable by the religious authorities has been their determination to pray aloud. This alone 'aroused the suspicion of some of the women nearby,' who 'reprimanded the group for singing prayers aloud, a practice which the onlookers said was unseemly for women.'[29] It was not the first time that women had attempted to challenge the religious jurisdiction of prayer at the Wall. In 1968, there had been a controversial attempt to hold a mixed (sexes) prayer service there. At that time, Mayor Teddy Kolleck had described the 'peace of Jerusalem' as 'all important.'[30] Twenty years later, he condemned the 'Women of the Wall' for 'waging a provocative fight and using prayer as a means of protest.'[31]

The 'peace of Jerusalem,' like the unity of the state of Israel, represents a singular goal for a governing body whose overriding concern is with the elimination of dissension. The pursuit of this goal reaches its zenith in Remembrance Day observations. Unity is the essential message of this ceremony: essential to the commemoration of the virtues of the ultimate sacrifice. There is no allowance in this agenda for the examination of sacrifices other than those associated with war. Diversions would only dilute the ability of the community to maintain consensus regarding the necessity for these sacrifices. In this context, it may seem virtually sacrilegious to remark that woman's participation has been sacrificed to religious propriety. Or that the entire theme of encompassment, based as it is on the inclusion of many via their representation in the few, excludes and thus cannot properly function as it was intended. Or that the metaphor of the family is a fiercely rigid pattern, representing only nuclear families in traditional roles. Nannerl Keohane suggests that the image of a father-figure President 'effectively perpetuates male dominance: the close association of authority with the father. The cluster of connotations that brings together God, the paterfamilias, and the head of

State is very powerful and difficult to break apart.'[32] Is it possible to imagine a woman as the President of the State of Israel? Would she be allowed to speak in the Remembrance Day services at the Western Wall?

Conclusion: 'Markers of Absence'

While it is true that the content of men's Remembrance Day speeches or readings is circumscribed, whether formally or informally (it would be difficult to imagine the bereaved father being allowed now to use the 1956 prayer that omitted mention of the Deity), men are, nonetheless, the only speakers — and thus, as I have argued, the only active participants — in this ceremony. Handelman and Katz characterize the symbols interwoven in the ceremony as 'markers of presence.' I contend that there must be an acknowledgment of the need to identify concomitant 'markers of absence.' These are not so easily evoked by the standard symbols of the ceremony: perhaps, as I have suggested, because encompassment only works on what it has included. The 'nesting' or layering of symbols breaks down when those symbols' meanings are predicated upon the exclusion of certain segments of the population. Once excluded from participation in this way, these members of society are not eligible to be encompassed, nor are there any recognized 'markers of absence' to make their exclusion more visible.

The 'Women of the Wall' have contributed to making visible and audible the protest against the monolithic symbolic power of the Wall and of those religious authorities, prescribing what is and is not acceptable, who include and who exclude. It is in their re-marking of exclusion and absence that the 'Women of the Wall' are seen to be so very provocative. The unanimity achieved on Remembrance Day is a powerful demonstration of political engineering and control of societal discourse. That unanimity is not on the line. But on a regular day, when singing women at the Wall provoke violence and the jurisdiction of the religious maintains its stronghold, when the female Knesset member is prevented from speaking, fissures appear not in the Wall, but in the authority of the State. The State, as it were, becomes voiceless, and it is left to the women rendered silent at the Remembrance Day ceremony to articulate the question, could the State authorize a woman to speak in this ceremony at the Western Wall? With all the deliberateness of the Remembrance Day ceremony and its unifying function, it seems an unlikely forum in which to raise such a divisive issue. But perhaps that is how the invisible and the silent work best — even if only to point out where the exclusions are working most effectively.

Notes

1 Edward W. Said, 'Criticism Between Culture and System,' in *The World, the Text, and the Critic* (Cambridge: Harvard University Press, 1983), 219.
2 Edward Shils, *Center and Periphery, Essays in Macrosociology* (Chicago: University of Chicago Press, 1975), 3.
3 Shils, 4-5.
4 Don Handelman, *Models and Mirrors: Towards an Anthropology of Public Events* (Cambridge: Cambridge University Press, 1990), 15-16.
5 Don Handelman and Elihu Katz, 'State Ceremonies of Israel – Remembrance Day and Independence Day,' in *Models and Mirrors: Towards an Anthropology of Public Events*, (Cambridge: Cambridge University Press, 1990), 191.
6 Handelman, 8.
7 Michel Foucault, 'The Order of Discourse,' in *Language and Politics*, ed. Michael J. Shapiro (Oxford: Basil Blackwell, 1984), 110.
8 Handelman, 12.
9 Handelman, 11.
10 Handelman and Katz, 203-4.
11 *Ibid.*
12 Handelman and Katz, 206.
13 Handelman and Katz, 211.
14 *Ibid.*
15 See Handelman and Katz, 208.
16 *Jerusalem Post*, 28 April 1952, 3.
17 *Jerusalem Post*, 5 May 1954, 1.
18 This echoes the identical phrase in the Passover ceremony. *Jerusalem Post*, 20 April 1953, 3.
19 *Jerusalem Post*, 27 April 1955, 3.
20 *Jerusalem Post*, 15 April 1956, 3.
21 The First Temple was built by King Solomon [970-930 BCE] before the Babylonian Exile.
22 Handelman and Katz, 207.
23 In each ceremony, one bereaved woman (mother or wife) and one bereaved man (father) represents the families of the deceased. I compared the ways in which these individuals were described in the newspaper articles. Over the course of twenty years (twenty different ceremonies), the ceremony was virtually the same: one bereaved man, one bereaved woman. The difference in the reporting was the degree to which the men were named, the women anonymous.
24 *Jerusalem Post*, 7 February 1989, 2.
25 *Jerusalem Post*, 13 March 1989, 2.
26 *Jerusalem Post*, 2 June 1989, 5.
27 *Ha'aretz*, 23 May 2000, online.
28 *Jerusalem Report*, 7 June 2000, online.
29 *Jerusalem Post*, 25 April 1989, 2. Their suspicion led them to bring in an usher to see if there was a man hidden in this group of singing women.
30 *Jerusalem Post*, 25 April 1989, 5.
31 *Jerusalem Post*, 25 April 1989, 2.
32 Nannerl Keohane, 'Speaking from Silence: Women and the Science of Politics' in *A Feminist Perspective in the Academy*, ed. Elizabeth Langland (Chicago: University of Chicago Press, 1982), 97.

18 Revisiting a Site of Cultural Bondage: JoAnn Gibson Robinson's *Boycott Memoir*

Ruth Ellen Kocher

This essay considers JoAnn Gibson Robinson's 1987 memoir, The Montgomery Bus Boycott and the Women Who Started It, *as a contemporary slave narrative, given Robinson's siting of herself as a narrator-witness in every sense. Robinson writes with an anticipation of cross-examination and marks her disclosures, as did traditional authors of slave narratives, as record — as verification of historical fact. Kocher finds most significant to Robinson's memoir a voice and narrative technique reminiscent of nineteenth-century slave narratives, and finds* The Montgomery Bus Boycott… *to be a contemporary continuation of that genre, despite the hundred years separating Robinson and the former American slaves who authored such testimonials. The essay focuses on the ways that such a memoir becomes a site at which we may revisit the subject of cultural bondage as it existed for boycotters in the mid 1950s and, consequently, representative of the witness' voice, a voice that is, itself, historically suspect.*

JoAnn Gibson Robinson's narrative, *The Montgomery Bus Boycott and the Women Who Started It*, serves as a textual site at which we may revisit the often brutal circumstances and heroic negotiations of the Civil Rights movement in America. As a verification and clarification of the 1955 events in Birmingham, her narrative differs from such documents as Martin Luther King Jr.'s 'Letter From Birmingham Jail,' offering not only a personal account of the boycott events but also a testimonial meant to withstand speculation and scrutiny. I find the difference between Robinson's narrative and others like King's emerges from her disposition as a narrator-witness in every sense: she writes with an anticipation of cross-examination and marks her disclosures as record, pertinent among all others. Robinson, herself, becomes the locus of our revisitation, and yet, she lends her account to us as historical record, beyond reproach. Perhaps most significant to Robinson's memoir is a voice and narrative technique so reminiscent of nineteenth-century slave narratives that I argue her text to be a contemporary continuation of that genre, despite the hundred years separating Robinson and the former American slaves who authored such testimonials.

To read *The Montgomery Bus Boycott* as a slave narrative undoubtedly requires us to re-negotiate our perceptions of slavery and what, in fact, it means to be a slave. We learn through this reading that we must accept such bondage as a tangible, physical reality whether the (female) black body is restricted by chains or, in the case of Robinson, by severe societal limitations that not only hinder mobility but subject her to a continually hostile and physically threatening environment. Once we recognize Robinson's text as a slave narrative, dependent on nineteenth-century slave narratives as a collection of incumbent voices, we may begin to understand more fully the precedent nature of the oppressive dynamics in place at the onset of the Civil Rights era. Robinson's memoir is a primary cultural site that allows us to interpret and correlate the events of the civil rights movement as a continuation of slave rebellion and abolitionist sentiments commenced in the nineteenth century — and also as a recurring cultural trope in African American writing. Such an interpretation comes in opposition to one that would frame the era as a static set of events, commencing in 1955 and ending with the assassination of King in 1968, and thus reveals an integral relationship between the nineteenth-century slave narrative authors and contemporary black activists such as Robinson.   The task of writing memoir remains one of the foremost challenges to the African American who aims to substantiate a traditionally undervalued, overlooked and forsaken existence.   In his essay 'Narration, Authentication, and Authorial Control in Frederick Douglass' *Narrative* of 1845,' Robert Stepto recounts perhaps the most famous of the nineteenth-century examples of authenticated captivity experience while directing us to the premise that 'the strident, moral voice of the former slave recounting, exposing, appealing, apostrophizing and above all, *remembering* his ordeal in bondage is the single most impressive feature of a slave narrative.'[1]   While Stepto emphasizes the act of '*remembering,*' the acts of 'recounting, exposing and appealing' seem to collectively address the relationship inherent in the way the speaker establishes ethical appeal, that is, the ways in which the speaker is or is not believable to the reader. As we know from Aristotelian rhetoric, the ethical appeal establishes 'the speaker's good character' and 'credibility.'[2] This concern for ethical appeal (ethos) as an example of an intrinsic rhetorical proof comes as one often subtly privileged in the slave narrative above other such proofs that rely on emotion (pathos) or argument (logos). In line with this idea, Stepto posits in another work, 'Distrust of the Reader in Afro-American Narratives,' that an additional feature of such texts is an inherent suspicion on the part of the speaker directed toward the reader. It would seem that for Stepto, the African American writer's distrust functions as an integral mechanism in the translation of memory to record when the personal account of the speaker in a slave narrative responds to a reader's ethical distrust of that speaker, that is, of the speaker's 'good name' and thus, 'credibility.' Stepto observes that this distrust works both ways, such that the narrator *anticipates* an audience's distrust of the speaker as well. In sum, the narrator's testimony of events relates a precarious position, that of the 'speaker of truths,' while it also connotes the uneasiness, as does Robinson's text, of a witness on display.

Francis Smith Foster also examines the witness-speaker in *Witnessing Slavery: The Development of Ante-bellum Slave Narratives*, detailing the fundamental elements of the slave narrative and the shifting form of the genre.[3] Foster makes two significant elements clear: the intent and agenda of the narratives' authors and the general sentiments of whites towards the narratives and the slaves themselves. Foster sees the narrative changing as the institution of slavery changed, becoming more explicit in representations of violence and human suffering as the abolitionist movement gained steam. In my comparison of Robinson's memoir to the slave narratives of which Foster and Stepto speak, I posit that in her 'attack' on the slavish institution of segregation, Robinson engages a trope of *repetition and revision*; she continually reiterates what has been record, revising that history by interjecting her own, individual experience. Her telling becomes a site, or locus, of cultural exchange between the historical reality that excludes her and a revised, experiential history that does not. Robinson's memoir is a modern slave narrative in terms of narrative function — she utilizes narrative distrust as a mechanism, positioning her personal account as the pivotal testimony that informs a historicizing of experience. As the freed slave made his ordeal public for the benefit of other slaves, Robinson speaks for other blacks bound by the chains of segregation. In effect, her memoir is personal, yes, but becomes as well part of our public record. Consequently, Robinson's disclosure finds a place in the continuum of African American narratives as another telling of the former slave writing herself into history to authenticate and validate her existence and experience.

In her effort to recount and expose, Robinson utilizes three specific means. First, as a participant in the Civil Rights Movement, Robinson names names, both as an endorsement of her narrative and as a means of disclosing the identities of those involved with the planning and implementation of the boycott: those for and those against. As these names actuate some endorsement of the text, they also function as an indictment of the white community's resistance to Black progress in the same way as do some slave narratives, according to Foster. Robinson uses such verification as a means of countering the distrusting reader to whom Stepto refers. Next, she discloses authorial intent early in the novel in much the same way as Douglass and other writers of slave narratives reveal to the reader their intention in 'telling,' an agenda that is greatly invested in the righting of wrongs and the correction or substantiation of public record — a historicizing of experience. Last, she locates experience chronologically, geographically, and through the hierarchical relationships of those who officiated the boycott. She discloses testimony of specific times, dates, and places during which key events took place, as well as the identities of important figures mediating such events — a move that ultimately speaks to the interrogative relationship between speaker and reader within the slave narrative.

Before speaking to the three most prominent slave narrative characteristics present in Robinson's memoir, I would like to address David J. Garrow's introduction to the work and the role it plays in contextualizing her document. Foremost, I mean to point out the parallelisms between Garrow's introduction and those we find in classic accounts such as Frederick Douglass' *Narrative*. Garrow begins by explaining how he came to know Robinson, noting that he met her in April 1984 after requesting an interview concerning her role in the boycott. The language of both the classic narratives and Robinson's memoir are so important to our comparative understanding of their relationship that I take the liberty of quoting extended portions of text throughout this essay in order to emphasize correlations in content and tone. For example, in this portion of an introduction written for Frederick Douglass by William Lloyd Garrison, we may discern precedent not only for Garrow's objective, but also for his approach. He engages the reader through the advocational relationship he establishes with the author:

> In the month of August, 1841 I attended an anti-slavery convention in Nantucket, at which it was my happiness to become acquainted with Frederick Douglass, the writer of the following narrative...It was at once deeply impressed upon my mind, that, if Mr. Douglass could be persuaded to consecrate his time and talents to the promotion of the anti-slavery enterprise, a powerful impetus would be given to it...I therefore endeavored to instill hope and courage into his mind.[4]

Like Garrison, Garrow speaks of Robinson's position to convey her experience while foremost suggesting his role as a primary agent in her doing so:

> I began to realize just how much original never-before-told historical detail there was about black civic activism in Montgomery...Here indeed, I realized as I read further into her manuscript, was an autobiographical account that not only deserved publication, but that could be perhaps the most important participant-observer account of the Montgomery protest that students and scholars of the American black freedom struggle might ever have available.[5]

As Foster posits that slave narrative authors at length deny personal involvement in the impetus to print their texts, Garrow suggests the same in his introduction. He is careful to point out that he questions Robinson with 'encouragement,' assuring the reader of her modesty towards authorship:

> Mrs. Robinson remains generally hesitant to claim for herself the historical credit that she deserves for launching the Montgomery Bus Boycott of 1955-1956. Although her story fully and accurately describes how it was she, during the night and early morning hours of December 1 and 2, 1955,

who actually started the boycott on its way, it is only with some gentle encouragement that she will acknowledge herself as 'the instigator of the movement to start the boycott.[6]

In a similar way, Olaudah Equiano, alias Gustavus Vassa, offers such a disclaimer to any praise he might expect for bravely publishing his own memoir in 1792:

> If, then, the following narrative does not appear sufficiently interesting to engage general attention, let my motive be some excuse for its publication. I am not so foolishly vain to expect from it either immortality or literary reputation. If it affords any satisfaction to my numerous friends, at whose request it has been written, or in the smallest degree promotes the interests of humanity, the ends for which it was undertaken will be fully attained.[7]

Even by the end of the introduction, the structural and contextual correspondence of Robinson's work to classic narratives such as Equiano's and Douglass' begins to emerge as a tonal framing spoken by an authorial agent to the engaged reader. In accordance with this design, Robinson embarks on the narrative with thanks and dedications to all those who stood up for the movement. Her words come as a familiar reminder to readers who recognize the directives of former slaves whose narratives were preceded by praise meant for abolitionist mentors and literary benefactors.

Distrust and Naming

Although we see in Douglass the inclination to name his various masters, Henry Louis Gates Jr., in his introduction to *Our Nig: or Sketches from the Life of a Free Black*, a text initially written in 1859 that also, inarguably, reads as a slave narrative, posits that 'not one other author before Harriet Wilson felt compelled to anticipate the "severe" criticisms of even the Northern Abolitionists.'[8] Gates suggests here that Wilson's anticipation of the readers' distrust of her would be unique within the genre of slave narrative. However, Gates' own edited collection, *The Classic Slave Narratives*, offers us some evidence to the contrary. In 1814, Olaudah Equiano published his own *Interesting Narrative* in which his dedication is thinly disguised as an elevation of ethical appeal. Equiano dedicates the work to his 'Lords and Gentlemen' and in the preface, like Douglass and Robinson, names names of 'whites in high regard':

> The subscription list of the first edition could boast, that it was graced with the names of a greater number of worthy characters that had before adorned the pages of any small

> book published in this country. Their Royal Highnesses the
> Prince of Wales, the Dukes of York and Cumberland; the
> Dukes of Marlborough, Bedford, Northumberland, &c; the
> Duchess of Buccleugh....[9]

Perhaps not as overt an appeal as Wilson's, Equiano's inclusion of this list of patrons serves to validate his telling as a grand assortment of aristocratic and imperial endorsements. Equiano did, in fact, anticipate doubt in response to his testimony. His counter discourse anticipates the 'severe criticisms' of his readership:

> An objection, but a very unreasonable one, has been raised
> against the author, for the account which he gives of his
> native country; his own noble extraction; and the manners,
> customs and religion of his countrymen. To many people it
> has seemed too circumstantial to be recollected by a youth,
> who was but eleven years of age when he was forced to visit
> foreign lands. But whoever will give himself the trouble of
> reflecting on what passed during his own infancy...could
> himself give a very accurate detail of their sports and
> usages.[10]

Like Equiano, Linda Brent begins her own telling in *Incidents in the Life of a Slave Girl* by entreating the reader to 'believe this narrative is no fiction.'[11] While Brent's narrative was published in 1861, two years after Wilson's, Douglass' *Narrative* precedes *Our Nig* as does *The History of Mary Prince* in which we are assured that 'It was written out fully, with...Mary's exact expressions and peculiar phraseology.'[12] While these numerous accounts may not anticipate 'severe criticisms' as explicitly as did Wilson's, we are hard pressed to ignore how these disclosures play into the cycle of distrust between reader and writer of the testimonial narrative. As a characteristic of the slave narrative, naming serves the author in various capacities but comes to one final purpose: to mark, through implicit collusion, other witnesses who can substantiate, verify, and endorse the personal disclosure of the author.

Even in her opening dedication, Robinson begins to name names: 'Mrs. A. W. West, Mrs. Alberta James, Mrs. Daisy Poole' — all women who can verify black efforts to shuttle boycotters back and forth across Montgomery.[13] This information becomes an important detail in the recognition of the black protest as a calculated movement of self-preservation. Such naming is an integral feature to narratives like Douglass' where his role of witness is compounded by his role as fugitive. He names names so that his white reading public may verify his testimony, yet at the same time exposes former masters as treacherous and himself as a criminal. Likewise, Robinson goes to great pains in the text to verify her testimony by disclosing even the smallest details of planning throughout the boycott. She does so in an effort to counter charges that the movement was serendipitous, an emotional compulsion of a people who could not think through such an elaborate exercise in civil disobedience. Her decision to address this yet unspoken character assault by a suspicious reader places her within a tradition of African American writers who acknowledge themselves as suspect given the context of racial abjection to which they have historically been lost. What we have in the telling of the slave narrative is a historical pattern of qualification meant to counter prospective attacks on the part of a reader who doubts the 'verifiable' truths proffered by a slave's own hand.

The Author's Agenda

The relationship between writer and reader is one that comes not so simply for slave narrative authors. The air of distrust apparent in such a relationship is underwritten first by the author's agenda. Consequently, in disclosing her authorial intent in the preface, Robinson assumes the role of a narrator who, like nineteenth-century narrative authors, means her disclosure to be understood as sociopolitical commentary. Her words aim to clarify for the reader a revised history in light of a flawed one. The writer of the slave narrative aims to make this 'correction' in a substantiating way, making her testimonial public and permanent. In his own statement of authorial intent, Douglass reminds us that 'we have been left long enough to gather the character of slavery from the involuntary evidence of the masters.'[14] Robinson, as well, counters the reader who questions her intent:

> I have chosen to record the facts of the Montgomery Bus Boycott for several reasons. The first is general: so that the world will know that black people of America are not, as stereotypes have depicted them for generations, a "happy-go-lucky," self-satisfied, complacent, lazy, good-for nothing race that has nothing good or worthwhile to offer society. I have attempted to relate the verifiable truth in every area of concern, so that the reader will know *why* fifty thousand black citizens walked off city transit lines.[15]

Robinson's barrage of stereotypical adjectives serves as an assault upon deplorable typologies. Her attack on the 'happy-go-lucky' fallacy may sound familiar to us as one Douglass also addresses:

> I have often been utterly astonished, since I came to the north, to find persons who could speak of the singing, among slaves, as evidence of their contentment and happiness. It is impossible to conceive of a greater mistake. Slaves sing most when they are most unhappy. The songs of the slave represent the sorrows of his heart; and he is relieved by them, only as an aching heart is relieved by its tears.[16]

Like Douglass, Robinson attempts to solicit justification through qualification of her acts. Why blacks walked off of the transit system in Montgomery becomes as much a part of Robinson's telling as the cruel conditions Douglass proclaims to be the common experience of his 'manacled brethren'; they, like Robinson, have no moral choice but to act in the interest of self-preservation.[17] Both writers are enabled to negotiate and mediate the ethical concerns and reactions of their readers *because* of their own participation in the events of their narratives. Such involvement reveals to the world a witness who is not a bystander but instead an agent, marking the writer's disclosure as historicized experience simultaneous to the written record — purpose and direction conflated at the moment the author puts pen to paper.

As Stepto points out in regard to the *Narrative*, Douglass authors his record in response to the reader's distrust of him — to the scrutinizing assessment of his ethos, his character. While we can benefit from a rhetorical analysis of Douglass' Aristotelian methodology in epidectic and/or ceremonial modes of discourse, we are better engaged as readers in understanding the nature of Douglass' (and Robinson's) reciprocating distrust. It seems that this motivating distrust, along with an impetus to transform memory and experience into testimonial account, moves the speaker to repetitiously verify the verifiable. In this way, the slave narrative's author, both classic and contemporary, reveals an agenda in the form of the cultural trope of *repetition* and *revision*. The trope functions to convey experience. The author reiterates verifiable details of previously recorded experience within this reiteration of the existing record. Robinson not only offers us the details of her activity, she supplies us with personal and emotional accounts of the mistreatment of blacks, in conjunction with intricate time frames and locations, compounding verifiable facts. In so doing, she makes claims in accordance with her authorial design, and simultaneously offers conclusive proofs as well. Her ethos emerges early on in the narrative and she foregoes the dialogic bantering that would lead us from speaker to listener, writer to reader, in a rhetorical battle of argumentative points. The monotonous cycle of presentation, refutation, qualification, and resignation is anticipated by Robinson and, through the use of repetition and revision, countered with inherent textual and factual support.

Time, Place, and Face

At the outset of the narrative, after she engages the reader in an ethical validation of her character, Robinson proceeds to give multiple accounts of objectionable treatment endured by numerous other black citizens of Montgomery, a foundational pattern of corroboration that serves to justify the imminent move to boycott. We learn of 'a group of men' abandoned at a bus stop after paying their fares and deboarding to re-enter through the rear exit, 'a mentally defective but harmless black man' who was beaten by a driver, even a driver who collects his own 'witnesses' to an incident where he closed the doors on a black woman before she had fully entered the bus, trapping her. Robinson uses geographical locus as an index of proof within the memoir, virtually citing the landscape as witness to her experience. She gives us numerous accounts in which she is careful to record street intersections, regions of the city and even, in some cases, specific bus routes: 'Buses to Cloverdale were usually crowded with these domestic helpers in the early morning and again in the late afternoon when they came off duty. Meanwhile, whites rode from home into town in the mornings and back again in the afternoon. Thus black passengers occupied the buses going one way and the whites the other.'[18] In citing geographical locations as integral aspects of the memoir, Robinson creates a record that potentially jogs the memories of her corroborators, placing them within a physical context that facilitates their own historicizing of experience, making the record collaborative.

Likewise, chronology becomes an important aspect of Robinson's telling, in the same way that details of times and dates are important in narratives like Douglass'. We are told of events in 1951, 1952, and 1954 that lead up to the decisive moment of the boycott on 5 December, 1955. Robinson cites an editorial in the *Advertiser* on 8 December of that same year detailing the recent boycott. She also directs us to a bus company manager's announcement that bus service in select boycotting neighborhoods would be discontinued, an obvious move on the part of white management to discount the black riders' concerns. Robinson notes that on Monday, 19 December, 'the appointed interracial committee met as planned at nine o'clock in...the Chamber of Commerce, to try again to find a solution,' but adds that, in lieu of finding such a solution, the motion to accept a number of proposals by black Montgomerians requested in that meeting by Dr. King was 'talked to death.'[19] Her dates appear as a persistent means of speaking the truths that have not been spoken previously, while providing a chronological framework to which a reader may refer and so qualify the disposition of her narration. It would seem that this strategy not only validates her testimony for the reader but, in this case, also emphasizes black Montgomerians' heart-felt desire for real reconciliation with, and accountability on the part of, whites in transportation management.

In her account of early attempts at management and mediation, Robinson seems to imply that the white negotiators apparently waited for the boycotters to become frustrated, perhaps even bored, with their campaign. In Robinson's account of minor concessions, such as allowing black passengers to at least temporarily occupy seats reserved for whites until those patrons boarded the buses, we are reminded of Douglass' warnings in *Narrative* against complacency brought about by the lure of temporary 'leisure':

> During these leisure times, those old notions about freedom would steal over me again. When in Mr. Gardner's employment, I was kept in such a perpetual whirl of

> excitement, I could think of nothing, scarcely, but my life; and in thinking of my life, I almost forgot my liberty. I have observed this in my experience of slavery — that whenever my condition was improved, instead of its increasing my contentment, it only increased my desire to be free, and set me to thinking of plans to gain my freedom.[20]

This insatiable drive to freedom from bondage characterizes the slave narrative — and Robinson's memoir — as a record of desire continually made trivial in the face of minor concessions by officials in positions of mediating authority. Because such personal and often emotional information may inflect her testimony as suspect, Robinson discloses many of her own 'verifiable' truths as part of a public record already in existence. As one example, she states: 'In 1956, the superintendent of a local hospital, which...treated many ...fight victims, told a reporter that since the boycott began, the hospital had fewer such patients. Thus the hospital official corroborated the WPC's (Women's Political Council) findings that bitter bus experiences could have caused...fights in the home.'[21]   Robinson brings not only public record into consideration here but public officials who, perhaps unwillingly, validate the author's ethical qualifications and the nature of her disclosure as viable. As a final, crowning means of such verification, Robinson includes a 'Glossary of Individuals' as well as a 'Chronology of Events' at the end of her memoir.

Besides her attention to chronology, geography and positions of authority, Robinson also appears to possess a genuine concern for re-corroboration, that is, straightening out facts that may have, in the years since the boycott, become skewed, exaggerated, or simply mistold. She assures us that 'Dr. Mary Fair Burks organized the WPC to fight segregation. Dr. Martin Luther King, Jr. and the ministers, along with Mr. E.D. Nixon, Mr. Rufus Lewis, and many others established the Montgomery Improvement Association. But they did not call the boycott.'[22] Within an otherwise modest proposal of activity and participation, a narrative in which Robinson and other women regularly defer to their male counterparts, she seems to stand her ground here, acknowledging Martin Luther King Jr.'s leadership while attributing the genesis of the movement to other sources. This move absolves Dr. King of direct involvement but at the same time leaves us to wonder, with a prompt from Robinson's title, more of the women who occupied the central battalions of the Montgomery conflict — a matter which deserves additional and significant investigation in and of itself.

We do eventually learn of Mrs. Maude Ballou, Mrs. Martha Johnson, and Mrs. Hazel Gregory, all of whom helped Robinson in organizational efforts along with 'hundreds of volunteers.'[23] But even these bastions of civil improvement are overlooked in public records before Robinson's memoir. Because these 'women who started it,' as Robinson so boldly points out in the memoir's title, are not recognized as true leaders, they merely become part of the female force *behind* the boycott. We are reminded of Robinson's attack on stereotypical representations of blacks as 'complacent, lazy, good-for nothing' people at the same time that she reveals their characteristic worth:

> Contributions came from around the world, either directly to the MIA [Montgomery Improvement Association] or through various churches whose ministers turned them over to the MIA. At the very beginning, the Finance Committee — a group of volunteers, men of means, honesty and purpose — took charge of the collections. These "selected persons" received the money, counted it, rolled it up by amounts and gave it to the treasurer. They accompanied the treasurer to the banking places where the money was safe in deposits.[24]

It is no narrative accident that Robinson so candidly explains the inner workings of the movement's financial network, the exactitude of contribution assessment and the ethical qualifications of the money handlers. Like Douglass, she accounts for even the minor details of character within her narrative, citing and inciting our speculative evaluations as readers. What do we know of the men who handled the money of the movement? We know that they were 'men of means — honesty and purpose' and that they were 'selected' by equally honest participants in the movement. While relegated to roles of support, the women seem also to wield some power in determining the direction the movement takes by choosing not only their leaders but also key participants in the boycott. Robinson reveals a collective pool of female strategists who carefully plan and execute the boycott that leads to their deliverance from the municipal bondage to which they are subject. Robinson's disclosure of intent informs her telling just as Douglass' description of his calculated escape discloses his 'contemplated start,' conveying a sense of urgency and necessity as well as meticulous preparation.[25]

Conclusion

Robinson's account of the Montgomery boycott unfolds as that of an active participant. She presents her memoir as a personal testimonial of events to which we have been privileged historically but, without the benefit of her personal account, about which we have historically been misinformed. Her memoir functions not as an appendage to historical artifact but instead as a retelling that situates her as narrator, as one who may be suspect, but as a witness who wields the power of substantiation and revision of public record. As the central witness in her slave narrative, like Douglass, Robinson demonstrates an obvious concern for the verifiable facts that allow us, as readers, to accept her testimony as a 'speaking of truths.' She ultimately reveals the names of her figurative captors: the white establishment that facilitates her bondage through continual passive endorsement of brutal treatment of blacks on Montgomery buses. We should recognize the methods employed here, the painstaking detail that Robinson submits as evidence of personal accountability, the attempts to throw off the chains of subjugation, demonstrated repeatedly throughout the memoir. We learn from this telling, as we learn from traditional slave narratives, that bondage comes in many forms, and that the spirit may be shackled as well as the body. The most important role for the deterred then, besides that of serving as their own emancipators, becomes the role exemplified by Robinson: that of witness, verifier of truths, and contributor to a collective history of which woman may finally become a part.

Notes

1   Robert Stepto, 'Narration, Authentication, Authorial Control in Frederick Douglass' Narrative of 1845,' in *Afro-American Literature: The Reconstruction of Instruction*, eds. Dexter Fisher and Robert B. Stepto (New York: MLA, 1979), 178-9.

2   James J. Murphy and Richard A. Katula, *A Synoptic History of Classical Rhetoric*. (Davis: Hermagoras Press, 1994)., 152-4.

3   Frances Smith Foster, *Witnessing Slavery: The Development of Ante-bellum Slave Narratives*. (Westport: Greenwood Press, 1979), 87-93.

4   Henry Louis Gates, Jr., ed., *The Classic Slave Narratives* (New York: Mentor, 1987), 244-7.

5   Gates, Introduction, xi.

6   Ibid.

7   Gates, 12.

8   Gates, Introduction, vi-vii.

9   Gates, 5.

10   Gates, 6-7.

11   Gates, 335.

12   Gates, 185.

13   Jo Ann Gibson Robinson, *The Montgomery Bus Boycott and the Women Who Started It: The Memoir of Jo Ann Gibson Robinson*, David J. Garrow, ed. (Knoxville: University of Tennessee Press, 1987), 3.

14   Gates, *The Classic Slave Narratives*, 252.

15   Robinson, 11.

16   Gates, 263.

17   Gates, 254.

18   Robinson, 34.

19   Robinson, 88-9.

20   Gates, 314-15.

21   Robinson, 37.

22   Robinson, 40.

23   Robinson, 64.

24   Robinson, 72.

25   Gates, 319.

Bibliography

Abrams, Lynn and Elizabeth Harvey, eds. *Gender Relations in German History: Power, Agency, and Experience from the Sixteenth to the Twentieth Century.* Durham: Duke University Press, 1996.

Acheson, Katherine O., ed. *The Diary of Anne Clifford 1616-1619: A Critical Edition.* New York and London: Garland, 1995.

Alcoff, Linda. 'Cultural Feminism versus Post-Structuralism, the Identity Crisis in Feminist Theory.' *Signs* 13, no. 3 (1988): 405-36.

Amussen, Susan Dwyer. *An Ordered Society. Gender and Class in Early Modern England.* New York: Columbia University Press, 1988.

Anthias, Floya and Nira Yuval-Davis. *Racialised Boundaries.* London: Routledge, 1993.

Arditi, Jorge. 'The Feminization of Etiquette Literature: Foucault, Mechanisms of Social Change, and the Paradoxes of Empowerment.' *Sociological Perspectives* 39, no. 3 (1996): 417-34.

Aulnoy, Madame de [Countess of Dunois]. *The Memoirs of the Countess of Dunois: Author of the Lady's Travels into Spain. Written by her Self before her Retirement By Way of Answer to Monsieur St. Evremont. Containing withal A Modest Vindication of the Female Sex, more frequently injur'd by imprudence and Misconstruction, then Defect of Vertue.* London, 1699.

———. *Memoirs of the court of England... To Which is Added, The Lady's Pacquet of Letters. Taken from her by a French Privateer in her Passage to Holland...* London, 1707.

Baillie, H. M. 'Etiquette and the Planning of the State Apartments in Baroque Palaces.' *Archaeologia* (1967): 169-99.

Banet-Weiser, Sarah. *The Most Beautiful Girl in the World: Beauty Pageants and National Identity.* Berkeley: University of California Press, 1999.

Beilin, Elaine. *Redeeming Eve: Women Writers of the English Renaissance.* Princeton: Princeton University Press, 1987.

Berlant, Lauren. *The Anatomy of National Fantasy: Hawthorne, Utopia, and Everyday Life.* Chicago: University of Chicago Press, 1991.

Bidyābhūsan, Jogendranāth. '*Mañce Bārāṅganā* [Prostitutes on stage].' *Āryadarśan* 4, no.5 (Calcutta, 1877).

Blair, Walter. Introduction to *Crockett at 200: New Perspectives on the Man and the Myth,* edited by Michael A. Lofaro and Joe Cummings, 3-6. Knoxville: University of Tennessee Press, 1989.

Blamires, Alcuin. *The Case for Women in Medieval Culture.* Oxford: Clarendon Press; New York: Oxford University Press, 1997.

Bloom, Harold, ed. *Cleopatra.* New York: Chelsea House Publishers, 1990.

Boland, Eavan. *Object Lessons: The Life of the Woman and the Poet in Our Time.* New York: Norton Publishing, 1995.

Bordo, Susan. 'Feminism, Foucault and The Politics of the Body.' In *Reconstructing Foucault: Essays in the Wake of the 80's*, edited by Ricardo Miguel-Alfonso and Silvia Caporale-Bizzini, 219-43. Amsterdam: Rodolpi, 1994.

——. *Unbearable Weight: Feminism, Western Culture, and the Body.* Berkeley: University of California Press, 1993.

Botkin, B.A. *A Treasury of New England Folklore.* New York: Crown Publishers, 1947.

Boureau, Alain. 'Richard Southern: A Landscape for a Portrait.' *Past and Present* 165 (1999): 218-29.

Braverman, Richard. *Plots and Counterplots: Sexual politics and the body politic in English literature, 1660-1730.* Cambridge Studies in Eighteenth-Century English Literature and Thought, 18. Cambridge: Cambridge University Press, 1993.

Briggs, Robin. 'The Theatre State: Ceremony and Politics, 1600-60.' *Seventeenth-Century French Studies* 16 (1994): 15-32.

Britonio di Sicignano, Girolamo. *Opera Volgare, intitolata Gelosia del Sole.* Naples: Sigismondo Mair, 1519.

Bromhall, Susan. ' "In my opinion": Charlotte de Minut and Female Political Discussion in Print in Sixteenth-Century France.' *Sixteenth-Century Journal* 31 (2000): 24-45.

Brown, Carolyn. *The Tall Tale in American Folklore and Literature.* Knoxville: University of Tennessee Press, 1987.

Brown, Elizabeth A. R. 'Authority, the Family, and the Dead in Late-Medieval France.' *French Historical Studies* 16 (1990): 803-32.

Brown, Terence. *Ireland: A Social and Cultural History.* London: Fontana, 1987.

Bynum, Caroline Walker. *The Resurrection of the Body in Western Christianity, 200-1336.* New York: Columbia University Press, 1995.

Caldwell, Patricia. 'The Antinomian Language Controversy.' *Harvard Theological Review* 69 (1976): 345-67.

Canfield, J. Douglas. *Word as Bond in English Literature from the Middle Ages to the Restoration.* Philadelphia: University of Pennsylvania Press, 1989.

Canfield, J. Douglas and Deborah C. Payne, eds. *Cultural Readings of Restoration and Eighteenth-Century English Theater.* Athens, GA: University of Georgia Press, 1995.

Carby, Hazel. *Reconstructing Womanhood: The Emergence of the Afro-American Woman Novelist.* New York: Oxford University Press, 1987.

Caudhurī, Darśan. *Uniś Śataker Nāṭyabisay* [Topics in nineteenth century theatre]. Calcutta: Pustak Bipani, 1985.

Cerasano, S.P. and Marion Wynne-Davies, eds. *Renaissance Drama by Women: Texts and Documents.* New York: Routledge, 1996.

Charnes, Linda. *Notorious Identity: Materializing the Subject in Shakespeare.* Cambridge, MA and London: Harvard University Press, 1993.

Chatterjee, Partha. *The Nation and Its Fragments: Colonial and Postcolonial Histories.* Princeton, NJ: Princeton University Press, 1993.

Chester, Pamela and Forrester, Sibelan, eds. *Engendering Slavic Literatures.* Bloomington, IN: Indiana University Press, 1996.

Cheung, King-Kok. 'The Woman Warrior versus The Chinaman Pacific: Must a Chinese-American Critic Choose Between Feminism and Heroism?' In *Conflicts in Feminism*, edited by Marianne Hirsch and Evelyn Fox Keller, 234-51. NY: Routledge, 1990. Reprinted in *Critical Essays on Maxine Hong Kingston*, edited by Laura E. Skandera-Trombley, 107-24. New York: G.K. Hall, 1998.

Chin, Frank. 'This Is Not an Autobiography.' *Genre* 18.2 (1985): 109-30.

Clifford, D. J. H. ed. *The Diaries of Lady Anne Clifford.* Stroud, Gloucestershire: Sutton Publishing, 1990.

Coffin, Tristram. 'Daisy Miller: Western Hero.' In *James's* Daisy Miller: *The Story, the Play, the Critics*, edited by William T. Stafford, 136-7. Scribner Research Anthologies, edited by Martin Steinmann, Jr. New York: Scribner, 1963.

Comensoli, Viviana and Anne Russell, eds. *Enacting Gender on the English Renaissance Stage*. Urbana: University of Illinois Press, 1999.

Cotton, Nancy. *Women Playwrights in England 1363-1750*. Lewisburg: Bucknell University Press, 1980.

Cunnally, John. *Images of the Illustrious: The Numismatic Presence in the Renaissance*. Princeton: Princeton University Press, 1999.

Curran, Stuart. 'Romantic Poetry: The I Altered.' In *Romanticism and Feminism*, edited by Anne K. Mellor, 185-207. Bloomington: Indiana University Press, 1988.

———. 'Women readers, women writers.' In *The Cambridge Companion to British Romanticism*, edited by Stuart Curran, 177-96. Cambridge: Cambridge University Press, 1993.

Czernik, Stanisław, ed. 'Dziewczyna na wojnie [A girl in war].' In *Polska epoka ludowa* [Poland during the era of the people], 275-6. Series I, no. 176. Wrocław: Biblioteka Narodowa, 1958.

Datta, Kiraṇ Candra. *Baṅgīya Nāṭyaśālār Itihās* [The history of the Bengali theatre]. Calcutta: Paścim Baṅga Nāṭya Ākādemi, 1996.

Dāsī, Binodinī. *Āmār Kathā o Anyānya Racanā* [My words and other writings]. Edited by Soumitra Caṭṭopādhyāy and Nirmālya Āchārya. Calcutta: Subarnarekhā, 1987.

Davies, H. Neville. 'All for Love: Text and Contexts.' *Cahiers Elisabethains* 36 (Oct 1989): 49-71.

Davis-Kimball, Jeannine. 'Warrior Women of the Eurasian Steppes.' *Archaelogy Magazine* 50, no. 1 (January/February 1997): 45-8.

Deveaux, Monique. 'Feminism and Enpowerment. A Critical Reading of Foucault.' *Feminist Studies* 20, no. 2 (1994): 223-47.

Difranco, Ani. *Not a Pretty Girl*. LP. Righteous Babe Records.

Dobson, Michael. *The Making of the National Poet: Shakespeare, Adaptation and Authorship, 1660-1769*. Oxford: Clarendon Press, 1992.

Dolan, Frances E., ed. *Taming of the Shrew. Texts and Contexts*. New York: St. Martin's Press, 1996.

Dorson, Richard. *America in Legend: Folklore from the Colonial Period to the Present*. New York: Pantheon Books, 1973.

———. *Davy Crockett: American Comic Legend*. New York: Arno Press, 1977.

———. *Jonathan Draws the Long Bow: New England Popular Tales and Legends*. Cambridge, MA: Harvard University Press, 1946.

Doza, Christine. 'Bloodlove.' In *Listen Up: Voices from the Next Feminist Generation*, edited by Barbara Findlen, 249-57. Seattle: Seal, 1995.

Dryden, John. *All for Love*. In *The Works of John Dryden*, Vol. 13, edited by Maximillian E. Novak. Berkeley: University of California Press, 1984.

Duindam, Jeroen. *Myths of Power*. Amsterdam: Amsterdam University Press, 1994.

Ellis, Grace A. *A Selection from the Poems and Prose Writings of Mrs. Anna Lætitia Barbauld*. Boston: James R. Osgood and Company, 1874.

Elshtain, Jean Bethke. 'Feminist Discourse and Its Discontents: Language, Power and Meaning.' *Signs* 7, no. 3 (1982): 603-21.

Evelyn, John. *The Diary of John Evelyn*. Edited by E.S. De Beer. Vol 4. Oxford: Clarendon Press, 1955.

Ferino-Pagden, Sylvia, ed. *Vittoria Colonna, Dichterin und Muse Michelangelos*. Vienna: Kunsthistorisches Museum; Skira, 1997.

ffolliott, Sheila. 'The Ideal Queenly Patron of the Renaissance: Catherine de' Medici Defining Herself or Defined by Others?' In *Women and Art in Early Modern Europe: Patrons,*

Collectors, and Connoisseurs, edited by Cynthia Lawrence, 99-111. University Park: Pennsylvania State University Press, 1997.

Fielding, Sarah. *The History of Ophelia*. London, 1760.

Fitch, Suzanne Pullon and Roseann M. Mandziuk. *Sojourner Truth as Orator: Wit, Story, and Song*. Westpo.t, CT: Greenwood Press, 1997.

Floyd-Wilson, Mary. 'Ophelia and Femininity in the Eighteenth Century: "Dangerous conjectures in ill-breeding minds."' *Women's Studies* 21 (1992): 397-409.

Fong, Katheryn. 'To Maxine Hong Kingston: A Letter.' *Bulletin for Concerned Asian Scholars* 9, no. 4 (1977): 67-9.

Foster, Frances Smith. *Witnessing Slavery: The Development of Ante-bellum Slave Narratives*. Westport: Greenwood Press, 1979.

Foucault, Michel. 'The Order of Discourse.' In *Language and Politics*, edited by Michael J. Shapiro, 108-38. Basil Blackwell: Oxford, 1984.

Frankenberg, Ruth. *White Women, Race Matters: The Social Construction of Whiteness*. Minneapolis: University of Minnesota Press, 1993.

———, ed. *Displacing Whiteness: Essays in Social and Cultural Criticism*. Durham: Duke University Press, 1997.

Friedman, Alice T. 'Wife in the English Country House: Gender and the Meaning of Style in Early Modern England.' In *Women and Art in Early Modern Europe: Patrons, Collectors, and Connoisseurs*, edited by Cynthia Lawrence, 111-25. University Park: Pennsylvania State University Press, 1997.

———. 'Constructing an Identity in Prose, Plaster and Paint: Lady Anne Clifford as Writer and Patron of the Arts.' In *Albion's Classicism: The Visual Arts in Britain, 1550-1660*, edited by Lucy Gent, 359-76. New Haven and London: Yale University Press, 1995.

———. Architecture, Authority, and the Female Gaze: Planning and Representation in the Early Modern Country House.' *Assemblage* 18 (1992): 41-61.

Frye, Joanne. *Living Stories, Telling Lives: Women and the Novel in Contemporary Experience*. Women and Culture Series. Ann Arbor: University of Michigan Press, 1986.

Frye, Marilynne. 'On Being White: Thinking Toward a Feminist Understanding of Race and Race Supremacy.' In *The Politics of Reality: Essays in Feminist Theory*, 110-27. Freedom, CA: Crossing, 1983.

Gage, Mrs. F.D. 'Sojourner Truth.' *Independent,* 23 April 1863.

Garnier, Robert. *Two Tragedies: Hippolyte and Marc Antoine*. Edited by Christine M. Hill and Mary G. Morrison. London: Athlone Press, 1975.

Gatens, Moira. 'Corporeal representation in/and the body politic.' In *Cartographies, Poststructuralism and the mapping of bodies and spaces*, edited by Rosalyn Diprose and Robyn Ferrell, 79-92. North Sydney, Australia: Allen and Unwin, 1991.

Gates, Henry Louis, Jr., ed. *The Classic Slave Narratives*. New York: Mentor, 1987.

Gent, Lucy and Nigel Llewellyn, eds. *Renaissance Bodies: The Human Figure in English Culture ca. 1540-1660*. London: Reaktion Books, 1990.

Ghoṣ, Giriś Candra. *Giriś Racanābalī*. Edited by Debīpada Bhaṭṭācārya. Calcutta: Sāhitya Saṅgsad, 1972.

Girouard, Mark. *Life in the English Country House: A Social and Architectural History*. New Haven and London: Yale University Press, 1978.

Goodwin, Sarah Webster and Elisabeth Bronfen, eds. *Death and Representation*. Baltimore: Johns Hopkins University Press, 1993.

Gordon, Linda. 'What's New in Women's History.' In *Feminist Studies, Critical Studies*, edited by T. de Lauretis, 20-30. Madison, WI: The Regents of the University of Wisconsin System, 1986.

Gray, Breda and Louise Ryan. '(Dis)locating "Woman" and Women in Representations of Irish National Identity.' In *Women and Irish Society: A Sociological Reader*, edited by Anne Byrne and Madeleine Leonard, 517-34. Belfast: Beyond the Pale Publications, 1997.

Gubar, Susan. 'What Ails Feminist Criticism?' *Critical Inquiry* 24 (1999): 878-902.

————. Critical Condition: Feminism at the Turn of the Century. New York: Columbia University Press, 2000.

Guth, Christine M. E. *Art, Tea, and Industry: Masuda Takashi and the Mitsui Circle.* Princeton: Princeton University Press, 1993.

Hall, David D., ed. *The Antinomian Controversy, 1636-38: A Documentary History.* 2nd ed. Durham and London: Duke University Press, 1990.

Hallam, Elizabeth, Jenny Hockey, and Glennys Howard. *Beyond the Body: Death and Social Identity.* London and New York: Routledge, 1999.

Hamer, Mary. *Signs of Cleopatra: History, Politics, Representation.* New York: Routledge, 1993.

Handelman, Don. *Models and Mirrors: Towards an Anthropology of Public Events.* Cambridge: Cambridge University Press, 1990.

Hannay, Margaret. *Philip's Phoenix: Mary Sidney, Countess of Pembroke.* Oxford: Oxford University Press, 1990.

Harding, Sandra. *Whose Science? Whose Knowledge? Thinking from Women's Lives.* Ithaca, NY: Cornell University Press, 1991.

Hauck, Richard Boyd. 'The Man in the Buckskin Hunting Shirt: Fact and Fiction in the Crockett Story.' In *Davy Crockett: The Man, the Legend, the Legacy, 1786-1986*, edited by Michael A. Lofaro, 3-20. Knoxville: University of Tennessee Press, 1985.

Hayakawa, Noriyo. *Kindai tennôsei kokka to jendâ.* [Modern imperialist state and gender]. Tokyo: Aoki Shoten, 1998.

Heal, Felicity. *Hospitality in Early Modern England.* Oxford: Clarendon Press, 1990.

Heldke, Lisa. 'On Being a Responsible Traitor: A Primer.' In *Daring to Be Good: Essays in Feminist Ethico-Politics.* Thinking Gender Series, edited by Bat-Ami Bar On and Ann Ferguson, 87-99. New York: Routledge, 1998.

Heywood, Leslie and Jennifer Drake. 'We Learn America like a Script: Activism in the Third Wave; or, Enough Phantoms of Nothing.' In *Third Wave Agenda: Being Feminist, Doing Feminism*, 40-54. Minneapolis: University of Minnesota Press, 1997.

Higgins, Patricia. 'The Reactions of Women, with special references to women petitioners.' In *Politics, Religion and the English Civil War*, edited by Brian Manning, 179-97. London: Edward Arnold, 1973.

Hill, George F. *A Corpus of Italian Medals of the Renaissance before Cellini.* London: British Museum, 1930.

Hill, George F., and Graham Pollard. *Renaissance Medals from the Samuel H. Kress Collection at the National Gallery of Art.* London: Phaidon Press, 1967.

Hirahara, Hokudo, ed. *Shinchû: Onna-daigaku* [The Great Learning for women. With new annotations]. Kyoto: Bunka-jihôsha, 1943.

Hirst, Michael. *Sebastiano del Piombo.* Oxford: Oxford University Press, 1981.

Hisada, Waki. *Kokusui-sahô* [Manners for genuine nationalists]. Sasebo: Sasebo Girls' Sewing School, 1937.

Hisamatsu, Shin'ichi. 'Sadô-bunka no seikaku.' [Characteristics of the culture of the tea ceremony]. 1947. In *Sadô no tetsugaku* [Philosophy of the tea ceremony], edited by Jikai Fujiyoshi, 52-61. Tokyo: Kodan-sha, 1987.

Hodgkin, Katharine. 'The Diary of Anne Clifford: A Study of Class and Gender in the Seventeenth Century.' *History Workshop* 19 (Spring 1985): 148-61.

Hogan, Charles Beecher. *Shakespeare in the Theater, 1701-1800.* Oxford: Clarendon Press, 1952-7.

Holdgate, Martin. *A History of Appleby.* Appleby: Dalesman Books, 1982.

Hollanda, Francisco de. *Four Dialogues on Painting*, trans. Aubrey F. G. Bell. Oxford: Oxford University Press, 1928.

Homans, Margaret. *Bearing the Word: Language and Female Experience in Nineteenth-Century Women's Writing.* Chicago: University of Chicago Press, 1986.

hooks, bell. *Feminist Theory: From Margin to Center.* 2nd ed. Cambridge: South End, 2000.

Hosmer, James Kendall, ed. *Winthrop's Journal: 'History of New England,' 1630-1649.* 2 vols. New York: Barnes and Noble, 1946.

Howe, Elizabeth. *The First English Actresses: Women and Drama 1660-1700.* New York: Cambridge University Press, 1992.

Huber, Elaine C. *Women and the Authority of Inspiration: A Reexamination of Two Prophetic Movements From a Contemporary Feminist Perspective.* Lanham, MD and London: University Press of America, 1985.

Hughes, Ann. 'Gender and Politics in Leveller Literature.' In *Political Culture and Cultural Politics in Early Modern England: essays presented to David Underdown*, edited by Susan D. Amussen and Mark A. Kishlansky, 162-89. Manchester: Manchester University Press, 1995.

Hughes-Hallett, Lucy. *Cleopatra: Histories, Dreams and Distortions.* London: Bloomsbury, 1990.

Innes, C.L. *Woman and Nation in Irish Literature and Society.* Hemel Hempstead: Harvester Wheatsheaf, 1993.

Inoue, Tetsujiro. *Teisei: joshi shûshin kyôkasho.* [Ethics textbook for girls]. Vol. 3. 1907. In *Kôtô jogakkô shiryô shûsei.* [Collected materials on girls' high school], edited by Reiko Yamamoto, vol. 10, 87-178. Tokyo: Ozorasha, 1989.

Jacquette, Jane. 'Contract and Coercion: Power and Gender in *Leviathan.*' In *Women Writers and The Early Modern British Political Condition*, edited by Hilda L. Smith, 200-19. Cambridge: Cambridge University Press, 1998.

Jaeger, Stephen C. *Ennobling Love: In Search of a Lost Sensibility.* Philadelphia: University of Pennsylvania Press, 1999.

James, Henry. *Daisy Miller.* Edited by Geoffrey Moore and Patricia Crick. New York: Penguin, 1986.

Johnson, Jeffrey Lawson Lawrence. 'Sweeping up Shakespeare's "Rubbish": Garrick's Condensation of Acts IV & V of *Hamlet.*' *Eighteenth-Century Life* 8, vol. 3 (1983): 14-25.

Juhasz, Suzanne. 'Maxine Hong Kingston: Narrative Technique and Female Identity.' In *Contemporary American Women Writers: Narrative Strategies*, edited by Catherine Rainwater, 173-89. Lexington, KY: University Press of Kentucky, 1985.

Kagotani, Machiko. *Josei to chanoyu.* [Women and the tea ceremony]. Kyoto: Tankôsha, 1985.

Kato, Etsuko. 'Bodies Re-Presenting the Past: Japanese Women and the Tea Ceremony after World War II.' Ph.D diss., University of Toronto, 2001.

Katz, Elihu and Daniel Dayan. 'Articulating Consensus: The Ritual and Rhetoric of Media Events.' In *Durkheimian Sociology: Cultural Studies*, 161-86. Cambridge: Cambridge University Press, 1988.

Keach, William. 'Barbauld, Romanticism, and the Survival of Dissent.' In *Romanticism and Gender*, vol. 51, edited by Anne Janowitz and Gordon Campbell, 44-61. New York: Boydell and Brewer, Inc, 1998.

Keeble, N. H. ed. *The Cultural Identity of Seventeenth-Century Woman: A Reader.* New York: Routledge, 1994.

Keohane, Nannerl O. 'Speaking from Silence: Women and the Science of Politics.' In *A Feminist Perspective in the Academy*, edited by Elizabeth Langland, 86-100. Chicago: University of Chicago, 1981.

Kibbey, Anne. *The Interpretation of Material Shapes in Puritanism: A Study of Rhetoric, Prejudice, and Violence.* Cambridge: Cambridge University Press, 1986.

Kingston, Maxine Hong. 'Cultural Mis-readings by American Reviewers.' In *Asian and Western Writers in Dialogue,* edited by Guy Amirthanayagam, 55-64. NY: Macmillan, 1982. Reprinted in Skandera-Trombley, op. cit., 95-103.

———. *The Woman Warrior: Memoirs of a Girlhood Among Ghosts.* New York: Vintage, 1976.

Kirsch, Arthur C. *Dryden's Heroic Drama.* Princeton, N.J.: Princeton University Press, 1965.

Kitazawa, Noriaki. *Me no shinden: 'Bijutsu' juyô hen'yô-shi nôto.* [The temple for eyes: the history of introducing 'art']. Tokyo: Bijutsu Shuppan, 1989.

Klarer, Mario. 'Woman and Arcadia: The Impact of Ancient Utopian Thought on the Early Image of America.' *Journal of American Studies* 27 (1993): 1-17.

Knecht, R[obert] J. *Catherine de' Medici.* London and New York: Longman, 1998.

Knight, Janice. *Orthodoxies in Massachusetts: Rereading American Puritanism.* Cambridge, MA. and London: Harvard University Press, 1994.

Koyama, Shizuko. *Ryôsai kenbo to iu kihan.* [Standards of 'the good wife and wise mother']. Tokyo: Keisô Shobô, 1991.

Kraft, Elizabeth. 'Anna Letitia Barbauld's "Washing-Day" and the Montgolfier Balloon.' *Literature & History* 4, no. 2 (1995): 25-41.

Kristeva, Julia. *The Kristeva Reader.* Edited by Toril Moi. New York: Columbia University Press, 1986.

Krontiris, Tina. *Oppositional Voices: Women as Writers and Translators of Literature in the English Renaissance.* New York: Routledge, 1992.

Kuchowicz, Zbigniew, Żywoty niepospolitych kobiet Polskiego baroku [Lives of Exceptional Women of the Polish Baroque]. Łódź: Wydawnictwo Towarzystwa Krzewienia Kulty Świeckiej Łódź, 1989.

Kumakura, Isao. *Kindai sadô-shi no kenkyû.* [Study of the history of the tea ceremony in modern times]. Tokyo: Nihon Hôsô Shuppankai, 1980.

———. *Chanoyu no rekishi: Sen Rikyû made.* [The history of the tea ceremony to Sen Rikyû]. Tokyo: Asahi Shimbunsha, 1990.

Lamb, Margaret. *Antony and Cleopatra on the English Stage.* Toronto: Associated University Presses, 1980.

Lamb, Mary Ellen. *Gender and Authorship in the Sidney Circle.* Madison: University of Wisconsin Press, 1990.

Landry, Donna. *The Muses of Resistance: Laboring-Class Women's Poetry in Britain, 1739-1796.* Cambridge: Cambridge University Press, 1990.

Lang, Amy Schrager. *Prophetic Woman: Anne Hutchinson and the Problem of Dissent in the Literature of New England.* Berkeley, Los Angeles and London: University of California Press, 1987.

Lazarre, Jane. *Beyond the Whiteness of Whiteness: Memoir of a White Mother of Black Sons.* Durham: Duke University Press, 1996.

Ling, Amy. 'Maxine Hong Kingston and the Dialogic Dilemma of Asian American Writers.' In *Having Our Way: Women Rewriting Tradition in Twentieth-Century America,* edited by Harriet Pollack, 151-66. London: Associated University Presses, 1995. Reprinted in Skandera-Trombley., op. cit., 168-81.

Lofaro, Michael A. 'The Hidden "Hero" of the Nashville Crockett Almanacs.' In *Davy Crockett: The Man, the Legend, the Legacy, 1786-1986,* edited by Michael A. Lofaro, 46-79. Knoxville: University of Tennessee Press, 1985.

———. 'Riproarious Shemales: Legendary Women in the Tall Tale World of the Davy Crockett Almanacs.' In *Crockett at 200: New Perspectives on the Man and the Myth,* edited by Michael A. Lofaro and Joe Cummings, 114-52. Knoxville: University of Tennessee Press, 1989.

Lord, George deForest, ed. *Poems On Affairs of State: Augustan Satirical Verse, 1660-1714.* 7 vols. New Haven and London: Yale University Press, 1963-75.

Loret, Jean. *La muze historique ou recueil des lettres en vers contenant les nouvelles du temps écrites à son altesse mademoizelle de Longueville, depuis Duchesse de Nemours.* 2nd ed. Paris, 1867.

Lyons, Bridget Gellert. 'The Iconography of Ophelia.' *English Literary History* 44 (1977): 60-74.

Mabee, Carlton. *Sojourner Truth: Slave, Prophet, Legend.* New York: New York University Press, 1993.

MacLeod, Catharine and Julia Marciari Alexander, eds. *Painted Ladies: Women at the Court of Charles II.* London: National Portrait Gallery; London and New Haven: Yale Center for British Art, 2001.

Mancini, Hortense, Duchess Mazarin. *Mémoires d'Hortense et de Marie Mancini.* Edited by Gérard Doscot. Paris: Mercure de France, 1987.

Mandell, Laura. '"Those Limbs Disjointed of Gigantic Power": Barbauld's Personifications and the (Mis)Attribution of Political Agency.' *Studies in Romanticism* 37, no. 1 (1998): 27-41.

Maus, Katharine Eisaman. '"Playhouse Flesh and Blood": Sexual Ideology and the Restoration Actress.' *English Literary History* 46 (1979): 595-617.

McArthur, Eileen. 'Women Petitioners and the Long Parliament.' *English Historical Review* 24 (1919): 698-709.

McCarthy, William. 'We Hoped the *Woman* Was Going to Appear: Repression, Desire, and Gender in Anna Letitia Barbauld's Early Poems.' In *Romantic Women Writers: Voices and Countervoices,* edited by Paula R. Feldman and Theresa M. Kelly, 113-37. Hanover: University Presses of New England, 1995.

McCarthy, William and Elizabeth Kraft, eds. *The Poems of Anna Leticia Barbauld.* Athens: The University of Georgia Press, 1994.

McCartney, Elizabeth Ann. 'Queens in the Cult of the French Renaissance Monarchy: Selected Studies in Public Law, Royal Ceremonial, and Political Discourse (1484-1610),' 2 vols. PhD diss., University of Iowa, 1998.

McClintock, Anne. 'Family Feuds: Gender, Nationalism and the Family.' *Feminist Review* 44 (1993), 61-80.

McEntee, Ann Marie. '"The [Un]Civill-Sisterhood of Oranges and Lemons": Female Petitioners and Demonstrators, 1642-3.' In *Pamphlet Wars.Prose in the English Revolution,* edited by James Holstun, 92-3. London, Frank Cass, 1992.

Meaney, Gerardine. 'Sex and Nation: Women in Irish Culture and Politics.' In *Irish Women's Studies Reader,* edited by Aibhe Smyth, 230-44. Dublin: Attic Press, 1993.

Mellor, Anne K. 'A Criticism of Their Own: Romantic Women Literary Critics.' In *Questioning Romanticism,* edited by John Beer, 29-48. Baltimore: The Johns Hopkins University Press, 1995.

Messenger, Ann. *His and Hers: Essays in Restoration and Eighteenth-Century Literature.* Lexington, KY: University Press of Kentucky, 1986.

Mitchell, David and Sharon I. Synder., eds. *The Body and Physical Difference. Discourses of Disability.* Ann Arbor: University of Michigan Press, 1997.

Morris, Christopher, ed. *The Illustrated Journeys of Celia Fiennes, 1685-c. 1712.* London and Sydney: Macdonald and Co., 1982.

Morrison, Mary. 'Some aspects of the Treatment of the Theme of Antony and Cleopatra in Tragedies of the Sixteenth Century.' *Journal of European Studies* 4 (1974): 113-25.

Mosse, George L. *Nationalism and Sexuality.* New York: Howard Fertig, 1985.

Mouffe, Chantal. 'Feminism, Citizenship and Radical Democratic Politics.' *In The Return of the Political,* 74-89. London: Verso, 1993.

Mukherjee, Sushil. *The Story of the Calcutta Theatres.* Calcutta: K P Bagchi & Company, 1982.

Nash, Catherine. 'Remapping and Renaming: New Cartographies of Identity, Gender and Landscape in Ireland.' *Feminist Review* 44 (1993), 39-57.

Nava, Mica. 'Modernity Tamed? Women Shoppers and the Rationalisation of Consumption in the Interwar Period.' *Australia Journal of Communication* 22, no. 2 (1995), 1-18.

Nicolson, Joseph and Richard Burn, *The History and Antiquities of the Counties of Westmorland and Cumberland.* London: W. Strachan and T. Cadell, 1777.

Nishiyama, Matsunosuke. *Iemoto no kenkyû.* [Studies on the *iemoto*]. Tokyo: Yoshikawa Kôbunkan, 1959.

———. *Iemoto monogatari.* [The tale of the *iemoto*]. Tokyo: Shuei-shuppan, 1971.

Nitobe, Inazo. *Bushido*: The Soul of Japan. 1899. Reprint, New York: Putnam, 1905.

Nudelman, Franny. 'Harriet Jacobs and the Sentimental Politics of Female Suffering.' *English Literary History* 59 (1992): 939-64.

O'Brien, Ellen J. 'Ophelia's Mad Scene and the Stage Tradition.' In *Shakespeare and the Arts*, edited by Cecile Williamson Cary and Henry S. Limouze, 109-25. Washington D.C.: University Press of America, Inc., 1982.

Och, Marjorie. 'Vittoria Colonna and the Commission for a "Mary Magdalen" by Titian.' In *Beyond Isabella: Secular Women Patrons of Art in Renaissance Italy*, edited by Sheryl E. Reiss and David G. Wilkins, 193-223. Kirksville, MO: Truman State University Press, 2001.

Ogasawara-ryû reihô. [Ogasawara's manners] (website). 1999. Available at www.ogasawararyureihou.gr.jp

Okakura, Kakuzo. 1906. *The Book of Tea.* Reprint, Tokyo: Charles E. Tuttle, 1956.

Painter, Nell Irvin. *Sojourner Truth: A Life, a Symbol.* New York: Oxford University Press, 1996.

———. 'Representing Truth: Sojourner Truth's Knowing and Being Known.' *The Journal of American History* 81 (1994): 461-92.

———. 'Sojourner Truth in Life and Memory: Writing the Biography of an American Exotic.' *Gender and History* 2.1. (1990): 3-16.

Patrick, Max. 'The Cleopatra Theme in World Literature up to 1700.' In *The Undoing of Babel: Watson Kirkconnell, The Man and his Work*, edited by J.R.C. Perkin, 64-76. Toronto: McClelland and Stewart, 1975.

Pepys, Samuel. *The Diary of Samuel Pepys.* Edited by R.C. Latham and W. Matthews. Vol. 8. Berkeley and Los Angeles: University of California Press, 1970-83.

Peterson, Carla. *'Doers of the Word': African-American Women Speakers and Writers in the North (1830-1880).* New York: Oxford University Press, 1995.

Porter, Roy. 'Love, Sex, and Madness in Eighteenth-Century England.' *Social Research* 53, no. 2 (1986): 211-42.

Potter, Lois. *Secret Rites and Secret Writing: Royalist Literature 1641-1660.* Cambridge: Cambridge University Press, 1989.

Pounds, N. J. G. *The Medieval Castle in England and Wales: A Social and Political History.* Cambridge: Cambridge University Press, 1990.

Pudaloff, Ross J. 'Sign and Subject: Antinomianism in Massachusetts Bay.' *Semiotica* 54 (1985): 147-63.

Purkiss, Diane. 'Producing the Voice, Consuming the Body.' In *Women, Writing, History 1640-1799*, edited by Isobel Grundy and Susan Wiseman, 139-58. Athens: University of Georgia Press, 1992.

Quinby, Lee. 'The Subject of Memoirs: *The Woman Warrior*'s Technology of Ideographic Selfhood.' In *Freedom, Foucault, and the Subject of America.* Boston: Northeastern University Press, 1991. Reprinted in Skandera-Trombley, op. cit., 125-45.

Quinsey, Katherine M., ed. *Broken Boundaries: Women and Feminism in Restoration Drama*, Lexington, KY: University Press of Kentucky, 1996.

Rabine, Leslie. 'No Lost Paradise: Social Gender and Symbolic Gender in the Writings of Maxine Hong Kingston.' *Signs* 12, no. 3 (1987): 471-92.

Raynaud, Christiane. 'Humanism and Good Government: A Burgundian Rendering of the Romuleon by Roberto Della Porta.' *Fifteenth-Century Studies* 24 (1998): 159-74.

Reumont, Alfred. *Vittoria Colonna, fede, vita e poesia nel secolo XVI*, eds. Giuseppe Müller and Ermanno Ferrero. Turin: Ermanno Loescher, 1892.

Richardson, Alan. 'Romanticism and the Colonization of the Feminine.' In *Romanticism And Feminism*, edited by Anne K. Mellor, 13-25. Bloomington: Indiana University Press, 1988.

Robbins, Sarah. '*Lessons for Children* and Teaching Mothers: Mrs. Barbauld's Primer for the Textual Construction of Middle-Class Domestic Pedagogy.' *The Lion and the Unicorn* 17, no. 2 (1993): 135-51.

Robinson, Jo Ann Gibson. *The Montgomery Bus Boycott and the Women Who Started It: The Memoir of Jo Ann Gibson Robinson*. Edited by David J. Garrow. Knoxville: University of Tennessee Press, 1987.

Roper, Lyndal. *Oedipus and the Devil: Witchcraft, Sexuality, and Religion in Early Modern Europe*. London and New York: Routledge, 1994.

Rose, Mary Beth. 'Where Are the Mothers in Shakespeare? Options for Gender Representation in the English Renaissance.' *Shakespeare Quarterly* 42:3 (Fall 1991): 291-314.

Ross, Marlon. *The Contours of Masculine Desire: Romanticism and the Rise of Women's Poetry*. New York: Oxford University Press, 1989.

Royal Commission on Historical Monuments, England. *An Inventory of the Historical Monuments in Westmorland*. London: His Majesty's Stationery Office, 1936.

Ryan, Louise. 'Negotiating Modernity and Traditions: Newspaper Debates On the "Modern Girl" in the Irish Free State.' *Journal of Gender Studies*.17, no.2 (1998), 181-97.

———. 'Constructing "Irishwoman": Modern Girls and Comely Maidens.' *Irish Studies Review* 6, no. 3 (1998), 263-72.

———. 'Furies and Diehards: Women and Irish Republicanism in the Early Twentieth Century.' *Gender and History* 11, no.2 (1999), 256-75.

Said, Edward W. *The World, the Text and the Critic*. Cambridge, MA: Harvard University Press, 1983.

Salmonson, Jessica Amanda. *The Encyclopedia of Amazons*. New York: Paragon House, 1991.

Sawday, Jonathan. *The Body Emblazoned: Dissection and the human body in Renaissance culture*. London: Routledge, 1995.

Schenk, Celeste. 'All of a Piece: Women's Poetry and Autobiography.' In *Life/Lines: Theorizing Women's Autobiography*, edited by Bella Brodzki and Celeste Schenke, 107-30. Ithaca: Cornell University Press, 1988.

Scher, Stephen K., et al. *The Currency of Fame: Portrait Medals of the Renaissance*. New York: Harry N. Abrams, Inc., 1994.

Shifrin, Susan. '"A Copy of my Countenance": Biography, Iconography and Likeness in the Portraits of the Duchess Mazarin and Her Circle.' PhD diss, Bryn Mawr College, 1998.

———. 'Undress, Cross-Dressing, and the Transgression of Gender in Restoration Portraits of Women.' In *Fantasy and Fashion: Essays on the History of Costume*, edited by Mary Leahy and James Tanis, 105-18. Bryn Mawr, PA: Bryn Mawr College Library, 1996.

Shils, Edward. *Center and Periphery, Essays in Macrosociology*. Chicago: University of Chicago Press, 1975.

Shiotsuki, Yaeko. *Wakai-hito no tame no sadô no hon.* [The book of the tea ceremony for young people]. Tokyo: Shufu-to-seikatsu-sha, 1973.

Shirane, Haruo, and Tomi Suzuki, ed. *Sôzô sareta koten.* [The invented classics]. Tokyo: Shinyôsha, 1999.

Showalter, Elaine. *The Female Malady: Women, Madness, and English Culture, 1830-1980.* 1985. Reprint, New York: Penguin Books, 1987.

————. 'Representing Ophelia: Women, Madness, and the Responsibility of Feminist Criticism.' In *Shakespeare and the Question of Theory*, edited by Patricia Parker and Geoffrey Hartman, 77-94. London and New York: Methuen, 1985.

Simpson, W. Douglas. 'The Town and Castle of Appleby: A Morphological Study.' *Transactions of the Cumberland and Westmorland Antiquarian and Archaeological Society* [CWAAS] n.s., 49 (1949): 118-33.

Skeggs, Beverly. *Formations of Class and Gender: Becoming Respectable.* London: Sage, 1997.

Smith, Sidonie. *A Poetics of Women's Autobiography: Marginality and the Fictions of Self-Representation.* Bloomington, IN: University of Indiana Press, 1987.

Smith-Rosenberg, Carroll. *Disorderly Conduct: Visions of Gender in Victorian America.* New York: Oxford University Press, 1985.

Stallybrass, Peter. 'Patriarchal Territories: The Body Enclosed.' In *Rewriting the Renaissance: The Discourses of Sexual Difference in Early Modern Europe*, edited by Margaret W. Ferguson, Maureen Quilligan, and Nancy Vickers, 123-42. Chicago and London: The University of Chicago Press, 1986.

Staves, Susan. *Players' Scepters: Fictions of Authority in the Restoration.* Lincoln, NB: University of Nebraska Press, 1979.

Stepto, Robert. 'Narration, Authentication, and Authorial Control in Frederick Douglass' Narrative of 1845.' In *Afro-American Literature: The Reconstruction of Instruction*, edited by Dexter Fisher and Robert B. Stepto, 178-9. New York: Modern Language Association, 1979.

Sterne, Laurence. *Life and Opinions of Tristram Shandy, Gentleman* (1760-1767). Vols 1-2. Edited by Melvyn New and Joan New. Florida: University Presses of Florida, 1978.

————. *A Sentimental Journey through France and Italy, by Mr. Yorick* (1768). Edited by Gardiner D. Stout, Jr. Berkeley and Los Angeles: University of California Press, 1967.

Stetson, Erlene, and Linda David. *Glorying in Tribulation: The Lifework of Sojourner Truth.* East Lansing: Michigan State University Press, 1994.

Stewart, Jeffrey. Introduction to *Narrative of Sojourner Truth: A Bondswoman of Olden Time, with a History of her Labors and Correspondence Drawn from her 'Book of Life.'* 1878. Reprint, New York: Oxford University Press, 1991: xxxiii-xlvii.

Stimpson, Catherine R. 'Ad/d Feminam: Women, Literature and Society.' In *Literature and Society*, edited by Edward W. Said, 174-92. Baltimore: Johns Hopkins University Press, 1978.

Straub, Kristina. *Sexual Suspects: Eighteenth-Century Players and Sexual Ideology.* Princeton: Princeton University Press, 1992.

Tanaka, Hidetaka. '*Sadô no kigôka to Shôwa yo-nen.*' [The tea ceremony as a sign and the fourth year of Showa], *Tokugawa Rinsei-shi Kenkyûjo, Kenkyû kiyô* 26 (March 1992): 193-217.

————. '*Sadô bunkaron no kôzô*' [Cultural theories on the tea ceremony]. In *Sadô-gaku taikei.* [Studies on the tea ceremony], vol. 1, edited by Sen Sôshitsu, 135-72. Kyoto: Tankôsha, 1999.

Tanaka, Sen'o. *Cha no bi: Nihonjin ni totte 'cha' wa naze bi na no ka?* [Beauty of tea: Why is the tea ceremony beauty for the Japanese?] Tokyo: Asahi Sonorama, 1976.

Tanenbaum, Leora. *Slut! Growing Up Female with a Bad Reputation.* New York: Seven Stories, 1999.

Thornton, Peter. *Seventeenth-Century Interior Decoration in England, France and Holland.* New Haven and London: Yale University Press, 1978.

Tiffany, Sharon W. and Kathleen J. Adams. *The Wild Woman: An Inquiry into the Anthropology of an Idea.* Rochester, VT: Schenkman Books, 1985.

Tobin, Lad. 'A Radically Different Voice: Gender and Language in the Trials of Anne Hutchinson.' *Early American Literature* 25 [1990]: 253-70.

Travitsky, Betty, ed. *The Paradise of Women: Writings by Englishwomen of the Renaissance.* New York: Columbia University Press, 1981.

Truth, Sojourner. *Narrative of Sojourner Truth: A Bondswoman of Olden Time, with a History of her Labors and Correspondence Drawn from her 'Book of Life.'* 1878. Reprint, New York: Oxford University Press, 1991.

Tsutsui, Hiroichi. *Kindai no josei chajin.* [Modern female tea masters]. *Kindai no sukisha: zoku chajin-den.* [Modern tea lovers]. Second series. Special Issue, no. 23. Kyoto: Tankôsha, 1997.

Underdown, David. 'The Taming of the Scold: The Enforcement of Patriarchal Authority in Early Modern England.' In *Order and Disorder in Early Modern England*, edited by Anthony Fletcher and John Stevenson, 116-36. Cambridge: Cambridge University Press, 1985.

Valiulis, Maryann. 'Power, Gender and Identity in the Irish Free State.' In *Irish Women's Voices: Past and Present*, edited by Joan Hoff and Moureen Coulter, 117-36. Bloomington: Indiana University Press, 1995.

———. 'Neither Feminist nor Flapper: the Ecclesiastical Construction of the Ideal Irish Woman.' In *Chattel, Servant or Citizen: Women's Status in Church, State and Society*, edited by Mary O'Dowd and Sabine Wichert, 168-78. Belfast: Institute of Irish Studies, 1995.

Van Lennep, W., et al. *The London Stage, 1660-1800: A Calendar of Plays, Entertainments & Afterpieces Together with Casts, Box-Receipts and Contemporary Comment.* 11 vols. Carbondale: Southern Illinois University Press, 1960-69.

Vickers, Brian, ed. *Shakespeare: The Critical Heritage, 1623-1800.* London and Boston: Routledge and Kegan Paul, 1974-81.

Visconti, Pietro Ercole. *Le rime di Vittoria Colonna corrette su i testi a penna pubblicate con la vita della medesima.* Rome: Salviucci, 1840.

Waddy, Patricia. *Seventeenth-Century Roman Palaces: Use and the Art of the Plan* Cambridge, MA: Massachusetts Institute of Technology Press, 1990.

Wagenknecht, Edward. *Eve and Henry James: Portraits of Women and Girls in His Fiction.* Norman, OK: University of Oklahoma Press, 1978.

Weedon, Chris. *Feminist Practice and Poststructuralist Theory.* Oxford: Basil Blackwell, 1987.

Weigman, Robyn. 'What Ails Feminist Criticism? A Second Opinion.' *Critical Inquiry* 25 (1999): 363-79.

Williamson, Marilyn L. *Infinite Variety: Antony and Cleopatra in Renaissance Drama and Earlier Tradition.* Mystic, CT.: Lawrence Verry, 1974.

Wilson, Carol Shiner. 'Lost Needles, Tangled Threads: Stitchery, Domesticity, and the Artistic Enterprise in Barbauld, Edgeworth, Taylor, and Lamb.' In *Re-Visioning Romanticism: British Women Writers, 1776-1837*, edited by Carol Shiner Wilson and Joel Haefner, 167-92. Philadelphia: University of Pennsylvania Press, 1994.

Wilson, Elizabeth. *Adorned in Dreams: Fashion and Modernity.* London: Virago, 1985.

Wilson, Harriet. *Our Nig; or, Sketches from the Life of a Free Black.* New York: Vintage, 1983.

Wilson, Katharina M., ed. *Women Writers of the Renaissance and Reformation.* Athens and London: The University of Georgia Press, 1987.

'Women's Rights Convention: Sojourner Truth.' *Anti-Slavery Bugle* (Salem, OH), 21 June 1851.

Wong, Sau-ling Cynthia. 'Autobiography as Guided Chinatown Tour? Maxine Hong Kingston's *The Woman Warrior* and the Chinese-American Autobiographical Controversy.' In *Multicultural Autobiography: American Lives*, edited by James Robert Payne, 248-79. Knoxville, TN: University of Tennessee Press, 1992. Reprinted. in Skandera-Trombley, op.cit., 146-67.

Wonham, Henry B. *Mark Twain and the Art of the Tall Tale.* New York: Oxford University Press, 1993.

Wynne, Sonya. 'The Mistresses of Charles II and Restoration Court Politics, 1660-1685.' PhD diss., Cambridge University, 1997.

Yelin, Louise. *From the Margins of Empire: Christina Stead, Doris Lessing, Nadine Gordimer.* Reading Women Writing Series. Ithaca: Cornell University Press, 1998.

Yuval-Davis, Nira. *Gender and Nation.* London: Sage, 1998.

Index

activism, political, of women, 10, 13-14, 25, 250, 252-3, 256, 259;
  and 17th-century English women petitioners, 10, 12-16, 20, 21n.
advocate, woman as, 30, 210
All for Love (Dryden), 94, 96-9, 102n., 196
Amazon, 156, 183-7, 190-1, 192n., 193n., 196
'American Girl,' 65-6, 71, 74
Anthony and Cleopatra (Shakespeare), 96-9, 196, 102n., 103n., 202n.
autobiography, woman's, 51-3, 56, 58, 62n., 132, 134, 169, 177n., 212

Barbauld, Anna Leticia, 4, 221-31
Binodinī Dās, 125, 128, 132-6, 137n.;
  writings of, *see* writings, of women
body, female
  African American, and Sojourner Truth, 26-7, 30-3;
  and analogy, 10, 16, 20;
  and dissent, 9, 12-14, 16-17, 20;
  as erotic site, 97, 99, 113;
  as maternal site, 16, 18-20, 56, 59-60, 81-5;
  as metaphor, 1, 9, 11, 19-20, 23n.;
  as 'monstrous,' 17, 20;
  as sexual site, 10, 14-15, 53, 59;
  as social site, 53, 55, 59;
  as text, 51, 53-60;
  'docile,' and 20th-century criticism, 11, 20;
  embodiment of 19th-century tall tale in Sojourner Truth, 1, 25-6;
  figurative use of, 1-2, 10, 16, 20;
  representation of lineage in, 53, 83-5
boundaries, gender, transgression of by women, 2-3, 12, 16, 22n., 54-5, 58-9, 61, 71-4, 79-81, 93, 96, 100, 183-5, 187-92, 195-201, 202n., 209-18, 221-2, 225, 230
  and cross-dressing, *see* cross-dressing, and transgression of gender boundaries

breast, woman's, iconography of, 96-7, 113, 155-6, 162n.

canon, women's place in, 68, 222
ceremony, and women's involvement in, 1-2, 4, 79, 83, 86-8;
  processional, 86, 171, 173-6;
  Remembrance Day, 233-44;
  tea, 139-49
Civil Rights movement, 4, 245-56
Cleopatra (Queen of Egypt), 2, 93-103, 196-200, 202n.;
  and Plutarch, 93-4, 100n., 101n.;
  role of, and cross-dressing, *see* cross-dressing
Clifford, Lady Anne (Countess of Dorset, Pembroke, and Montgomery, Baroness Clifford, Westmorland and Vesey), 3, 167-82
clothing, *see* dress; *see also* reassemblage
Colonna, Vittoria, 3, 153-66
  and humanism, 3, 153-5, 157-61;
  and Pietro Bembo, 157, 159-60;
  and references to antiquity, 158-9;
  and references to Sappho, 156-9, 162n.;
  as patron, 154-6, 158-9, 162n.;
  iconography of, 153-8;
  iconography of, and Raphael, 156, 159, 162n.
cross-dressing
  and controversy of prostitute-actresses in 19th-century Bengali theater, 128;
  and transgression of gender boundaries, 56, 58, 128, 185, 187;
  on stage, and *Caitanyalīla* (Ghos), 128;
  and role of Cleopatra in Restoration England, 96-7;
  and wild woman archetype, 185, 187

Daisy Miller (James), 2, 65, 68, 70-4, 76n.
dissent, role of women in, *see* protest, role of women in